Robert Love's Warnings

T0366844

EARLY AMERICAN STUDIES

Series editors:
Daniel K. Richter, Kathleen M. Brown,
Max Cavitch, and David Waldstreicher

Exploring neglected aspects of our colonial,
revolutionary, and early national history and culture,
Early American Studies reinterprets familiar themes
and events in fresh ways. Interdisciplinary in character,
and with a special emphasis on the period from about
1600 to 1850, the series is published in partnership with
the McNeil Center for Early American Studies.

A complete list of books in the series
is available from the publisher.

Robert Love's
WARNINGS

SEARCHING FOR STRANGERS
IN COLONIAL BOSTON

Cornelia H. Dayton
and Sharon V. Salinger

PENN

UNIVERSITY OF PENNSYLVANIA PRESS

PHILADELPHIA

Published by
University of Pennsylvania Press
Philadelphia, Pennsylvania 19104-4112
www.upenn.edu/pennpress

Printed in the United States of America
on acid-free paper

1 3 5 7 9 10 8 6 4 2

Library of Congress Cataloging-in-Publication Data
Dayton, Cornelia Hughes.
Robert Love's warnings : searching for strangers in colonial Boston /
Cornelia H. Dayton and Sharon V. Salinger.—1st ed.
p. cm.— (Early American studies)
Includes bibliographical references and index.
ISBN 978-0-8122-4593-6 (hardcover : alk. paper)
1. Boston (Mass.)—History—Colonial period, ca. 1600–1775.
2. Warning out (Law).   3. Strangers—Massachusetts—
Boston—History—18th century.   4. Migration,
Internal—Massachusetts—Boston—History—18th century.
5. Boston (Mass.)—Social conditions—18th century.   6. Love, Robert,
1696 or 1697-1774.   I. Salinger, Sharon V. (Sharon Vineberg).
II. Title.   III. Series: Early American studies.
F73.4.D39   2014
974.4'6102—dc23
2013041216

Endsheets: William Price, "A New Plan of ye Great Town
of Boston in New England in America, with the many
additional buildings, and new streets, to the year 1769"
(Boston: 1769).
Map image courtesy of the Norman B. Leventhal Map Center
at the Boston Public Library.

To our friends and mentors
Gary B. Nash and Stanley N. Katz
and to the memory of
Alfred F. Young

CONTENTS

❖

Contents

✿

Prologue

A Walking Day

LATE IN THE MORNING OF Wednesday, July 9, 1766, Robert Love pushed his chair back from his mahogany desk; tucked notepaper, quill, and inkwell into the pouch attached to his belt; and stuck his head outside to assess when the approaching thunderstorm might arrive. Deciding to delay no longer, he put on his hat; alerted his wife, Rachel, that he was heading out on his rounds; and stepped out of his house into the shadow of the Hollis Street Church.

For the past eighteen months, Love had walked the streets of Boston a few days each week to warn strangers. Now in his sixties, he had recently been hired by the town to visit "all such Houses & Families as he apprehends Entertains Inmates or Strangers." On this particular summer day, Love intended to call first on housewright Joseph Scott, who lived a few blocks to the south. He knew that Scott often boarded apprentices and employees.

As Love rounded the corner onto Orange Street, he nearly collided with Patrick Bonner, a lame and almost blind stranger. Bonner was plodding slowly north, begging as he went, with a written brief hung around his neck explaining his circumstances. Love called to Bonner to approach so that he might ask a series of questions. The stranger reported that he had arrived the previous day, having come all the way on foot from Londonderry in New Hampshire, and that he had no regular place of residence. Love wrote down the information and then verbally warned Bonner, in his Majesty's name, to depart the town in fourteen days.

Love continued south, covering the two short blocks from Hollis to Pleasant Street and turned right toward the commodious house owned by Scott. Eighteen months earlier, the man had gone bankrupt, but now his

affairs were in order. Love rapped loudly on the door and was greeted by
Ann Scott, Joseph's wife. Love was a frequent caller and did not need to
explain his errand. Ushered into the parlor, he waited until the household's
new lodger, David Hunt, appeared. The young man answered Love's queries readily—he had been in Boston since early May, had come directly
from his hometown of Tewksbury, and was learning the housewright trade
with Mr. Scott. After his training, he intended to return home to his family.
Love recorded the information and pronounced the verbal warning.

By the time Love left the Scotts', it was approaching noon, and the day
had become unbearably hot. He had developed a powerful thirst and appe-
tite. Because his perambulations through Boston on this day would include
a visit to the almshouse, located west of the town center, he set his sights
on the Horseshoe tavern, at the corner of Common and School Streets. He
headed north on Clough Street, crossed Frog Lane onto Common Street,
and followed the east edge of the town common northward. The most
remarkable features on the landscape were the three hills that rose to the
west.

Love took a right turn on School Street, passed a few storefronts, and
entered the Horseshoe. He nodded at acquaintances, ate a bit of bread and
cheese washed down with a pint of ale, and, before leaving, consulted with
the tavern keeper and patrons about whether they knew of any recent arrivals to town. At the tavern doorstep, he turned left, crossed Long Acre, and
continued on to Beacon Street, pausing momentarily at Johonnot's distillery to establish a delivery date for his liquor supply. The selectmen had
recently granted Love a retailer's license that allowed him to sell small
quantities of liquor from his house. From the distillery, it was a few steps
to the northeast corner of the Common, which housed the almshouse,
workhouse, bridewell (house of correction), and public granary. Love
passed through the gate in the fence that surrounded the almshouse and
knocked on the door of the main building to enquire of the keeper, Samuel
Proctor, if strangers had recently been admitted who had not yet been
warned. Proctor reassured Love that no stranger had been taken in since
his last visit.

Skirting the Trimountain area, Love continued north on Tremont Street
and bore right on Hanover Street, which took him into the North End,
where he planned to call on Sarah King. King's husband, a boat builder,
had died in 1757, leaving behind a minimum of household possessions.
Since then, widow King had earned income by taking in lodgers. For Love,

the visit was productive. He warned two parties. George Beatty, a silver-smith, and his wife, Nancy, had arrived four days earlier with Captain James Scott in the brigantine *Lydia* from London. Love knew Beatty. He had warned him the previous year, when the man was visiting for a few months to scout out his prospects for settling in Boston. Love also interviewed Peter Rose, a shoemaker, who had arrived on the same brig with the Beattys. With warnings delivered and notes written, Love bid good day, donned his hat, and continued his perambulation.

Love headed southward into the town center, through Dock Square, and down Marlborough Street, poking his nose into doorways and alleys in search of strangers. And because it was Wednesday, he turned south on Newbury Street to pause at the White Horse tavern. He ordered a pint and enquired of the keeper, Joseph Morton, about the Providence wagon, since the White Horse was its only Boston stop. Morton informed Love that Dixey Brown, the wagon driver, had delivered the mail but had carried no passengers. The wagon would return the next week.

A breeze refreshed Love as he covered the last few blocks to his lodgings. He passed the Liberty Tree, where the scene was quiet during the summer heat. As was his wont when walking this narrow stretch, he strolled down the short streets to his left, which led to Walker's, Kneeland's, Harvard's, Bennet's, and Allen's wharves. There was always the chance of spying a newcomer among the dockworkers. But on this afternoon, his tour was to no avail. With the first clap of thunder, Love made the final turn onto Hollis Street and headed for home.[1]

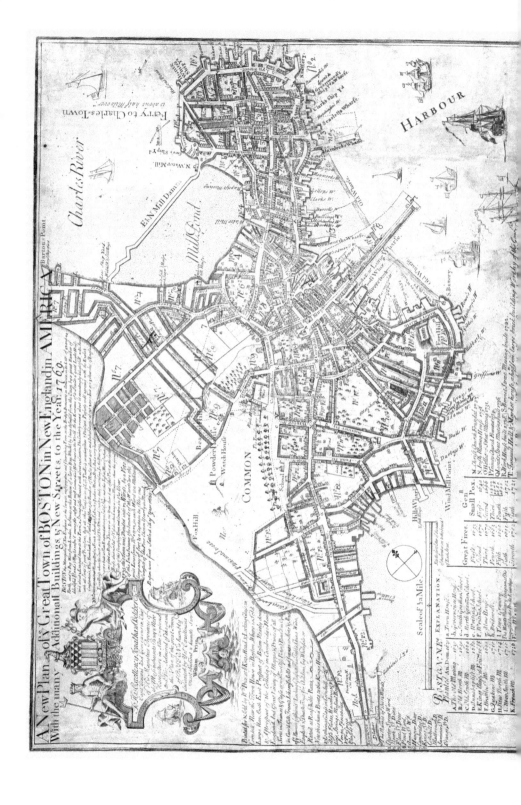

❖

Introduction

THE JOB ROBERT LOVE performed had no name. He was one of several Boston residents appointed in the mid-1760s to walk the town's streets and wharves "to warn Strangers out." Despite the fact that such minor officers had been in place for thirty years in the province's largest ports, New Englanders never created a title for them. We will simply call them warners. Each warning presumed that the newcomer did not have legal inhabitancy in Boston and gave notice that the town was not liable to relieve the stranger should he or she become indigent. Warners thus enacted a legal gesture designed to safeguard the town's treasury. This ritualized use of warning was distinctive to the New England colonies, although it grew out of English settlement and poor laws. To fulfill his trust, Love knew that what mattered legally were both the verbal pronouncement, you are "Warned in his Majestys Name to Depart this town of Boston in 14 Days," and the subsequent writing of the stranger's name in town and court records.[1]

We are able to follow Love as he perambulated Boston because of the remarkable scope and detail of his written warnings, consisting of slightly over twenty-four hundred separate entries naming some four thousand men, women, and children. The showpiece of Love's archive is his earliest personal logbook, which survives in the collections of the Massachusetts Historical Society (Figures 1 and 2). Its entries stretch from January 1765, when he took up the office, to August 1766, when he had filled the pages. In his pocket-size journal, sixty-eight-year-old Love inscribed 426 entries, each dedicated to a person traveling alone or a family group, naming 688 persons in all. Even though subsequent logbooks are not known to be extant, a nearly complete set of Love's warnings up to his death in April 1774 can be reconstructed. Love copied out his logbooks word for word on the warning warrants he received each month from the town clerk and then

FIGURE 1. Robert Love's surviving record book, 1765–66.
Image courtesy of the Massachusetts Historical Society.

submitted to the county court. Thus we can follow Love as he walked the streets of Boston for his full nine years and three months of service, a period that coincided with the peak of warnings-out in colonial New England.[2]

Love stood out among other warners for the obsessiveness with which he tackled his task. In his first two years, in which he shared the post with two others, Love was responsible for nearly two-thirds of the people warned in Boston.[3] His success led to his being appointed the town's sole warner in 1768. Unlike his colleagues, who recorded minimal information about strangers, Love noted the name of every child or member of a family group, their method of travel (by land or sea), their lodgings in Boston, and, in some cases, additional particulars ("a baker" by trade, "Clothed in rags," "wants to go to Halifax"). The details allow us to trace people moving across borders as well as profile Boston's landlords, both rich and poor. We are also brought much closer to the encounter between the warner, the newcomer, and bystanders because we can detect the questions Love asked and the ways in which Bostonians aided him. Woven into Love's warning records are the dislocating effects of war and the heightened political tensions that gripped Boston from the Stamp Act protests of 1765, to the town's

FIGURE 2. Flyleaf, Love's 1765–66 record book.

Image courtesy of the Massachusetts Historical Society.

occupation by British troops beginning in 1768, to the Tea Party in December 1773. Simply put, Love's records permit us to appreciate the varieties of people on the move, the reasons Boston absorbed them, and the disruptions wrought by imperial policies.

This study updates Josiah Henry Benton's classic overview of how warning worked in the various New England colonies and how the practice varied from town to town. Our focus is on Boston and Massachusetts, the province that originated the warning system used throughout New England. Only Rhode Island adopted different procedures. Whereas Benton passed quickly over warning's European origins, we investigate its roots in sixteenth- and seventeenth-century plans for alleviating poverty and organizing municipal government more effectively. Understanding the ideological origins of warning illuminates why Massachusetts and its neighbors continued the arduous process of registering strangers long into the eighteenth century. We underscore a crucial aspect that many historians have missed: warning was the hinge in a distinctive, two-tiered welfare system in which the province's taxpayers paid for the relief of needy strangers. These recipients of aid were called strangers not because they were unknown to local residents but because they had legal settlement outside of Massachusetts and thus were not entitled to *local* poor relief. Love's job was to interview recent arrivals to determine whether they had settlement in Boston, and, if not, to warn them. If in the future they needed shelter or medical assistance in Boston's almshouse, the overseers of the poor searched for their names in the warning ledgers and then admitted them on what was called the province poor account. The province treasurer covered their expenses. Warning thus shifted the cost of aiding the unsettled poor from the town to the province.[4]

The link with the province poor account refutes older characterizations of warning as a manifestation of New Englanders' stinginess and aversion to outsiders. By itself, warning barred no one from staying in town, finding employment, buying a house, or marrying. The practice did put newcomers on notice, however. On the rare occasions when authorities decided to physically cast persons out, they followed warning with a removal warrant. Rather than a gesture meant to exclude, warning facilitated the province's policy of making available a larger pool of welfare funds for Britons and non-Britons, native born and stranger, than existed elsewhere in the empire. Rather than gatekeeping, warning encouraged the movement of people and laborers across town borders. In the legal jargon of the day, it rendered the strangers "harmless" to the town, protecting local taxpayers from the burden of strangers who became indigent. Warning allowed employers and landlords to hire and lodge workers without worrying that their welcoming of newcomers imposed a financial risk on the town.[5]

Because warning created long lists of newcomers, it may be tempting to view it as a prototype for modern, bureaucratic surveillance systems. Yet there is little evidence that authorities used it as a means of social control. During its heyday, warning was not used to monitor religious and political iconoclasts. Nor did warnings mostly indicate transiency by singling out the landless and rootless. Among the thousands warned, sons and daughters of the propertied middling sort were far more numerous than people with no foothold in the region. These sojourners understood warning not as a stigma or threat, but as part of the bureaucratic management of the province's dual set of poor accounts.[6]

This book, as an extended interpretation of Love's warning records, seeks to illuminate our picture of who was marked as a stranger in the years following the Seven Years War, who was moving across town and colony borders, and why. One of our major goals has been to capture how sojourners' stays in Boston fit into their life experiences. We have generated biographical sketches for hundreds of ordinary and marginal people. Boston officials, like their counterparts in other towns, warned not just those in immediate need of poor relief but also those who might need help in the future. In an era with no savings accounts or health insurance, people's need for a stay in the almshouse might be only an injury or illness away. Love's observations shed new light on the beggars, strollers, and homeless of eighteenth-century North America and the mobile middling sort.[7]

Love's own biography was more like those he warned than the other Bostonians who served as warners. He neither held other town offices nor accumulated great wealth. Were it not for his extraordinary records, Love would have escaped notice. He was chosen as warner, we can surmise, because he had two rare gifts: an unusually adept visual memory for human faces and a tenacity for record keeping. While these traits did not lead to fame and fortune, they turned Robert Love into one of the most thorough chroniclers of people on the move in the eighteenth-century Atlantic world.

CHAPTER 1

Mr. Love's Mission

WHEN ROBERT LOVE walked out of Faneuil Hall on January 25, 1765, he discarded the veil that hides so many ordinary colonial Boston residents from sight. A few minutes earlier, the gentlemen selectmen at their weekly meeting had placed "Mr. Love"—as the minutes would always refer to him—within the ranks of minor officialdom and hence the written records of the town. The setting was the selectmen's chamber on the imposing building's second floor—a room to which Love would frequently report over the next ten years. To get there, he would bypass the market stalls on the first floor, climb the corner staircase, and, rather than turning right to enter the large hall where town meetings convened, wait near the stairs to be ushered into the heated chamber for his brief meeting.[1]

The minutes explain why Love had been summoned: "Mr. Robert Love being recommended as a suitable Person to have the Charge of warning such as come from other Towns, to depart Boston in the Time prescribed by Law—was this Day appointed . . . and sworn to the faithful discharge of his trust." No clues reveal who brought the sixty-eight-year-old Love to the selectmen's attention or by what networks of patronage or winds of chance he acquired this part-time post. But clearly, Love was appointed to plug a hole: the selectmen expressed their distress with a previous appointee who had been "found guilty of great neglect in the Warning [of] Strangers." And in this final week of January 1765, they appointed two new men, including Robert Love, and confirmed a third to the same trust.[2]

It was also on January 25 that Love began his long official association with William Cooper, the town clerk. Cooper's desk in the selectmen's room was the focal point where all minor officials of the town converged to submit their reports and accounts. For Love and other petty officers with limited education, Cooper may have appeared a daunting figure, with his exquisite penmanship and exceptionally orderly records. This son and brother of Harvard-educated Congregational clergymen served forty-nine years as town clerk. On that wintry January day, after Love had been sworn into office, the selectmen turned to Cooper, directing him to write out for Love his formal orders:

> You [are] to make enquiry after all Strangers, and other Persons who shall hereafter come into the Town and reside here that are not Inhabitants, and all such of them as you shall apprehend are in low Circumstances you are immediately to warn to depart this Town in (14) fourteen Days, or [to] give security to the satisfaction of the Selectmen, and this you are to do without any further direction, and when you have done the same you must Report it to the Selectmen that they may give such other Orders respecting Such Persons as they shall Judge proper.[3]

Cooper and Love met regularly in the months and years to come because among Love's most important obligations were picking up monthly warrants from Cooper and delivering his written record of warnings to the town clerk for rerecording in the official town book. Love also became a fixture at selectmen's meetings, passing on information about newcomers who needed aid and landlords who entertained strangers.

At the time Love became a warner, the selectmen set up a competitive incentive system for the three men who were to warn. The sum of £53.6s.8d. for "a Years service" was to be divided among them "in proportion to the Number of Persons each have warned." Through his assiduity, Love took home the most money. Starting in September 1768, the town relied solely on Love to warn strangers and paid him directly—£20 for every six months of service.[4]

Taking advantage of the fact that Love and his fellow warners would be walking the streets of Boston to identify strangers, the selectmen added "Street Dirt" to the objects they should be on the lookout for. Love was "to take notice of such Persons as shall carry Dirt Dung Carrion or any Rubbish into the Streets or Lanes of this Town." The selectmen hoped that Love and his compatriots' inspections of the streets would both prevent such smelly "Nusances" from being dumped and lead to prosecutions of those who did the dumping. How diligently Love pursued this additional duty in 1765 and following years is not recorded. His surviving notes focus on strangers, not on rubbish dumpers.[5]

Love's mission to warn strangers had its origins in two legal assumptions central to the social vision of the English colonies' founders. The first held that voters in the towns (or their annually elected selectmen) should be empowered to reject newcomers seeking long-term residence in their community. In 1637, John Winthrop, the first governor of the Massachusetts Bay Colony, articulated the principle: "If we here be a corporation established by free consent, if the place of our cohabitation be our own, then no man has right to come into us, etc., without our consent." Winthrop wrote that the puritan settlers' desire to "provide for our peace" and "preserve the welfare of the body" justified that "we should take notice of" strangers and "lawfully refuse to receive such whose dispositions suit not with ours." Although the governor's remarks arose from a suddenly urgent desire in 1637 to bar from the colony radical Protestants who were seen as heretical ("such as would . . . infect others with dangerous tenets"), his wording mirrored the language adopted in the earliest town covenants and ordinances. A good example is found in the announcement penned by Dedham's founders: "we shall . . . keep off from us all such as are contrary minded, and receive only such unto us as may be probably of one heart with us." The impulse to screen newcomers was intimately bound up with the strong communal and utopian goals of the New English settlements, where, it was hoped, like-minded yeoman families could live godly lives, prosper, and keep peace among themselves.[6]

Allied with this tenet that town fathers ought to act as gatekeepers was the ancient English concept of legal inhabitancy. Every subject of the monarch possessed inhabitancy in one town or jurisdiction—and one only. This brought with it the right to receive support from the town (drawing on its tax revenues) if one became indigent. Thus, legal settlement offered men, women, and children a *lifetime claim* to poor relief. The place where they could draw on relief funds might change through their life cycle if they moved and established settlement in a new locale.[7]

Several paths led to legal settlement in colonial Massachusetts. Children born to married adults took their father's settlement, whereas out-of-wedlock children were given settlement in the town of their birth. An enslaved person had the same settlement as his or her owner. "A woman by marrying acquired the settlement of her husband." For newcomers to the province and residents who wished to change their settlement, the primary route was to seek approval by the vote of the selectmen or the town meeting.[8] An additional route, which we call the backdoor method, involved uncontested residency. A 1659 law (not yet using the language of warning) stipulated that if a newcomer were allowed to reside in a town "for more than three months without" being notified that the town was unwilling to have them "remain as an Inhabitant" and subsequently being escorted out, then they would be accounted a legal inhabitant and afforded relief "in case of necessity." The would-be inhabitant had to take no special action (beyond arriving and staying put); settlement was gained because town officials failed to act. In 1701, the three-month period was extended to twelve months. When Love accepted his mission on behalf of Boston in January 1765, one of his goals was to prevent newcomers from seizing the backdoor route to inhabitancy.[9]

The word *warned* came into use in the 1660s and 1670s, carrying the specialized meaning of giving notice to a stranger that he or she was being denied inhabitancy and should depart the town. The Dorchester selectmen used it as a verb in April 1668 for newcomer Francis Oliver, and, in a similar vein, Plymouth townsmen voted later that year that "John Everson be forthwith warned to depart the towne with all Convenient speed." The colony law book of Plymouth, compiled in 1671, enacted the same three-month policy that was in effect in Massachusetts, making clear that a newcomer must be "warned by the Constable" or a selectman in that time frame in order to be denied the entitlement to town poor relief. In Boston, the first such use was in 1683.[10] By the early eighteenth century, the language of warning was used with respect to strangers in English towns across Massachusetts, New Hampshire, and Connecticut. In eighteenth-century parlance, it was as common to speak of *warning* a newcomer as it was to refer to warning him or her *out*. By the time Josiah Henry Benton published his book about the practice in 1911, attaching the directional preposition "out" had come to seem second nature to chroniclers of local New England history. To them, the practice appeared through the mists of time and memory as quaint and rather odd.[11]

In the Bay Colony, the late seventeenth-century decades constituted what we might call the warn-and-remove period. The laws dictated that town officials who wished to block the backdoor route to inhabitancy had to take two actions: verbally warn newcomers and, next, seek court authorization to physically remove any warned person who did not leave on his or her own initiative. Warning was thus promulgated to compel newcomers literally to leave town. In a major revision of its laws in 1692, Massachusetts, newly a royal province, made the step of physical removal optional. From this point on, the verbal warning itself became a bar to settlement, as long as the constable who delivered it made sure that a written record was "returned" to the county court of general sessions. Towns had the option of following up the warning with a warrant from a local justice to physically escort out any stranger who lingered fourteen days after being warned. But for the warning to have legal force, physical removal was no longer necessary.[12]

In towns smaller than Boston and Salem, the work of warning was carried out largely by one man: the town constable. Warning strangers was just one among the myriad of the constables' assigned duties. Typically these men were also responsible for summoning town meetings, collecting town and church rates, and arresting tax evaders and suspected criminals. Given the many tense situations into which a constable was obliged to step, it is not surprising that this was the annual town office that New England men most often tried to avoid. Warning out was probably not the most charged or burdensome of a constable's tasks: in a country town such as Rehoboth prior to the 1760s, authorities issued on average one to six warnings per year. When Love assumed the role of warner in 1765—a post that was in effect one of a specialized constable—he was rehearsing the roles and routines that hundreds of New England settler men before him had filled.[13]

As officials in the region began to practice warning, local variations emerged. For example, in Middlesex County but infrequently elsewhere in the province, warnings were called "cautions." Court clerks in Middlesex and Essex Counties, but not in Suffolk, which included Boston, recorded each town's list of cautions in the sessions record books. In the late 1600s, some towns told strangers they should depart within five, six, or eight days. After 1730, Boston consistently used fourteen. Rehoboth's warrants contained no specific time frame but sounded like banishments: strangers were told "to Speedily Depart . . . and Not Longer Reside therein." Roxbury and Stoughton selectmen in instructing constables whom to warn consistently noted the landlords with whom strangers were staying or from whom they were renting. In returning warrants, only Love, working for the region's largest town, gave residential neighborhoods or approximate addresses for those he warned.[14]

Constables and specially appointed warners like Love were not the only legal agents making up the region's defensive front against intruding and possibly dangerous strangers. By the time that Love began his rounds, two lay groups in the society had considerable experience identifying strangers: ship captains and the local residents who took sojourners into their houses. By the mid-seventeenth century, captains of vessels arriving in Boston were required to bring all newcomers for an audience before the governor or deputy governor. In 1701, the selectmen took over the receiving function. Each ship captain was to submit to them a "perfect list . . . of all passengers . . . and their circumstances so far as he knows" them. The selectmen could, and often did, "demand" that the captain carry away or post bond for any passenger who was "impotent, lame or otherwise infirme, or likely to be a charge."[15] A 1724 amendment made even more explicit the sorting process that occurred on ship decks: the captain was exempt from giving security for passengers who were able-bodied workers of good character or who could "make it appear" that they were bringing £50 of productive property into the colony.[16]

In the eyes of Massachusetts law, the townsfolk themselves, whose tax burden would increase if the poor rolls mushroomed, were a second line of defense. As in England, newcomers were formulaically cast as "obtruding themselves" into towns and even households. Despite the presentation of strangers as dangerous intruders, town residents were responsible for inviting them into their households—as apprentices, boarders, hired hands, nurses, or sojourning kinfolk. A 1723 statute introduced a system of written notification: any resident "entertaining" a newcomer was required to submit a slip of paper to the selectmen, recording the strangers' names, "the time they first received them, . . . the place from whence they last came, together with their circumstances, as far as they can," or else pay a £5 fine. In Boston and other towns, the notification process often worked in tandem with a warning out order. For example, a Mrs. McDaniel informed the Boston selectmen at their December 9, 1741, meeting that "One Alexander Ross with his Wife and three Children are lately come into this Town from Andover, that they lived sometime at her House . . . & that they are very poor." The officials' immediate response was to direct that the family be warned.[17]

At the level of practice, town officials and residents focused their attention not on newcomers of obvious wealth but on those of "low circumstances." These two words were a key phrase in Love's job description and

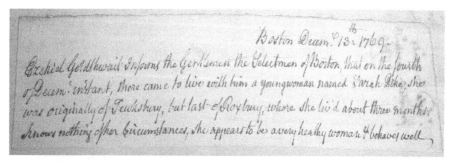

in the directions given to constables in many Massachusetts towns. The
phrase was often used interchangeably with "likely to be chargeable"—
meaning likely soon to be in need of poor relief. Warners like Love and
residents who took in strangers were primed by local directives and custom
to judge strangers for signs of near poverty. They assessed by their gaze—
sizing up clothing, shoes, baggage, hands, faces—and by verbal inter-
rogation.[18]

Notification slips provide a fascinating window onto this process of sizing up strangers because townsfolk sometimes listed the newcomer's personal property, inserted adjectives to indicate the "quality" of the person's
skills, or spun small narratives about the migrant's travels (Figure 3). Moreover, notification slips submitted by town residents were more likely even
than Love's warnings to reveal the purpose for a stranger's sojourn. To read
the slips is to enter the world of circulating people, very much like those
who encountered Love on the streets and wharves of Boston. We espy men
and women arriving in New England towns for short-term work or a pre-
arranged indenture, and renting a chamber or leasing a small house while
trying to establish themselves in a trade.[19]

In the following sampling of notification slips, the voice is that of the
landlord or kinsman who took in the sojourner, dutifully reporting to the
selectmen so as to avoid a fine. Typically, the notifications began with a
phrase such as "These Lines are to inform you that" on "13 Day of Nov'r
last I took into my House" so-and-so.[20] The description of the landlord's
new lodger or tenant then follows.

- "hiered [by me] . . . a spinster a hansom yong woman"[21]
- "he is a weaver and his wife a good Spinner and they Call themselves Newlights"[22]
- "as to her Surcumstances I am unacquainted with them but thus far I can Say according to what Experience I have had She is a very notable woman for bisness"
- "as for any Estate I know not of any he hath beside Some household Stuff, one Cow & one Swine"[23]
- "a sister of mine . . . belong to Providence Town not having eny estat besids moveables"[24]
- "she was bound to me till this day and now her time is out"[25]
- "I have Hired" "one Cato Fair a Negro man" "for Six months & no more & as to his Circomstances he Informs me that he Hath a peace of Land at Natick which befell him by his wife on to which he Intended to go as Soon as his time is out with me"
- "a Child of about 2 years old. . . . She came from Sudbury & is under Low Circumstances"[26]
- "an aged inferm Woman," "taken into . . . [my] Family on charity, [she] came from Hallifax a few Days since, but [was] born in this Town"[27]
- "I took into my House as a Boarder . . . a young man Last from Worcester a Cordwa[i]ner By trade & if it Suts you may Let him have your Custum as he is a good workman"[28]

In notifying selectmen about out-of-towners, inhabitants were well aware of the high likelihood that their lodgers would be warned. On occasion, landlords indicated that they welcomed the warning mechanism. When George Farrar informed the Weston selectmen that he had taken in "John Parks & Anna his wife and their Son John," he added: "I Desire you to warn them out of Weston according to Law they Being under Low Circumstances and by so Doing you will Greatly oblige your fri[e]nd & humble Ser[van]t." Note that Farrar was not asking that the Parks be removed from town; rather, he was observing that a verbal warning would prevent the family from later claiming inhabitancy and bidding to receive poor relief from the town. In contrast to Farrar's explicit request that his boarders be warned, notifiers more often adopted a neutral, reportorial tone, leaving the matter up to the selectmen's "discresion." But quite often, as these examples reflect, they wrote as if recommending and justifying the sojourner's presence in their midst, pointing to their good character or occupational talents. Thus, the collective recognition at the heart of many warning scenarios, in country towns and in Boston, was that sojourners were more often than not useful additions to the town, not polluting intruders. For New Englanders, whether they received lodgers or were sojourning themselves, warning for the most part was a routine, nonstigmatizing practice.[29]

Monitoring the flow of sojourners presented Boston with a much larger challenge than country towns where selectmen saw fit to issue only a handful of warnings each year. Even in the early eighteenth century, Boston officials faced the certainty that scores would arrive annually; by midcentury, it was hundreds.[30] The population of Boston was six thousand in 1690, rose to 16,500 by 1742, and hovered between fifteen and sixteen thousand in the 1760s. Especially from the 1670s on, during King Philip's War and the frequent French-inspired raids on settlers in the district of Maine, Boston officials were conscious that their town was not only "the principal seat of trade" in the region but also attracted far more refugees and newcomers than any other town in the colony. In 1679, and again in 1687 and 1701, the town made special pleas to the General Court for colony laws that would allow for more satisfactory regulation of the influx of strangers. Each time, they explained that because "Our Town" was "so Populous" and newcomers tended to shift "from place to place" within the town, the three months often elapsed "before they be Descovered" and thus "the law makes them Inhabitants." One day after the 1701 resolution to this effect, the General Court (then in session in Boston) responded with a law extending the time towns had to warn strangers to twelve months.[31]

In the earliest decades when warning was in use, Boston officials had a tendency to moralize when returning to the court the names of those they found unacceptable for admission to inhabitancy. One person was "said to be very prophane & of a bad report," another "of a vitious [vicious] conversation," and a third criticized because she "refuseth to goe to her husband." In the eighteenth century, comments about newcomers' character all but vanished, replaced by the pragmatic tone of landlords welcoming renters and residents taking in "strangers" who were known to them. For example, "Mr. John Fleet informs that he has taken into his Family as a Maid Servant one Esther Crawford, who came to this Town from Townsend at the Eastward; she . . . was received by Mr. Fleet the 3d of Dec."[32]

Aiming to be responsible town governors, Boston officials sorted new-comers into four types: those in immediate need who were sent to the almshouse for succor and medical care; those whose occupations and wealth made them attractive and safe candidates to be admitted as inhabi-tants; disorderly transients who were encouraged to move along, prose-cuted as vagrants, or physically removed; and those able-bodied men, women, and children who needed to be verbally warned but could stay. That many in this latter category stayed—whether for a few months or a few years or a lifetime—needs to be emphasized because too often the words "I warn you to depart" have been interpreted literally by modern researchers. A few historians have traced small sets of individuals warned, establishing that many continued to live in the town where they received the command to depart. As we explore how warning worked and how it interacted with the delivery of poor relief, Lawrence M. Friedman's words become our mantra: warning out "was not a sentence of banishment, but a disclaimer of responsibility."[33]

Boston's two-story stone almshouse was the largest among the few such institutions that existed in colonial Massachusetts. Eighteenth-century almshouses in the large seaport cities were all-in-one lying-in hospitals, medical clinics, homeless shelters, and old-age homes. Although many of the town's poor preferred to remain in their domiciles and receive outrelief (direct payments in cash, firewood, or other necessities), incomers far from home or without settlement in North America might look on admittance as a boon. Securing shelter and diet in the almshouse, especially in the winter months, could mean the difference between survival and dying in the streets.

In Boston, unlike New York and Philadelphia, town officials could admit "strangers" to the almshouse without financial qualms. In the eigh-teenth century, Massachusetts regularized a system for extending charity to nonresidents. Each year, some of the provincial rates paid by taxpayers throughout the colony went toward what was called the province poor account. Unique to the Bay Colony (and neighboring colonies who copied it), the account, making up a hefty chunk of the province's annual budget, was set aside to provide relief to strangers in distress—men, women, and children who had no settlement in Massachusetts. Boston received by far the largest number of such needy sojourners. If they were injured or impov-erished—either on or after arrival—the selectmen and overseers of the poor almost never gave them outrelief but admitted them to the almshouse. Thus, at any given time the "House," as it was referred to, accommodated some of the town's poor and others called the province poor.[34] The major reason that Boston and other towns worked hard to identify and warn strangers was to create a written index by which the overseers could know which treasurer to charge for a particular indigent person.[35]

Another category of newcomer to Boston managed to cross the threshold into inclusion in town membership. Early in the eighteenth century, skilled tradespeople or household heads bringing with them substantial amounts of personal property had a very good chance of success when petitioning for inhabitancy. Soon after arriving from London in 1744, watchmaker James Atkinson was admitted, having proven to the selectmen that he had "brought with him upwards of Five Hundred Pounds Sterling" and was "a Gentleman of a good Character."[36] Other new arrivals could gain inhabitancy if they secured one or two prosperous Bostonians willing to post large bonds to ensure the stranger and his or her family members would not become town charges. These actions were typically tied to a newcomer's successful petition to open a shop in town.[37] Given that granting town inhabitancy was an early version of conferring corporate citizenship, it is noteworthy that eighteen unmarried women, either arriving solo or as heads of household, were admitted.[38]

The frequent wars between England and France from the 1680s until Love's years as warner meant that travelers "of the French Nation" who arrived in the province were subject to special procedures and scrutiny. Thus, they were not formally warned but were handled in parallel fashion. A statute required French subjects to obtain license from the Governor's Council if they wished to spend time in the colony. In addition, they were almost always interviewed by the selectmen and required to post security. Ideally, they were to spend the few days between debarking in Boston and their meeting with the governor in quarantine at their lodgings—not allowed to walk the streets. In practice, only a handful of the two dozen or so French arrivals were deemed dangerous enough to warrant rejection, such as two men suspected in 1742 of being engaged in "illegal Trade" who were required to "Depart the Province by Thursday next." Others, once their circumstances were known, were permitted to "tarry." These included occasional deserters from troops stationed in New France, several travelers seeking passage from one part of New France to another (for example, from St. Christopher's to Louisburg), and one John Baptist Maginel, who was challenging the seizure of his vessel by a Rhode Island privateer and came to Boston to "obtain a Lawyer, Not being willing to Trust to Rhode Island Lawyers" in his circumstances. Some of these sojourners had been in Boston for weeks or months before the governor or the selectmen got around to calling them in for an audience. Hence we see that, although colony officials had strong measures at their disposal, in the eighteenth century they rarely reacted to foreigners' presence with deportation or banishment.[39]

The audience that Frenchmen were required to attend had its parallel for all newcomers in that the selectmen initially chose to handle almost all admissions and warnings themselves. On hearing that a stranger had arrived in town, the selectmen summoned him or her to appear before them in person. The encounter often went like this: "William Robinson Cabbinet maker being present [at the selectmen's meeting] Sayes he came over from London into this Town w'th Capt Beard in Septemb'r Last & br[ough]t his wife w'th him. The Sel[ect]men do now warn him to depart." This practice of face-to-face meetings indicates the intimacy of scale that Bostonians attributed to their community in the earliest years of warning. However, in the 1710s, the selectmen began a retreat from acting as their own warners. By the 1720s, they had in place at least one townsman to help them identify strangers. The earliest example came in March 1690, when they instructed the town's bell ringer and clock keeper, Robert Williams, to go "about the Towne at least once a month or oftn'r as may be occasion to inquire after New Comers into the Towne & informe the Select men at theire monthlie Meetinges for which he is to be paid" £12 for one year. In the first decade of the eighteenth century, strangers were sometimes warned twice—once by the warner and again when they appeared before the selectmen. From 1715 to at least 1723, John Marion, a deacon of Boston's First Church, although never formally appointed, warned strangers, typically on specific orders of the selectmen. By the 1720s, the selectmen were finding that it was no longer "practicable for [us] to come to the knowledge of" incoming strangers without having a man dedicated to searching them out. Here commenced the ritualized layer of governance that would continue through Love's tenure: a warner walking the town's streets, interviewing noninhabitants, and regularly reporting to the selectmen.[40]

Twelve men served as warners prior to 1765. The selectmen chose for the job men with whom they were familiar—reliable minor officeholders, adherents of the orthodox church, tradesmen. What is unusual in their profile is their age at appointment. Most minor town offices were filled by residents in their late twenties and thirties; hogreeve, for example, ritualistically went to young men who had just married. For the responsibility of identifying strangers, older men were deemed appropriate. The first four appointees were in their forties, but Deacon Marion was sixty-three and his successor a year younger. Thereafter, the average age was fifty-four. At sixty-eight, Love shared the spot as oldest at time of appointment with Captain Isaac Dupee, who served temporarily in 1760. The position was not a sinecure awarded to deserving codgers. The selectmen expected conscientious and energetic performances from the paid warners. Maturity in years brought long familiarity with the town's population, detailed knowledge of its alleys and hiding places, and the standing to recruit many townspeople as informants. All these attributes were crucial to success on the job.[41]

From 1730 on, the selectmen elaborated the record-keeping systems relating to warning. In 1737, they directed the town clerk "to keep an Account of such Persons as shall from time to time hereafter be Warned to depart the Town." The separate ledger devoted to warnings would allow town officials to check whether someone had been warned previously. In 1744, the warrant system was introduced. At the start of each month, the town clerk wrote out a warrant addressed to the man delegated to warn, leaving space on the first page for the warner to fill in (after the fact) the names of those he warned. This made it appear that the selectmen had ordered him in advance to warn those individuals. In the 1750s, worrying that "the good & Wholesome Laws made for . . . preventing Strangers coming among us" were "often transgressed," they put what was probably misguided faith in printing and distributing many copies of the province law requiring landlord notification, hoping Bostonians would thereafter "conform to the Act." In their view, town residents all too frequently ignored their legal duty to report newcomers they lodged or rented to. Finally, the board recognized that the overseers of the poor needed help in sorting out which of the indigent were properly the town's poor and which could be billed to the province. From 1756 on, the overseers would receive a monthly copy of the list of those warned; if someone they were about to admit to the almshouse had been warned, then the relief recipient could be assumed not to have settlement in the colony and could be accounted a province charge.[42]

Having access to well-organized records was not the only solution. Time and again, the selectmen found that the men they relied on to identify strangers were not always up to the task. In autumn 1743, at their very first meeting in newly erected Faneuil Hall, they lamented that John Savell, their attender and warner, was neglecting to "strictly observe the Province Law . . . for warning Persons out of Town." They hoped that they had found a diligent warner in Thomas Williston. He was a cordwainer and member of the First Church whom they had previously entrusted with the minor town posts of bell ringer, clock winder, grave digger, watchman, and messenger-runner. But Williston was replaced after only five months with yet another man who ended up disappointing his employers. Finally, in December 1743, after "some discourse with Deacon W[illia]m Larrabee," the officials believed they had identified the right man for the job. Even so, from this moment on, whoever was warner was required to report weekly to the selectmen's chamber in Faneuil Hall.[43]

At Larrabee's death, Abijah Adams took over as the town's sole warner, serving from 1757 until 1762, during part of which time he was also clerk of the Faneuil Hall market. An incident that occurred at the marketplace reveals something of his temperament as a town official. A man testified that one summer he saw "Mr Adams . . . turn persons out of the market Yard near the market House for asking A price for good Butter that was not Agreeable to him." The deponent reported further that he had observed Adams "sundry times kick over womens Panniers for refusing to pay for standing" in the yard, and "Drive men on horsback out of said yard By caning their Horses." If Adams was verbally rough in his encounters with strangers he warned, the selectmen may have replaced him with Love knowing that he would bring to the job a more courteous and less peremptory manner. Moreover, in a time of increasing poor relief costs, the town could not afford to put warning in the hands of a man like Adams, who in the early 1760s neglected to warn for months at a time.[44]

By Adams's and Love's tenures, the demands on warners intensified. The numbers of persons warned doubled during the 1750s. The problem abated somewhat in the early years of the 1760s, but the influx was even more dramatic in the 1765–69 years, when warnings doubled yet again (from their late 1750s peak), reaching their highest for the colonial period. In 1734, John Savell might warn out only four parties in a given month, whereas by 1756 and 1757, Larrabee and Adams were warning fifteen or more in most months. In the spring and summer of his busiest year as sole warner, 1768, Love's monthly average was thirty-two. At the same time, the town's outlay for poor relief was skyrocketing, from annual levels below

£730 before 1751, to sums of £1,300–1,900 sterling during and after the Seven Years War.[45]

The escalating numbers of strangers arriving in Boston were part of a widespread trend on the Atlantic seaboard. The colonial population was growing at the astounding rate of 28 percent per decade. Furthermore, as trade and commercial networks expanded and urban centers grew in size, the short-distance movement that had always existed between rural locations, small towns, and cities intensified. In the 1760s, hundreds of demobilized regimental soldiers who had seen action in Seven Years War wandered from seaport to seaport, hoping to find steady work or a passage home. At mid-decade, Love took up the job of warner when the challenge of identifying strangers was more daunting than ever before.[46]

A CLOSE look at the everyday working of the warning out system and its evolution in Massachusetts helps us to see that it was not the harsh, exclusionary measure depicted by some. Too often, chroniclers of early New England, whether devoted antiquarians or modern academics, have taken literally the words uttered to strangers and assumed that newcomers were rejected by insular puritans. That, however, is not how warning worked in practice. Warning was a mechanism that allowed newcomers who were acting peaceably and who had often found work to stay in town without their presence raising the specter of dependence on the town's future poor-relief resources. At its core, warning out was an act of fiscal accounting and a recording device establishing the line between a town's budgetary responsibilities and the province poor account. Dramatic proof of this came in the aftermath of an amending law passed in 1767. Echoing a parliamentary statute passed eighty years earlier, the new law eliminated the residency or backdoor route to inhabitancy. A newcomer now had to make "known his or her desire" to become an inhabitant and be approved by a town vote.[47]

On its face, the 1767 law would appear to have released Massachusetts towns from warning. Yet the practice continued because it was the hinge of the province's poor-relief system. In order to make aid available to those who had no legal inhabitancy in Massachusetts and yet avoid burdening the towns, officials needed an interview-and-recording system that differentiated the settled from unsettled poor. Whenever a person needed assistance, overseers of the poor consulted the warning rolls. If they found that the needy person had been warned, then they were authorized to charge the stranger's relief to the province. Warning, working hand-in-hand with the province's formalized, two-tiered poor-relief system, carefully monitored newcomers so that charity could be extended to the deserving poor, both local and foreign.

Defining warning out chiefly as a matter concerning town and colony treasuries, though important, provides too narrow a view. As we will see, the warning system, although often described as yet another marker of New England's peculiarity and Puritanism, took its purpose and spirit from a long tradition of Christian social ethics and secular humanism. It reflected a desire to bring to the townscape what reformers of the era called a "culture of discipline." In their vision, one important ingredient of a disciplined, well-governed town was a network of personnel—overseers of the poor, selectmen, warners, watchmen—all of whom would acquire an intimate knowledge of residents' needs, skills, and vices, so that the town could respond appropriately. Robert Love joined this constellation of watchful, civic-minded souls at the moment when more people than ever before were arriving in the harbor town. He fulfilled the selectmen's nearly century-long quest for an adept, consistent, and conscientious searcher for strangers. He was indeed well suited for the post with no name and obscure origins.

CHAPTER 2

The Warner

WHAT ARE WE to make of an early New England immigrant from Ireland who got into trouble as a young man for threatening to break open a man's head and yet by his late seventies earned public praise for the "tender Affection" residing in his breast? The trajectory of Robert Love was not unlike that of many peripatetic men in the British Atlantic world whose episodes of youthful rabble-rousing gave way to orderly household governance. As an Ulster Scot with some useful social connections, Love secured a modest foothold in the colonies. If in his early years he felt like an outsider, by the end of his life, having proved himself of great value to the local authorities, he had garnered respect if not genteel status. Tracking Love and his immediate family members through his forty-odd years as a Bostonian provides an object lesson in the patchwork way in which lower-middling sorts in colonial port towns earned their livelihoods. Comparing Love's social profile to those of other warners illuminates why he took on the perambulating mission at age sixty-eight and why he fulfilled it with such tenacity.

ALL indications are that Love was born in County Antrim, Ireland, in 1696 or 1697. The most important clue is that his brother, Richie, with whom he was closely associated as a young adult, was born there. Richie Love immigrated to Boston as a young man sometime before November 1719. In that month, he made a very good marriage—to Copia Bridge, the daughter of a recently deceased minister of Boston's First Church. Copia's father had been educated at Oxford, received an honorary masters of arts from Harvard College in 1712, and was counted among the intellectual elite of the Bay Colony. Richie's younger brother, Robert, arrived in Boston with a ready network of kin and allies to help him get established.[1]

More is documented about the transatlantic journey of Rachel Blair, the woman who would become Robert Love's wife. The daughter of David Blair of Ireland, she crossed the Atlantic in 1718 with two siblings, Elizabeth and James. Five days after their August 17 arrival in Boston, the selectmen issued an order that the newly disembarked passengers be warned—thus, informing them they would not become legal inhabitants by mere residency. The young Blairs joined extended family in Boston, including their cousin William Blair, a prominent merchant, his wife, Mary, and son William. If her family reassured her that the warning had no real sting for propertied newcomers, perhaps Rachel was not alarmed at the verbal command "to depart the town in fourteen days." But she surely was able to recall her encounter with the practice when, years later, her husband became the man in charge of issuing such warnings.[2]

Robert Love and Rachel Blair were part of a major wave of immigration from Ireland to the North American colonies. Approximately four thousand persons left for New England between 1714 and 1720; the largest number traveled in the same year as Blair—1718. And almost all who left the northern province of Ulster were Scottish in heritage, their parents or grandparents having moved from Scotland to Ireland under favorable settlement conditions offered by the English. Known in this era as Presbyterians, these settlers were Protestants with Calvinist leanings—and thus their theological and world views aligned with those New England puritans. One factor pushing Scots to leave the counties of Antrim or Londonderry in the early eighteenth century was the desire to escape from almost a century of warfare; another was an economic climate that combined high rents and prices with low wages. Many of the new arrivals from Ulster disembarked in Boston but then moved to frontier lands in New Hampshire and the District of Maine, serving as buffer between Indians allied with the enemy French and the settled portions of southeastern New England. Robert Love was one such emigrant.[3]

The first we know of Robert Love on the western side of the Atlantic is his arrival on November 14, 1720, in a frontier area of coastal Maine, then referred to as "the eastward" part of Massachusetts Bay Colony.[4] Called upon to testify in a land dispute a few years later, Love recalled arriving at "Rowsick in Kennebeck River." He had landed by sloop in the rudimentary settlement of Georgetown on Arrowsic Island, located at the mouth of the Kennebec and just east of Casco Bay, 150 miles from Boston by water. Love was headed to one of "Sundrie houses built along upon the River" north of Arrowsic, toward Richmond. His brother, Richie, having purchased a thousand-acre tract there from Colonel Edward Hutchinson, had just discharged his tenant and given Robert management or "Posession of the farm and Dwelling house," where, Robert testified, he "Lived with five or Six Servants and Cleared Land & Planted a Number of Acres." As a contemporary observer explained, these lands, newly resettled by Britons after the Treaty of Utrecht in 1713, provided "vast quantities of Pipe Staves, Hogshead and Barrel, Pine Boards, Plank, and Timber of all sorts" to Boston and other points.[5]

If Robert could have managed his brother's estate along the Kennebec without interruption in the 1720s and beyond, he might have become a prosperous farmer or merchant "down east." Instead, two dramas unfolded in the year 1722. In alliance with other Ulster Scots, Love got himself in trouble with the law, and as Love himself wrote, "the Indian war happened," such that all the settlers along the Kennebec were forced to leave their lands.

Threatening and abusing a deputy sheriff and another man; joining a riotous group of non-Englishmen who obstructed, assaulted, stabbed, knocked down, and cursed the pair; harassing the resident justice of the peace; evading arrest: these were the accusations made against the youthful Love in York County Court in 1722. While the context for the dispute remains obscure, Love's mob, as we will see, was protecting one of their own—trying to prevent an arrest. What the incident also demonstrates is that the human landscape of the Arrowsic Island area had become bitterly divided between "Englishmen" and non-English, including the Ulster Scots.[6]

Narratives of the two-part fracas survive only in the accounts of those who were attacked, or their allies. They open with Deputy Sheriff Abraham Ayers arriving in Georgetown in March in the company of Thomas Newman. Newman, who at the time was styled a tallow chandler but later became a merchant, was a resident of the town. Although Newman was the eventual target, Ayers tasted the ire of some local men that first day, when he was "denyed entertainment" by the local innkeeper and at the same time had a firelock cocked and aimed at him by the inn holder's associate, Lodowick Macgowen. The more serious confrontation occurred two days later, at nine or ten o'clock Monday morning. The same locals, accompanied this time by five others, including Robert Love, overtook Newman as he was crossing over a causeway to Esquire Penhallow's wharf, aiming to board a waiting sloop. The men asked Newman "if the Sheriff had any warrant ag't any of them." Skeptical about Newman's answer that he "did not know of one," two of them declared that "no Officer should dare to touch any man in that River."[7]

At the wharf, according to Newman, he was struck several times with the hilt of a sword, stabbed in the left leg, and held down by Love and others before a swipe of a blade glanced his head, leaving a gash. "The affray . . . ended" when Newman was "rescued by one of the Selectmen and other Englishmen." They hustled him into the forecastle of the sloop, whereupon the mate produced a blunderbuss to ward off the attackers and shouted that he would not suffer "any but English to Com where" Newman was. Deputy Sheriff Ayers, arriving at the scene, was held off by an attacker, Samuel Rodgers, who was wielding a large walnut club and bidding him, "keep off." It was at this moment that Love had his speaking part: he "told Mr A Ayers that if Esqu[ire] Penhallow gave him a Crooked word he would Break his head as soon as any man." To top off the indignities committed, Macgowen announced "that none but a Rogue would help Newman," and a former constable ran up, egging on the attackers by shouting, "Kill him a Rouge [a rogue;] Kill him."[8]

Temporarily at least, Macgowen, Love, and their associates—all Ulster Scots, evidently—may have gotten what they wanted. As one of the victims in the attack warned, unless all eight of the accused men were arrested and convicted, "no Officer can Officiate as Sheriff" in Georgetown "without great danger of his Life." Only two of the eight were ever tried (Macgowen and Rodgers), and that was because, turning up in Boston in June, they were promptly arrested and made to post £50 bail. Robert's brother, Richie Love, who now identified himself as a merchant, served as one of their bondsmen. The defiant rioters would also have been pleased that the special target of "the Irish" men's fury, Thomas Newman, decided that, for his self-preservation, he must "Remove my family from George Town." Within three months, Newman had resettled in Boston. From there, he worked for at least another year to push authorities to capture the remaining men, but other dramatic events intervened.[9]

Just three weeks before the "Barbarous & Riotous" actions of Love and his associates were to be presented to the York County grand jurors, Norridgewock Indians, a band of Abenaki who had their base at a bend in the Kennebec eighty miles upstream, traveled southward, propelled their canoes to the waterways at the river's mouth—an area called Merrymeeting

Bay—and sacked houses and mills and captured men, women, and children. In all, they took sixty-five hostages. Robert Love gives us a glimpse of the scene on Arrowsic Island: they "took my Self Captive [and] Plundered my house of all my Goods as also [S]triped my Servants of their Cloathing." The raiding party's goal was to harass the "English" enemy sufficiently that the colony of Massachusetts Bay would release four sachems held prisoner in Boston. Bringing the pillaging to a stop, the raiders made a gesture they hoped would convince the colonial leaders to release the Indian prisoners: they freed all but five of the settlers. One of the five men taken northward as a hostage was Robert Love.[10]

Love experienced captivity in "removes"—eighteenth-century parlance for stages. At first, he was held with fellow captive Henry Edgar at the central village of the band, Norridgewock on the Kennebec. Later in 1722, probably before winter, he was moved into Canada, in all probability passed on by his captors to an Abenaki village that no English rescue party would dare approach. The other captives were similarly dispersed, George Hamilton to the Mohawks, and Zachariah Trescott to St. Francis and then Montreal. Ironically, Love's fellow hostage Trescott was the lieutenant of the Georgetown militia band and one of the "Englishmen" who had been summoned to testify against Love and his mates in the riot case. The hostages were told that they would be freed when the Bay province released the Indians imprisoned in Boston. Trescott wrote several letters appealing to Governor Dudley of Massachusetts, asking that he effect the exchange so that Trescott and his comrades could be returned home. The swapping of prisoners never happened. Instead, various middlemen based in Albany paid ransoms for the release of the Anglo captives and advanced sums to pay the expenses of their journeys through Albany to Boston.[11]

Love may have been the first of the captured men to make his way to Boston. In May 1723, he petitioned the House of Representatives, requesting that they reimburse Peter Schuyler in the sum of £75.7.3 New England currency, the amount Schuyler had "advanced for him in Canada and Albany for his Redemption, Expenses and Charges in returning home." Of Dutch heritage, Schuyler was a colonel of the Albany militia, longtime commissioner of Indian affairs for that city, and expert in Indian languages and affairs. Together with his brother, Colonel John Schuyler, he negotiated the release of many captives. No doubt to Love's great disappointment, the house rejected his petitions—in 1723, and in 1724 when he tried again. His frustration must have been aggravated by the knowledge that the General

Court authorized at least partial reimbursements for his fellow hostages and those who had aided them. Perhaps, the legislators denied the young immigrant's plea as a rebuke and a substitute punishment for his part in the Arrowsic fracas.[12]

With his petitions denied and unable to return to his brother's lands in Maine, Love moved to Portsmouth, New Hampshire. It was here or in Boston, we surmise, that he married Rachel Blair in 1723 or 1724. Soon after, their first child, Ann, was born. Love now described himself in legal documents as a tailor.[13] After a few years in New Hampshire, Love moved his wife and young daughter to Boston, arriving sometime between winter 1727 and summer 1728. Given that Love was a newcomer intending to establish permanent residence and evidently not wealthy enough to post a £100 bond, it is reasonable to expect that he would have been warned to depart. However, no records of Boston warnings survive for most of these months, indicating either that the records were lost or that officials did not bother to warn any strangers in that stretch of time. The intriguing possibility remains that the man who became Boston's best warner lived in the town "under warning," as did many other eighteenth-century newcomers— allowed to settle, work, buy property, and vote, but destined not to receive poor relief paid for by the town, should he need it.[14]

The family's move to Boston may have been prompted by the aftermath of the sudden death of Robert's brother Richie in 1724 at a young age. Richie left behind two sons, William Richie (known as Billey) and Ebenezer, whose fates would have been of concern when their remarried mother, Copia, died in 1727. In August 1728, Billey, then nearly eight years old, came to live with his uncle Robert (who became the boy's legal guardian) until he was apprenticed to printer Thomas Fleet two years later. The lad brought a few furnishings with him: "a Bedsted with a Small feather bed[,] Bolster & a Ruge with an old Blankt." In Love's reckoning, his brother's estate owed him £40.16.0 for "Dyet & lodging & Clothing" of Billey, plus an additional £7 to cover the expenses of nursing the boy through measles, smallpox, and a bout with swollen legs that kept him in bed for six weeks.[15]

Nephew Billey joined the young couple's household just as Robert and Rachel's own children were arriving. In the pattern followed by so many white settler women, Rachel gave birth regularly every two years from 1731 to 1737, producing three sisters and one brother for Ann. Then came an agonizing stretch of time: four children in a row, born between 1739 and 1745 and whom the couple named Jane, Robert, Catharine, and (again)

Jane, died at some point in infancy or childhood. While it was not uncommon for parents to lose children to throat distemper or other illnesses, this
cluster of deaths must have marked a dark passage in the Loves' fifty-year
marriage.[16]

The Loves' religious choice is telling. Richie and Copia Love had their
infants baptized at Old South (the Third Church), while Rachel and Robert
affiliated with the First Church, located on Cornhill, close by the Town
House on King Street, at the heart of the city. Most significantly, Robert
and Rachel did not defect from the Congregational fold when, in 1729,
Boston's first Presbyterian church was established, attracting many of the
recent migrants from Ulster. John Moorehead, the church's minister, had
been born near Belfast, Ireland, in 1703, and educated at the University of
Edinburgh; he thus shared with Robert Love his country of birth, cultural
heritage, and age cohort. By not choosing to worship in Moorehead's
church, the Loves indicated they found New England congregational practices congenial. The association may also have blunted some of the prejudice manifested toward "Irishmen."[17]

Gauging the level of Robert's and Rachel's piety is difficult. Neither
became a full member of the First Church in an era when many attended
but declined to give the relation of faith that was required for full membership (and receipt of communion). We do not know the regularity with
which they attended worship services in the Old Brick meetinghouse or
how they reacted to Thomas Foxcroft's and Charles Chauncy's sermons. At
his death, Love, like almost all New Englanders, owned one Bible; no other
devotional tracts or books were listed among his possessions. But if he
attended worship on the Sabbath faithfully, and perhaps the occasional
Thursday lecture, Love, even though he never rose to a position of responsibility such as deacon, surely benefitted from the social networks among
congregants. This was the congregation that earlier in the century had produced two deacons and one sexton who were assigned to warn strangers. It
may have been a deacon, minister, or prominent lay member who recommended Love "as a suitable Person to have the Charge of warning." At least
one of the seven selectmen who appointed Love in 1765, merchant Benjamin Austin, was a full member of the First Church.[18]

In his more than forty years as a Boston resident, Love acquired considerable familiarity with the legal system. Like most middling sorts, his
involvement entailed ordinary, not dramatic, activities. In the probate area,

besides serving as guardian, he was named as one of two estate executors
by nephew Billey, who died at age thirty-seven.[19] In civil litigation, Love
was a defendant three times and a plaintiff twice in debt cases. He and his
son David periodically hired Boston lawyer Robert Auchmuty—a fellow
Ulster Scot who attained high social prominence. Indeed, Auchmuty sued
them each on separate occasions to collect his fees.[20]

In one suit, a file paper has survived that allows us a glimpse of how
Love made his living in Boston. Love sued to collect £9 from a Providence
man who between August 1752 and March 1753 had purchased many items
related to head wear: "10½ ounces Brown Hair, . . . Near 10 oz. White Horse
Hair," 7 ounces short goat hair, many silk cauls, thread cauls, and some
curled tails and head ribbons. Evidently, by the 1750s Love had developed a
specialty as a trader in hair, caps, and ribbons.[21] It is possible that he sold
his wares not just out of his lodgings but also as an itinerant, carrying an
assortment in a box or portmanteau. Whether he continued such trade on
through his years as a warner is not clear. As a retailer, he ranked well
below Boston's major storekeepers, merchants, and importers, and, as with
so many urban toilers of the lower middling sort, his business never
attained the volume or visibility to warrant his advertising in the newspapers.

A tailor, a trader, a retailer in liquor: Love cobbled together a living as
best he could. Like many in the middling and lower sorts, he did not have
a consistent professional identity throughout his adult life. He seems to
have given up the tailoring trade by his thirties in favor of petty retailing.
Like nearly all propertied colonists, at any one point in time he owed
money to several people and was also a creditor—selling goods on credit
or loaning money at interest. Love made a speculative investment in western lands in the 1740s, acquiring a few tracts and division rights in Monson,
an unsettled district west of Worcester. By the time of his death, the six
parcels were the most valuable asset in his possession.[22] In summer 1766,
Love made his first bid to retail small amounts of liquor from his South
End domicile; this was a standard means by which urban residents produced income or supplemented other endeavors. For the sixty-nine-year-
old Love, newly appointed a warner on the incentive system, the application
perhaps signaled that he was giving up trade in horsehair. Initially, the
selectmen turned him down; perhaps there were too many retailers of spirits clustered in the neighborhood. But a year later, in 1767, the license was

granted, and (as happened in many households), the wife, in this case Rachel Blair Love, though not the named licensee, dispensed most of the drams.[23]

Understanding the patchwork nature of Love's ways of making ends meet and knowing that the town fathers wanted older men for the job help answer the question of why at the age of sixty-eight Love would take on a post that required him in all seasons to walk the town streets in search of strangers. Encouraged by the competition among the three men, Love from the start took home about £40 a year. This became his official annual salary from autumn 1768 on, when the competition dropped out. Forty pounds was a sizable sum—and a significant salary in an era when clergy often received £100 and few adults had a guaranteed, predictable income. By warning hundreds of strangers each year and keeping meticulous records, Love won the continuing esteem of the gentlemen selectmen, ensuring that he would stay in the post.

From the early 1760s, and perhaps long before, Robert and Rachel Love lived in a rented house on Hollis Street "near Dr. [Mather] Byles Church" (Figure 4). This placed them in what Love in his warning records called "the southerly part" of Boston—the southernmost part of the South End and the Twelfth Ward. The Loves lived footsteps away from the South End's major north-south road—called Orange Street in this neighborhood and Newbury Street further north. In a 1763 petition to the town about the area's infrastructure, Love and other signers called it the "only avenue" to town and a "very commodious [one] for those who come to supply and trade with the Town." In one direction, the street led to the Neck and the Roxbury gate. In the other direction, it was just under a mile's walk to the town center. Since peninsular Boston narrowed at the intersection of Hollis and Orange Streets, the Loves reached water in one to two blocks when they headed out their door to the east or west. They were not far from the Liberty Tree at Newbury and Essex Streets.[24]

That Love was a renter and never owned land in Boston set him apart from the other men appointed warners in the eighteenth century. Yet he was hardly alone among Boston residents as a whole; close to two-thirds of legal inhabitants never entered the deed rolls.[25] Without a parental house to inherit or a windfall large enough to leverage a mortgage, the Ulster Scot was content to convert his modest surpluses into loans to his grown children and a smattering of material comforts.

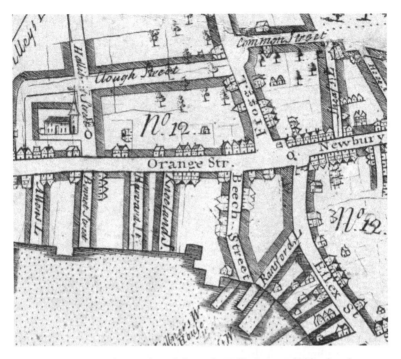

FIGURE 4. Robert and Rachel Love's Hollis Street neighborhood.
Detail from William Price's 1769 map of Boston.

Map image courtesy of the Norman B. Leventhal Map Center at the Boston Public Library.

The possessions owned by Love at his death fill in considerable detail about his domestic life and social status. The appraisers did not divide their one-column list by room, which means we do not know how many chambers and stories the Loves occupied. At their late stage of life, one bedstead, with a suit of curtains and valuable bedding and pillows, was sufficient. The saw, ax, cleaver, box of irons, and wedges indicate that Love kept up the woodsman's skills he had relied on while on the Maine frontier; presumably, he continued to split his own wood. The nearly nine ounces in silver items and £2 in "Old Gold" were easily stored forms of moveable wealth favored by most long-lived, propertied colonists. The patriarchal emphasis of the household is revealed in the single arm chair: these were by custom in colonial homes reserved for the male head. The couple's one looking glass was by then common to middling colonial households, but aspirations to gentility were reflected in three mahogany pieces of furniture, and we see the Loves' adoption of new beverage tastes in the coffeepot and mill.[26]

The household's thirteen chairs, five tables, thirty-two pounds of pewter, seven candlesticks, and chafing dishes—in addition to material objects owned by almost all households such as a jack and spit, pots, ironware, china, glasses, earthenware, tinware, knives and forks—are the accoutrements often found in spaces used for entertaining paying customers. They suggest that Love and his wife may have stretched the limits of his retailer's license to serve food and drink indoors. Or perhaps these were kept on hand to entertain members of the large Love brood. By the time they reached their seventies, Robert and Rachel had five grown children and ten grandchildren living in town.[27]

Some of the items owned by Love at his death can illuminate his activity as a warner. Perhaps he used the "Glass Lanthorn" to walk the nearby streets of an evening. Three desks are an unusually high number for a man with no higher learning. It may be that he purchased these with his warning earnings, having found it necessary to have several places to write and store logbooks and papers, not just the large mahogany desk. Love's clothes tell us something of how he appeared to others. Not atypical of ordinary colonists, he had a limited wardrobe. Besides "sundry cloathing," the appraisers itemized seven pieces, most of which were men's outerwear, used for venturing abroad: a blue cloak, one "surtule" coat, a black coat, hat, wig, one pair of cloth breeches, and one pair of leather breeches. These reflect his in-between status: part laboring sort (leather breeches), part middling sort who was often in the company of town notables (thus the wig).[28]

How did Love's Ulster Scots heritage affect his prospects in Boston and his carrying out of the warning job? Although Love's Maine sojourn was marked by English-Irish tension, prejudice against Irish-born Protestants who conformed to New England ways, as did the Loves and the Blairs, seems not to have manifested itself in Boston. Many who arrived in the 1718–20 wave prospered, including some of Love's male kinsmen.[29] With regard to his late-in-life post as warner of strangers, Love's Scots heritage may have been apropos in two ways. Among Lowland Scots, the semantic sense of warning as a legal notice to remove from the premises was in use from at least 1504. Love of course did not bring the term to colonial New England, but he may have been quite comfortable rolling it off his tongue. Second, his heritage would have included familiarity with the notarial tradition. Notaries were more central to legal practice in Scotland than in

England. From the 1500s onward, Scottish notaries emulated their continental peers by keeping registers containing verbatim copies of all land instruments, contracts, and other documents they drew up for clients. The repetition involved in notarial habits helps explain why Love wrote out the same phrase in each logbook entry and in duplicate sets, "Warned in his Majestys Name to Depart this Town of Boston in 14 days."[30]

We do not know if Robert Love was tall or short, wide at the waist or slim, or facially scarred by smallpox; he may very well have spoken with a Scottish brogue. We imagine that he carried himself with pride and with a calm sense of authority leavened by curiosity about and compassion for many of the wanderers he encountered. His authority was not that of a learned scholar or a member of the local gentry, but he could be confident knowing that he worked hard and effectively to earn his salary. Unlike constables who carried a black staff to signal their authority, Love bore no physical marker of office. But the most salient phrase that he publicly gave voice to and obsessively wrote in thousands of warnings was "in his Majestys Name." We suspect that he felt considerable personal satisfaction in being able to speak on behalf of King George III while on official business. Intensifying political developments in Boston would not have changed that: until late 1774, most American colonials remained loyal to the king and hopeful that the monarch would help reverse the colonies' mistreatment.[31] Besides, Love clearly had a strong sense of civic belonging: by perambulating the streets and acting as warner in these years, he was conscious that he played a significant role in the scheme of town governance, joining the selectmen, overseers, constables, and men of the watch in protecting the town.

Confident because of his conscientiousness, Love had no other advantages to pave the way toward winning the selectmen's favor. The three other men occupying the warner's position in the decade before the revolution had all been born in or near Boston, followed their well-established fathers into lucrative tradesmen's careers, owned urban tracts, and held several town offices. John Sweetser was a successful peruke maker who owned his North End house. Cornelius Thayer's father had been a deacon of the First Church. Isaac Peirce, who replaced Love in 1774, was born in Boston to a rope maker. Besides retailing strong drink, Peirce operated a distillery, and at his death in the 1790s, he left a substantial estate that totaled well over £1,000 and included several town properties. To these men, the warning position, with its dependable remuneration, was not as much a prize as it was to the more modestly positioned Love. Sweetser, for example, was able to forego the income supplement provided by warning; he resigned when his daughter Abigail married and could no longer keep his shop and house.[32]

Another perspective on Love's place in his adopted hometown comes from sizing up the fates of his children. Their adult lives in Boston reveal quite a bit about their father, given that his life from the 1750s on was intertwined with theirs. Not one of the five who grew to adulthood ever needed poor relief. None acquired great wealth or social prominence. In their profiles, they occupied various gradations in the broad middling swath of the society. Tellingly, none of the next generation of Loves became loyalists, thus reinforcing clues we find in Love's warning records that their father would have sided with rebellion against Britain had he lived longer.

One of the first-generation Loves achieved social mobility, but it was not Robert and Rachel's sole surviving son, David. Born in 1733, David lived only until the age of forty; thus, not only did he miss the Boston Tea Party by a month, but he predeceased his father by half a year. At age twenty-eight, David married Margaret Forrester in Boston's Presbyterian church. They had two surviving children, who inherited small portions from their grandfather Robert Love's estate. Active in debt litigation, David Love was styled in the records sometimes as bookkeeper, other times as yeoman. He carried on business dealings not just in Boston but with men in Plymouth County and in New Hampshire. At least once, he journeyed from Boston by ship. We know this because in 1763 he was sued by Boston shipmaster Bellingham Watts for goods that David Love had arranged to ship to Boston from a distant place, plus return passage for himself and "his Servant Boy . . . James Crawford." That distant place was New Providence in the Bahama Islands, where David sojourned in spring 1763. What took this bookkeeper to the Bahamas (besides business) was doubtless his tie to cousin Ebenezer Love, a printer who had been raised in Boston but had moved to Nassau by 1758, eventually becoming a merchant and Speaker of the legislative assembly. Perhaps never financially secure, David may have engaged in petty trading jointly with his father and turned to him often for credit. At the time of his death, he owed the elder Love the sizable sum of £107.4.9 lawful money, but Robert's administrator had little hope of ever receiving payment.[33]

Two of Love's daughters married middling tradesmen. The second eldest, Rachel, chose rope maker Samuel Emmons. He had been baptized in the First Church as had she. They continued as Congregationalists but eschewed the First Church, preferring to have their eight children baptized by the Reverend Jonathan Mayhew in Boston's West Church. During Robert Love's lifetime, they lived near the South End ropewalks. But in the 1780s, with three adolescent children still at home, Emmons found himself unable to work at his trade even "one hour in a day" because of his "having had several touches of the Palsey" (meaning that he had suffered several small strokes). At this juncture, the family was renting a house on Fish Street in the North End, where Samuel had "opened a Shop for the supply of Seafaring People." He petitioned the authorities to obtain a license to retail liquor from the shop, explaining that his wife, Rachel, "has her health & is well calculated to attend" that business. Thus, Rachel Love Emmons ended up pursuing the same part-time calling followed by her father, her mother, an aunt, and her older sister.[34] Little is known about the adult life of her sister Elizabeth, who married George Ray in 1763 at age twenty-eight, beyond that she bore at least one son and outlived her husband. Later in life, she moved in with her wealthier sister Agnes; she was still living in that South End house upon her death at age fifty-seven.[35]

Ann Love remained unmarried. Her single state is not necessarily an indication of her unattractiveness as a partner. Boston, like all port towns in the region, had more women than men of marriageable ages. Ann found various ways to make a living and pay the rent. Age fifty by the time her father died, she probably had lived with or near her parents, caring for them as they aged and helping them to retail liquor. Her reputation as a capable businesswoman is reflected in the probate judge's choice of her—rather than a male kinsman or associate—to be the administrator of her father's estate. (At that time, in April 1774, her mother, Rachel, was perhaps ill; she appears to have died the following year.) After her parents' deaths, from September 1776 onward, Ann was licensed to "dispense . . . Spirits at her Shop in Orange Street" "beyond [the] Liberty Tree." This South End location was very near to—but not the same as—her parents' shop and residence. It seems that, in effect, Ann inherited the family license. By summer 1784, she had "removed" to Water Street, closer to the town center. When Ann died eight years later, in her mid- or late sixties, her death was noted in three newspapers.[36]

Of the surviving children of Robert and Rachel, it was the youngest, Agnes, who made the most advantageous partnership. At twenty, she married housewright Samuel Bradley. Shortly thereafter, he purchased a large brick house on Essex Street in the South End, where they brought up four children. The son born in 1769 was named John Wilkes Bradley, indicating the family's fulsome support for American resistance to parliamentary taxation, a resistance that the famous Briton John Wilkes championed. When Samuel died in 1770 at age thirty-eight and Agnes became administrator of the estate, her father was surety on the £1,000 bond. As a married woman, Agnes had lived in considerable comfort. Her husband's brick dwelling house (valued at £200) contained delftware, pictures, desks, a Bible and six other books, leather-bottom chairs, a clotheshorse, thirty-seven pounds of pewter, three feather beds, ten silver spoons, new silver shoe buckles, and a silver watch. As a widow, Agnes took as her dower the front end of the house, including the shop, and lived there until her death at age fifty-three. Unlike some northern elites, the Bradleys had not foresworn slaveholding. One "Negro Girl" appraised at £13.6.8 was part of Samuel's property; her name and her fate went unrecorded.[37]

As a youthful immigrant arriving in the Americas with little or no capital, Robert Love followed the well-trod path of occupational versatility to make a decent living for his family. As a tailor turned trader-in-horsehair, with his wife dispensing small drams, and occupying a well-paying town office in his last ten years of life, he managed to accumulate enough property to bequeath to each of his children a £15 legacy—a modest but not insignificant sum on a par with that of many small farm families. Love owned £70 in personal property when he died (which translates into £52.5 sterling). This was eight pounds lower than the median personal wealth held at death by Boston artisans in one of the more prestigious trades—construction— who had died in the previous decade. Love must have been assessed at least as one rateable poll in the 1771 provincial tax—the only one that survives for his lifetime—but the listing was among pages that are missing.[38]

In the social classifications of the time, Love would have been understood as a member of the lower middling sort. Compared to his contemporary George Robert Twelves Hewes, the Boston shoemaker whose life has been vividly chronicled by historian Alfred F. Young, Love was perhaps only a notch or two more economically secure. Hewes inherited only £2.17.4 when his father died suddenly, and, as a young married man in 1770, he endured a spell in debtors' prison when he was unable to pay off a £6 tailor's bill. In contrast, Love was able to pay the few court judgments that went against him, but this was less a result of his success in business (retailing small goods was similar to shoemaking in being low status and insecure) than of his being in his thirties and older when he was sued. White, male New Englanders' overall worth rose progressively through the decades of their adult lives.[39]

An important difference between the shoemaker Hewes and the warner Love was in their sense of themselves as Bostonians. Hewes, who came of age in the 1760s, held no town offices, belonged to no organizations (not that there were many open to a young, unpropertied shoemaker), and joined street protests only gradually, sparked by the presence of troops in 1768. Despite his politicization in key events such as the Tea Party, Hewes took with him no warmth toward his natal town when he moved his family to Wrentham after the Revolutionary War. Love on the other hand, while he too was absent from the rolls of fire companies and private associations such as the Scottish and Irish Charitable Societies, emerged as a familiar civic figure and spokesman for the town as warner in the last decade of his life. As with many ordinary white men of the times, the nature of his political life can be only hazily sketched. It is unclear if he qualified to vote in town elections. To do so, an adult man needed £20 in rateable estate besides the poll in the provincial tax; Love's small "stock in trade" as a trader may not have met the requirement. He held none of the other categories of assessed property—livestock, slaves, urban property, or acres that were in tillage, pasturage, meadow, or salt marsh. His unimproved land in Monson would not have counted. This must have been disappointing for an immigrant who seemingly identified strongly with the city and whose wife and children chose to return to Boston after evacuation and to die there.[40] Yet many of Boston's middling male residents were in a similar position: at most, eleven hundred voted, indicating that many among the remaining twenty-three hundred did not qualify. The situation changed starting in 1770, when protest leaders periodically encouraged all residents of Boston and neighboring towns to gather as "the Body of the People" to address particular crises. Thus, normally disenfranchised men and women increasingly participated in community decision making.[41]

From our vantage point, the subtle gradations among the middling and working sorts in eighteenth-century cities can be difficult to detect and parse, but to urban denizens at the time they would have been clear. It is easier for us to identify the social circles in which Love did *not* move (or even aspire to join) than the ones in which he engaged as a social equal or revered elder. Take the selectmen who were his employers. He served them faithfully, paid them proper deference, and probably conversed comfortably with them about certain aspects of town affairs. But the social divide between them was very clear. They were wealthy "gentlemen" whose social sphere excluded middling types like the Loves and their grown children. Love's exclusion was most clearly signaled on semiannual visitation days, when the selectmen, overseers, and magistrates were joined by specifically invited other gentlemen of the town to walk the wards and inspect public buildings such as schools and almshouse; in the evening they adjourned to a festive dinner at Faneuil Hall. As mobilization to combat the British clampdown on Boston increased, only a few of the town's prosperous and politically gifted artisan-entrepreneurs such as Paul Revere were included in the tavern gatherings, formal dinners, and country outings of elites that were chronicled in great detail by the gossipy diarist and well-connected merchant John Rowe. Dress would have marked the divide, too. It would have been neither socially appropriate nor economically possible for Love to wear the silk, embroidered waistcoats, or ruffled shirts of the town's best sort. A blue cloak, only two pairs of breeches, and a hat and wig were adequate for a plain man and for a warner's perambulating duties.[42]

ROBERT Love may have been a man of plain style, modest holdings, and rustic penmanship, but he earned unusual attention on the occasion of his death in the spring of 1774. This distinction did not occur at his funeral, which was, befitting the times, a restrained affair. In protest of punitive British policies, Bostonians had agreed to abandon the wearing of black clothes for mourning. Instead, the widow Rachel and her three grown daughters would have worn black bonnets while the men and boys donned armbands of black "crape." The burial ritual began at the deceased's house in the South End. There, over the coffin, Charles Chauncy, minister of the First Church, likely said a prayer.[43] The men who lifted the coffin and bore it to the cemetery probably included Love's sole surviving son-in-law, Samuel Emmons, and his three closest business associates: distiller, militia colonel, and former selectman Joseph Jackson; shopkeeper and "gentleman" Joseph Bradford; and distiller Ebenezer Sever. The ritual at the cemetery was kept to a minimum. Either honoring her father's wishes or recognizing his frugality, Ann in administering Love's estate did not arrange for a gravestone to be erected for her parents.[44]

What was unusual was the obituary published on the day of Love's funeral in the *Boston News-Letter* and the *Massachusetts Gazette*. Most death notices that appeared in newspapers of the period were short. They transmitted name, age, and perhaps occupation, as in "Mr. Elisha Eaton, Housewright, aged 39." Such lines were embedded in a paragraph listing some of those who had died in the previous week, arranged by location: At Boston, at Roxbury, at Barbados. Printer-publishers (who were often the authors of the notices) included more descriptive information only in certain situations: when there was a sudden death owing to a catastrophe or accident; when the deceased's marriage had been very long or the offspring unusually numerous; and sometimes, not always, if an adult man had been eminent in public service, a woman was notable for her piety and good works, or a youth had had a promising career in front of him.[45]

Thursday, April 28, was publication day for the *Boston News-Letter*. The *News-Letter* had the distinction of being the oldest newspaper published in the British American colonies, having been established in 1704. Since 1734, its printers had been appointed by the governor and council to print the province laws and other documents—a plum assignment. Bostonians knew that of the four weekly newspapers published in town, the *News-Letter* was politically the most conservative, committed to printing governmental activity and presenting politics from a royalist perspective. Indeed, Richard Draper, the paper's owner and printer in 1774, had added the king's arms to the masthead eleven years before.[46] Draper's paper published the first and the fullest obituary out of five that appeared noting Love's death; we do not know why. Perhaps the warner often dropped by the two-room printing house on Cornhill and Newbury, close by the Town House. Perhaps the two men forged a friendship over their interest in newcomers to town. Politics evidently did not unite them; Draper became a Tory in 1776, and the Loves did not. In any event, the anonymous author of the *News-Letter* obituary wrote as if speaking for many Bostonians about Love's character:

DIED. Mr. Robert Love, at the South-End, aged 77. In whose Breast true Friendship and tender Affection had laid a Foundation, which, added to a sincere honest and upright Mind, made him well esteemed and respected by all that knew him. His Funeral is to be this Afternoon, at 4 o'Clock, when the Friends and Acquaintance of the Deceased are requested to attend.[47]

The praise of Love's character was not boilerplate language copied from other death notices. It belonged to a long English and New England tradition of elegizing boys and men by praising their capacity for friendship and sympathy. The wording reflects the heavy cultural emphasis placed in the eighteenth century on literate, pious men's development of sensibility—"a refinement of moral feeling" that was seen as honing the deployment of one's rational faculties and disposing one "to acts of humanity and benevolence." The encomium tells us that because of his service to the town, and perhaps because of other acts of sociability that have gone unrecorded, Love had become a valued Bostonian by the time of his death. His position as warner, even though it was not mentioned in the obituary, had raised him to notability.[48]

CHAPTER 3

Origins

ROBERT LOVE'S SEARCHES for strangers grew out of early modern European debates over how best to organize public charity and govern cities. The Massachusetts solution drew largely on seventeenth-century English settlement law and parish experimentation. But Bay Colony officials did not simply copy English procedures. In adapting humanist and Reformation goals to New World conditions, they innovated, elevating an obscure legal writ to serve as the lynchpin of a welfare regime that was arguably more effective than many others.

All British colonial cities contended with influxes of laboring people, disabled seamen, and distressed travelers. Aghast at rising poor relief costs, officials in New York and Philadelphia were unable to convince provincial authorities to share the costs of aiding needy strangers. Adopting warning would have helped them do so. And yet these colonial leaders drew on the same legal heritage and expressed just as intense concerns for the poor as their counterparts in Massachusetts. Partly an exploration of what warning was and was not, partly an exercise in comparative legal history, this chapter addresses what set New England's approach apart.

COMPARING warning to techniques used in continental Europe to mark strangers illuminates the choices made by Massachusetts. Some early modern municipalities closely monitored strangers' entrances *and* exits. In the Vatican-controlled town of Avignon, visitors were issued a ticket by the border guard to be submitted to their innkeeper. Within three days, the traveling party was required to appear at the town hall to register their names. There they received yet another piece of paper to take back to their innkeeper, who would tender it to authorities when the travelers departed. One young visiting scholar wrote of this rigmarole, perhaps tongue in cheek: "that is how they maintain good order, so that they know at all times what foreigners are in their town." In contrast, the interviewing of strangers in Massachusetts was not chiefly directed at foreigners—subjects of a ruler other than George III—and newcomers received no badge or documentation to carry with them.[1]

Nor did warning generate internal passes marking certain classes. In Leipzig and other early modern German towns, some residents—poorer renters who lived in low-rent neighborhoods—were called "paper citizens," *Zettelbürgers*, "because they were required to have paper permits bearing their landlord's surety" while moving around the city. A similar system existed largely as a racial marker in British America, not affecting warned strangers in Boston who were perceived to be white, but rather directed at indentured servants and slaves and all people of color moving about after the curfew of nine o'clock at night.[2]

Warning bore little kinship to schemes that imagined all residents should be tagged. Johann Gottlieb Fichte opined in 1796 that in "a well-regulated police state," each citizen should at all times be recognizable "as this or that particular person," and to that end every person "must carry a pass . . . in which his person is accurately described." Jeremy Bentham advocated that all persons should have their name and place and date of birth tattooed on the wrist. Jean Bodin saw universal registration as a route to identifying the idle and the dangerous. As a register, the warning ledgers created a very incomplete census. At best, the lists functioned to divide Boston's population into three groups: legal inhabitants (who were implied by their absence from the lists), sojourners with settlement elsewhere in the province, and those from outside the colony. Warning had the same purpose as Nuremberg's and Bern's marking of local versus stranger paupers. In those cities, the local poor were given badges and listed in town books, indicating their right to public support or license to solicit alms, while the foreign destitute were supposedly banished.[3] The Massachusetts system worked differently and was more capacious in extending alms. The recording of names permitted relief given to the unsettled (those without legal inhabitancy) to be charged to the province rather than the town.

In sum, warning was a rather relaxed registration system. It did not stem from bureaucratic fantasies of establishing an all-seeing gaze or total control. It did not prevent eighteenth-century Boston from being a fairly porous place. It was less an oppressive instance of surveillance than a means of clarifying who could make a claim on which relief funds.[4] To assess how distinctive warning was both in the context of western European history and in the Anglo-American legal tradition, we need to take a closer look at English approaches to poor relief and settlement.

In his 1911 history of warning out, lawyer and amateur historian Josiah Henry Benton Jr. argued that the concept of settlement-by-residence reached back to Saxon England and even further—to ancient German customs and "the remote villages of the Aryan East." Benton cited evidence that the Teutonic village communities of England followed the rule that if a "stranger remained . . . without challenge" and without being removed for "twelve months, he was from thenceforth allowed to dwell in peace and security."[5] If this is accurate, it is not clear how long such a one-year residency requirement lasted past the Norman invasion and into the medieval period. The ecclesiastical court records of the late 1400s contain rare deployments of the verb "monuit" (Latin for *warn*) as a command to depart. The context was not that of strangers intruding into a parish, but sinners convicted of serious crimes (sorcery, adultery) and punished partly by being banished from the parish.[6] In seeking the legal origins of warning out, we do better turning to the sixteenth- and seventeenth-century landscape of welfare experimentation and law than to the far distant past.

In England and Europe in the 1500s, authorities put into place a variety of new poor relief schemes. In the medieval period, the onus was on the pauper, who was expected to secure a source of alms. Poor relief was a patchwork affair, with monasteries limiting themselves to aiding a customary number of local poor (twelve, for example) annually and offering short-term lodging and alms to beggars or travelers in distress. Personal alms giving—whether offered spontaneously when one encountered a plaintive soul or given ritually at the church steps or wedding feasts—was the general rule. Critics of this haphazard system lamented that such habits of indiscriminate alms giving meant that much-needed relief never reached many of the deserving poor—those disabled in accidents, those chronically ill, the infirm elderly—unless they were out on the roads begging.[7]

As early as the 1520s, humanists expressed deep compassion for the plight of needy persons and advocated that poor relief be secularized and its delivery rationalized. An influential plan for the Flemish town of Bruges, circulated by Juan Luis Vives, envisioned that officials canvas the city in order to understand the various categories of poor within the walls and then establish discrete institutions and methods of aid for each. Propertied city residents were to be cajoled into contributing to a poor fund. Descriptions of Vives's plan and one implemented in Ypres, another Flanders port town, were translated and published in England, thus shaping early discussions about how to address poverty. The Catholics and Protestants who embraced these ideas were convinced that a disciplined and rational approach to poor relief would lead to one of their vaunted goals for earthly godliness—effective stewardship.[8]

During the reign of Elizabeth I, England departed from Continental practices by mandating collection of funds for the poor in all parts of the kingdom: these were the now-famous poor law statutes passed in 1572, 1598, and 1601. Yet, even with the establishment of such a radical policy, advocates of reform in England recognized that national enforcement mechanisms were weak and thus initiative and willpower had to be exercised at the local level. Puritans were often at the forefront of the ongoing attempts to implement effective systems of poor relief, taking their cues from Calvinist communities across Europe. Following the model set in Geneva, Bordeaux's two thousand Calvinists forged a notably efficient poor relief system for their coreligionists. Features included weekly meetings of elders to identify needy recipients and twice-weekly visits to sick persons. In addition to this intensive investment of lay personnel in knitting their beleaguered community together through a pattern of visiting, the French Calvinists' aim was to "make it possible for the poor to help themselves." Assistance usually took the form of temporary supplements aimed to help craftsmen secure employment or tide families through periods of serious illness. Many English parish officials were already adopting this model by appointing overseers of the poor and instructing them to be in close communication with needy residents.[9]

The most energetic efforts to implement effective welfare regimes occurred first in towns such as Norwich and Ipswich in the 1570s. Municipal leaders began by taking a detailed, parish-by-parish census of the poor and working poor, listing "the name, age, occupation and dwelling of every man, woman and child." The next steps included sending small numbers away to their place of legal settlement, placing youths with masters, reestablishing a small orphanage, and dividing the city into wards for better oversight of the needy. Norwich pursued several additional planks of poor relief reform: increasing the amounts that could go to individual recipients, organizing a well-run workhouse, forbidding begging altogether, and strictly enforcing settlement regulations. Their campaign approach hinged on the assumption that only by a rigorous patrolling of the town to remove those who did not belong could officials offer generous and systematic relief to the poor.[10]

Although Anglican leaders were included among those advocating these innovative improvements at the local level in advance of parliamentary action, puritans (or the "godly," as they called themselves) brought a particular religious zeal to urban reform efforts. Inspired by the model of John Calvin's Geneva, they believed, as one cleric wrote, that God would watch over them "in special manner," and ensure that they would "escape . . . many dangers." Besides systematizing the delivery of relief, reforms that signaled a godly city included providing education for young people, punishing vice, eliminating disorderly alehouses, and providing for clean water and swept streets.[11]

Whether cities and parishes took an early initiative or were jarred into action by the laws making poor rates compulsory, new attention was directed to the monitoring of incomers. Localities turned to four methods, none of which yet had statutory backing. These portend the techniques later used in Massachusetts. One was the interview with the local officials. For example, in Leicester starting in 1562, "no stranger could be admitted as a tenant" until he was examined by the mayor and the ward's aldermen to discover "from when he comyth & what honest behavior such forren person or persons be of." To get newcomers before the aldermen, however, one usually had to search them out—a second mechanism in the parish's new toolkit. Thus we find references to "searchers"—men whose task resembled that of Boston's Robert Love. Ipswich was very early in this respect, implementing a compulsory poor rate and instructing the bailiffs in 1557 to "order searchers for new commers into the Towne, and idle persons and vagabonds." By the 1580s, constables in each ward were to "make search every month for needy, impotent and vagrant p'sons, and therof make certificate that they may be settled according to law." In the Surrey parish of St. Savior, Southwark, in 1606 two men were paid twenty shillings each to be "surveyore[s] of Inmates" for the year.[12]

Besides searching for newcomers and interviewing them, some towns used a third mechanism to minimize the poor rolls: they gave newcomers who were not abjectly indigent the chance to give security (in the form of a bond) that they would not become chargeable. A fourth approach involved fining landlords who entertained or rented to lodgers for more than seven days without notifying town leaders. All of these mechanisms—

searching, interviewing, demanding security from strangers, and putting restrictions on landlords—became elements of New England's warning-out system.[13]

With a string of statutes starting with the Settlement Act of 1662, Parliament laid down a set of national policies for the monitoring and removal of intruding inmates. These statutes introduced both the certificate (a sort of worker passport) and an enumeration of ways to gain settlement in a new parish—by paying taxes, holding office, and paying over £10 in annual rent, for example. From 1685 onward, no longer could a newcomer gain inhabitancy by residing in a place for a certain time without detection. And yet parishes continued to monitor migrants, conducting "prudential" examinations so that their place of settlement would be on record should they ever need relief.[14]

Taken together, the statutory and local practices in place by the early 1700s in England took cognizance of at least six groups of people on the move—including servants contracted for one year, demobilized soldiers, and "certificate men." In other words, the measures constituted an interlocking system, the regulatory details of which often emerged from litigation between parishes. The ins and outs of settlement law—when a person was removable, what writ must be used, when children's settlement followed their parents—occupied 230 pages in the eleventh edition of Richard Burn's much relied upon justice of the peace manual published in 1769.[15]

In contrast to England's complicated regulatory matrix, Massachusetts adopted a single law (in 1692) and a single registration system (warning) to encompass the diverse types of mobile people. Building on reformers' ideas and on seventeenth-century English practice, legislators introduced two unique features. One was the province account—a truly radical commitment by the state to extend alms and relief to incoming strangers and sojourners. This novel fiscal arrangement, often unnoticed by scholars, provided a fix for the aid that parishes and municipalities extended to travelers and sojourners who had no local settlement. The second departure from English and European patterns was the provision that the verbal warning to depart in itself was sufficient to block one from gaining settlement. With this, Massachusetts did away with formal settlement hearings before justices of the peace and decoupled warning from removal. When forty-year-old James Miller walked all the way "By Land" from New York to Boston in autumn 1767 and was warned by Love on the very day he entered the port town, the language of the warning sounded as if King George himself had commanded the lame and "poorly" Miller to "depart this town of Boston." But Miller and everyone in earshot knew that he could stay and that being warned meant being put on notice with respect to settlement.[16]

Warning in eighteenth-century Massachusetts paralleled English settlement examinations that did not lead to removal. Both operated as insurance for the local governing unit (parish or town) in case the newcomer stayed and at some point became needy. A great many Britons moved frequently, crossing parish lines, often over short distances. Establishing an individual's settlement was often not a simple matter. In a typical English examination, justices asked a string of questions similar to but more extensive than the ones posed in Boston:

Where born? Where Father was settled? If ever apprenticed? To whom? for how long, how long served? . . . If served as a yearly Servant? for how long? . . . if married? How many Children? their Ages, Sexes and Names? If rented any House or Land? how much rent? Whether ever Rated to the poor? What Parish Land in or Rates paid?

In England, the migrant was typically put under oath when answering about what was his or her last place of legal settlement. In New England, no oath was applied. Both practices established prima facie evidence that the person had settlement elsewhere. Both practices allowed for a flow of labor into the town and avoided the expense entailed by physical removals. Given that yearly censuses of parish or town populations were not conducted, keeping a running log of those arriving enabled parishes and towns, when necessary, to distinguish settled from unsettled inhabitants.[17]

Settlement examinations in England and the issuing of verbal warnings in New England could operate as a valve. Local authorities could use the various means at their disposal to increase or diminish the flow of laborers over their boundaries depending on the needs of local employers. In good economic times, for example, towns might relax their attentiveness to settlement restriction. Moreover, labor needs, while important, were not the only consideration. Especially in certain rural areas of England, sojourners were monitored to prevent accelerated depletion of the commons—woods, wastes, and grazing land that many in these communities depended on. In the north Atlantic seaboard colonies, the sustained demand for white laborers or settlers outweighed anxiety over the commons. An urban seaport like

Boston, experiencing at midcentury the out-migration of many native-born artisans and workers, had few incentives to follow up verbal warnings with removals.[18]

Despite the affinity between warning in New England and settlement examinations in old England, a major difference occurred in the realm of vocabulary. Warning, in its specialized meaning of ordering noninhabitants to depart a legal jurisdiction, is absent from most English legal sources. It appears in neither parliamentary legislation nor English dictionaries of the period. It is mentioned in only one of the many legal manuals published in the seventeenth and eighteenth centuries to help parish officers and justices of the peace understand the statute and case law pertaining to the poor. The exception is Richard Kilburne's book entitled *Choice Presidents* [Precedents], which included "A Warrant to warn one to depart out of a Parish . . . or to give sufficient Security to indempnifie the Parish." Kilburne's sample warrant gives us the clue that warning to depart was not entirely unknown in local English practice.[19]

The warning warrant and the verb *warn* crop up occasionally in English parish and town records. Officials in Ipswich, East Anglia, a region of puritan strength from which many seventeenth-century New England settlers came, used the verb in a December 10, 1578, order: "searches shall be made forthwith [by Constables] for new Commers, . . . and to . . . warne new Commers to depart the Towne." Evidence suggests that warning warrants were sometimes issued at the parish level in the seventeenth century in hopes that the recipient would depart without having to be removed. By the early eighteenth century, the writ was no longer in use.[20] The overall picture, then, is that English officials rarely relied on the language of warning. Yet New Englanders formulating their own policies toward intruders and strangers starting in the 1670s knew of the term and understood its utility as a preremoval mechanism. They expanded its use such that it became their chief instrument for monitoring immigration and protecting community resources.

In terms of practice, Massachusetts was not departing in dramatic ways from the parent country. Yet in settlement law as in other areas, the province steered an independent route in terms of statutes, neither incorporating nor revising the relevant parliamentary laws.[21] For example, towns began using certificates in the 1680s, at the same time that England increasingly embraced them, but the province never mentioned the practice in its law books as other colonies did. Certificates were useful in situations in which a person with settlement in Massachusetts was presently living in a town other than where she or he had inhabitancy. Issued after the two towns had corresponded and agreed on the facts of the case, the document functioned as a contract between them. When widow Susanna Hewes moved from Boston—where she had been receiving relief—to neighboring Roxbury in order to live in her married daughter's household, the Boston selectmen wrote to their Roxbury counterparts that they "acknowledge[d] . . . Hewes as an Inhabit[an]t of Boston" and would cover any reasonable charges that had to be expended on her behalf. In England, certificates were typically prospective—they identified the migrant worker's parish of settlement, where he could return if he needed relief in the future. Given that the vast majority of people on the move in the Bay province were not currently chargeable, the most suitable and economical device to protect a town's poor relief funds was a simple verbal warning.[22]

Overall, the aim of settlement law in both regions was *not* to prohibit mobility but to help communities protect their resources and channel poor relief to deserving locals and, when circumstances demanded it, impoverished outsiders. All European jurisdictions struggled with the influx of laborers from the immediate hinterland and places farther afield who might fall ill and become needy. In an era when secular governing units had taken on responsibility to care for the local poor, how was a Christian polity to respond? The solution in Massachusetts was the province account. It originated when the province took financial responsibility for the upkeep of white settler refugees burnt out of their houses and towns in King Philip's and King William's wars of the late 1600s. The account's statutory basis was a 1701 law providing that passengers arriving by sea who fell ill on the passage would be relieved "at the charge of the province." This was soon expanded to include any sick person not "belonging to any town or place within this province" who was unable to pay their own medical bills.[23]

By the 1760s, the province poor account had become an entrenched and fiscally significant aspect of Massachusetts governance. Town authorities who extended public aid to a needy stranger became accustomed to petitioning the governor and council for reimbursement. They were rarely refused; after the medical and other bills were scrutinized, the province treasurer was authorized to make payment. Sickness and infectious disease were not the only conditions covered; neediness that arose out of indigence, pregnancy, physical and mental disability, and old age led to care being given and the province picking up the tab. After being duly warned in

Uxbridge in autumn 1759, Betty Trifle and her "bastard" daughter Mary continued to reside in town. They were constantly in need of aid because Betty suffered from an incapacitating mental disorder. The province treasurer reimbursed the town for their care until at least 1777. In Medway, the overseers of the poor arranged for the care of John Williams, a native of Exeter in old England; when he made known that he was "desirous of returning" there, the assembly ordered that he "be transported as soon as may be to Great Britain at the charge of this Province."[24]

By far the largest payouts from the province account each year went to Boston. One-third of the city's almshouse residents were on the province charge. In the fiscal year 1769–70, the selectmen received £677 sterling for the relief strangers received while in the house. In addition, the treasurer divided £171 between the almshouse keeper and the institution's physician for special ministrations to these inmates. In that year, the Boston-based expenses accounted for two-thirds of the total annual province poor outlay of £1,040. In other pre-revolutionary years, the annual bills for the province poor ranged from £813 to £1,073 and made up about 10 percent of all province appropriations, excluding payments to fund the public debt.[25]

Like warning, the province account system was capacious. It covered the towns' expenses for housing and upkeep for the roughly eleven hundred Acadians forced to endure eleven years of internal exile in Massachusetts starting in 1755. Legislators estimated in 1763 that the province's costs for caring for Acadians had mounted to £10,000. When some Massachusetts towns such as Natick refused to categorize Indians who had been longtime residents as town poor, the province account stepped into the breach. After the revolution, the numbers of formerly enslaved persons facing impoverishment rose. Unable to find work and denied legal settlement in the towns where they grew up, many African New Englanders admitted to the almshouse were counted as state charges.[26]

In adapting their settlement practices to the colonial social landscape, New Englanders made warning a flexible instrument. Massachusetts warnings accommodated a broad range of persons: unmarried male and female youths entering short-term work arrangements, families relocating, Britons who had served in the Seven Years War, and beggars and strollers. Inspired by civic betterment schemes on the Continent and in England, province lawmakers transformed an obscure warrant into a recording mechanism that permitted sizable amounts of aid to support both the town poor and sojourning strangers.

LARGE port towns along the eastern North American seaboard faced explosively rising relief costs due to influxes of newcomers. By 1770, New York and Philadelphia had populations larger than Boston's and greater inmigration. To Love's way of thinking, these port cities warned strangers just as Boston did. Twice, he wrote about a stranger who had recently arrived from one or the other city: "he Lived Some years" there and was "Never Warned Out."[27] However, the vocabulary of warning is absent from the minutes of the New York mayor's court and the Philadelphia Common Council. Was Love mistaken?

Since neither New York nor Pennsylvania instituted a province poor account, we would not expect them to have resorted to a registration system like warning that entailed diligent searchers and scads of paperwork. For the most part, taxpayers in these major seaports were expected to absorb the costs of the relief offered to the nonsettled. Indeed, city authorities forgave the jail costs and fines of petty criminals who were not province inhabitants and paid the passages home by land or sea of many displaced colonists and Britons. They also admitted strangers in distress to their overcrowded almshouses, frequently begging their legislatures to help cover the costs.[28]

New Yorkers and Pennsylvanians did not mobilize to create province poor accounts to relieve the undue burden borne by taxpayers in their major cities. Conversely, Massachusetts taxpayers accepted and did not protest the tax responsibility represented by the province account. Politics, and the identity of those who would be aided, supply an explanation for this difference. At its genesis, funds from the Massachusetts province account went to colonists who had lost their homes in wars with Indians and France. Because these needy came from towns in all parts of the province, legislators supported drawing down provincial revenues for their relief. Only later did the bulk of such compensation cover outsiders and get funneled mostly to Boston. In the mid-Atlantic colonies where the inmigration of Britons, Germans, and other Europeans was phenomenally high, the seaports' assembly representatives never managed to mobilize sufficient support for a dual accounting system from colleagues representing rural, interior townships.

But even without dual poor relief accounts in place, local jurisdictions outside New England could have drawn on legal precedent and used warning.[29] Although scholars have associated warning exclusively with New England, this equation needs reexamination. The most likely place to find warning deployed as a legal step potentially leading to removal would be in the legal papers filed with the county sessions courts relating to pauper support suits.[30] In Chester County, just west of Philadelphia, one finds the occasional use of the verb *warn*. On at least six occasions from the 1720s to the 1750s, officials in various townships warned strangers to depart in the same way that Massachusetts towns did. An overseer in Concord recalled how, in 1726, the overseers handled the case of Margaret Power, who was originally from Ireland and came "to reside among us"; we found "that She was a transient person . . . very old [with] no viseble estate to support her." Her grown son, a "transient," also living there, must have been unable to maintain her. The overseers interviewed Power, and upon discovering that she could not give security for indemnifying the township should she become chargeable, they warned her to depart and explained that "She Should not have any Settlement here." Rather than petition to have the elderly woman removed, the Concord overseers obtained a court order requiring the county commissioners to acknowledge that "her Support and maintenance ought to be at the publick Charge" of the County; they refused to comply. Other litigation in the county shows overseers using warning as a prerequisite to obtaining removal orders; they followed the form laid out in the English legal manual *Choice Presidents*.[31]

Warning strangers thus occurred in at least one local jurisdiction in Pennsylvania, albeit in a limited fashion. Associated with removal, the verb *warn* crops up intermittently only in two genres of documents: overseers' testimony and removal orders by justices of the peace. By the 1760s, it was no longer in use. The word is not found in the quarter sessions docket books, the life narratives that "poor and Impotent" persons gave when submitting to settlement examinations, or the pertinent 1718 and 1734 statutes. Thus, surviving references to warning are so rare and obscure that they have been missed by historians of colonial Pennsylvania.[32]

The Chester County evidence suggests that the warning writ was used as a precursor to removal in parts of British America other than New England at least sometimes, especially in the early decades of the eighteenth century. In New York, eastern Long Island communities founded by puritans adopted the warning practice, but other townships seem not to have done so. The units charged with dispensing poor relief in Virginia and the Carolinas (Anglican parishes) and Maryland (counties) are described by scholars as not bothering much with removals.[33] The level of government higher than the locality entrusted with care of the poor—such as the county—occasionally acknowledged an obligation to cover relief costs for individuals lacking settlement in the colony. But these ad hoc reimbursements were few and far between.[34]

The exception may be South Carolina, where an alternative path was forged to provide for both strangers of free status and those whites who were considered the town and colony poor. Wealthy St. Philip's parish in the major port of Charles Town shouldered the double costs of caring for the town poor *and* aiding the nonsettled. Some strangers were housed in the poorhouse, disabled sailors were given passage home, backcountry settlers fleeing Indian raids were succored. The assembly reimbursed the parish infrequently. Rather than create a province poor account and deploy warning to differentiate legal inhabitants from nonsettled folk, the legislators and the vestrymen (who were often the same men) dispensed aid on an ad hoc basis—whenever whites were seen as deserving.[35]

The South Carolina–Massachusetts comparison raises a thorny issue about levels of public relief. In polities' efforts to fashion what they perceived to be effective welfare regimes, what constituted generosity to the needy? Historians argue that poor relief for white residents of South Carolina was more generous than in the north, supporting "a reasonable standard of living rather than merely subsistence" and marking off an entitlement denied to persons of color. Charles Town pensioners received on average 8 shillings, 7 pence per month (which exceeded the estimated cost of food by three shillings), whereas their counterparts in Boston and Philadelphia received between four and six shillings monthly (an amount that fell short of the cost of food). To conclude from this comparison that the major concern of northern authorities was "reducing expenses" rather than relieving want and suffering belies the evidence. Everywhere, elites, clerics, and overseers believed that the principles of Christian charity guided their efforts.[36] In all parts of the British Atlantic, those in control of governance condoned a political order that visited the most entrenched impoverishment and the most sustained denial of human rights on enslaved men, women, and children. The modest geographical comparisons presented here suggest that we need a more fine-tuned calculus of where the boundaries of sympathy were drawn in the colonies and a better understanding of the tax and donation schemas undergirding public and private relief.[37]

In the eighteenth century, the largest British American mainland ports experienced rapidly growing Euro-American populations and sizable in-migration from the nearby countryside and often from abroad. Each struggled with the problem of distinguishing poor relief for residents and strangers. What stands out is how long one of these towns, Robert Love's Boston, and a set of colonies, Massachusetts and most of its neighbors, monitored newcomers as a means of extending Christian charity to all of the deserving poor. Anyone sojourning in or moving to a town in the region could expect to receive a verbal warning to depart. Authorities and lay people alike understood that this legal gesture saved towns from uncontrollable poor relief without impeding the movement of people. Warning coupled with the province poor account was the innovation that most distinguished Boston from Ypres and Norwich, Paris and Lyons—cities with much praised and much advertised welfare systems inaugurated in the sixteenth century. Nowhere else in the West did taxpayers in a jurisdiction as extensive as Massachusetts prove willing to pay what were in effect two poor rates. And unlike South Carolina, which could boast making the highest payments to the town poor, the Massachusetts system made it possible for people of color to claim aid.[38]

Was the warning system "puritan"? Yes and no. Its impetus and its staying power can be explained by religious and civic commitments of the puritan-minded men and women who founded and provided leadership for most of the New England colonies. But the ideas behind the system were not uniquely puritan. In adopting the practice of searching for strangers, New England settlers followed reform ideas that had found widespread approval among seventeenth-century English elites—puritan and non-puritan alike. In this era of municipal experimentation, certain towns like Norwich and Boston stood out for the thoroughness of implementation. Hiring searchers, expecting overseers to walk their wards, maintaining a large almshouse, and using watchmen to ensure the Lord's Day was not profaned required volunteers and a few paid townsmen to commit huge amounts of time. In England, many towns "fell far short of the ideal," and by the 1640s most had abandoned any comprehensive program.[39]

As a warner who walked the streets almost daily and identified up to 420 strangers per year, Robert Love epitomized this "constant supervision" that early modern visionaries knew was requisite to maintain a well-ordered town. To the rituals of perambulation that greased the system, New Englanders could afford to add an element. Because of phenomenally high literacy rates among adult white men, walking *and* writing were paired tasks that could be asked of the low-profile men who filled the posts of night constables and warners. Just as Love with his phonetic spelling and inelegant penmanship filled out hundreds of pages, night constables such as Isaac Townsend and Valentine Sullivan took pains to detail in monthly journals the drunkards and domestic disputes they encountered on their watch.[40] The walking, warning, and recording that became Love's drill in his older years announced that Boston adhered to its particular vision for disciplining the urban landscape far into the eighteenth century.

CHAPTER 4

Walking and Warning

No MEMOIRIST RECOUNTED how it felt to be accosted and verbally warned to depart. Diaries, letters, and travel accounts contain no descriptive scenes of warnings. Despite their formulaic character, Love's notes divulge quite a lot about the warning encounter. They reveal the warner's rhythms of walking and warning, including the gaps of time between when newcomers arrived and when Love found them. They allow us to partially overhear the conversations he held with strangers, and to perceive the reactions of the warned. Most answered Love's questions in a straightforward manner, but some were cantankerous and set him on edge. Others talked a blue streak, divulging their faraway birthplaces, Atlantic journeys, and hopes for the future. Occasionally they asked advice about work or lodging. Bystanders and landlords joined in these exchanges, making Love's capsule biographies a collective product. Indeed, the meticulous paper trail that the warner left underscores the layered way in which local knowledge of strangers was compiled. Love could successfully fulfill his mission on behalf of the town only through careful attention to a series of personal transactions: with the strangers he warned, with his network of informants, and with the officials he reported to.

Love took care to write down what he believed was the salient information he gathered from each stranger. In each entry, the warner followed a ritualized sequence. While adherence to this particular ordering of information would not have mattered to his employers, the repetitive act was probably a helpful mnemonic device for Love as a record keeper. His most fulsome records contained: the names of strangers in the group; where they were "last from"; the date they entered Boston; whether they came "by land" or "by sea," and, if the latter, the name of the captain and the ship; with whom they were lodging and in what neighborhood; additional information such as occupation or personal appearance; and the words of the warning (Figure 5, for two entries).

A good example is his record of an encounter with a Frenchman in early August 1766:

> Larance Gillerest Last from QueBeck Come to town July 26 1766 With Captn. David Weir in the Scooner Rainbowe he is a Baker to traid he Entends to Work Journey work if he Can Gett itt to Doe Warned in His Majestys Name to depart the town of Boston in 14 days.

Many entries are shorter. Love recorded occupations for only a small percentage of the travelers. "By land or sea" information could be left out for the numerous people who walked into Boston from nearby Massachusetts towns. And at times Love was forced to be terse because the subject refused to tell him much. Hence, in September 1765: "William Doty Last from Plymouth Come to town yesterday he would not tell me Where he Lodged."[1]

Love, although a minor town official appointed to act in lieu of the selectmen, seemed proudly conscious of his ability to present himself as an agent of George III. As he walked the streets, alleys, and docks, and visited landlords and tavern keepers in search of strangers, the public nature of his job followed him throughout Boston, legitimizing a considerable amount of what otherwise would be snooping and verbal badgering. Love did not take along just his voice (was it stern or kindly, mellifluous or croaking?) and his powerful memory for faces. He also must have carried his warning book, or at least some place where he jotted preliminary notes before transferring them into his calf-bound logbooks. Given the crowded conditions of the town, Love's individual acts of warning were witnessed by many townspeople and thus were public performances. His pen and paper were physical artifacts marking the warner's efficacy as an agent of the king.[2]

Surprise was one tactic that Boston officials had at their disposal. In smaller country towns in Massachusetts, strangers often knew in advance that they were about to be warned. Selectmen first issued a warrant naming newcomers who needed to be warned. After a gap of a few days, the town constable set out to find the strangers, display the warrant, and verbally

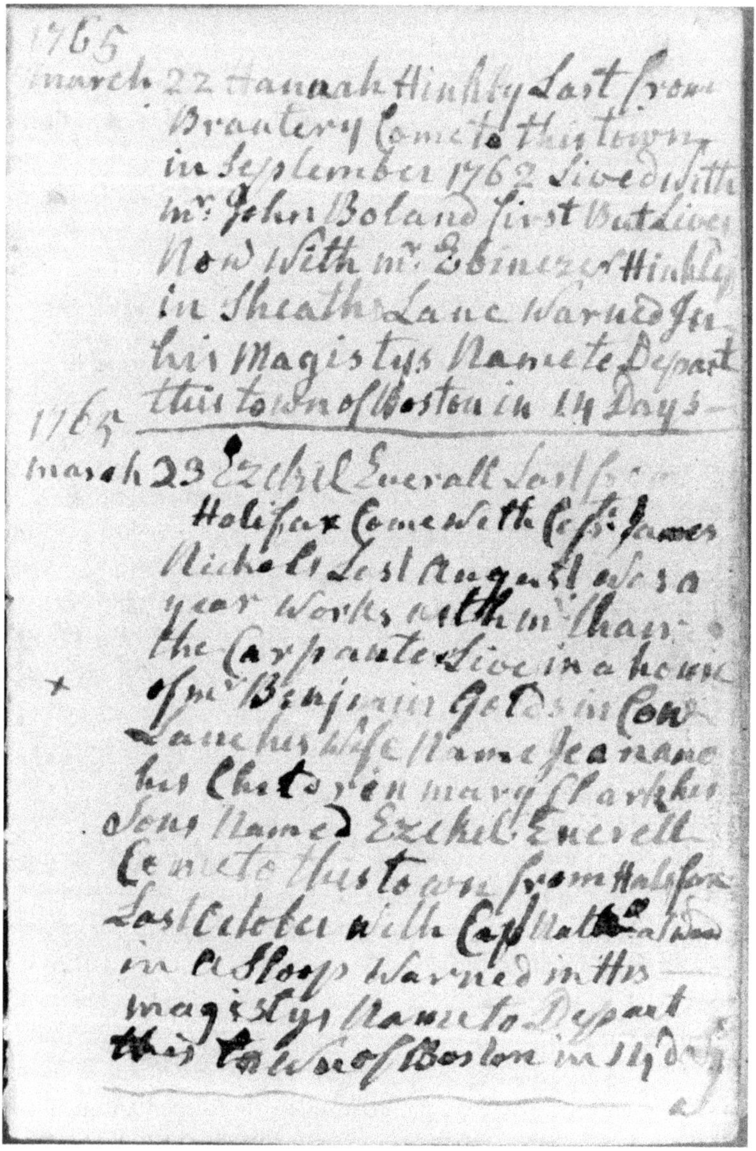

1765
march 22 Hannah Hinkly Last from
Brantery Came to this town
in September 1762 Lived with
mr John Boland first But Lives
Now With mr Ebinezer Hinkly
in Sheath Lane Warned in
his Magistys Name to Depart
this town of Boston in 14 Days

1765
march 23 Ezckel Everall Last from
Holifax Came with Capt James
Nichols Last August was a
year Works with mr Cham
the Carpanter Live in a house
of mr Benjamin Getes in Cow
Lane his wife Name Jeanane
his Chel in mary Clark his
Sons Named Ezekel Everell
Came to this town from Halifax
Last October with Capt Math
in a Sloop Warned in His
Magistys Name to Depart
this town of Boston in 14 Days

FIGURE 5. A page from Robert Love's 1765–66 record book.
Image courtesy of the Massachusetts Historical Society.

warn them "to Depart out of town."[3] The gap must have given noninhabitants the opportunity to evade the constable, if they so wished. However,
in the long run, if the sojourner stayed in town, warnings undoubtedly were
served. Love and his fellow warners in the provincial capital had the power
to issue warnings without getting prior direction from the selectmen.[4]
Hence a Boston warner could arrive unannounced at tenements or workplaces. He could hail unfamiliar figures in the street and demand that they
state their business in Boston, their place of legal settlement, and the day of
their arrival.

Newcomers found it hard to hide from the indefatigable Love. The
intervals between a stranger's arrival and the day on which Love found and
warned him or her reveal just how good he was at his job. Love warned an
astonishing 63 percent within one *month* of their arrival. He encountered
20 percent on the first or second day they were in town, and another 19
percent within the first week. Only 4 percent of the strangers had been in
town ten months or more. Of course, despite his assiduity, Love must have
missed spotting some sojourners, but given the high turnover in the urban
population, chances were good that they left town on their own accord
within a year.[5]

The quickness with which Love identified newcomers is of a piece with
other evidence that he was a man with a remarkable memory. Historians
recognize that, given the paucity of personal written records relative to
modern times, eighteenth-century denizens had well-developed oral memories. Court records reveal that many could recall conversations and business reckonings from years past in fine detail, when these became a matter
of serious dispute or litigation. Similarly, residents of port cities would have
built up an impressive memory bank of the faces, gaits, hats, clothes, voices,
and laughs of all who lived in the neighborhoods where their own living
quarters and workplaces were located. Those who regularly perambulated
all parts of the city and had an incentive to memorize faces, as Love did,
might come to believe that they "knew every person white & black[,]
men[,] women & children in the City . . . by name."[6] While Love might
not have claimed such encyclopedic and intimate knowledge, he had to
have carried with him on his walks an extraordinarily acute "facebook" of
the permanent and recent residents of Boston.

Unfortunately, Love rarely described the faces, physical attributes, or
clothing of strangers. Based on his notes, a sketch artist would not have
enough information to draw portraits of the warner's interlocutors. If we

were able to interview Love at the end of a warning day, he doubtless could have enumerated the height, physique, countenance, and togs of the person freshly entered in his logbook. Over and over again in the runaway notices posted in colonial newspapers, masters and ship captains displayed their intimate knowledge of what employees wore at any given moment. Love's short-term memory must have been similarly acute. The hundreds of young people flowing into Boston varied in body type and skin tone: thick-set, slender-bodied, straight-limbed, pretty tall, of swarthy complexion or pale. People of all ages were sorted by whether they were smooth faced, or "pock freckled" because of smallpox. A man "of middling Age" might be wearing "his own black Hair, tyed with a black Ribbon," while the woman accompanying him was "of thin Visage" and had "a wide Mouth, large Teeth, thick Lips." Love was used to hearing stammers and other speech impediments, and many accents, including some like his own: a sailor who deserted a brig in Boston harbor in 1764 was said to be "born in the North of Ireland, and speaks like a Scotchman." Finally, Love saw before him an enormous array of clothing: patterns of stripes, checks, flowers, and plaids; textures of velvet, leather, homespun, and superfine broadcloth; great coats, waistcoats, and petticoats of blue, green, red, purple, calico, and cinnamon; buttons and buckles galore; distinctive cravats and capes; lots of gray yarn stockings; and hats and shoes of all varieties.[7]

The shape of a nose or a tell-tale, well-worn jacket might have jogged Love's memory when he warned a sojourner for a second or third time. At least seventy repeaters appear in his warning records. To be warned more than once usually meant that the stranger had come into Boston, left, and returned. Love's decision to warn a party more than once reflects his thoroughness and his awareness of the legal and welfare ramifications of travelers' changing circumstances—such as place of settlement or economic standing. On the occasions when a household head spent time in Boston alone and then returned some years later with his family, the original warning would not have covered the man's dependents. Hence Hugh Thompson earned warnings both on his solo sojourn in town in the winter of 1766 and eighteen months later, when he lodged at the Sign of the Jolly Sailor with his wife and three children shortly after they all arrived from Scotland. More commonly, duplicate warnings were issued to people who were perpetually on the move on the North American continent and were needy in some way. William Harris (begging, an old man, very poor) circulated so often to towns in Pennsylvania and Rhode Island then back to Boston that Love warned him four times.[8]

Although Love was not explicit about where he encountered strangers and delivered his warnings, he allows us to infer the location. For the 14 percent of his warnings that were delivered on the very day the traveler arrived in Boston, almost all seem to have taken place in the streets.[9] Often, Love caught the newcomer while he or she was in motion across the town landscape, heading toward a specific destination. John Green and John Smith were among those who knew in advance where they would be staying. Green told Love that he was "Gowing to Work With [laborer] Rodger Mcknights." Smith was walking northward from the gate at Boston Neck to join his wife, Mary, who was already in town and lodging "att David Powers Neer the North Battery." Some brand new arrivals admitted to Love that they had come to the port town not with secure prospects but with vague hopes of work or succor. Mary Chatot had walked in from nearby Brookline and told Love that she "was Looking for a place to Live att in town." Incomers may have looked to Love, as a longtime Boston resident, to play the broker's role, pointing them to a likely employer or affordable lodging. Whether he did so is not revealed in his warning records.[10]

Others whom Love found on their first days in Boston were down on their luck and told the warner that they did not expect to be in Boston long. Love judged William Rodgers, who had served in the colonial militia in 1757, "a verry Old man and verry Rag[g]ed." The old soldier reported that "he Wants to Go to Marthers vinyard has a Brother their." Jenkin Conway, who had been discharged from Colonel John Whitmore's regiment in late 1762, "Wants a pasage to England." Love's conversations with poor or disreputable new arrivals were at times reminiscent of a negotiation. As the selectmen's agent, Love must have cautioned men he found begging or women he suspected of loose morals that the town could prosecute them for vagrancy (punishable by a term in the workhouse). The threat was effective. Constable Isaac Townsend reported that on a winter night in 1765, the watchmen found "a Stranger . . . asleep on Bradfords Wharff being m[u]ch intoxicated with Liquor whom we kept till Morn[;] inquiring where he belong'd he said to Marblehead & had been fasting all Day & laid him[self] down to sleep He was perswaded to putt off in the first boat by [our] telling him he would be taken up as a Stroling Person."[11]

Indeed, several disreputable newcomers pledged to Love that they would leave town in a few days, in effect notifying the town through the warner that they need not be prosecuted or forcibly removed. With this strategy, they bought themselves a few days to solicit alms or do business. About Richard Griffin, who had arrived "this day" from Philadelphia by land, Love wrote: "he is an old man and a beggar[;] he has promised me that he will depart this [town] in 2 or 3 days." On Margaret Lemey: "she is a stroling womon or[i]ginally belonged to Exeter," New Hampshire, who had come to Boston from Portsmouth; "she promesed to Return their as soon as posable." In one encounter in March 1770, Love ventriloquized for the selectmen. Lee Wolfindine had come in by land from New York two days earlier: "he is a Kind of a Crasey man he has No place of Abode but . . . Lodges in the WatchHouses and makes a Grate noise with Boys in the Streets & in the town house[.] I told him he Must Get a pasage to England soon or he must Return soon to New York again."[12]

While it was in the streets that Love most often encountered migrants arriving "this day," one of his chief strategies for discovering who had entered Boston days or weeks before was to frequent landlords' establishments. Like warners before him, Love would have been told when he took office that he was to "Visit all such Houses & Families as he apprehends Entertains Inmates or Strangers."[13] That Love did so regularly is indicated by frequent clusters found in his records of strangers staying at the same location warned on the same day. For example, on a day in May 1772 and again in mid-July 1773, Love recorded back-to-back warnings for solo men who had come to town at different times and were now staying with the retailer Enoch Brown in his house on Boston Neck. The likelihood is that, rather than meeting the colodgers on the streets, Love went to Brown's to interview and warn these men. Occasionally, Love was explicit: he wrote that he "found" widow Elizabeth Hardwick, who had come in from nearby Braintree, at her son-in-law's house in Back Street.[14]

Love's records offer few internal clues to indicate the hours of the day when he issued warnings. Twice he specified that the encounter occurred after dark. "I found" William Johnston "Looking for Lodging in the Night"; the warner probably led or directed the man to Daniel McKeen's South End house, where he ended up lodging. On a Tuesday one March, Love recorded that a strolling couple, last from Scotland, "came to town this Evening" and promised him that they were "Gowing Eastward" on "the morrow morning." In three cases, he remarked that it was morning when he found and warned a stranger drunk in the streets. Presumably, the great bulk of Love's interviews with strangers occurred in daylight hours.[15]

We do know the frequency with which Love walked and warned, and the days of the week and seasons of the year when he was most active and successful. Over his years as warner, Love for the most part recorded only one or two warnings on a given day, indicating that he did not generally spend the whole day scouting for strangers. He typically found strangers to warn two to three days in a row, then skipped a day or two. Love warned slightly more groups on Thursdays than on the other weekdays, and slightly fewer on Saturdays. He generally observed the Sabbath by not issuing warnings on Sundays, but on seventeen occasions he made an exception— perhaps discovering a stranger while on the way to worship with his family at the centrally located First Church.[16]

The puritan founders of the colony disdained traditional European and Christian patterns of declaring no work for common laborers on feast, harvest, and saints' days. As an adherent of the Congregational church, Love would have been aware of their insistence that men and women work on December 25 and not observe Christmas. Yet cultural practices in Massachusetts had changed in Love's lifetime; by the 1760s New Englanders increasingly celebrated Christmas and refrained from labor. In his first year on the job, Love's warning of two families on December 25 can be read as his honoring the old New England way. But ever after, he gave warnings a rest when that day came around, as he did on New Year's Day except in 1772 and 1773. On the public days of fasting and thanksgiving proclaimed by the governor in ritual fashion each April and November, Love for the most part did not warn. In contrast, when civic or political events occasioned large gatherings, such as town meetings, provincial elections, Pope's Day processions (November 5), or celebrations of the Stamp Act repeal, Love often took advantage of the large gatherings and street activity to warn several strangers.[17]

The busiest months of warning matched those when the temperatures were mildest and the harbor was filled with ships—May to September. Fifty-one percent of Love's warnings fell in these months, while January and February engendered the lowest monthly totals. This seasonal pattern reflects the ebb and flow of labor in and out of the town rather than the warner's hesitation to step out onto the winter streets wearing his heavy cloak.[18]

Inquiring into the emotional tenor of the exchanges between strangers and warner opens a series of questions. Were newcomers startled, annoyed, perplexed, or humiliated by the ritual? Consider that Love's contemporaries would have heard the verb *warn* to mean one was put on notice, not that one had to leave imminently. Furthermore, sojourners to Boston who had grown up or lived in towns in Massachusetts, Connecticut, or New Hampshire were well acquainted with the warning practice, and they would have anticipated a warning by Boston officials if they appeared to be coming to live. British subjects were well-acquainted with the laws of settlement and were probably quick to grasp why Love needed to record their particulars. Many whom Love questioned revealed extraneous details about themselves—their trade, how long they had lived in their last place of residence, their exact route to Boston, their future plans. The great majority of migrants spoke truthfully and without evasion. Some probably engaged the warner and bystanders in lengthy conversation. For most, the warning ritual was a fairly benign and inevitable aspect of sojourning in Boston.

Yet warning had its ominous side. As legal authorities of the time put it, once a newcomer heard the words "I warn you to depart," he or she was considered to be "under warning" while remaining in Boston. The great bulk of warned strangers were welcome to stay. For them, the process registered their presence, allowed them to enter the town's workforce, and insulated local taxpayers from future charge. Boston officials pursued removal warrants against only thirty solo travelers or families between 1765 and 1775—the decade during which about three thousand parties were warned. As with other regional hubs, Boston needed a continual influx of laborers. Moreover, physical removals were time consuming, labor intensive, and expensive (given that most removed persons could not pay the costs). Boston acted in parallel with other towns in keeping them to a minimum.[19]

Love did not personally escort the unwelcome strangers out of town, but he was sometimes asked by the selectmen to arrange removals. To do so, he presented a petition on behalf of the selectmen to a Boston justice of the peace, claiming that, as in the case of pregnant Lydia Gammons, "although She has been Warned According to law for more than fourteen days past to depart," she had refused to do so. If all was in order, the justice would grant the requested warrant, ordering any constable to apprehend the named party, and—at their own charge, if able to pay—carry them to the Massachusetts town where they were believed to have settlement, to be delivered there to the selectmen or overseers.[20]

Removal orders omitted the reasons for expulsions, but the types and profiles of those removed suggest what prompted such dramatic action. Few solo men were the subject of such orders. If he was able-bodied, a male newcomer's usefulness as a laborer apparently protected him from removal. If deemed a common beggar, stroller, or vagabond, he could be "taken up" by any petty official such as a night watchman and carried before a justice of the peace, convicted of a misdemeanor, and committed to a short stint of labor at the workhouse. As was the case elsewhere under British settlement law, the costly procedure of removing "strangers" was reserved for certain types of families and solo women. Studies of English parishes have shown that recently married couples with young children were the demographic group most likely to need public support. In Boston, most of the fifteen families removed appear to have been impoverished, young parents with children under age ten. In two cases, there were aggravating causes: the warned strangers, both Irishmen, who had been arrested for burglary a few months after their arrival in town, jailed, and convicted as felons.[21]

Women might be removed if they behaved in an outrageous and disorderly manner. Lucy Pernam, a black resident of Newburyport, was warned at least once and removed twice. She provoked authorities by episodically becoming intoxicated and threatening to burn down the town. Others merited removal if they were notorious for bearing children out of wedlock. Katherine Green, an Indian last from Stoughton, provoked Love's ire with her promiscuous behavior with men of color; he did not wait for a removal warrant. "Come to town yesterday [a Sunday] Between meetings I then Charged her to Gett out of town Early on Munday morning[.] Was all Night in a Lighter Boat with 4 Negor Men[.] Att 9 [I] found her and Carried her Over the Neck." Nearly all of those carried out had come in from Massachusetts towns and were returned to the town where they were believed to have inhabitancy. In the mid-eighteenth century at least, officials rarely if ever invoked the legal process of removal for the large numbers of sojourners arriving from outside the province.[22]

Cognizant that strangers' warning histories could help determine which fund would be charged for a pauper, Love at times noted whether a stranger had been warned in a previous place of residence. Moses McIntosh had lived in several Massachusetts towns before arriving in Boston in late 1770, but because he had "been Warned in his Majestys Name out of them *all*," he was admitted to the Boston almshouse on the province account. Daniel Tombs and his wife and child had been "warned out from" Roxbury, their last abode, so Love had to dig deeper: "the[y] Orig[in]lay Belonged to Hopkintown and [were] Born their." In contrast, free black Elizabeth Chase "properly belongs to Roxberry," proclaimed Love, because "she lived [there, prior to the 1767 law] 1 year and a half without being warned out of town."[23]

A small subset of Boston's newcomers courted eviction by greeting Love defiantly. These resisters "refused to tell" where they had come from or where they lodged and sometimes even to give their names. Love encountered Robert Gray on a January day; the man had arrived eight weeks earlier from Scotland: "he says He Lodges Neer Mr. Cooper's Meetinghouse But He Refuses to tell the people['s] Names." The warner added an unusual, judgmental aside: "the Man Apears to Be a Bad man." Most contrary of all was Samuel Fosdick, "a Verry Old man & Verry poor & Verry Cross[;] he would Not tell where he Lodged in town But said he Would Live in town and NoBody Should hinder him he had places anofe [enough] to lodge att." While refusing to give Love a name or past place of residence might be read as a survival strategy or as a sign of mental illness, it likely just as often reflected the traveler's adoption of an irascible public persona in the face of poverty, disability, social alienation, and kinlessness.[24]

In the face of resistance, Love could be very persistent. One April day, he came across a transient man who "Would Not tell his Name and Was Very Angrey." The indefatigable warner shadowed the man around town or hung about where the stranger loitered. "After Wa[i]ting upon him" the great part of the day, wrote Love, he finally "told me his Name" (Michael Vane) and "I Warned him."[25]

The locution "I warned" was a telling deviation from Love's routine wording, which followed the formula, "warned him in His Majesty's Name." The phrase crept into Love's writing exclusively on occasions when the stranger he encountered was resistant, begging, or seemed dangerous. We can hear the warner's agitation in this rather choppy entry: "Davison Johnston Last from providanc Come to town this Day he Says he has No Certain place of aboade he is pretty shabby in his Clothing he Says he has no money I Warned him." Love likely lapsed into the first-person unconsciously. It signaled his heightened emotions when coming face-to-face with the most unkempt and unruly of the town's incomers, those whose behavior suggested they could become extra burdensome. Strangers who hollered and screamed in the night or who begged openly and defiantly clearly rattled Love. Inserting himself into the warning declaration by writing "*I* warned *him*" suggests his need to differentiate and distance himself from the person being warned. The "I" may also reflect Love's sense of himself as a pious Congregationalist obligated to enforce moral codes whenever possible. In inscribing himself as active agent in these cases, the warner was in essence wagging his finger and evoking his office and ability to inform the selectmen of immoral behavior.[26]

Indeed, in order to deliver a moral judgment of the person in front of him, Love occasionally wrote himself into the narrative section of his entry. Love encountered Anna Caterina Boma "in the streets." He had doubts that she was truly a peddler; rather, she *"pretends* to be a pedler." Furthermore, her word was not to be trusted: "she Said first She came from New London But Afterwards She Said She Belonged to New york." Love's coda: "I belive She is as bad a woman as can be." On another occasion, Love wrote without further explanation: "he is a man I Do not Like Verry Well." And of Archibald Conaway, who "Would Not tell his Business But said he had Something to Advertis"; "I Do not Like the Looks of the man."[27]

One gets the sense that Love, as a fastidious record keeper, was offended when he found himself thwarted in collecting information. Because of drunkenness, impudence, or mental disability, strangers sometimes gave "very slender" or "poor" accounts of themselves, preventing Love from writing down where they had a place of settlement, where they were last from, or why they had come to Boston. Love may have placed his hands on some of these defiant street people, gripping their arms or giving them a shake to wake them out of drunken stupors. "A Kind of Crasey man" whom Love came across in August 1770 "Would Give no Acco't of himself where he Belonged But Disaired [desired] I Would Let him Goo." The wording suggests that the stranger perceived that Love was holding him, either physically or metaphorically.[28]

Strollers would have been especially worrisome to town and province officials. Because these men and women had "no settled place of abode" (in other words, no regular domicile and no traceable town of legal settlement), the province would have to pay if they became utterly disabled. Love had a favorite adjective for the male strollers. Jonathan Lawrence, "a tinker to traid" with "No Cartain place of aboad" but who originally "Belongs to Scotland" is "what me [may] be Called a Stroling Impidant Man." Former British army soldier William Filch made it a "Business of Beging from house to house" and was not just impudent but "verry Bould." John Ewing, who had come in from Lyme in the neighboring colony of Connecticut, was, according to the warner, "a Lying Drinking man and verry Impident[;]

he Says he Values Noboady." Love's desire to extract accurate information appears to have been sabotaged by these recalcitrant, rude strangers, resulting in unpleasant encounters that were fraught with friction.[29]

At times, Love wondered if his leg was being pulled or if the stranger had been deliberately deceptive. Polly Smith "says she Come to town yesterd[ay]: But I have heard She has Been in town Before" behaving promiscuously. Love sometimes wondered if he could trust those who claimed to have been castaways or captured by the Indians and held for years. He may have doubted that the stranger who called himself Abraham Colden was truly "the Natrell [natural, meaning illegitimate] son" of the governor of New York. Surely Edmund Mott, "a very poor man and very poorly clothed," was hallucinating when he boasted that "he Can Live Without Eating." A lack of worldly knowledge tripped up one fifteen-year-old who presented himself as Nicholas Hebier, born in Landersang in the German lands. He made the mistake of reporting that he had been "3 years in France in Paris from which place he says he Come *by Land*" to Boston. Love concluded: "I Take him to be a Runaway servant."[30]

Sometimes Love was able to unmask the deceiver. Aliases were a tool that marginal working people and traffickers in petty crime might adopt to evade detection. Love spotted the strategy being used by several women. In October 1767, he warned a woman a second time in seven months, identifying her as Mary Thompson and explaining that previously she had given him "the Name of Mary White Which Was a fals Name." Love's three warnings of Nancy Shays show that she had been circulating through towns in the Boston area: Cambridge, Charlestown, Westborough. After arriving in Boston in the fall of 1771, Shays was sentenced to a spell of labor in the workhouse for some unspecified misbehavior, and then given shelter at the almshouse. A year later, she returned to town, finding lodgings with a succession of residents. On their third encounter, Love reported that "She Calls herself Now by a falls Name Nancy Dasson." Her choice of alias was a defiant pun that would have been transparent to Love, given that Nancy Dawson was a famous English hornpipe and jig dancer of the 1750s and 1760s, appearing at London's Covent Garden and other stages. A ballad written in her honor to a Scottish fiddle tune boasted: "Of all the girls in our town / The black, the fair, the red, the brown,/That dance and prance it up and down, / There's none like Nancy Dawson."[31]

When presented with a mystery, Love could turn himself into an energetic investigator, stretching his researches over several days. In August

1768, he warned one mentally disturbed woman whose name he never learned even though he "Asked her several times while she Was aboute in the town." In May 1772, Love had perhaps his most extensive experience playing detective after he visited the almshouse and discovered a male infant who had recently been taken in. Love learned that the "man Child" had been found abandoned on Boston Neck. Somehow the warner was able to track down "the Womon that Nursed the Child about 8 or 9 Weeks . . . whose Name is Mary Hodlcy" at hcr lodgings in New Boston. She told him that "their Was a man," John Twing of Cambridge, a blacksmith, who paid "her for Nursing said Child" and then carried "it away with him"—before it was found abandoned. With this information, the town of Boston had someone to pursue for the cost of the child's upkeep. Love also had been able to discover that the infant was "Never Babtised therfor" he could give it "No name."[32]

The case of the abandoned infant reminds us that Love surely relied on the audience present at any warning scene to give him information. At warnings, it was not only the stranger who answered questions, but also landlords, employers, relatives, and bystanders. Mistress Candace, in Middle Street, had recently taken in her brother William Haley, formerly a Boston resident who had "Been Gon 30 years." "She Wants to h[ave] him taken Care of By the Gentlemen Selectmen of Boston," wrote Love. A three-way conversation unfolded when Betsy Mumford, "a girl," received her warning. Benjamin Clark, the brazier and merchant, was present, and in front of Love he told Betsy that "She behaved verry Loosly" when she had previously lived in Boston with the leather dresser John McFadden. Mumford's response to their grilling was to refuse to tell where she was currently lodging. Infrequently, Love encountered a Frenchman or Dutchman who could not speak English. Latinate place names, the use of mime, and some rudimentary knowledge of French may have allowed Love to fill in some of the blanks on these strangers, but bystanders may have provided translation help. In the case of Frenchman John Gosey, who had arrived in a small sloop from Cape Breton, Love wrote: "the man Could not Speak English he talks of Gowing to England."[33]

Unnamed observers helped Love to profile strangers of dubious reputation. "I am told," Love wrote about Charles Lee, who had come to Boston three months earlier, that "he is a man of No Business But Idles his time away." Similarly, Joseph Smithers, a maker of leather breeches lodging at a victualler's in Wing's Lane, "has been taken Notis by many to be Idling

Abou[t] the Warfes in town." On finding Azubah Mason "with a Number of Boys Making Game of her," Love reported that "She Semed to all the people to Be Quite Crasey or Light headed."[34] Such entries make clear that Love, as warner and investigator, often queried many people in the process of warning a stranger. The encounter was a public one, and the extraordinarily detailed information contained in Love's recorded warnings reflected the individual and collective insights of many Bostonians.

Love's skill as warner entailed not just finding strangers and getting them to talk but also making decisions about potentially chargeable people whom he need not warn. Besides newcomers of high status and obvious wealth, two groups appear to have been passed over. New Englanders who visited Boston in familiar patterns, lingering briefly, did not merit warning. These included adults called to the sickbeds or deathbeds of close relatives; captains of coasting vessels based in nearby ports who unloaded supplies on Boston's wharves; the country folk who sold their products and food-stuffs at the weekly town market; and middling residents of the region who made purposeful shopping trips to the city for themselves and neighbors. Love made the bet that these visitors were leaving quickly. If they lingered, he would find and warn them.[35]

The seamen who shipped out of Boston harbor did not receive warn-ings. On his rounds, Love would have easily identified them by their wide, baggy red breeches made of rough nap and smeared with tar, their distinc-tive jackets and Monmouth caps, and their tattoos and tanned skin. Their speech too betrayed them, since it was full of "technical terms, unusual syntax, distinctive pronunciation, and a generous portion of swearing and cursing." Love treated most sailors as exempt from warning for several reasons. Not only did mariners based temporarily in a port sleep on ship-board, but the commander of their ship was legally responsible for them. New England shipmasters recruited largely from their hometowns or nearby coastal towns. Thus, when sailors disembarked in Boston at the end of their contracts, they were either already in their hometown or were head-ing out of town. Love must have warned a few who left their maritime employment for work and lodgings on Boston's waterfront, but he made no comment on their seafaring pasts. For Boston officials, the familiar col-lective of ordinary seamen did not threaten to add measurably to poor relief outlays.[36]

IN becoming the best searcher-for-strangers that Boston had ever seen, Love did not walk the town unaided. He gleaned information about where to look and whom to look for from several types of informants. Landlords, including the owners of taverns that offered lodging, were frequent founts of information. The Boston-based ship captains who made regular runs to other ports were probably inured to Love's pestering them about their passengers. In these pre-stagecoach days, the only regular public transport conveying travelers to and from Boston by land was Mr. Dixey Brown's "Providence Wagon." Brown's single stop in Boston was at the Sign of the White Horse in the South End, where the travelers usually stayed for their first night. Love often intercepted new arrivals there either on their first or second day in town.[37]

Some of Love's most important contacts included men who served the town in various official capacities. Foremost on this list were his immediate employers, the selectmen. Given that the warner attended most of their meetings on Wednesdays, he got wind of landlords giving notice that they had taken in a noninhabitant and of selectmen authorizing almshouse admissions for distressed strangers. In a handful of cases, Love followed up with a warning delivered anywhere from a day to a month later. Just as often, however, Love's warning came first and was followed by the land- lord's notification or the selectmen's action. For example, Love warned Mary More on May 5, 1770, and six days later her landlord, Mr. John Knee- land, appeared before the selectmen to declare that he had taken her in twelve days earlier.[38] Or take Love's September 1765 warning of a man last from Jamaica with sores on his feet who "Wants to Gett in" to the alms- house: on the very next day, the selectmen ordered that the lame stranger be received into the house.[39] On the same day in May 1768 on which Love warned a family of four, recently arrived by ship from Lyme, Connecticut, and lodging with a man on King Street, the warner attended the selectmen's meeting to inform that these strangers were "poor Indigent Persons." Immediately sending for the owner of the sloop that had transported the family to Boston, the selectmen were pleased with the captain's pledge "that he would carry" them "back again to Connecticut or in case of failure that he will answer for all damages."[40] Although Love and the selectmen clearly traded information about strangers and their circumstances, it is a testa- ment to Love's efficiency that he rarely had to be told or tipped off in order to warn. More often, it was his act of warning that brought—or had the potential to bring—town leaders' gaze on the plight of newcomers.

Other officials with whom Love interacted had duties that required them, like him, to walk the streets of Boston and record their observations.

Each of the twelve wealthy men who served as overseers of the poor was assigned to a ward—a neighborhood they were instructed to "walk" at least monthly in order to inspect the poor and decide on the distribution of outdoor relief in the form of firewood and other vital provisions. The gentlemen overseers typically lived in their ward and walked it often, becoming intimately acquainted with its denizens and turnover in its population. Love would have been acquainted with individual overseers not least because they frequently attended selectmen's meetings. Furthermore, we can assume that overseers quickly got word to Love when persistent beggars haunted the streets of their ward or strangers of low circumstances moved into a tenement.[41]

The constables who managed the night watch were a second important source of information for Love. Here was yet another set of petty officials who recorded in writing the results of their human encounters on their walking rounds. Unlike Love, who was free to perambulate Boston as he wished, watchmen were required to follow particular routes. The men of the South Watch, for example, were to walk "To Deacon Eliots Corner, to Hills Still house to the Bull wharf up Summer Street to the Old South meeting house." The South Watch was one of four zones, each with a watch house and a designated constable in charge. Starting in 1761, the selectmen had ordered each constable of the watch to "keep a fair Journal of your doings every Night, how you find the state of the Town, and who of the Watchmen are on duty, and Report to the SelectMen every Wednesday." Their lists of disorderly nighttime miscreants rarely overlapped with those warned, but this does not mean that they did not pass on tips to Love about newcomers they found sleeping on the docks or in alleys or barns but had no need to write up.[42] Love netted at least one stranger, and probably many more, in this way. In May 1768, "Mr Walas the Constable" "Brought to me" Peter Murray, who "has been a Soldeir att the Havanah"; he was "Drunk."[43]

As a mode of governance, the twinned rituals of perambulating and writing prized in eighteenth-century Boston—carried out by night constables, gentlemen overseers, and warners—occupied a middle landscape between the gatekeeping and wall walking of medieval cities and the overlapping systems of personal identification central to the modern bureaucratic state. To ask the middling householders who served as head night watchmen to keep journals was to rely on the high literacy rates of colonial

New England. Writing undergirds modern governance, permitting codification of subjects in order to scrutinize them, collect obligations, and deliver services and rights. During Love's tenure, the technology of Boston's partial registration system was embodied in non-elite men's feet, voices, logbooks, and quills.[44]

At the end of each month, Robert Love sat down at his desk to fulfill his duty to report his findings. This entailed considerable copying. All in all, the warner wrote his warnings in four discrete places. First were Love's rough notes, which no longer survive. Second were his entries in his leather-bound journals. These books he purchased at some expense from a local printer; the town did not supply them nor did they claim them as public records. Love called these logs his "books." They were arranged chronologically, not alphabetically, and he would read back through them if he had a dim remembrance of having previously warned (say, a year or two earlier) a stranger he had recently encountered.[45] Third, with a thoroughness unrivalled by his counterparts in the job, the warner copied his logbook entries, with all the details, onto the monthly warrant that William Cooper, the town clerk, had issued to him.[46] And finally, our doughty scribbler copied the month's warnings, again word for word, onto a double sheet that would be sent to the overseers of the poor.[47]

Soon after making these careful copies, perhaps choosing an evening when the selectmen were to meet, Love placed the folded warrant in his leather pouch, donned his wig and cloak, and strode out of his house, heading northward on Orange Street. His destination was roughly fifteen minutes away—William Cooper's desk in the selectmen's chamber in Faneuil Hall. In his genteel hand, Cooper would copy the most relevant information from Love's logbook entries (names of the members of the party, where from, when arrived) into the alphabetized town warnings ledger. In the years 1765–68, when three men were warning strangers, Cooper must have checked his ledgers to ensure he was not entering a duplicate.[48]

Finally, it was Love's duty to deliver the completed warrant into the hands of the clerk of the court of general sessions. Having completed copying the names of those he warned onto the warrant, Love always finished off his return by writing the date and an official declaration: "I have Warned all of the Above Named persons to Depart the town of Boston in fourteen Days or Give Security . . . p[e]r Robert Love." Before he could deliver the warrant, the warner often had to wait until the sessions court met. Once again, he walked from his lodgings in the South End to the center of town, this time to the courthouse. Gaining entrance to the building, he dutifully delivered his warrant to the court clerk, who dated it, marked it as Love's "return," and filed it.[49] Thus did the many souls who encountered Love in the port town's streets and lodging places officially become nonsettled residents of Boston.

CHAPTER 5

The Warned and Why They Came

NEARLY EVERYONE WHO earned a warning from Robert Love was a British subject. Unlike New York and Philadelphia, New England at midcentury experienced very little direct emigration from England or Europe. And yet Love's records uncover a remarkable array of travelers, arriving on foot and horseback, by farm cart and wagon, and aboard the coasting vessels that carried on the region's provisioning trade. The eldest of Love's strangers claimed to be eighty-four years old; the youngest was about ten weeks old—an abandoned "man child" receiving care in the almshouse. Family groups as large as twelve encountered the warner; more numerous were youths and adults who appeared to be on their own. Some strangers were present because of the singular political and military events of the 1760s and 1770s. Other types had been coming to sojourn in Boston for decades.[1]

Colonial Boston has presented historians with a quandary. Why would so many people circulating within British America bother to go there? Struggling with population drain and a stagnating economy, Boston had been eclipsed as the most populous colonial city by more dynamic ports on the mid-Atlantic coast. Love's warnings unscramble the puzzle, elucidating the many ways that the town beckoned.

Sojourner is the most suitable term for Love's strangers. They were people on the move for a wide range of purposes with diverse fates ahead of them. Some we can think of as travelers—they stayed in town briefly, soon returning from whence they came or moving on with a destination in mind. A small set were classic migrants—those who intended to settle in Boston. The greatest number were sojourning in town for a few months or years. Among the sojourners, Boston attracted two sorts also on the move in early modern England. Unmarried youths and other adults with secure footholds in a region often moved short distances to cities for training or work; they have been described as "betterment" sojourners. "Subsistence" migrants, those with little property and "impelled by pressures of survival and economic necessity," tended to journey longer distances, trying their luck in various urban places.[2]

The image persists among social historians that the roads leading to Boston during "the generation before the Revolution" were crowded with the second sort: "destitute and unemployed persons" who failed to find jobs in the economically hard-hit seaport.[3] Love would beg to disagree. He described only 19 percent of parties warned as down-and-out. He wrote down the particular attributes of neediness of these unfortunates, calling them variously poor, sick, begging, disabled, dressed in rags, disordered in mind, idle, and strolling. The warner's remarks are, of course, not a perfect index of profound neediness: some of those he termed disabled were employable, and some strangers were surely in distress unbeknownst to him. Those he labeled needy fit the profile of subsistence sojourners: two-thirds of them came from outside the province, a much larger percentage than in the overall population of warned. Beyond illuminating what it meant to be in the lowest of circumstances in pre-revolutionary Boston, Love's observations strongly imply that the majority of newcomers were not drifting, destitute travelers, but purposeful ones.[4]

Another clue that betterment sojourners outnumbered subsistence ones is that the greater New England region, including the eastern Canadian provinces, provided three-quarters of warned incomers to Boston. Massachusetts was the source of half of Love's strangers, and the surrounding New England colonies together with the Canadian provinces supplied an additional 24 percent. In this, Boston was like English provincial cities, which drew most intensely from the nearby villages and smaller country towns. The largest contingent—nearly five hundred parties—reported that they were last from other towns in Boston's county, Suffolk. Thus, they had come the shortest distances. No wonder that Roxbury, just outside of the gate on the Boston Neck, contributed more "strangers" than any other province town. The seventy-four solos and thirty-three families in this stream had the best vantage point for gathering information by word of mouth about advantageous employment, rental, and marriage prospects in Boston (Figures 6 and 7).[5]

Midcoast Maine and Canada's maritime regions, notably Nova Scotia, were as closely tied to the Massachusetts capital as nearby counties such as Plymouth and Essex. In the forty years prior to 1765, the English population

FIGURE 6. Locations warned strangers were "last from." This figure includes all parties warned by Love except ninety-seven, for whom the information is missing or illegible.

Base map derived from Esri Data and Maps, 2012.

of these coastal "down east" regions had shot up, with many of the new settlers emigrating from long-settled towns in the eastern part of Massachusetts. Vast tracts in Maine were owned by Boston's wealthiest merchant and gentry families, who mobilized kinsmen, retainers, and eager tenants to improve the land. Because the Penobscot region provided the great bulk of Boston's enormous firewood needs, sloops plied the down east waters constantly except in winter. Nova Scotia was similarly an important part of Boston's economic hinterland or catch basin, given residents' extensive mercantile and familial ties to the Bay province. Love's warnings reflect the density of voluntary human traffic between Boston and these coastal nodes, as fisherfolk, servant youths, and families relocated or opted to sojourn in Boston after living part or all of their lives in Casco Bay, Halifax, or Annapolis Royal.[6]

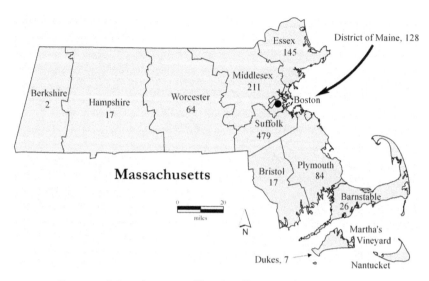

FIGURE 7. Warned strangers "last from" a Massachusetts location.
The numbers refer to parties warned, not individuals.

Base map derived from Esri Data and Maps, 2012.

Sojourners came directly to Boston from the rapidly growing cities of
New York and Philadelphia and other American sites outside the northeast,
but in such modest numbers that they made up scarcely one-fifth of the
warned. Only 5 percent of incomers to Boston captured in Love's logbooks
arrived from England, Scotland, Ireland, Europe, or Africa. Without a
doubt, New England flunked the test as a magnet for long-distance migration.[7] But Love's narrative notes about sojourners indicate that relying
solely on the raw figures exaggerates New England's insularity. Although
Boston was not their first destination in the New World, Scots, Englishmen,
and Protestant Irish did circulate through its streets.[8] Owen Kelley and his
wife and son had been headed to New York from Ireland when they were
"cast away near Carolina"; later they turned up in lodgings in Boston's
South End to tell Love their story. Three "Dutch" men (meaning German
in heritage) had probably been born or resident in colonies that drew Germans in large numbers.[9] Others had crossed national and imperial boundaries to enter British territory. Of Charles and Christine Jamison and their
son, Love wrote: "They are very poor and are begging; they came from
Lisbon in Portugal to Philadelphia and from there to this place." Some

from distant lands had resources and know-how about getting along with English colonists, while others were truly down-and-out. Josey (José) Desilver was a "portigee," last from Roxbury and lodging in Boston with a deacon. In contrast, Anthony Serron was an East Indian with no money or lodging. Serron's efforts to beg were hampered by what seemed to the warner to be a "stupifide" state. Peter Peterson was less adrift but had no local connections: he had most recently been in Stockbridge in the western part of the colony and explained that he was "prusin By nasion . . . [and] Wants to folow Labrouring Business in this town."[10]

The mix of accents and nationalities on Boston's streets was affected by the proximity of colonial territories that had until recently been governed by France. "Franch" people (as Love wrote and perhaps pronounced the adjective) were not uncommon. Their relaxed reception in Love's day contrasts with wartime periods earlier in the eighteenth century, when French men entering the town had been quarantined as enemy foreigners. Like many of the Britons and European-born strangers in Love's records, a goodly number of the French did not enter from territory once encompassed by New France. Rather, they had been living and circulating in the British colonies.[11]

In responding to Love's query about where they were "last from," travelers provided information that must be interpreted carefully.[12] Especially for Massachusetts-born incomers, the place they named was often their place of legal settlement. At other times, it merely specified where he or she had most recently lived, worked, or visited.[13] Love might signal this by writing "last from Roxbury but properly belongs to Medfield." Longer entries revealed the many moves that some made in order to maintain subsistence. Polly Nichols was "last from Roxbury," having moved from Braintree to there, and from York in England to Braintree. She "was Born in Old York which is her proper place." Such notations, resembling an English settlement examination, were important because if the warned newcomer stayed in Boston and needed relief, the selectmen would have a jump start on determining the person's "proper" place of settlement and thus who should pay.[14]

Both betterment and subsistence sojourners were often solo travelers, not journeying with kin. Among Love's strangers, a strikingly high proportion came as solos—74 percent. Earlier in the century, when smaller numbers were warned annually and when Boston was formally offering town inhabitancy to men with desirable skills, families had predominated. By the 1760s, not only were more youths from yeoman New England families traveling short distances on their own, but also, in the wake of the Seven Years War, displaced veterans and other wide-ranging subsistence seekers sent the numbers and proportions of solo male travelers to all-time highs. Of the parties Love warned, 47 percent were solo boys and men and 27 percent were solo girls and women.[15]

Thinking of these people on the move as "solos" carries hazards. Most solo travelers arriving from New England locations were firmly connected to kin, community, and work networks in the region and should not be imagined as "alone" in social terms. Moreover, being accounted as traveling alone by Love did not mean one was unmarried. Love sometimes explained that a woman arriving by herself was coming to join her husband. In most cases, only by pursuing biographical research can we ascertain a traveler's marital status. The manner in which a stranger traveled to Boston is often obscured by counting strangers as solo. A fifteen-year-old girl or boy might well have been accompanied by a parent, older sibling, or acquaintance with short-term business in the city.[16]

Women's and men's movement streams as solo travelers were distinctive. Slightly more girls and women than solo males entered Boston from Massachusetts locations overall and from Halifax in maritime Canada. This suggests the existence of a strong demand for female workers, probably in service positions for which we have little direct documentation in the form of indentures or work contracts. The warning records for 1765–73 show that Boston was annually absorbing on average seventy-eight solo females, and most of them young and unmarried.[17] Indeed, from the two closest towns, Roxbury and Dorchester, women made up 60 percent of all incomers who arrived on their own.[18] The pattern seen here, of females equaling or outnumbering males in entering towns from the nearby countryside, echoes that of many early modern English towns. In an urban setting, women could find domestic service posts or earn a living by huckstering, retailing drams, or doing washing. If not boarding with their employer, laboring-class women often shared lodgings or chores in cooperative "housefuls." Relatively cheap houses and rooms to hire made this possible.[19]

As everywhere in the early modern Western world, the greater the distance traveled, the fewer women making a journey without any kin or not in the company of husbands. While constituting up to half the solo stream from the province's towns, girls and women were only one-fifth of those who came in from the rest of greater New England and 10 percent of those from outside the region. Love noted only eleven girls or women came "alone" on shipboard to Boston from overseas; three had a husband or uncle serving in the British army in the Americas, and another came as a servant to customs commissioner Henry Hulton. Indeed, just over 90 percent of the solo female travelers into Boston came from the New England–Canada region. Traveling from afar greatly increased the likelihood that a solo woman would appear to be in distress or to have chosen a vagrant's life. One-third of the fifty-six solo women incoming from outside the greater New England region were in some sort of need. In contrast, 6 percent of solo females "last from" a Massachusetts town were so described. This is testimony that youthful women's circulation within the province was betterment migration rather than born of desperation.[20]

Love warned solo male youths and adult men at an average rate of 123 per year. One-third arrived from a location outside of New England and Canada. Signs of poverty or distress almost equally affected those boys and men traveling from afar as solo males "last from" a Massachusetts location. Nearly one in three, compared to one in ten for female parties, appeared to be in trouble or soon ended up in the almshouse or workhouse. Thus, the public face of impoverishment and physical disability in the mid-eighteenth century was more male than female.[21]

Most of the solo men and male youths were able-bodied and arrived expecting to work. Love reported occupations for 144 white men, including fifteen shoemakers, twelve barbers, nine peddlers, eight servants, seven bakers, seven laborers, seven tailors, and six each of carpenters and masons. Sometimes he indicated the flexibility of men's training and work, as in the case of Michael Amblert ("he is a baker to traid and a WistedComber"). Of course, many more interviewed by him had a trade, and others were coming to Boston for artisanal training, but their occupations went unrecorded. Strangers' landlords occasionally provide clues to their trades. For example, barber Theodore Dehone, who attracted clients to his shop on King Street, lodged solo male strangers on five occasions, and it is probable that all of them worked for him.[22]

Family groups or household clusters made up slightly less than a third of the parties warned. They were far less likely to show signs of neediness than solo male travelers and were slightly less prone to have come from afar. Among the many types of traveling households, spouse pairs and spouses with children predominated. But Love also ran into adult women with offspring, families or adults accompanied by servants and others not kin, and sibling pairs. The average number of offspring accompanying parental pairs was 2.5. Since historians calculate that on average white, married couples in colonial New England had 7.5 children, with 5.3 children surviving to the age of twenty-one, the size of traveling households indicates that many of these parents were young. A few, however, told Love that they had with them only some of their minor children, having placed others elsewhere.[23] Sometimes, parents were on the move with a grown child and her offspring. Abraham and Ann Rhodes, last from nearby Milton, arrived with "his" daughter Mary March and her child Alice; Love explained that March's "Husband is Gon and Left her." Intergenerational groups like this one and other blended families or stepfamilies caught the warner's attention because if the province later extended relief to the children, Love's notes might allow them to identify paternity and trace the deceased father's last place of settlement.[24]

The eighty-nine mothers traveling with one or more offspring remind us that the recent war had widowed many New England women, especially young women. Love called only ten of these mothers widows, but surely more than that number had lost their husbands. At least thirteen of these travelers were presently married; according to Love, their husbands had preceded them to Boston. Elizabeth Fillis came into town with daughters Nancy and Phoebe; their destination was the house near the windmill on Boston Neck that Elizabeth's husband had lived in since June. Sarah Berry, in contrast, had come to Boston with a daughter because she "had left her husband" (due to his abuse?) in Roxbury; Sarah was now in the bridewell for some undisclosed disorderliness. A few other women were on their own because their husbands had absconded. We might expect more of these female-headed parties to have been in bad straits; yet the percentage of them identified as needy nearly matched the percentage of solo women travelers similarly described.[25]

Love's lack of formal education, his phonetic spelling, and his Ulster Scots background help explain the idiosyncratic written markers he used for people of color. He described just under 5 percent of the warned as "Negor," "malato," or "Indin."[26] Educated Bostonians, such as town clerk William Cooper, used more standard orthography for these descriptors. Love's negative associations with Indians and blacks show occasionally in his entries, particularly in his insinuations that certain Indian and black women were promiscuous and thus disorderly. But most of the 104 entries convey information about the newcomers without moral judgment. Strikingly, Love described few blacks and Indians as ragged, poor, disabled, or needy in some other way. It appears that to counteract the prejudices and ill will harbored by many whites, people of color dressed and conducted themselves on the road and in Boston to avoid undue scrutiny. Furthermore, Love accorded these New Englanders a measure of respect by recording first names and surnames for all but a half dozen. When meeting Boston's warner, these men and women had the freedom to identify themselves quite differently from owners and employers who regularly denied them surnames or names they chose for themselves.[27]

Nearly all of the folks labeled nonwhite arrived solo.[28] A very high proportion came from a New England location (85 percent), with almost two-thirds reporting they were last from a Massachusetts town. Constantly vulnerable to kidnapping and wrongful enslavement, free people of color in the late colonial period did not venture far from communities in which their character and life histories were known. Nor was Boston yet a magnet for indigenous or African-descended travelers from colonies to the south. On the other hand, the 1760s and 1770s witnessed an untold number of enslaved New Englanders freeing themselves by walking away from their human owners or negotiating the end of their coerced labor. Many came to the region's largest town in search of work and fellowship with the eight-hundred-odd black and Indian residents whose domiciles could be found in all wards. Indian women and men often moved between two worlds—to and fro to towns where they could pick up jobs, pay debts, or sell baskets, and to native enclaves in the woods where community life and celebrations could take place free from white scrutiny. The English concept of settlement in a fixed place clashed with Algonquian patterns of movement, which were seasonal and clan based. Increasingly cast as a wandering people, their journeys reflected survival strategies that remained incomprehensible to colonists.[29]

African-descended persons on the road, but not Indians, were often questioned about their legal status. Love assumed that Indian persons were free, despite the frequency of natives' enslavement or forced indenture following from seventeenth-century military defeats, debt, and poverty. Only in the case of nine-year-old James Mohawk did the warner explain that a Boston man had "Bought" the boy's "time till he is 30 years old."[30] Of the sixty-eight solos or household heads whom he described as of African heritage, Love labeled thirty-six free and seven enslaved. Rather than using the

word *slave*, which white New Englanders tended to avoid, he resorted to a
vocabulary of ownership: "she properly belongs to Mr. Seth Barnes."
Enslaved persons' situations were in flux in the Bay province during the
three decades before the 1780 state constitution was interpreted as abolish-
ing slavery. Some found that they could pass as free by leaving owners and
moving a few towns away. Slave owners often deemed pursuit not worth
the expense. Others formerly enslaved who had reached advanced age were
fending for themselves because masters had released them without formal
manumission papers or financial support. Love sometimes chose phrasing
that reflected the uncertain climate: the stranger "says" she or he is free. In
other cases, his narration marked the stranger's status as ambiguous: Mingo
Otis, a "very Old" man, had been in town two months and "Gowes about
sawing Wood[;] his Late master's" name was Mr. Isaac Otis of Scituate.[31]

The skewed sex ratios of New England's black and Indian populations
(more black men than women, more Indian women than men) were
reflected in Love's encounters. This was most striking with respect to Indians on the move: Love warned twenty-eight women arriving solo and only
six solo males. The region's Indian male population had diminished dramatically. Epidemics took both sexes; in addition, men suffered heavy mortality as enlistees in provincial campaigns against the French. Enclaves such
as Natick had in the recent past contained over one hundred Indians; by
the mid-1760s only a few dozen Indians resided there, with women outnumbering men by three to two. Thus, Indian women went to port towns
seeking both employment opportunities and potential mates. Marriages
between native women and black men were on the rise. In Boston, which
housed the largest cluster of African-descended people in the region, black
males outnumbered females by 1.68:1, according to a 1765 population count;
in some smaller eastern towns, the male-female ratio among blacks was as
high as 2:1. No wonder Love warned slightly more solo black males than
females.[32]

Most of the warned can be pegged as middling and lower sorts. But
Love, despite his instructions to warn only those of low circumstances,
warned a few who were positioned near the top of eighteenth-century social
ranks. Whispers of future bankruptcy or concern over each household's
dependents may have prompted him to give notice to a titled gentlewoman
and a Harvard-educated cleric. Sarah Walter Hesilrige had grown up as the
minister's daughter in west Roxbury among the most elite and highly educated families. She had married Robert, the son of Sir Arthur Hesilrige,

baronet, whose English Civil War–era ancestor had been an "active parlia-
mentarian and friend of Oliver Cromwell" and a possessor of land grants
in New England. Sir Robert succeeded to the baronetcy on his father's death
in 1763 but did not inherit a share of familial land, perhaps because he lived
most of his adult life in the colonies. It is not clear why he was not with his
wife in 1766. Love's entry shows that in April of that year, Lady Hesilrige
moved into a rented house on Long Lane with her two daughters and
Sepro, an enslaved woman. She continued to reside in the Boston-Roxbury
area until her death in 1775 at age thirty-nine. Surprisingly, Love styled her
"Mrs" (for Mistress) rather than "Madam" or "Lady," the highest honor-
ifics for women and to which arguably she was entitled.[33]

Love's warning of the forty-three-year-old cleric John Carnes and his
nine dependents is more understandable. Upon graduating from Harvard
College in 1742, Carnes, the son of a Boston pewterer, lacked family links
to the ministerial elite except through his wife, Mary Lewis. Classmates
and observers described him as "silly," of small talent, and burdened by
"displeasing" manners. After two short pastorates in country towns characterized by unhappy parishioners and inadequate compensation, Carnes evidently decided that the ministry was not for him. In spring 1765, he moved
his large family and a servant maid from Rehoboth (the site of his final
pastorate) to Dedham, a town near Boston. There they rented a house and,
in the routine manner of newcomers, received warning. Fifteen months
later, the lapsed parson brought his household to Boston and rented a
South End house, expecting to carry on the owner's previous practice of
retailing liquor. The Boston selectmen initially denied Carnes's license
application. They relented two years later, as Carnes was by then an established grocer and dry goods retailer. In 1776, the former cleric moved his
family to Lynn, and Carnes's topsy-turvy life in these, his final, decades
vindicated Love's warning. Though the former cleric saw his children marry
well and was even chosen as a justice of the peace and delegate to the state
legislature, he suffered financial reverses and died in poverty.[34]

Betterment sojourners, strolling couples seeking alms, African New
Englanders shedding slave status, and the occasional high-ranking householder who might tumble in rank: these categories do not encompass three
groups on the move owing to imperial policies and conflicts specific to the
middle of the century. Acadian families encountered Love in Boston in 1766
not because they were voluntary sojourners in New England, but because
they were finally released from a decade of internal exile and misery in

interior Massachusetts towns. Eleven years earlier, the British government and army had forcibly expelled these French farmers from Nova Scotia. Similarly, the warning records enhance our knowledge about Boston under military occupation by British troops from 1768 to 1770. The warner focused not on the soldiers but on their dependents—wives, sweethearts, and children—and the often desperate conditions faced by military families on the move. Finally, even though military engagements in the Seven Years War had ended in the Americas in 1760, demobilized regimental soldiers circulated for years among the major port towns looking for work and often for passage home to old England.

HUNDREDS of people entered Boston every year in the pre-revolutionary decade to sojourn or settle. Historians have been skeptical that the city could have absorbed so many, especially during the postwar depression of the 1760s. Even before the Seven Years War, the city's economy had stalled; many native artisans, discouraged about prospects for drumming up enough trade, left for opportunities elsewhere. However, even in this climate, Boston beckoned to middling folk and the working poor.[35]

Boston's economic trough had lasted for two decades, in contrast with the growth occurring in the large mid-Atlantic port towns. Whereas Boston had once led "in shipbuilding, the leather trades, meat-packing, hatmaking, the axe and hardware manufacture, cheap export furniture," and chaise making, "only the furniture and carriage business remained profitable." While New York built a thousand houses in ten years to accommodate newcomers and Philadelphia witnessed an even bigger building boom, perhaps twenty residential structures went up each year in Boston. Dozens of rental units might stand vacant. Bostonians' confidence in the stability of their mercantile firms was shaken when a cascade of prominent traders went bankrupt in 1765. Not only were British lenders calling in overseas debts, but the war's end also meant that New Englanders were no longer called on to supply boots, bread, and rum for thousands of troops and sailors. As a consequence, many artisans, laborers, and dockworkers were out of jobs or plunged into underemployment.[36]

To compound matters, the West Indian trade, an important sector of Boston's economy, was hard hit when Parliament's new Sugar Act took effect in 1764. The act effectively ended the lucrative molasses smuggling long engaged in by Boston merchants. This development "convulsed" the economic prospects of shipowners, sea captains, and sailors active in the trade, along with associated tradespeople such as coopers, rope makers, and blacksmiths. The center of town was still struggling to recover from the devastating fire of 1760 that had consumed hundreds of structures. In these years, too, Bostonians bore a larger tax burden than residents of other major seaports. This was due partly to the structure of the province's tax system and partly to Boston's rising annual expenditures for the town poor. All these developments took their toll on the port city's residents. The median personal wealth left at their death by Boston craftsmen in various trades was significantly lower than that of their New York and Philadelphia counterparts.[37]

Boston also stood apart from the other port cities because of its imbalanced sex ratio. Most of the so-called surplus women were widows. Indeed, historian Alfred F. Young believes that Boston earned the title of the widow capital of the British Atlantic world. Relative to mid-Atlantic and southern colonies, Massachusetts contributed soldiers disproportionately, following the long sequence of colonial wars. Since women's means of earning were dramatically more constrained than white men's, many of the town's widows required some form of poor relief and many of the town's eight thousand children experienced not just fatherlessness but poverty.[38]

Boston's place as the largest urban center and seaport in the northernmost sector of British America helps explain continuing in-migration. Towns such as Newport, Hartford, Portsmouth, Montreal, and Halifax were considerably smaller in population. Scale alone created opportunities—more potential customers, patrons, and allies; more work possibilities; denser networks of information; more chances to book ship passage. The ever-widening stratification of wealth in colonial society and the fashion of emulating European aristocracy meant that urban gentry demanded and could pay for servants, retainers, and skilled craftsmen. The high turnover in population, endemic to urban centers in England as well, meant that there was a continual need for infusion of journeymen, laundresses, and dockworkers to replace those who had left.[39] Simply put, the movement of men, women, youths, and children in and out of Boston was a dynamic inherent to the relationships between commercial urban centers and their hinterlands. Boston was like Nottingham, Leeds, and London in drawing "unskilled young people" who "served as the infantry of town life, . . . working as tapsters in inns, servants in household and shops, doing dirty jobs like sweeping chimneys and cleaning latrines." Indeed, "without such an influx towns would not have been able to function effectively."[40]

Five general motivations drew strangers to Boston. At times, of course, these overlapped. Securing work and acquiring training brought the greatest number. Many youth came because it was a critical hub in the regional labor market and because the dense interconnectedness of New England families provided them entrée to employment that unskilled strangers arriving from afar were less certain to secure.[41] Some of the strangers who did not come to work told Love that they would be in town only as long as it took to find a conveyance to their desired destination. Boston represented for them the most convenient point of embarkation. Except in the winter, several ships a month might clear the harbor bound for the British Isles. Such departures were nil or rare from the region's smaller ports.

Large urban ports served as havens and gathering spots for like-minded and closely related people. James Darby provides an example of intercolonial Quaker networks. Warned on the day he arrived from Philadelphia, the down-at-the-heels Darby indicated that that he was looking for work as a "smith" and planned "to Lodge att freind Samul pop[e']s." Seventy-six-year-old Pope, a blacksmith who owned a house and shop on Hollis Street near Love's lodgings, was a member of the Boston Quaker Meeting. Members of the Pope clan often took in new arrivals, many of whom may have been Quakers.[42] Cities were also frequently sites of family reunification, as family members moved together and apart and together again. Isaac Hammon came in autumn 1771 to live with his mother, Mary, who had been warned by Love four months earlier. Both had lived last in nearby Newton; Mary's husband was presently working in Connecticut. Husbands joined wives, and vice versa; young children were escorted into town to become part of new stepfamilies; elderly parents came to live with a married son or daughter. Of course, a bustling urban entrepôt could also offer a place to hide, at least temporarily. Some of the Indian and black New Englanders warned by Love were eluding punitive masters and constrained existences in smaller towns. Confederates in burglary might bide their time in town until a warehouse or merchant's house appeared unguarded.[43]

A small portion of the warned aimed to resettle in Boston even though its economy was not booming. The Reverend Mr. John Carnes, profiled above, is an example of a career migrant, if a somewhat odd one. He gave up his previous work as a parson to take advantage of urban conditions, where he had access to affordable rental lodgings and customers for a retail business. Others arrived with uncertain plans and ended up staying. Families with slim resources relocated to early modern cities because there all family members, no matter their age, could find more opportunities for casual employment than in smaller places.[44]

Finally, the capital was a draw for beggars and others in need. Cities were better locations to beg or seek alms than smaller towns. A strolling couple might evade detection more readily than in rural villages. Boston's almshouse offered free medical care and food and housing that tided hundreds through difficult winters. Some ailing wanderers surely came to Boston because they knew that the province covered relief to all incomers in need.

THE men, women, and children warned in Boston did not seek out the destination willy-nilly. As the largest urban hub in the region, Boston readily absorbed laborers, especially domestic servants and journeymen. This was the case both when economic growth was stagnant and when shipyard work and overseas commerce were picking up, as occurred in 1770.[45] When we set Boston in the context of early modern English cities rather than measuring it narrowly against New York and Philadelphia, we see why many types of people flocked there and why they were welcome. Without Robert Love's detailed notes, differentiating sojourners from settlers, youths from ancients, and native-born beggars from Britons seeking passage home would be all but impossible.

❁

Interlude

A Sojourner's Arrival

IMAGINE AN ENTERPRISING young man, disembarking on the seven-hundred-yard-long wharf that dominated the inner harbor. Stiff from his passage from Halifax, he decided to perambulate the entire town before seeking lodgings.

The Long Wharf, lined on one side with imposing warehouses, led straight to the political and commercial heart of the town. As our traveler walked west along King and then Queen Streets, he could gawk at the brick mansions of some of the town's wealthiest residents, count the shop signs for a dozen barbers and peruke makers, and take in the steepled structures of the Town House and the First Church. Nearby, on the streets radiating out from this central corridor, were several more churches (including the modest Quaker meetinghouse and the small Huguenot place of worship), two school buildings, substantial taverns, and many structures housing retail businesses in which the proprietors lived over their shops. Devastated by a 1760 fire and containing residents with the highest median wealth of the town's inhabitants, this central section sported predominantly brick structures.[1]

Streets were congested in the town center, and no less so in the North and South Ends. Our newcomer would mimic other pedestrians by keeping when possible to the center of the street, and yet he would find himself frequently jumping aside or taking refuge in shop doorways to escape being run over by the "carts, waggons, drays, trucks, wheel-barrows, and porters . . . continually obstructing" one's passage.[2]

Pushed along by the flow of foot and wheeled traffic, the youthful traveler could not miss spying the courthouse and stone jail to his left as he ventured down Queen Street as it bent slightly northward. If he turned right on Tremont and then on Hanover Street, he would soon cross the bridge over Mill Creek and enter the North End. Packed with almost twice the number of people as the town's central district, the North End offered quite a different social landscape. Although some prosperous Bostonians such as Paul Revere lived here, the district was—measured by median household wealth—"the poorest section of town." Over half the residents in the wards at the northern tip of the peninsula lived so modestly or precariously that they did not own the house, shop, or £20 in merchandise that would make them liable for the province's property tax. This distinctive section, wedged between the harbor, the Charles River, and the Mill Pond, was a beehive of industry. Located here were most of the shipyards, along with the workshops of craftsmen in trades supporting shipbuilding and maritime commerce. Living and working cheek by jowl were sea captains, common seamen, sailmakers, coopers, tallow chandlers, and caulkers. If our traveler walked northward on Fish Street, following the harbor's curving shoreline, he would pass a wharf every few hundred feet: Clark's, Gallop's, Heywood's, Hancock's, Hutchinson's, and more. The boys of Boston, when not detained at school or by errands for their parents, could be found darting "to and fro beneath bowsprits and mooring lines." By making a northwesterly loop on Ship and Lynn Streets the traveler would reach the dock serving the Charlestown ferry. Then he might head away from the water for a block, climb Copp's Hill to view its burying ground and panoramic scenes of the harbor, and stroll eastward on Love Lane (not named after our warner's family). By turning right on Middle Street, one ended up back in part of the town center.[3]

From there, Cold Lane was the best route to the West End, the most sparsely settled section. The traveler might walk the curve of Green Lane, turning north on Leverett Street and passing two more shipyards before arriving at Barton's Point, the town's most northwesterly tip. By backtracking through the district, which was also called New Boston, and turning right on Cambridge Street, our sojourner would come upon Dawson's Cold Bath set in a "large Fruit Garden" near the water. Here gardeners and orchard owners Joseph and Sarah Dawson tried to attract "the Gentlemen and Ladies" to "spend an Afternoon" walking and taking "the Benefit of the Air," sipping tea or coffee, and surveying the array of fruit trees, flower plants, and seeds for sale.[4]

Between Cambridge Street and the high ridge of three peaks that made up the Trimountain, there were several streets laid out and a ropewalk or two, but few buildings or habitations. As the traveler passed the ropewalk on Belknap Street, he might notice people of African descent on the streets. A few men ran boardinghouses here that drew blacks and Indians from across New England. Bostonians muttered that bawdy houses were to be found nearby, hence the nickname of one of the hills: Mount Whoredom. The curious youth would probably be game to make the steep climb up Temple Street in order to reach the highest spot on the peninsula: 140-foot Beacon Hill. This peak was one of three in a row that gave Boston a distinctive profile when viewed from afar. Standing next to the beacon (a sixty-five-foot-tall crane, used for signaling danger to the surrounding countryside) and the great guns placed on the summit, visitors could "overlook all the Islands in the Bay, and descry such ships as are upon the Coast" (Figure 8). Below to the southwest was the forty-four-acre Boston Common. This large space was used largely for pasturing cattle and militia training. Except for a tree-lined promenade along one border, it had not been prettified. Left in its natural state, the Common was thought to offer a healthier environment than the city streets.[5]

Clambering down the south slope of Beacon Hill on a cow path lined with cedar trees and shrubs, our explorer could spot a number of elegant mansions, with extensive gardens, spread out along Beacon Street. If he kept going in a southeasterly direction, he would skirt the northeast side of the Common, putting the almshouse, workhouse, and town granary cluster on his left. Now he was entering the large expanse of the South End. Heading east on Milk Street would allow a circumnavigation of the district, allowing the walker to view the enormous ropewalks stretching along Hutchinson Street, note the South Battery jutting into the harbor, and then climb one of the steep lanes eighty feet to the top of Fort Hill to see its timber military works, thirty-five guns, and barracks housing Captain Jeremiah Green's company of soldiers. Then, winding southwesterly along the shore, the traveler passed a long series of wharves and distilleries, punctuated by Windmill Point.[6]

Sparsely settled up until the 1750s, the South End was now the fastest growing district in Boston, with the number of inhabitants and artisans rivaling the North End. Yet in places it featured open space, with pastures, orchards, gardens, and barns integrated into large house lots.[7] The walk down its main north-south artery, Newbury Street (called Marlborough and Orange in some sections) and approaching Frog Lane, led into a neighborhood of great elms, one of which in 1765 became the ceremonial center

FIGURE 8. This view of Boston from the top of Beacon Hill shows the Common in the near distance, the South End and Boston Neck in the middle distance, and the Dorchester hills on the horizon. "South-east View of Boston," by Samuel Hill, *Massachusetts Magazine*, 1790, p. 640.

Image courtesy of the American Antiquarian Society.

of the town's resistance to British policy—the Liberty Tree. After another long block, our newcomer would pass only a few doors from the rented quarters on Hollis Street of the man paid to identify and warn strangers, Robert Love.

Farther down Orange Street was a fortified wall with openings—a checkpoint for travelers arriving in Boston by land. If the newcomer chose to venture farther, he would pass through the opening designed for pedestrians (there was a separate one for carts) and find himself on Boston Neck. Here the urban clutter and cacophony were gone. The narrow strip of land was so close to sea level that the spring tides often washed over sections of the road. Except for a few taverns, a small house with a barn, and some outbuildings, no other structures appeared on either side of the paved cart path. The open land here was used for saltworks, pasturing townspeople's bulls, and the occasional horse race. A stretch of the path was lined with trees—alternating buttonwoods and elms. The gallows for the county of Suffolk stood on a small knoll, at a site that could accommodate the hundreds, even thousands, of people who attended corporal punishments and hangings. Shaking off this reminder of the brutal justice meted out to keep the king's order, our youth might very well opt to seek lodging for his first few nights in Boston at the George Tavern. He would thus end up sleeping just a stone's throw away from the Roxbury gate, which marked the bounds of Boston and which was the entrance point for visitors and newcomers who arrived by land.[8]

CHAPTER 6

Lodgings

IN HIS WARNINGS, Robert Love created a prose map that plotted the many
kinds of lodgings found by newcomers. Rebecca Anderson and her two
children were living in a chamber of John Bartlett's; Thomas Frasier's shop
was hired as living quarters by a shoemaker and his wife, fresh from London; Anthony St. John was working for and living with the baker John
Lucas. Bartlett, Frasier, and Lucas were among many hundreds of Boston
residents identified by Love as landlords who took in "strangers." The ros-
ter of their names and locations exposes not only the town's social hierarchy but also the seaport's streets, alleys, and structures. Much remains in
the shadows. The indefatigable warner reported where strangers could be
found on the urban grid but not if they lived upstairs or down, in a handsome house or a backyard hovel, in one room or more, with decent furnishings or almost none. Love's goal, after all, was to enable the selectmen to
find the sojourning stranger, if they chose to do so, or to reprimand a
landlord who had failed to give notification.[1]

Lining Boston's streets were roughly two thousand buildings of irregu-
lar shape and size. A late eighteenth-century account observed that "two
contiguous Houses are seldom found of the same height." Most blocks
sported a jumble of structures, with large and small residences found next
to the town's seventeen churches and innumerable shops and taverns.
Despite ordinances requiring new construction be of brick, the majority
of dwellings were wooden, two-story affairs. William Price's astonishingly
detailed 1769 map (produced on the endsheets of this book) reveals that on
the west side of Marlborough Street in the two blocks between West Street
and Rawson's Lane, for example, the buildings ranged between one and
three stories and were nearly continuous, with few yards or passageways

between them. Throughout the town, gambrel roofs were a common architectural feature, found on both modest houses and the grandest residences. The latter could contain as many as twenty-six rooms and were often set back from the street and surrounded by handsome gardens.[2]

Love's testimony that two-thirds of warned newcomers secured lodgings is powerful evidence that the great majority of people listed on Boston's warning rolls were not abjectly poor. In all, Love named nine hundred town residents who accommodated 1,482 warned parties. Some newcomers were prosperous enough to rent spacious quarters for their families. Many more arrived without much visible capital, but at least they carried with them sufficient coins, paper money, social credit, kin connections, charm, or potential as an employee to convince a Bostonian to house them.[3]

Love's phrasing sorts the living arrangements of strangers into four types. The majority "kept with" a landlord, meaning they lodged inside his or her dwelling and probably lived as part of the household. For this group, the warner used a range of verbs: "lives with," "lodges at," "lives and works for." A second type consisted of boarders, some of whom rented a chamber from a Bostonian. Third were new arrivals without long-term living arrangements, staying temporarily at an inn. A fourth group could afford to "hire" houses. This profited the rentiers of Boston, particularly merchants who had invested in multiple properties. John Hancock, for example, whose elegant residence was at the base of Beacon Hill, owned a rental house a few blocks eastward.[4]

For those "living in" others' households, Love's notes rarely indicate whether the newcomer was paying rent, exchanging services for room and board, or staying with kin or friends on a nonpaying basis. The proportion staying with kin appears to have been quite small: 5 percent of the warned parties with landlords shared their landlord's surname or told Love that they were lodging with relatives. These arrangements—living in, boarding, renting—could overlap, of course. Early modern cities were full of subtenants, and the warner's information allows us to see the layering of living arrangements. It was not unusual for him to explain, for example, that Ruth Scott "keeps now with the widow Dorothy Turner" who "lives in a house of Mr. Josiah Quincy."[5]

Love's landlords remind us of the many ways in which urban dwellers earned livelihoods—by speculating in real estate, managing wharves, or operating disorderly houses. Their biographical sketches not only evoke the vast assortment of Bostonians with whom Love interacted and kept stashed in his memory bank; they also bring into sharp relief the town's social hierarchy—its better, middling, and lower sorts. Landlords, whether long-time stakeholders in the city or short-term sojourners, are a key to unlocking what brought people on the move to Boston and what their experiences were like on its crooked streets.[6]

THE Boston residents who provided lodging for warned strangers represented all strata of society—from the governor to laborers, from octogenarians to young married couples, from mansion owners to garret dwellers. They included Congregationalists, Anglicans, Baptists, Quakers; Sons of Liberty and Bostonians who would become loyalists. Love named 779 individual men and 121 individual women as landlords. Fourteen black men and three African-descended women appear among the group, but not a single Indian.[7] In terms of occupations, tavern keepers vied with merchants for the most frequently represented, not just because they offered overnight accommodations but also because they relied on live-in employees. Seventy percent of the named landlords appear only once in Love's archive, and often the warner's notes are the only surviving evidence that these men and women resided for part of their lives in Boston. The city was experiencing very high rates of population turnover in the middle of the eighteenth century.[8]

While the landlords' dwellings, rental properties, and inns were found all over Boston, nearly 60 percent were located in the South End. Given that Love lived in the district, his familiarity with the neighborhood's denizens partly explains why he identified more strangers as lodging there than elsewhere. However, the warner's reporting bias is not the only factor. According to one historian's calculations, the South End held one-third of the town's population in 1771. A disproportionately large number of newcomers may have found lodgings in the southerly part of Boston because the district was the largest of the four named zones (North End, town center, South End, West End). It encompassed one-third of the peninsula's land mass and nearly all the area designated by four wards of the town's twelve. Moreover, during Love's tenure as warner, the South End witnessed a modest housing boom, drawing newcomers and enticing settled residents away from the two most densely populated sections, the North End and the town center.[9]

As was quite common in eighteenth-century seaports, many Boston landlords were renters not house owners. One historian figures that with

FIGURE 9. Isaiah Thomas was the only Boston newspaper publisher to include
woodcuts in his advertisements for houses to be let or sold. This one
is from the *Massachusetts Spy*, November 22, 1771.

Image courtesy of the American Antiquarian Society.

the average price of a residential building set at £100–130, a schoolmaster
or a laborer (with annual incomes of £100 or £45, respectively, and no
recourse to lending institutions) would have needed to save for ten to fifteen years to buy a lot with a house. With the town's uncertain economy
and land prices fluctuating at midcentury, many would have "concluded
that property ownership, though obviously desirable, was not worth the
risks involved, compared with other forms of economic activity and with
the need for cash or credit."[10]

Newcomers looking to rent relied on word of mouth, made inquiries
when they observed a vacancy, or consulted newspapers. Almost every issue
of the weekly news sheets carried at least one advertisement for a "genteel
House" or a "commodious Shop" to let or for sale. Houses meriting the
cost of advertising were described as two or three "rooms on a Floor," with
paved yards and other outdoor amenities (Figure 9).

Rooms available for lodgers were also cast as refined: "Two genteel
Apartments to be Lett, for the Benefit of Civil Society," read one 1770
notice. An available chamber might be "ready furnished" or unfurnished.
Some advertisers of such lodgings added that boarding or half boarding
was also offered. This might be "in a sober" or "quiet family," designated
only for "single Men" or "young ladies and Misses" (near "the best

Schools"), or suitable for both "Gentlemen and Ladies."[11] For those of very modest means, the Manufactory House, a large building on Tremont Street owned by the province, was rented out by the room.[12]

Love indicated how he perceived the social standing of landlords by what titles he attached to them. The warner honored the respectable status and civic standing of most male landlords by bestowing them with the standard honorific "Mr." or the appellations to which they were entitled, such as Capt., Dr., the Rev., Deacon, Maj., Col., and Esq. He withheld "Mr." for almost all landlords perceived to be African in heritage, for some Quakers (reflecting their renunciation of titles), and for roughly seventy onetime hosts who were probably short-term residents and of marginal status. Quite a number in this last group had Irish surnames; others lived in disreputable or liminal spaces—near the waterside, near the pesthouse, on a dock. If Love was unacquainted with a landlord, he might write: "keeps att one Samuel Dunbars upon Wintworths warfe."[13] Such entries, in which Love subtly cast the landlord as an impermanent, alien presence, are greatly outnumbered by ones in which the warner showed his familiarity with established townsmen. Love reeled off the occupations of many landlords with ease—"Mr. Thomas Crafts, the painter"—and signaled that particular domiciles were well known to town officials: a family of five "live[s] in the house with Widow Hoskins" near Fort Hill.[14] For landladies, Love recorded a title 90 percent of the time: Mrs. Rachel Newman, the Widow Waldo, Madam Pollard. In Love's notations, the three free black women who lodged men or women of color did not rate an honorific.[15]

Life-cycle stage, not simply wealth or occupation, often helps explain why some urban residents took in "strangers." Recently married couples needed wet nurses, nursemaids, and caretakers for growing children. Elderly propertied folk required attendants. Waitstill Jones, a Dorchester native, was "taken into" the family of Captain Mungo Mackay as a servant when she was nineteen. The Mackays—he a sea captain born in the Orkneys, his wife a Boston native—had been married less than two years, and their first child had been born seven months earlier.[16] The young lawyer John Adams had moved from the town of Braintree to rented quarters in Brattle Square, Boston, with his wife, Abigail, and their two toddlers in spring 1768. In the following months, Adams was often away riding circuit, or attending the admiralty court in Boston. The next spring, soon after the birth of their third child, the household hired young Sarah Marshall of Milton. At the other end of his adult life was Judge Samuel Welles, one of the richest men in Boston and a widower. In fall 1770, five months before his death at age eighty, he took into his mansion to live with him a Needham woman, probably as a caretaker.[17]

Both landlords and newcomers might change locations within the town from year to year. Sawyer Michael Condon tended to lodge solo travelers with Irish surnames like his own. In 1765, Condon, then in his thirties and with a young family, lived near James Griffin's wharf in the South End. Two years later, the Condons were residing close to a North End wharf; and in 1770, Love placed them in the West End of town.[18] In some forty cases, Love noted that a warned party lived first with one Bostonian and then with another. When she first arrived in town, Mary Davis "lived with one Mr Robison a tanner to traid, [but] she lives now [five months later] with Mr Peter Boyer," the jeweler, on Cold Lane. Such moves reflected not just the search for satisfactory housing at the right price but also the fluidity of the labor market. The youthful workers whom Love warned were typically not bound by one-year contracts as they would have been in England. They often signed up to work for short stints. If working conditions proved uncomfortable, they felt free to walk off the job in search of a new position.[19]

Only occasionally does Love take us inside the doors of warned strangers' lodgings. In his warning of one mother-and-daughter pair, the warner referred to a shocking indoor tragedy. On the previous Friday morning, the strangers' landlady, the widow Mary Cranch, was found dead in the house the women shared. As the jury of inquest put it: she, "being intoxicated with Liquor, fell down a steep pair of Stairs in her own House, and broke her neck."[20] Far more pleasant memories of boarding in Boston were recalled by the Scottish physician Alexander Hamilton, who wrote a travel account of his American journeys. The landlady of his genteel boardinghouse, a Mrs. Guneau, was an excellent source of information about the town, and a fellow lodger, a Frenchman, was the most lively "and merry companion ever I had met with." In Boston, as in other cities, many landlords must have served as fictive kin to their lodgers, giving them referrals, extending credit for small purchases, and offering various pointers to ease their adjustment.[21]

Love's list of landlords provides our best access to pre-revolutionary Boston's social hierarchy. Love and the selectmen who employed him would have known most of these town residents for their personality traits, political leanings, and willingness to abide by local ordinances. They would have effortlessly sized them up according to the system of sorting social status at the time—better, middling, and lower—and the subtle gradations within each "sort." The better sort was the smallest, making up about 5 percent of city residents. Love would have placed the wealthiest and most socially prominent family heads in this category—the learned clerics, the high office holders ("Esquires"), and many of those who styled themselves merchants and "gentlemen." The vast middling group mapped roughly onto those possessed of more than £40 in property, although the lines between the lower-middling and the lower sort blurred, especially for working and artisan men in their youths who had few possessions. The lower sort included the visibly poor, the near poor, and laborers with shaky access to steady work in the bottom rung of society. Many such men and women had no taxable wealth and no estate probated after their deaths, such that we can rarely capture the material circumstances of their lives.[22]

High social status and wealth tended to go hand in hand. Boston's elite men often came from well-established local families who financed their educations and started them off in business or a profession. They tended to intermarry and socialize mainly with one another. The men met at public houses that catered almost exclusively to them, and they formed clubs for eating, drinking, and conversation that were by invitation only. The women exchanged visits, often traveling through the city streets by chaise, accompanied by servants. These Bostonians, unlike the preponderance of city residents, were accustomed to owning horses, extensive libraries, silk clothes, silver plate, and luxurious furnishings. Merchant John Rowe's chatty diary, kept during the pre-revolutionary years, offers a fulsome account of the socializing of this stratum. Rowe's circle included some forty landlords mentioned in Love's warning records. But some of the most prominent Boston households—such as the Bromfields, Hutchinsons, and Vassals—are missing. While all of these families employed many servants and workers, we can imagine several reasons why they fail to appear in the warnings. Their employees must have included enslaved persons, lifelong retainers, Boston-born locals, and short-term, seasonal hires who happened not to be warned.[23]

Among the most visible elites in the town were those holding high office. In a royal colony such as Massachusetts, the governor was arguably at the apex of the social order. Francis Bernard took up the post in 1761. He had an Oxford education and lawyer's training that enabled him to discourse comfortably with Boston's learned men and women. Forced to defend and implement imperial and parliamentary measures that aggrieved the populace, he found his eight-year tenure increasingly rocky. The governor entered Love's records once as a landlord: in May 1767, Elisha Tilden, last from Stoughton, was living in the Province House on Marlborough Street with "his Excellency"; Tilden was probably a young servant.[24]

Wealthy landlord Robert Pierpoint was an active player in the Boston real estate market. A native of neighboring Roxbury, for almost all of his adult life Pierpoint was a prominent resident of Boston's South End. Indeed, he was chosen to replace Samuel Adams as Boston's tax assessor in 1770—a post that only wealthy men were asked to fill. As with many of the colonial elite, he did not start adult life as a gentleman of leisure. Pierpoint was a housewright turned merchant who eventually styled himself in documents as gentleman and, finally, esquire. Over a forty-year period, he was involved in fifty-three property transactions within the town's bounds. Often a landlord, he received eight warned families in rental properties and took eight solo men and women into his residence near the fortified gate leading to the Neck. One of the solos was a young carter, last from Nova Scotia. In most months of the year, merchants like Pierpoint needed employees for a range of tasks, including moving goods about town.[25]

Not all of the better sort had been born in the colonies. When he left his native Exeter in England and arrived in Boston at age twenty-one in the 1730s, John Rowe had enough capital to purchase a warehouse on the Long Wharf, launching a career that made him one of Boston's most eminent merchants. He managed the cargos of ships of all kinds—coasters, West Indian provisioners, and brigs that crisscrossed the Atlantic. His landholdings included many tracts in Boston and elsewhere in New England. An Anglican, he maintained close friendships with fellow churchmen who later left Boston as loyalists. At the same time Esquire Rowe befriended and worked on the merchants' committee side by side with many townsmen who became identified as patriots. He was a longtime fire warden, selectman, auditor of the town's accounts, and justice of the peace. Rowe stayed in Boston throughout the siege and the war years and died there in 1787. Rowe's tenants may chiefly have been well-connected families seeking genteel lodgings. Love's records depict one such renter. Lucy Remington Hobby, accompanied by two of her children and her "negro man Peter," occupied Rowe's house in Williams Court near Dock Square for at least a year in 1767–68. Hobby was the daughter of a well-known Cambridge judge and the recent widow of the congregational minister in the town of Reading. She was of gentle status but did not have great wealth.[26]

The mansion house of one "gentleman" landlord was located not in the peninsular part of Boston but on one of the islands in the harbor. Henry Howell Williams, the son of a colonel, had the lease of Noddle's Island from the town. The Williamses' nine children were born and raised on the island, which covered more than a square mile and was located over a mile from the Long Wharf. Williams must have managed a sizable retinue of servants, workers, and tenants on Noddle's, in part to entertain the clergy and other local dignitaries who frequently visited, and in part to manage the scores of cattle, horses, and sheep pastured on the island's hills. In 1764, Squire Williams advertised a reward for capture of an eighteen-year-old Irish runaway, a fellow who "speaks good English" and "has a very remarkable Cut or Scar in his left Nostrils." In 1767, the grandee publicly warned poachers that if they continued to trespass, "coming to gun . . . after Game" and killing his sheep, "they may depend on being dealt with" at law. In April 1768, Love recorded that Joseph Porter with his family of eight were installed in a house on the island. Porter was probably serving as a tenant farmer—and offering a hand in spotting poachers.[27]

Learned professional men—mostly clergymen, but sometimes lawyers and physicians—were accorded high status in puritan-inflected Boston. In 1764, young attorney Samuel Quincy and his wife, Hannah, took into their house Nancy Hinkley, a young woman who had grown up in Quincy's hometown of Braintree and whose ship master father had recently died in the West Indies, leaving a tiny estate. She probably worked for the Quincys as a nursemaid or housekeeper. Her landlord had won a reputation while a Harvard student for witty verse, and his legal practice was growing. His future included sitting for a Copley portrait, quitting New England forever as a loyalist, and practicing law in the British West Indies. Hinkley married ten years later in Boston; she and her husband, a ship captain, raised five children in the North End and eventually managed the Pine Tree tavern in Dock Square.[28]

Several clerics with interrupted careers are found among the landlords to warned strangers. Penuel Bowen, whose name means "face of God," had been called to be the colleague of the Reverend Samuel Checkley at Boston's New South Church in 1766, where young Bowen was expected to enjoy a long career. But he resigned unexpectedly at age twenty-nine in May 1772, announcing that he would be better suited to "a sedentary and studious

Life" free from pastoral duties. Love's records establish that Bowen made a living in the following years by opening a shop in Newbury Street. There he and his wife took in two (probably young) men from nearby towns as lodgers. The career of Samuel Mather did not entail becoming a shopkeeper, but its trajectory was as surprising to onlookers as that of Bowen. "Sammy" was a son of the famous Cotton Mather, whose biography he published. The younger Mather married well and settled into a house in the North End and into the pastorate at Boston's Second Church, located nearby. Perceived as being too tolerant of beliefs inimical to his forefathers' Calvinism, he negotiated to be dismissed from the pulpit in 1741 and took one-third of the congregation with him to start a new congregational society. For over forty years, the group limped along under his ministry, ridiculed by some Bostonians for its small size (twenty to thirty regular attenders) and for its leader's "dull pedantry." Lawyer and wit Robert Treat Paine famously claimed that his dog ran away after hearing Mather preach. In summer 1772, Love warned a family of five, who had recently arrived from Philadelphia on the sloop *Molly*, living in a house owned by Mather in Fore Street.[29]

Most members of Boston's gentry can be sorted into the familiar categories of congregational or Anglican, patriot or tory, merchant or divine, old New England family or new wealth. Occasionally, a worthy chose a path that deviated dramatically from the patterns typical of his kind. Nathaniel Appleton was born in Boston in 1731 to a congregational clergyman, graduated from Harvard, and went on to become a prominent merchant and leading Son of Liberty. With his family growing, in summer 1772 he took in Susanna Vose of Milton to live with them. Differentiating himself from the many slave owners among the town's elite whom Love knew as landlords, Appleton had a few years earlier published a pamphlet passionately denouncing slavery. This was a stance that some staunch puritans—such as Judge Samuel Sewall—had taken early in the century; but in the 1760s, few wealthy New Englanders saw owning slaves as unethical.[30]

The middling sort in early British America were those who earned what was known in the period as a decent competency. Competency meant not being obliged to work for wages; and it meant accumulating enough over one's adult lifespan to leave a decent inheritance for one's children. The yeoman farm families who owned land, livestock, and tools, and used family labor and neighborly exchanges to produce the household income are the iconic colonial middling sorts. Their urban equivalents were master artisans, sea captains, and shopkeepers who, after passing through apprenticeships or other youthful training, inherited or built up enough capital to purchase or lease a shop, work yard, or vessel. In Boston, they might rent their living quarters for part or all of their adult lives. If they owned their domicile, they were typically not involved in many real estate transactions. In any eighteenth-century city, many subtle gradations permeated the middling sort. At the lower end of the range were men like Love who pieced together a modest living by moving through several occupations (tailor, trader, liquor retailer, public servant). At the upper end were master craftsmen such as landlord Joseph Calef, a tanner who later moved to the suburbs; on his death, he styled himself a gentleman and owned possessions valued at £1,265.[31]

The middling landlords in Love's records more frequently "lodged" or rented rooms to warned strangers than offered houses to let. Take, for example, the fifteen housewrights (house builders) who lived in the South End and collectively provided lodgings for thirty-one warned parties—eight families, twelve solo women, and eleven solo men. All but two of these strangers were taken into their landlords' homes. Benjamin Eddy, who found success both as a housewright and wheelwright, lodged eight parties from 1765 to 1771—three solo women, one married couple, two solo males, and a nine-year-old Indian boy whose time Eddy "Bought . . . att the South." Love's notes do not tell us how old Eddy's female lodgers were or if they served as maids or wet nurses, but external sources reveal that one of the male lodgers was an apprentice. David Parker was a fifteen-year-old lad from Roxbury when he arrived in Eddy's household in 1765 and was still serving his term there in 1770 when he took a ball through the thigh at the Boston Massacre. The South End housewrights illustrate the range of wealth levels achieved by men in this line of work. John Preston, who rented houses to two warned parties, died at the end of the century worth £1,785, while his colleague Joseph Scott possessed one-tenth of that when he died at age fifty-four. In an eighteen-month stretch, Scott took in two solo male lodgers and two large families, such that his house in Pleasant Street was quite crowded; at the time he and his wife, Ann, had several young children.[32]

Shoemaking ranked among the "meaner"—thus less capitalized, less prestigious—of the trades. Because it did not require a large indenture fee or initial investment, orphan boys from impoverished backgrounds could

apprentice to learn the business of cobbling (repairing shoes) and cord-
waining (making shoes "bespoke" for customers) and open a shop in
rented quarters. Many never made an adequate living and died with under
£50 in tools and household items. Some of the twenty-odd shoemaker landlords in Love's records cannot be traced further in Boston records; these
men may never have made it out of the lower sort. For example, David
Murray never managed to establish his own shop, remaining a journeyman
during the fifteen years in which he lived with his wife and children on
Blower's wharf in the South End. His body washed up on the beach near
the Neck on an August day in 1771. The jury of inquest discovered that on
the previous evening, the shoemaker had gone out to Castle William in a
boat with tobacconist John Wilson; on the way home, the two men got into
a fierce fight that led to Murray's death. Wilson was tried for murder and
acquitted. Murray left no probated estate.[33]

In contrast, several of the Boston shoemakers listed as landlords by Love
established themselves as solid members of the middling sort by the time
they reached their fifties. John Shepard advertised that he had "lately
employed a Number of Hands from Europe" in his shop on Ann Street to
make fancy shoes of "Silk, Stuff, or Leather" "equal in Goodness to any
imported from Great-Britain." Perhaps Jacob Wilson, who came last from
Schoharie, New York, and lodged with Shepard in 1766, was one of these
workers. Shepard's possessions were not those of an ordinary cobbler; they
included several houses, a twenty-year-old enslaved woman, Phillis, and a
"Silver Snuff-Box, with a Jewish Pebble Stone upon the Lid, the inside
washed with Gold." When Hezediah Coley, another North End shoemaker
who lodged a few workers, died childless in 1769, he left a will stipulating
that "at the Death of my Wife" their enslaved man Caesar "shall Be free
from all Pepell and have a bed and six Chears one silver spoon and £5
lawful money."[34]

Middling men in the leather trades emerge in the warning records as
especially likely to hire and take in as lodgers solo men. Leather dressing
involved oiling, drying, and finishing tanned pieces to prepare them for
artisans such as bookbinders, breeches makers, and shoemakers. Five South
End leather dressers or breeches makers between them took in seventeen
solo males in Love's warning years. One of these master artisans and landlords, John McFadden, also leased and ran the town's slaughterhouse,
which was next to the water not far from Liberty Tree. Three of McFadden's
lodgers were in the leather trades; one had lived last in Delaware, one in

Philadelphia, and the third had arrived eleven months earlier from Ireland. McFadden's counterpart in the North End was William Dawes. Dawes took in five solo male travelers in the years 1771 and 1772, doubtless to serve as workers at his business near the town dock. This landlord became known in American lore as "Dawes the patriot" because he rode across the Neck through Roxbury to Lexington on April 18, 1775, while Paul Revere took an alternate route.[35]

Substantial artisans such as chandlers, glaziers, and rope makers often managed workshops or small manufactories that occupied significant square footage in the urban footprint and might include several sheds and outbuildings besides a shop or warehouse. As landlords, these property owners had more options for housing tenants and workers than most urban residents. Glazier James Cunningham had one widow living in the garret of a house he owned near his residence on Newbury Street at the same time that four soldiers' wives with three children between them lived in a house in Cunningham's yard. Saddler Sutton Byles owned a house, mud flats, and a wharf at the intersection of Castle and Orange Streets, three blocks south of the Hollis Street Church, where his cousin was the parson. Byles probably employed several of the solo males whom Love noted were boarding with him. He also allowed a French baker and his family to "lodge in fields" he owned near the windmill on the Neck.[36]

Ship captains, also known as master mariners, often left the sea by age forty and turned to keeping shops or taverns. At least twenty-seven ship captains appear as landlords lodging or renting to warned strangers. They are more easily identifiable by occupation than many other middling householders because Love gave them "Capt." as a title and because the Boston news sheets printed their names under the regular shipping news. Only a handful took in more than one warned party, and, surprisingly, during their active sailing years, they rarely lodged newcomers to whom they had given passage. Captain George Mitchell was in his fifties, married, and childless in the mid-1760s when he and his wife Sarah took in two family groups and three solo women, only one of whom had arrived on the captain's forty-ton sloop *Charming Molly* on one of Mitchell's frequent runs to and from Nova Scotian ports.[37] The life of one of his younger colleagues in the trade, landlord Abiel Lucas, is a sketch of downward mobility. Born to a prominent Plymouth County man, Lucas moved to Boston with his family of five in 1765 (earning a warning from Love). He commanded various coasters for the next few years but was posted as a

bankrupt and absconded debtor in 1768. By 1771, the year before his death
at age thirty-four, he was back in town but owned no rateable property and
was working as a tidesman for the customs officials, searching incoming
ships for smuggled cargo.[38]

When it came to the thirty-odd keepers of Boston's inns listed as landlords, it appears that Love did not use "lives with" and "lodges at" interchangeably. Those "living with" a tavern keeper had often done so for
months, while those "lodging at" a public house had typically done so for
less than two weeks. We can conclude that "living with" entailed working
for or staying in the family of the innkeeper while "lodging at" meant
that the newcomer was a paying customer. For example, Cord Cordis, the
proprietor of the British Coffee House on King Street acted as landlord to
both types—a solo male lived "with him" and a family lodged "at" his
establishment.[39]

Given the size of their establishments and the need to accommodate
people and horses and to transport guests within the town, proprietors
of commodious public houses required employees with a range of skills.
Longtime innholder Joseph Morton offered for hire "a young man who
understands the taking Care of Horses and driving a Carriage." One can
easily imagine such a lad managing or working at the stable of an inn on
Newbury Street described for sale in 1772: on the lot was "a large commodious Dwelling-House . . . also a Hatters Shop, between which is a Cart-Way
leading into a large Yard, wherein are Barns for keeping Horses, a Well of
Water . . ., and a good Garden." Such establishments would also need
cooks, washerwomen, and maids. Hence, one-third of the solo "strangers"
whom Boston's tavern keepers took in to live with them—and presumably
work for them—were women.[40]

The amenities, physical size, and reputation of taverns and their less
numerous counterparts, boardinghouses, varied according to the nature of
their clientele. Located at the Roxbury entrance to Boston, Gideon Gardner's George tavern, where our putative young traveler bedded down on
his first night in Boston, was a large establishment set on eighteen acres
including a shop, orchard, meadow, and tenements that could be rented
out. The tavern building could accommodate forty for private dinners.[41]
Gardner and his successor, Thomas Brackett, both Freemasons, were
favored by their brethren as hosts of the St. John the Baptist feast every
June. A tavern on the Neck had an advantage over those catering to the

genteel in the town center: when snow fell "fast," Boston gentlemen gathered for sleigh rides out to Roxbury and around Jamaica Pond, stopping on the Neck "at Gardners" on the way home. The tavern grounds accommodated entertainments such as that of a Yorkshire man who stood on two, then three horses' backs and galloped them "full Speed."[42] In the Love years, Gardner was landlord to two warned women who lived with him, one lodger who was looking for laboring work, and five families who rented the tenements.[43]

Nearer to the gallows on Boston Neck lived Ephraim and Mary Perry who drew to their house a very different clientele than the freemasons' favorite tavern with its elegant garden and fine assortment of wines. With the Perrys as with many of the landlords and New England–born sojourners in Love's records, it is hard to peg the family's social status—was it middling or lower? The couple had lived in Ephraim's natal town of Sherborn, then Holden in Worcester County, and finally Weymouth, before arriving (and being warned) in Boston in 1764 with six children. They stayed in Boston five years and then moved to Maine. Leasing town land on the northeastern part of the Neck, the Perrys may have earned some income by clamming, since the lease included the mud flats to the low water mark. Love's records indicate that they ran a boardinghouse or unlicensed inn: they put up twenty-two warned parties, more than any other landlord. Their lodgers did not stay with them for very long, perhaps because they could not afford to do so: ten of them were described as needy (almost blind, cut in the leg, old, poor) or lacking in resources (for example, unable to afford ship's passage). A few had profiles as strollers who went town to town, looking for opportunities to beg. Thus, it appears that the Perrys made their living by collecting a few shillings and pence from foot-weary travelers who came into Boston over the Neck. So did the enterprising Enoch Brown, a storekeeper and liquor retailer on the Neck who had nineteen warned parties, mostly solo men, living with him over a six-year period. Brown's live-ins probably worked for him; they stayed at least a couple of months; none were described as down-and-out, and most were from middling yeoman families in nearby country towns.[44]

Love was well acquainted with widows in various parts of town who had taken over their husband's licensed inns or forged a reputation as offering decent boarding arrangements. Because female heads of household appear infrequently in probate inventories and the surviving provincial tax rolls, it is often unclear to what social status the landladies belonged. Many were probably of the lower-middling sort, not unlike Love's daughter Ann, who never married and earned a living partly through retailing small amounts of liquor. For widows who as wives had run liquor retailing shops, the ability to continue running the establishment after their husband's death was not guaranteed. It took Rosanna Moore four years to get a license in her own name even though she testified that while her husband was alive, "the shop was almost wholly managed by her, and no complaint [of irregularities was ever] made." With license on hand, Moore lodged three solo men at her establishment in 1765 and 1766, and a shoemaker's family lived in a house she owned near the Liberty Tree in 1773.[45]

Boardinghouse was not a label yet in use, but Boston storekeepers, auctioneers, schoolmistresses, and others offered meals along with lodging rooms. The warner noted that Mrs. Robicheaux, "a franch woman [who] Lives now at New Boston and keeps Lodgers," was putting up a fellow Frenchman and probable Acadian Peter Dousett in October 1768.[46] Widows Agnes Osgood, Mary Culbertson, and Margarett Butt housed thirteen lodgers among them, including six who had stayed with them two months or longer. These women's economic circumstances varied. Butt owned a wooden house rated to be worth £16 in annual rental income. Culbertson went unrated and never obtained the liquor retailing license she sought; her lodgers included two peddlers.[47] Love identified two schoolmistresses, Elizabeth Taylor and Elizabeth Dinsdale, as taking in between them three solo females (one was a niece of Dinsdale's). It is not clear what sorts of schools they ran or whether their lodgers were students.[48]

The lower sort included tradesmen who toiled throughout their adult lives but failed to acquire their own shop or to accumulate enough to leave legacies to their children. Elisha Holmes fits this profile of the respectable working poor. At his death in 1774, the forty-three year-old Boston housewright owned goods valued at £27, consisting of little more than a few beds, some silver teaspoons, and a chest of tools. The Holmeses had married in Brookline, raised their first two children in Cambridge, where they were in covenant with the First Church, and then in spring 1765 moved to Boston. Love found them living "in the house with" another young housewright, Stephen Rodgers. Rodgers was more prosperous than Elisha Holmes: he soon sold his Orange Street house and moved to the western part of the province. The Holmeses remained in the South End, renting, and baptizing four more children at Boston's First Church. Over a four-year period, they

served as landlords for seven live-in solo travelers, all from nearby towns—
five women and two men. One was a widow in her sixties; another was a
young man in training as a housewright; one was a Roxbury wig maker.[49]

A few landlords made use of the Boston almshouse. John "Androwson,"
whom Love noted was a Dutchman (thus of German descent), told the
selectmen that in May 1766 he had embarked from Waterford, Ireland, to
Newfoundland, and from thence to Boston in September. Soon after, he
spent five weeks in the almshouse, which seemed to get him back on somewhat steady footing. Love's records show that two years later he was living
at "Mr. Go[u]ld's in the North End" and acting as landlord to "a franch
Gerrell [girl]" who came from Halifax on "one of the transports that
Brought the [occupying] Soldiers Bagage."[50]

During Love's years as warner, sixteen prosecutions went to trial against
Boston residents allegedly keeping disorderly houses. Six of these defendants show up as landlords in the warning records. From Love we learn the
locations of their allegedly "ill govern'd" tippling spaces and other details
about their urban lives—information absent from the court records.[51] The
charges against Rachel Hubbard in 1765 quoted formulaically but colorfully
from the relevant statute; these phrases recurred with slight variation in
other cases. Hubbard, the widow of a block maker, was convicted by the
jury of maintaining over the previous nine months a disorderly house,
where she "Entertain'd . . . idle" persons suspected "of evil fame & Conversation, as well Negro Slaves," permitting them to "remain in her . . . house
at unseasonable times" night and day, "quarrrling fighting tipling & drinking to Excess, & otherwise misbehaving themselves," to the disturbance of
the king's subjects. Fined £10 and required to post £20 promising good
behavior, Hubbard avoided being jailed by posting bond together with her
mariner son. The house where this iniquity was said to have occurred was
an "old" one with deficient chimneys at the head of the ropewalks off the
South End's Cow Lane. Here Hubbard had taken in lodger George O'Bryant—who was soon exposed as a horse thief. By 1769, widow Hubbard was
selling Lignum-Vitae at another South End location. Thirteen years later,
she entered the almshouse together with one of her widowed daughters.[52]

Were these disorderly houses sites for women making a living by prostitution? It is possible, but there is little evidence. None of the proprietors
were charged with running a bawdy house, and none took in a series of
girls and women to live with them. When Love wrote of "bad" women,
he generally placed them out and about the town—in the streets, keeping

company with men on boats—not in interior spaces. Prosecutors even in puritan Boston had turned a blind eye to prostitutes and brothels for decades. Both existed in the town, without a doubt, but they have left few traces.[53]

A substantial volume of unlicensed ale, fermented cider, and rum sales must have taken place in Boston, especially given the difficulty laboring people often had procuring a license. Grog shops, licensed and unlicensed, were the main source of everyday beverages for ordinary folk who could not afford to buy and store the hogsheads of Madeira, wine, and rum ordered by the better sort. Townspeople were encouraged by law to inform on unlicensed sellers and thereby earn some cash, but doing so usually broke unspoken codes of neighborhood loyalty. Only two women and ten men were hauled into court for selling without a license in the pre-revolutionary decade, and their cases were handled in a routine manner. All defendants confessed or pleaded nolo contendere and accepted the £2 fine. Three of them surface as Love landlords taking in one lodger each, and at least two of them had recently arrived in Boston and been warned. They listed their primary occupations variously as victualler, laborer, yeoman, trader, and mariner.[54]

White New Englanders condemned their African-descended neighbors to the lower sort by their denigrating attitudes toward them and by customs and structures that restricted black men and women to domestic and menial work.[55] Yet black New Englanders were well aware of the social and economic gradations in their small communities. Two landlords, Scipio Fayerweather and Tobias Locker, owned small tracts with houses adjacent to the ropewalks on Belknap Street in the West End. Fayerweather managed the feat of becoming a landowner only six years after being manumitted and bequeathed £3 plus his bed and bedding. A few months before making the purchase, the laborer, then in his forties, married with several adolescent children, and a communicant at the Brattle Street Church, took in Patience Nickols, "a free negro man's wife, she works at the tayler's traid." After becoming a landowner and moving to the West End, he lodged a black couple accompanied by their three grandchildren. By 1771, Fayerweather had erected a second building in this newly and sparsely settled part of town—a house that he rented to a black family arriving from Rutland in Vermont.[56]

Like his neighbor, Tobias Locker referred to himself as a laborer in court documents and deeds. Town records reveal the varied nature of his work:

in 1769 Locker had spent a week leveling the ground around the courthouse and jail complex on Queen Street and "cleansing the vault," earning two shillings, four pence per day. On his deathbed in July 1783, Locker wrote a will bequeathing all he owned to his "Beloved Wife Margarett." She held on to all or some of the estate; at her death, the residuary legatee named by her husband—boatbuilder Boston Smith—received it, including half of a wooden house. In their prime, Locker and his neighbor Fayerweather had together defied the town authorities, who blocked almost all pathways to entrepreneurship and wealth that black men and women might have seized. From 1762 on, the selectmen repeatedly found the two men in contempt for failing to work the requisite days repairing the public highways that was seen by whites as a suitable substitution for militia and watch duties, civic obligations that were exclusively open to white males.[57]

Another African New Englander dwelt at the far west edge of the hilly West End and welcomed strangers there. The house occupied by Joseph Bill, a free black in his late sixties in winter 1766, was probably a rickety, wooden building. It was situated in newly laid out blocks that had few inhabitants. Love identified it as "near the pest house," a building at the water's edge where smallpox patients were cared for and quarantined. Bill's house was also near or on Mount Whoredom. Between February and July, Bill welcomed five solo people of color, four of them women. Lydia Horton, an Indian last from Stoughton, had been in town only a week but told Love that she had come "offen before." Twenty-two-year-old Sarah Burnee, the daughter of Nipmuc Indian Sarah Muckamugg and a black man, Fortune Burnee, arrived in August in the company of another Indian, Martha Fegin. Another winter boarder was Patience Peck, whom Love described as a free mulatto and "a Bad woman" who "Comes after Negor felows." Was Bill operating an unlicensed tavern where men could find women and pay for sex? Whatever the case, within a few months, the establishment probably closed its doors as "Jo Bill," at age seventy, was admitted to the almshouse. He died there on May 22, 1767.[58]

Not all of Boston's blacks lived on the Trimountain. Nine lived in the North or South End, in addition to the eight Love placed in the West End. Scipio Gunney styled himself a trader. In two of the three years he appears in Love's records, he was renting a house from Captain Hopestill Foster in the South End, not far from where the warner lived. Gunney soon became a full communicant at Old South. In the mid-1760s, a few years after becoming free, Gunney lodged five warned parties, including a kinswoman,

Eunice, who was enslaved to a Plymouth man. Daniel Halsey, a mathematical instrument maker, rented a house on Fore Street in the North End and
occasionally took in white lodgers. Like the handful of others who plied his
trade in Boston, Halsey would have made, sold, and mended hourglasses,
compasses, Hadley's quadrants, and surveyors' tools.[59]

The kin connections among Boston's and New England's blacks were
dense. Abraham Millrow and his wife, Elizabeth, rented at about the same
location as Gunney (and may have preceded him in the same rented house).
In a six-month period, they took in three solo female lodgers, one of whom
was of African descent. Across town, in New Boston, Esau Millrow and his
wife and daughter came to lodge in January 1767 with Cato Jeffries and his
wife of two years. While still enslaved, Jeffries had married freewoman
Arminia Millrow. The exact nature of the kin relation between householder
Abraham and incomer Esau is unclear, but their simultaneous residence in
town in separate households is a reminder that with few chances to rise
from the lower to middling sort, African New Englanders greatly depended
on fellow blacks opening their houses, larders, and knowledge of survival
skills to one another, whether blood kin or fictive kin.[60]

WALKING the eighteenth-century city in the company of the diverse townspeople who offered lodgings takes us to street corners, doorsteps, back
alleys, wharves, and hilltops long gone. In the physical city that Love knew
so well, Beacon Hill had not yet been "greatly mutilated," dug down for
gravel and dirt to fill in the Mill Pond. To its west, Mount Vernon (also
known as Mount Whoredom) would likewise be shorn of its top sixty feet,
starting in summer 1799, when a syndicate of wealthy men laid out streets
and large lots. From Fort Hill's eighty-foot elevation in Love's era, cannon
thundered their salute on auspicious military victories; a century later, only
the base remained. Thirty years after Love's death, the mudflats lining the
Neck would be filled in with gravel, laying the foundation for the widening
and eventual obliteration of this distinctive narrow strip marking the
boundary with Roxbury and nearly making an island out of colonial Boston. None of the perimeter of the town as Love knew it remains. Wharves
disappeared long ago under landfill, and the western coast succumbed to a
landlubber's Back Bay crossed by railway lines. One researcher's map of
revolutionary-era Boston notes only eleven buildings that still stand, and
none are in the South End that was Love's most intimate milieu.[61]

Greeters not gatekeepers: this is the image of landlords that arises from Love's hundreds of entries. Of economic necessity, Boston was, like towns its size in England and Scotland, porous. The practice of taking in lodgers was pervasive. Men and women from every economic stratum and virtually every occupational category offered accommodations in order to generate rent, have domestic or other work performed, and fulfill cultural expectations of mutual support owed kinspersons and business and religious associates. Tracing the landlord-tenant relationship reveals, too, that far from placing an undue strain on the town, the great bulk of the "strangers" who arrived in Boston were readily absorbed into the town's economy and built environment.

CHAPTER 7

Sojourners of the Respectable Sort

SUSANNAH HALL CAME into Boston at age seventeen from her natal town of Newton, the eldest child of Josiah and Abigail Hall. She had been in town three weeks before Love warned her. He found her living, most likely as a servant, in the household of wealthy South Ender Robert Pierpoint, who was not her kinsman. Susannah's father was a weaver and settled landowner who served in minor town offices. Upon his death in 1786, his estate was valued at £395 in land, livestock, and movables, placing him firmly in the middling ranks of colonial society. Susannah remained in Boston for some time, married there at age twenty-one, and then relocated with her husband to her hometown to raise a family.[1]

Hall was joined by many who like her were traveling in response to the rhythms of their life cycles and the regional economy. Boston's warned strangers came overwhelmingly from middling households or the respectable lower sort. They had not been forced into a life of tramping; they were hardly without prospects. They had often arranged their work and lodgings in advance. Most seem to have held the vision that they were capable of attaining a decent competency during their adult lives. Robert Love warned them not because they bore signs of poverty or "low circumstances" but out of the belief that nearly anyone in society might suffer injury, illness, or unexpected misfortune and need relief.[2]

Love crossed paths with these sojourners at least once, often soon after they had arrived. He may have seen them again on the streets and noticed when some were named in marriage banns and others advanced from journeyman to master craftsman. But most were not persisters, and the warner had no need to be concerned with the manner or timing of their exits from town. A wealth of records kept by other colonial scriveners—registering births, deaths, taxes, and the like—often captures the fates of many of these respectable sorts. For their life stories and the role that Boston sojourns played, we need not let Love have the final word.

WILLIAM Doty and Elisha Goodenow illustrate the most common profile of males who made their way to Boston alone. These Massachusetts-born youths came for work and returned to their hometowns to marry.[3] Fourteen-year-old Doty hailed from a long-established Plymouth family. He arrived on a September day in 1765. By 1776, if not years before, he was back in Plymouth for his marriage to Abigail Sylvester. William became a mariner like his father. On his death in 1813, he left a substantial estate consisting of real estate worth £940 and personal goods including a Hadley's quadrant.[4] Elisha Goodenow of nearby Sudbury was twenty-nine at entry into Boston in May 1765; he did not stay more than a few years. By 1769, he was back in Sudbury, where he married, carried on a modest business as a trader, inherited a few acres on his father's death in 1788, and shared the care of his elderly, bedridden mother, before dying at age sixty-two.[5]

For some incomers, the Boston sojourn was but the first step in a peripatetic life. Vassell Sabin left his birthplace in Bristol County at age twenty. In Boston, he lodged, and perhaps worked, at Joseph Morton's White Horse tavern. Three years later, he married in Attleborough, a town adjacent to his hometown. He and his wife, along with an apprentice boy, then settled temporarily in Wrentham, several miles to the north. By 1771, they resided in nearby Stoughton as tenant farmers. Sabin died in Attleborough in 1804. Such mobile households of modest means were commonplace in the middle and latter parts of the century.[6]

Asa Haven was even more mobile over longer distances. He moved at least six times in his short adult life, following his warning in Boston at age twenty-three. His mobility was shaped by conditions shared by many of his male peers: a father who died long after Asa married, an expectation that he and his siblings would never inherit more than a few tools, and the lure of frontier towns in the central and western parts of the province. At first, he and his wife, Eunice, lived in a string of Worcester County towns in relatively close proximity to their natal towns. By the second year of the Revolutionary War, they had moved to Blandford, in the western part of the state, from which Haven enlisted; he died two months into his military service.[7]

"Lads" were much in demand. The few newspaper advertisements seeking workers stressed youthfulness: "WANTED, a strong hearty honest young Lad, in the Appothecary's Business"; "a Lad . . . of Ten or Eleven Years old" (by a tavern keeper); "A Smart, active Boy, from 12 to 14 years old, as an Apprentice to a Barber." Boys from adjoining towns, whose residents enjoyed strong familial and business connections with Bostonians, often completed one or more work stints in the capital before they reached the age of majority. A lad named Prince George from the north parish of Braintree (later Quincy) was taken in at age nine by Samuel Adams, who gave proper notification to the selectmen. At some point, the boy returned to his hometown, but by age fifteen, Love found him back in Boston, living and probably working with blacksmith and axe maker Thomas Trott.[8]

What determined the end of a young man's stay in Boston? The exact day on which these men departed is rarely known. Some would have left Boston when their period of work—an apprenticeship or a seasonal arrangement—was over. News of a family member's death or illness might recall them to their natal village. Others departed when they had accumulated cash sufficient to launch them in married life. The trigger for Solomon Goodale may have been early receipt of part of his inheritance. Solomon was twenty-one in the spring of 1766, when he came to Boston from his hometown, Marlborough, in Worcester County. His father, Nathan, was a well-established yeoman with sufficient tracts and wealth to provide for all of his eight children. But it was only to Solomon, the youngest, that Nathan gave some of his portion prior to writing his will in 1778. This may have been a ploy to reclaim Solomon from the city. The gift was probably what took Solomon to the distant frontier town of Conway, where he settled, served in the local militia and the Continental army, and raised a family.[9]

Not all New England male youths were fortunate enough to inherit land. In the eighteenth century, the long-settled towns in the eastern part of the Bay province were experiencing a population squeeze on arable land that forced many young men to move far from their parents and acquire land largely on their own hook. Simeon Pratt's father, a tanner, died a year after Simeon's birth, leaving a modest estate (house, barn, tan house, five-acre home lot, a horse, many books). When the estate was divided among the heirs some fifteen years later, Simeon received his small portion in cash. This Needham lad soon departed to serve an apprenticeship in Weston, but this arrangement may have ended a few months later, when Pratt at age twenty-one came to Boston, where he lodged with tanner Samuel Bass. Pratt eventually settled as a tanner in Roxbury. All this young man inherited from the father he barely knew was his trade, not his start in adult life or his status as an adult landowner.[10]

Although Levi Ames came from a "credible" family, to use the parlance of the time, he disgraced his kinfolk. Spending his early childhood in the Middlesex County town of Groton, he was cautioned by his widowed mother never to repeat the small thefts he indulged in. Little did Love know when he met Ames, then age fourteen and staying with a South End barber, that the lad would six years later swing from Boston's gallows after a long string of thefts and burglaries. It is likely that the warner was in the throng of seven thousand or so who crowded Boston Neck in October 1773 to see the now-repentant Ames "turned off."[11]

Hadley, on the Connecticut River ninety miles west of Boston, was the home of John Clark, a small landowner of Ulster Scot heritage in his mid-twenties. One July day, he temporarily left his very pregnant young wife to venture to Boston. We do not know why he made the trip, but he promised Love that he would "goo out of town in a day or two." Four days later, Clark's first child, Sarah, was born; he may have arrived at his homestead just in time to learn that his wife had been safely delivered.[12]

Joseph Tyler, the son of Dedham's congregational minister, represented a category of warned solo males of middling status who stayed in Boston for a while, establishing households before moving elsewhere. Tyler came at age sixteen, placed as an apprentice or trainee with a prominent Boston house builder. Town records indicate that thirteen years later he had attained independent status as a housewright. He later moved his family to the District of Maine.[13] David Hide, who arrived in his early twenties from Hampshire County, became affiliated with the venerable Brattle Street Church; he and his wife had their first children baptized there in the early 1770s. A few years later, the Hides moved west to the newly incorporated town of Monson, where David's father had settled. The younger Hide achieved considerable prominence, owning a substantial house and serving as selectman, town clerk, and representative to the general court.[14]

The romantic and marriage history of the uniquely named sojourner Unite Cox provides several twists on the path followed by Tyler and Hide. Cox, a cordwainer, was in his forties when he encountered Love in October 1767. He refused to identify the town he belonged to or last came from. The history he hid from Love included his birth in Dorchester and life as a farmer and householder in Malden, where he and his now-deceased wife had had at least eight children born to them in the 1740s and 1750s. After his first wife's death, Cox evidently came often to Boston searching for a partner. His banns of marriage to one woman were published in 1763, but no marriage ensued. In May 1767, his banns with Sarah Dickinson of Boston were "forbid." Four months later, in the Baptist meetinghouse, Unite married a Boston resident who shared his surname. The following spring, Cox appeared in the sessions court, where he unsuccessfully contested the charge of forty-year-old Dickinson that he had fathered her newborn. With no spouse to contribute to her wherewithal, Dickinson, with her child, sought shelter in the Boston almshouse.[15]

Housewright John Stutson, warned in 1763 at age twenty-three, was one of a strikingly small proportion of the warned single men from middling families who lived out their lives as Boston residents. In part, the convulsions of the American Revolution, particularly the occupation of the town by British troops in 1775 and the siege of the city by George Washington's army, forced many townspeople to evacuate lest they be seen as abetting the enemy. Evacuees lived temporarily in interior towns such as Worcester, and many never returned to Boston.[16] Stutson, a shipwright's son from Hingham, was among those who stayed. He raised a family in the North End, held town office, and became a militia captain and an officer in the town's artillery company. A family genealogist boasted that Stutson "built the Dome of the New [Charles Bulfinch–designed] State House." At his death in 1799, Stutson owned $5,500 in town real estate and $893 in movable goods and cash.[17]

Peddler Michael Hogan had little property when he died, but he managed to avoid relying on poor relief. He had lived in two other sizable towns, Salem and Providence, before entering Boston in late summer 1768 carrying a box with goods he planned to "Sell upon a WheleBarrow." Soon after, Hogan established himself with a peddler's shop at the South End. He did not live long enough to see the War for Independence start. During a stretch of ninety-degree days in August 1771, newspapers reported his sudden death by heatstroke.[18]

Like boys and men, the girls and women arriving in Boston alone came primarily for work opportunities. Mary Woodhouse, a Milton lass who came to serve in a North End household, was only ten. But most, like the solo males in the warning records, were between fifteen and the late twenties. Laundering, nursing, cooking, sewing and mending, and above all, maid service in private residences and taverns were in constant demand in the port town of sixteen thousand.[19]

Wealthy merchant Nathaniel Glover, whose large household on Orange Street included two enslaved persons, notified the selectmen in autumn 1765 that he had "taken into his Family as a maid Servant," Eleanor White, from Pownalborough. Love warned her eleven days later, identifying her landlord but omitting, as he did in most entries for solo women, any details about her employment. Only rarely did he describe the sort of domestic work taken on by warned women or the difficulties they might face if abruptly dismissed. Lucy Barker, a widow, came "to town . . . to be a housekeeper for a Gentleman in the south end." Chloe Short, "a malato Womon last from Grafton" but previously of New London, was nursing an unnamed women "in the Back Side of" the widow Culbertson's house. Frances Ledeer embarked in London with her new employer's wife and children for the trip to New England after having agreed to serve in customs commissioner Henry Hulton's Brookline household for "one whole year." Ledeer found herself unable to find another position nearby when Hulton "discharged her" and "would give no recommendation." She came to Boston, lodged with a widow, and continued looking for work.[20]

Some of the solo women sojourning in or moving to Boston pursued jobs other than domestic service. Some must have set themselves up as petty shopkeepers—in the sort of small establishment found throughout the town for which the proprietors never bothered to advertise in the news sheets. Immediately on her arrival "by land" from Philadelphia, widow Mary Scramp went "about peddling," Love noted. She had made the overseas passage from London four years earlier. Eight months later, this new Bostonian married a local shopkeeper's son.[21]

Many young women sojourning in Boston found marriage partners. Despite Boston's imbalanced sex ratio, incomers from villages and small towns encountered a sizable youthful labor force which was continually being replenished. The warned women who married in Boston met with a variety of fates. Hannah Flint never left. Not quite three years after her arrival, she married twenty-two-year-old Jesse, son of her Boston landlord, Ephraim Perry. Both Hannah and the Perry family had previously lived in the town of Sherborn, Massachusetts, suggesting that Flint's ties to this family had been long-standing. Hannah would not make the move that Jesse did to Vermont later in the century, as she died in Boston in 1770 and was buried alongside their one-year-old infant.[22]

Sabra Cobb's trajectory was more typical than Flint's in that she married in Boston but then moved away. Cobb arrived at seventeen to live in the household of her newly arrived married sister. Six years later, she made a marriage that secured for her the status of a genteel lady. Her chosen was John Emerson, a Harvard College graduate and son of a congregational minister. Lore has it that Sabra unsuccessfully pleaded with him not to accept a call to become parson in the frontier town of Conway, New Hampshire. There, in a settlement carved out of the woods before their eyes, they raised many children. Susannah Hall, whom we met earlier, followed a slightly different path out of Boston. Four years after her arrival, she married a man then "of Boston" in King's Chapel, but he, like Susannah, had been born in Newton. The couple promptly decamped for Newton, where their first children were born.[23]

Pregnancies outside of marriage placed young women in vulnerable positions. Six days after she was warned by Love, Kate Sullivan had sex with laborer Michael Welch in Boston. Or at least that was the day—April 25, 1768—she later specified as when conception had occurred of the infant girl she gave birth to the following January. Welch had shipped himself off as a sailor by the time Sullivan confessed to her sin in court and received a sentence of ten lashes.[24]

Mary Gay's out-of-wedlock pregnancy led to her being charged with the capital crime of infanticide. Arriving in Boston at the start of 1771, Mary lived with her brother-in-law Daniel Whitney, and her sister Sarah, in the small house with barn that they rented on Boston Neck. Possibly a traumatic event, such as having a secret affair with or being sexually coerced by her landlord or a familial intimate, caused the young woman to "disown" being with child throughout the following fall and winter. Early on the morning of April 13, 1772, a newly born infant was found dead in the bed with Mary. Legal protocol dictated that a jury of inquest be called; later in the day, coroner Robert Pierpoint, who lived a short walk away, reported the male jurors' suspicion that the child had died due to Mary's deliberate neglect. Mary was in too weak a condition to be taken to Boston's jail. For the next twenty-three days, deputized men took turns keeping a twenty-four-hour watch, ensuring that Mary not "make an Escape from Justice." The prosecution against Mary fizzled, as did most of the relatively rare, late eighteenth-century infanticide cases against white women. Mary was taken to prison in a hired chaise on May 7, but no trial ensued. At some point, she was discharged.[25]

The stream of girls and women warned as solo travelers included individuals whose destination was Boston because their family head was resettling there or because Boston was the hometown they had left for a while. When the Hinkleys (last from Braintree) and the Clarks (last from Londonderry, New Hampshire) moved to Boston, they arrived singly or in clusters, over the course of a year.[26] In other cases, Love warned young women who had been born in Boston; a spell living elsewhere might mean they had lost their Boston inhabitancy. Given a world in which family members frequently changed locations out-of-step with one another, Love often left out the details and let a brief reference to kinship suffice: Mary Unchet's arrival from Halifax was explained by his observation that "She is Daughter to a Confectioner at the South End."[27]

Widowed and married female travelers arriving alone often came for the prosaic reasons of work opportunities or family reunification, but sometimes there was another trigger. Jane Kingston had been several months in Boston, using a garret chamber on Gibbons Court as a shelter from domestic violence: "she says she has a husband and 5 Children at Woster . . . But he has Used her so Ill she Could Not Live With him so Come to this town." Widow Elizabeth Hardwick, last from Braintree, had fixed on a familiar answer to old age: Love found her living in the family of one son-in-law and explained that she rotated "among her Children" who had households in Boston.[28]

In any given year, Love warned some two hundred children and young adults whom he accounted as traveling alone and as belonging to the respectable sort. Unknown to one another on entry, some of the strangers must have met—if not at their lodgings or workplaces, then in the marketplace, public worship places, or the streets. Many of these exchanges would have been salutary. But the encounter between a child, Betty Allen, and a journeyman, John Ward, both receiving warning in the second half of 1765, was not. In August, nine-year-old Betty came into Boston with her younger sister Tamar from their natal town of Weston. Love noted that their father had died and that they were coming to live with their mother, Mary, and her new husband, Robert McCurdy, who rented a house near the windmills in the South End. In mid-December, Love warned Ward, a Hartford man in his mid-twenties who was two weeks into his stint as a journeyman and boarder at wig maker John Piemont's on King Street. Two days before Christmas, at a house on one of the wharves just north of Faneuil Hall, Betty was sexually assaulted by Ward, the "journeyman-barber," with "grievous" physical injury resulting. The printer of the *Newport Mercury*, in reporting Ward's arrest, opined that the man awaited "the just sentence of his demerit."[29]

Had Betty been lured off the streets or kidnapped in daylight hours by John Ward aided by unnamed associates? The details are unknown because the testimony of the witnesses at Ward's trial was not recorded. Ward may have been one of those eighteenth-century men who believed that a girl-child could consent to and welcome sexual play. The outcome of Ward's trial mirrored that of other cases involving very young accusers and white male defendants who were not cultural outsiders.[30] Acquitted by a jury on a count of rape, Ward pleaded guilty to the lesser charge of making "a Violent Assault With an Intention her . . . to Ravish & Carnally Know, and Other Enormities." On a Thursday in May, the court's sentence was carried out: Ward sat on the gallows for an hour with a halter about his neck, doubtless being jeered at by a crowd, "and was afterwards severely flogg'd 20 Stripes." The bench also decreed that he suffer a year's imprisonment and pay the prosecution costs. But come summer, with Boston's jail about to be dismantled and rebuilt, Sheriff Greenleaf negotiated what was in effect banishment for Ward. "The Commander of one of his Majestys Ships now in Harbour . . . Consented to take him on board" and sail away with him.[31]

Unlike the many solo males warned in Boston who could choose when to leave town, John Ward suffered deportation as a convicted criminal. He may have never again seen his native Connecticut. Betty Allen seems to have survived the assault. She may be the Elizabeth Allen who married in Boston in 1774. If not, she probably joined her mother and stepfather when they moved to Maine. Despite the trauma she endured, in the end Betty's, not John's, was the more common life-story outcome for thousands of New Englanders of the middling sort who made Boston one stop on their peregrinations.[32]

LIKE many white New Englanders, Indians and blacks came to Boston seeking work, marriage partners, and reunion with family members. However, they faced additional difficulties exacerbated by the suspicious, demeaning attitudes that most white New Englanders held of Indians and blacks. Furthermore, at least in authorities' eyes, almost every element of their lives was uncertain and unfixed—names, marriages, residences. Their urban sojourns were not tied as clearly to life-cycle patterns as was the case for incoming white New Englanders. Indeed, if we could attach ages to most of these travelers, it is likely that they would turn out to be on average slightly older. Thus, Love's warnings confirm that New Englanders of color were more peripatetic over their life courses and faced even poorer prospects for attaining competency than whites not born into privilege.

Some African New Englanders traveled to Boston in kin clusters, apparently in the midst of transitioning from slavery to freedom. Cuffee and Grace Luce came to Boston with three of their grandchildren and lodged in the West End house of Scipio Fayerweather. They had long been slaves in the household of west Roxbury clergyman Nathaniel Walter; he married them in 1745 and heard them own the covenant when he baptized them along with four of their children in 1749. Love's entry tells us that by 1770 they had taken a surname and most likely were claiming free status.[33] Similarly, Scipio, another enslaved Roxbury man, used a surname (Feittis) and established himself and his wife of two years in a rented South End house.[34]

Most of the couples, according to Love, were "both negors" or "both Indians." Not however, Solomon and Sarah Wamsquan: "he is a Indin his Wife is White Woman." Marriages between whites and Indians were not prohibited by the provincial statute that banned unions between whites and blacks, but "custom frowned on" them, and they are usually absent from official marriage records. This couple's union, however, was recorded. The Natick town clerk noted that Solomon, a Natick Indian then in his mid-twenties, wed Sarah Jones, "a transient person," in 1759 in the neighboring town of Sherborn. The couple came into Boston with two of their children, but since Love warned them on the day they arrived, we have no clue where they lodged or how long they stayed. It may be that this family avoided the indebtedness and poverty that plagued Solomon's widowed mother, Sarah, in the 1760s and 1770s when the town of Natick claimed that, due to her many moves, she had "no Pretentions to a legal Residence." Dislocation and neediness marked the other two interracial couples mentioned in Love's warnings. Of William and Deliverance Parker, last from Newport: "she is an Indin Womon; they are Begers." Elizabeth Meers was in town without her husband, Aaron Collins, "a free Negor Man." She "Lives Now in" the almshouse, where the couple's one-year-old daughter soon died.[35]

The women of color who traveled alone into Boston lived peripatetic lives. For several, Boston was at least their third residence within the past few years. Elizabeth Chase had recently lived (and presumably worked) in Roxbury, establishing inhabitancy, and then Dedham. Sarah Fletcher had worked in New York City and then in Wrentham, Massachusetts. Chloe

Short had "Belonged to" both the Connecticut port of New London and the Massachusetts country town of Grafton. In contrast, Dinah Gummer's adult life pivoted back and forth between two towns. This "free Negor Woman" had grown up in Boston. As a youthful slave of John Clough, deacon of the Hollis Street Church, Dinah came into contact with William Gummer, a man newly freed by his master, the pastor in a town twelve miles west of Boston. After their 1745 Boston marriage, Dinah evidently lived for two decades in Sherborn, from which she reentered Boston and received warning in 1766—whether as a new widow, the records do not say. Two years later, Gummer, yet again "of Sherborn," married former slave Prince Vitter of Natick.[36]

Women might cross town lines in their efforts to marry or preserve marital ties. Both Short and Sarah Prince married black men held as slaves by wealthy Bostonians. One wonders what strategies these women of free status used to cope with a legal and social system that denied full conjugal rights to the enslaved. At weddings, Massachusetts ministers were known to use special vows declaring that the tie would last as long as it was "consistent with" the obligations a servant owed to his master and as "God, in his Providence, shall continue your . . . abode in Such Place (or Places) as that you can conveniently come together." In his warnings of Prince and freewoman Phyllis Dinn, Love ignored their recent in-town marriages (one to an enslaved man, one to a freeman) in that the surnames recorded for the women did not change after the weddings and the husbands went unmentioned. However, in one of these cases, the lodging locations confirm that the spouses were living together. Love's elision of the women's marital status provides further evidence that white New Englanders often perceived marriages among nonwhites as precarious and contingent.[37]

Indian women encountered similar marital complications. Molly Surrance, a "free Indian" according to her marriage record, had wed Cato, a "negro servant of the Governor's," in Boston in 1763. Four years later, Love warned her after she reentered Boston from Roxbury, where her husband worked on Governor Bernard's Jamaica Plain estate. Like many couples of color, these spouses often had to live apart. Molly was not able to earn and save enough to purchase and thus free her spouse. By October 1768, it is likely that Molly had died or been forced to take a live-in position where she could not bring the couple's son. This child, the namesake of his father, was delivered to the Boston almshouse, where he died.[38]

For Lucy Pernam, trouble stemmed from inside her marriage. Because of it, she would become the only black woman in colonial Massachusetts to be granted a marital separation. In June 1766, when Love warned her, Lucy had not yet filed her divorce petition. Since marrying Newburyport truckman Scipio Pernam and bearing a daughter earlier in the decade, Lucy had met with a host of troubles. Scipio punished her severely for what he and white male neighbors claimed was "remarkably wild profane" and threatening, often drunken behavior. Not only did he beat her, turn her out of doors, and block her from entering the house to tend to their daughter, but he arranged for her to be confined in the town workhouse for months at a time. Finally, according to Lucy, in spring 1765 in utter disregard for her free status, he sold her to a local butcher, who had her spirited to the Hudson River for resale. Managing to escape after several weeks of bondage, Lucy came to Boston, which she started using as a base from which to return to Newburyport in her attempts to see her daughter. Even though some observers believed that she was "distracted" (mentally disordered), most whites sided with Scipio in decrying her as a willfully "Vile" and disorderly woman who would someday act on her repeated threats to set fire to town buildings. Boston officials concurred: twice they ordered her physically removed from town. Lucy's adult life was marked by dramatic juxtapositions. On the one hand, she was left destitute and forlorn by Scipio (who failed to pay the court-ordered alimony) and increasingly found herself in irons (in Ipswich, Boston, and Newburyport). On the other hand, Pernam displayed legal savvy—hiring Boston lawyer Benjamin Kent, for example—and she at times was given shelter and succor from a network of sympathetic blacks and whites. Her many confinements and the labels she bore by the time of her death at the end of the century—"Raving," "negro wench"—signal that for African New Englanders, rage and mental illness, when combined with quotidian struggles for survival and dignity, were a deadly mix.[39]

Two warned Indian women were among the last of their particular matri- and patri-lines to hold land in Natick, where John Eliot had gathered one of the original Praying Towns to attract natives willing to adopt Christianity. By the 1760s, pressured by indebtedness and loss of hunting grounds, many Natick Indians had sold their land to English settlers. Moreover, the remaining Indian population was heavily skewed to widows and orphaned children. Both of the women who encountered Love had been baptized in the Natick church and orphaned young; each inherited ten or more acres from their fathers and other kin. Mary Waban acquired enough schooling to be able to sign her name at age fifteen. By that time, she was living in Newton, serving or apprenticed to the family of Enoch Parker. At age thirty-three, Waban sojourned in Boston—her purpose and length of stay are unknown. Within six years, she had relocated to Barre in northern Worcester County, where she married an enslaved black man, Stepney.[40] In contrast, we know why Rhoda Babesuck Wamsquan was in Boston for three weeks in November 1765. Married in Natick four years earlier at age twenty-one, Rhoda had since been living in New Haven, Connecticut, with her husband. She came alone to Boston—by ship, the easiest way—because she had recently enlisted a Natick-area man well versed in legal affairs to help her, as he put it, sell "her Land in order to Paying her debts and Procuring a horse for her to Ride." In fall 1765, their efforts "were disappointed," but the sale was approved by the General Court the following year. When Rhoda, who appears to have remarried after 1766, died in Natick only three years later, the administrator claimed that she owned no personal goods at all.[41]

Beulah Speen's story speaks to the high mortality among men of color in these decades and whites' lack of comprehension of many New Englanders' blended heritage. Love labeled her "a negor Woman" and noted that she was last from Needham (where she probably had been bound out to serve a white family in her teenage years) and was living with a black woman, Hitty Winship, in the North End. He omitted or was ignorant of other relevant facts. First, Beulah's mother was Lydia Speen of the Natick Indians and a landowner there. Second, four months after arriving in Boston, Beulah, at age twenty-three, had been married in Christ Church to Saul Rogers, slave to schoolmaster and Harvard graduate Richard Pateshall, who ran a private school in the town center. Saul must have died soon after, as Beulah was back in Natick in 1770, where she married into the Waban clan but mourned her second husband after a year. Only with her third marriage, to Nicodemus Gigger, did Beulah become a mother. She died at age fifty-eight, having outlived her husband by four months.[42]

Many of the black and Indian men of free status were as mobile as the solo women of color. Anthony Diego's comings and goings earned him two warnings in Boston. This "tall Negor" first appeared in 1768 from England; when Diego reentered the town in summer 1771, he was coming from Natick. Henry Travel had lived in New York City and Albany prior to his

Boston visit in September 1768, when he found lodging and probably work with the saddler Sutton Byles. He returned to Boston three summers later, this time from nearby Bridgewater, expecting to be employed as a laborer. Jacob Cromwell, "a Negor man and free," had lived the past two summers in Roxbury but was originally from New Jersey.[43]

A few men of color earned a measure of fame or even infamy for their actions in the volatile period just before the revolution. Age twenty in the summer 1767, Ebenezer Ephraim, a Natick-born Indian, told Love that he was in town "to Dow Labring Work." On the day he arrived from Medford, he secured lodging with Gideon Gardner on the Neck. In 1775, as a resident of Worcester, he signed up for an eight-month stretch with the provincial service and was one of fifteen Indians who fought at Bunker Hill.[44] In late 1766, Love warned a young enslaved man who gave his name as John Francis. Francis obtained his freedom during the next few years while living in Boston, after which he styled himself first Peter Frizer and then John Peters. This is the John Peters, small-time grocer and "trader" of Boston, who married the African-born poet Phillis Wheatley in Boston's Second Church in 1778. Wheatley's biographers agree that this marriage was disastrous for Phillis, given that Peters appears to have been an inveterate con man and neglectful husband.[45]

Only one among the warned blacks and Indians can be documented as settling permanently and dying in Boston. John Brown, a black man, came to Boston in autumn 1770 from London in the company of two prominent white Bostonians; his relation to them is unclear. He was a young man of about twenty. Two years later, Brown was living in the South End when he served as landlord to a free black woman warned by Love. His marriage soon after (not to his female lodger) was sponsored by the Hollis Street Church. Brown evidently served in the Revolutionary War, as upon his death in January 1820 he left household items worth $25 and $38 from the Pension Office. His funeral was from King's Chapel. An obituary notice called him "a man of colour, aged 67; an honest and industrious man."[46]

PROSPEROUS families migrating to Boston, like those of Ebenezer Allen and Peter McNabb, often brought their household or work-related laborers. Allen came with not only his wife, Meribah, and daughter Mary but also an apprentice and a journeyman. Five male servants accompanied shoemaker McNabb when he relocated from Halifax to Boston in 1769 and established himself at the Sign of the Boot on King Street.[47] Arriving from her home in

Martha's Vineyard two months prior to her wedding in Christ Church, widow Mercy Chase brought an entourage that included two children, a "negro man of hers named" Prince, and an Indian woman, Violet. Coffee-house operator Abigail Stoneman brought two daughters and two enslaved persons with her when she took over the license of the Royal Exchange tavern on King-Street. She stayed for nineteen months before returning to her Newport, Rhode Island, base. In these cases, each wealthy household head had declined to give a bond absolving the town from future charge related to members of their retinue. Love warned not because he feared the family governor would become indigent but because he realized that servants and slaves might decide to quit these households, after which they might require aid.[48]

Relocating a large household, whether temporarily or permanently, was costly and often occurred in stages. Prosperous mariner Jonathan Nutting hired a house in spring 1766 for his wife, four children, and a "servant lad"; this sojourn occurred in the midst of the family's relocation from Cumberland, Rhode Island, to Cushing, Maine. Shoemaker Ashbel Anderson of East Windsor, Connecticut, traveled by sloop from Hartford with his wife, daughters, and sister-in-law; all six lodged at the White Horse tavern. The purpose of their trip went unrecorded; soon, the Andersons returned home.[49]

Many families teetered on the margin between sustaining themselves through casual employments and needing public relief. Luke Ament was a baker in his mid-thirties, arriving from his birthplace, New York City, with his wife, Elizabeth (Billings), and sons Eldart and William. What seems to have precipitated the family's move was Ament's falling deeply into arrears in paying the ground rent on the house lot they occupied on the Manor of Fordham. Henry and Mary Williams had lived "on[c]e att Marblehead" and twenty different places in all and yet Love in the spring of 1767 saw them as purposeful workers, not idle strollers. Before entering town, Henry had arranged employment with a Boston brazier. The work stint did not last long. In the following March, the couple reentered town and earned a second warning. This time, Love's comment was bleaker: "They have No place [of] aboade But Goes aboute a pedling."[50]

For shopkeepers and artisans, previous residence in London was seen as advantageous in attracting clients. Elizabeth Simmons disembarked on Long Wharf in November 1768 with her husband, a silk dyer, but he may have died shortly afterward, as he disappears from the record. More than a year later, Simmons paid for a newspaper notice acquainting "the Ladies" that "she understands clear Starching Lawns, Muslins and Gauzes, Net-Work and Scotch Cambricks, as well as if done in London." Simmons, who worshiped at King's Chapel, was also letting out unfurnished rooms and boarding "single Men" at the house she rented opposite the Brattle Street church. Within a month of arriving from London with his wife, brazier and silversmith George Beatty, whom we met in the Prologue, was advertising that he "makes all sorts of Pocket Books, with . . . Clasps both in Silver, Brass & Mettal, Gentlemen and Lady's Twezer Cases, Bodkins, Tooth & Ear-Pickers . . . —Likewise, mends broken China." In 1775, the Beattys remained loyal Britons: George took up arms to support the British troops occupying Boston and later did so in New York; eventually he and his family resettled in Quebec.[51]

Despite the dislocations of the period, some families settled in Boston and stayed. When Ephraim Richards of Weymouth moved to the city at age twenty-five with his wife and sister-in-law, he was making a career switch from yeoman farmer to spermaceti (whale oil) refiner. He was appointed to serve on Engine No. 9, engaged in a handful of real estate transactions in the South End, and had four children baptized at New South Church. Smallpox struck Ephraim down at age thirty-six; as an obituary put it, he "left a sorrowful widow and six children to mourn the loss."[52] Two men in their forties, Moses Bradley and Augustus Moore, sold their properties in Haverhill and Sudbury respectively and became successful inn holders in Boston. Bradley died in his Prince Street house in 1794, styling himself "gentleman" in his will. Moore, an Anglican and a loyalist, decided not to evacuate with the British in 1776. He managed to avoid prosecution and by 1782 was in enough favor to be awarded the license to run the Lamb tavern on Newbury Street.[53]

As with solo incomers, families on the road could be persons who had been born in Boston or lived there previously. Rope maker James Forder and his wife, son, and maid arrived on a sloop from Philadelphia in June 1765. This couple had been married from Boston's First Church in 1757; this time, they stayed until at least 1771. Similarly, William Winter, when warned by Love, was reentering the town in which he was married and he and his wife were born. Love did not mention that Winter was a well-known notary public and auctioneer. The Winters' first ten children had been baptized in the Hollis Street Church between 1740 and 1761. But in spring 1762, Winter had advertised for sale his house, land, and brick stores near the head of the town dock, and moved his family to Cambridge. The Winters' son Francis had just matriculated at Harvard College. For almost all his undergraduate career, the young man lived in a rented house with his parents and young sisters before they returned to Boston.[54]

Religious enthusiasm of a particular stripe drew a succession of young couples to town starting in spring 1767. The male household heads included one very wealthy Boston-born merchant, Colburn Barrell, and two recent Yale graduates who upon graduation had appeared headed for careers as orthodox Congregational ministers. Love may have been inspired to warn them because of a well-advertised tenet of their newly found faith community. Followers of Scottish Calvinist preachers John Glas and his son-in-law Robert Sandeman believed that it was "unlawful to lay up Treasures on Earth," including purchasing a house. Instead, one should rent lodgings, cover familial living expenses, and distribute surplus wealth to the poor. Like many Reformation-age groups, they were convinced that their communal rituals—in their case, breaking bread together, exchanging the "holy Kiss," and washing "one another's Feet"—copied practices of the earliest Christian disciples. Sandemanians, as the sect was known in North America, never attracted many adherents, but the oddities of their scriptural interpretation and worship provoked established Boston ministers, like the First Church's Charles Chauncy, to publish refutations.[55]

Love's encounter with Sandemanians began when he warned forty-six-year-old Sandeman in April 1767. By then, Sandeman had been in the colonies for over two years, preaching and gathering small congregations in Boston, Portsmouth, New Hampshire; and Danbury, Connecticut. (One observer described him as "of middling Stature, dark Complexion, . . . has not a melodious voice, . . . yet has something which deforces attention.") New England converts met with much censure from their families and acquaintances. Consequently, they traveled to seek out each other's fellowship and lingered in towns with clusters of coreligionists. Over a period of five years, Love warned at least six married couples who espoused Sandeman's views; they usually lodged with members of the church. Some stayed a few months and then emerged as stalwart Sandemanians in places such as Portsmouth and New Haven. Others, like David and Ann Mitchelson, stayed and became pillars of the Boston Sandemanian Society, evacuating with the British in 1776 because their faith insisted that Christians owed obedience to their secular ruler, George III.[56]

COMING to Boston for the respectable sort might mean relief—from an abusive spouse, the tedium of a parental household, or a country town's oppressively small marriage pool. The city at midcentury offered wider choices than other New England towns—not just in types of employments but in styles of public worship and in entertainments ranging from the street pageantry celebrating special days (the king's birthday, Pope's Day, the Stamp Act's repeal) to having one's face "taken" in crayon for two guineas. Although some newcomers were an injury away from seeking shelter at the almshouse, most had a family base, worldly goods, and social credit to pave their way. Robert Love, that retailer of drams, horsehair, and ribbons who had long made a livelihood through a patchwork of trades, must have seen himself in many of the strangers. As a youth, he had tried to make a go of it on the banks of the Kennebec River and then in the port town of Portsmouth. Like most of those he warned, he had shifted locations not out of desperation and poverty but because he had good reason to believe that each move would help his family attain a competent living. And as with many of Boston's newcomers, kin connections shaped his decisions. While the Ulster Scot immigrant had experienced many vicissitudes of life by the time he reached his late sixties, he had managed to stay securely among the respectable working and middling sorts. As warner, he came to know, more deeply than previously in his life, the faces and stories of many who endured extreme hardship. Despite the praise lavished on him posthumously for his capacity for "tender Affection," Love did not invariably summon empathy for the plight of Boston's strangers.[57]

CHAPTER 8

Travelers in Distress

"THE MAN IS a mason to traid and verry poor"; "she Apears to be a verry Helpless Womon"; "they say they lost all they had"; "he is a young man . . . in distress": these traveling folk were among those whom Robert Love flagged as begging, sick, destitute, drunk, dressed in rags, physically disabled, mentally disturbed, old, idling, strolling, thieving, lodging out of doors, or lacking a place of abode. Such strangers made up nearly one-fifth of all parties warned by Love. Most were not locals; they had often traveled from afar by foot. Except for the strollers, men arriving alone predominated. Some came to Boston seeking immediate relief. Others, despite a lame hand or a recent shipwreck experience, found lodging and work, avoiding dependence on the province poor rolls. Still others moved quickly out of town.[1]

Examining Love's descriptions gives us a rough portrait of the neediest of Boston's sojourners. Four types of distressed persons emerge. In one group were those unambiguously displaying neediness: they were begging, their clothes betrayed impoverishment, or they could not afford lodging. A second group made their hardship known by either requesting relief from town officials, such as passage home, or obtaining a stay in the almshouse. Sometimes acting as broker between the needy stranger and the selectmen, Love became well acquainted with the inmates and rhythms of the almshouse. A third traveling type manifested signs such as mental illness, physical handicaps, sickness, and old age that could entail an inability to earn a living and lead to destitution. Fourth, the warner commented on those whom many in his society saw as the immoral poor: drunkards, strollers, idlers, and disreputable types in trouble with the law. Analyzing the stories these diverse strangers told and the life histories that can be generated for some, this chapter illuminates the range of tribulations that could propel any member of the lower-middling sort or working poor into homelessness or a roving, property-less existence in the British Atlantic.[2]

BEGGING was an unmistakable signal of need. It was also illegal in colonial Massachusetts. Knowing the law, beggars mostly eschewed boldness, pragmatically engaging in less obtrusive mendicancy as long as they could get away with it. One strategy was to broadcast the reason for one's plight. Mary Miller told Love that two months earlier she had been "burnt out" of her dwelling in a village on the Hudson River. A young man claimed that "the Owner of the Land where he Lived [at the eastward] Drove him from the place" he had occupied. Another tactic was to reassure the warner that one was passing quickly through town. Love wrote of William and Margaret Robinson: "beging Strolers . . . are Gowing Eastward and promies to sett out the morrow morning." Yet some felt entitled to ask for alms. One elderly, almost naked vagrant declared "he Would Bege in Spite of anyBody."[3]

Despite the official condemnation of begging, subtly different categories of beggars were present in colonial North American cities. Solo men were observed "beg[g]ing money," "beg[g]ing for healp," and begging "his Bread." That an adult, in Love's terms, might be "a complete beggar [and] not able to get his bread" implies that others were understood to be begging seasonally, for only part of their income, or as a temporary strategy when in dire straits. Some were identified as permanent beggars whose activity was fairly continuous and practiced beyond Boston. Abial Wood is "Lame in his Legs with Sores . . . and is Beging from Every Boady he meets," wrote the warner. Peter Barker, a frail man of seventy-three, was observed "Beging from Door to Door." Love knew that John Davis was hardly alone in going "aboute the Country Beging." Elderly William Harris had come by land from Pottsgrove, Pennsylvania, "begging all the way."[4] The warner expressed surprise when he came across a young or "stout" man pleading on the streets for alms or "all in rags."[5]

People brazen or desperate enough to try begging in Boston's streets and alleys tended to come from farther afield than the bulk of warned sojourners. The seven reporting that they had been soldiers, whether in the country or the regular service, were all last from a distant town—in Connecticut, the middle colonies, or Quebec. Among solo beggars, only one-quarter had come last from a Massachusetts town, while one-third told Love that they hailed from greater New England. These findings indicate that adults who relied on begging circulated through a fairly large region including the major towns. Patrick Bonner, for example, who was "almost blind," came at least twice to Boston from different towns in New Hampshire. On the first occasion, he was begging and offering passersby "a Small Brife [brief]" or piece of paper that chronicled his misfortunes in a bid for charity. William Simpson, an elderly man with "no Setled place of Aboad," circulated between towns in Connecticut and Boston, collecting three warnings from Love.[6]

Although most beggars were colony outsiders, some province residents ventured to Boston to try their hand at asking for alms on the streets. Jonathan Whittemore from Malden appeared before Love on a spring day in 1766, all in rags. His was a somewhat sad life. Although he grew up in solid circumstances on the family farm, married at age thirty, and had eight children, Jonathan had never held a trade or been able to support his family sufficiently. Age sixty-one, with children aged five to fifteen, he told Love on the day he crossed Boston Neck that "he Come to town one purpose to beg." Love likely ordered him to refrain from open mendicancy or move quickly out of town. Whittemore was soon back in his place of settlement, Needham. After his wife died in 1771, the elderly Jonathan spent the last fourteen years on the town poor roll, boarded out to various families.[7]

William Bowen presented a similar portrait of an "old Man" at loose ends, but it was his shabby clothes not an attempt to beg that gave away his neediness. A former schoolmaster whose charges had habitually played tricks on him and who was fated to die in poverty, Bowen was one of eighty-five persons whose torn garb or paucity of clothing was remarked on by Love.[8] Ninety percent of these unkempt strangers were solo men on the move. Love's usual adjectives for them were "ragged" and "poorly clothed," but he was not shy about using the adjective "naked." As with other Anglo-American writers, he used it to indicate "almost Nacked for want of Close [Clothes]," as he explained in a particularly fulsome entry. Thus, the person who was "almost naked" may have displayed many tears in his stockings or shirt or lacked the conventional outer garments that people of middling and better sorts wore according to the season.[9]

Given that clothing was one of the most important clues to a stranger's material wealth and prospects, it loomed large in the warner's criteria for assessing if newcomers were "of low circumstances" and inclined to end up on poor relief. Lacking the proper clothing for one's station or trade indicated the absence of female kin, hired help, or friends who could assist with mending. Thus, it was not surprising that Davison Johnston, who had no money with him and "No Certain place of aboade," was "prety shabbey in his Clothing."[10]

Love ratcheted up his language from "poorly clothed" or "pretty poorly dressed" to *very* ragged (and variants indicating extremity) in two-thirds of the warnings that referred to clothing. These travelers bore overt marks of destitution and were barely surviving. The young man Thomas Willard, very poorly dressed, "Wanted to know if the town would help him" as he had been continuously sick with fever and ague. Mary Chilman arrived "quite Destitut" from Halifax and was forced to lodge out of doors; Love noted another sign of her poverty—she was "bare footed." Thirteen of the ragged and almost naked were begging. Most of these probably shared the plight of Edmund Toye: having trudged in from Marshfield in Plymouth County on a cold day in early November, "he lodged in a pesture [pasture]" his first night in town, "being so poorly Clothed Nobody would Lodge him."[11]

Like Toye, some of the rootless folks whom Love encountered on their first days in town were forced to lodge out of doors or in barns. Peter Highnots, a baker by trade, had made his way to Boston on a recent circuitous voyage: from London to South Carolina to Marblehead and by land to Boston. On one of his first two nights there, noted Love, he "lodged in the Street." Love recorded his discovery of nine other men and two women who did the same; most had come in between May and October and had been in town only a few days.[12]

Bostonians at times refused to take in ragged wanderers, who were often also ill, fearing infestation, put off by intolerable smells, and aware that they might never be paid. Silas Giles, "almost Naked," had been in town one week before he met Love; he had lodged in the streets the whole time "Excepting one Night he Lodged in the Widow Elisabath Ervin[']s att the head of the Long Warfe." For the eight nights since his arrival from New York in May, Moses Shipsces, who had lost a limb, had the dropsy, and was bereft of money, was "obliged to Lye in the Streett." An eighteenth-century story that resonates even more closely with the modern category of homeless urban dwellers was that of William Ferrell. Warned by Love on a day in late July 1768, he insisted that he had been in town since the previous September; for eleven months, he "lodged abroad in the streets." Ferrell had once worked as a barber; Love observed that he was "verry poor," ragged, and lice ridden ("Lousey").[13]

Those without money for lodging might try to persuade the town and provincial authorities to pay for their overseas passage home to the British Isles or to subsidize their journey by land to a distant North American destination. Love encountered wool comber John Taylor on the day he arrived from Philadelphia in autumn 1767, noting: "he wants a passage to England if the Overseers of the Poor Would pay for itt." The town fathers appear not to have taken up Taylor's cause, but they did assist others when convinced that helping the stranger reach his or her desired destination would save the town and province from recurrent expense. Mary McCarthy arrived in Boston from Quebec in summer 1770, eight months pregnant, seeking her husband in vain. On the day Love warned her, she was admitted into the almshouse on the province account, where she soon gave birth to a daughter. Her stay in the house ended after seven weeks, when she applied for and was granted a sum of six dollars to assist her and her infant's "return to Canada by Land."[14]

A remarkable number of strangers who were in no condition to move on found refuge in the town's sizable almshouse—the largest in the region. The almshouse was located just west of the town center, on the east edge of the town common, in a complex of public buildings that included the even larger workhouse edifice, a small bridewell, and the public granary. Built of stone and brick, with segments dating from 1686 and 1742, the two-story almshouse had a long, narrow footprint. No illustrations or blueprints survive, but other records tell us there were thirty-three "apartments" (sleeping chambers) besides the requisite refectory and lodging space for the keeper and his family. Designed to house 130 to 160 persons comfortably, the inmate population hit a pre-revolutionary high of 260 during the winters of the mid-1760s. This meant eight persons per room—often, a large family lodged with two single women—and many in each bed, as was standard eighteenth-century practice.[15]

Despite the crowded conditions, the almshouse meant food, shelter, and medical care. For many poor folk, it served as a maternity hospital and the only place where one could receive treatment for broken limbs, gonorrhea, or mania. Given the province's welcoming policy, it is not surprising that some strangers came to Boston "to get in to" the almshouse. Anthony McNeil believed that a stay would enable him to recover from his pleurisy; he was arriving from Newport, Rhode Island, and was very poor. McNeil evidently never entered the house, but two lame men who hoped to "be Cured" there were admitted a day or two after being warned, with Love doubtless alerting the selectmen and overseers, whose say-so secured alms-house admission.[16]

Love witnessed some of the dramas unfolding within the almshouse walls because he visited the building every few months. He issued verbal warnings from there on at least forty-five occasions. Love's first known foray to "the house" (as the overseers termed the almshouse) in search of strangers was in his third month on the job. In late March 1765, he delivered a warning there to forty-year-old Richard Leader, who had "been in the armey." Leader had arrived the previous December from Cape Breton, initially lodging with a shoemaker in the South End. But sickness forced him to stop working and seek relief. On March 20, the day before Love found and warned the veteran, he was admitted to the almshouse. Six months later, Leader left the house; he then disappears from Massachusetts records.[17]

On his visits, we can imagine Love first passing through the gate in the tall fence that surrounded the almshouse building, and then stepping into the narrow house to seek out the keeper, Samuel Proctor. Proctor, or Proctor's wife, Hannah, who served as cokeeper and matron, could direct him to "stranger" inmates who had not yet received the town's warning. Love would have sought out the individual or family group in their chamber; perhaps he sat down while he asked them his standard set of questions. To David Dolbeare and his family, Love added a twist to his usual words and revealed his typical spelling and pronunciation for the institution. He verbally warned them "to Depart this town or Allamshouse" in fourteen days.[18]

The strangers on the move who sought the house's shelter included youthful, solo travelers who had run into trouble, distressed mothers and fathers traveling with small children, and pregnant women who had no family in New England to support them during childbirth and several weeks of lying-in. Most took advantage of the house's accommodations only once, but others had repeat residencies. On average, their stays lasted four months; occasionally they topped two years. George Gutteridge, age thirty-five, who, Love wrote, "Has Been in the Armey and is sikley," was admitted in June 1767 "till he Recovers his Health," which turned out to be only one week. John Fitzgerald arrived in Boston from Newfoundland sick, was admitted to the almshouse, and died there one month later, at age twenty-one. Lame youth Edward Davis, admitted at age twenty, remained for two and a half years.[19]

Disabilities such as mental distress, blindness, and deafness, might mean that a stranger needed charity or succor in the almshouse, but that was not always the case. Then as now, an individual's experience of mental and psychological affliction could wax and wane. When Love warned twenty-nine-year-old Joseph Norcross one June, the warner did not sense anything amiss. Norcross had come to town to live in his brother-in-law's large family. By the following winter, however, the Boston selectmen became aware that Norcross was "distracted" (the preferred regional idiom for mental illness); they sent Love to negotiate for the stranger's return to his natal town. Norcross's relatives explained that the man suffered from a disorder that was much worse in winter than summer and that he was already under guardianship as a "non compos" person who could not be trusted to engage rationally in buying and selling. He would return to his hometown of Weston and live out his life there, unmarried.[20]

Love's sense of the range of mental disorders and intellectual deficits that could befall a person emerges in his phrasings. Besides deploying the adjectives of "crazy" and "distracted," Love wrote that a person might appear stupefied, "underwitted," or "a Lit[t]le out of his head." When strangers acted "Verry Od[d]e," Bostonians were put in the position of puzzling out their condition. Love was on guard for men faking distraction in order to win sympathetic treatment or alms. Anthony Ferdinando, a "portygee," "pretends to be Disstracted." Prince Sturgis, the scion of a wealthy mercantile family with roots in Cape Cod and Boston, "Either is or pretends to be Crasey." In the case of the "verry troubelsome" workhouse resident John Dwyer, Love left the assessment to the keeper, Joseph Lasenby. After three weeks, Lasenby concluded that although the man "pretends to be out of his head att times . . . he is Not." Within a few months, the town fathers arranged for Dwyer, a recent immigrant from Ireland, to be removed to his last place of residence, Portsmouth, New Hampshire.[21]

Love expressed less doubt in the cases of those who gave voice to their hallucinations or set the townspeople on edge by screaming through the streets at night. At the almshouse, Love listened to George Carroll, a Briton lucid enough at times to remember that he had been born on the Isle of Jersey. But on the day Love warned him, Carroll was "posse[sse]d with [Vi]asions that the Divel is Coming to Carry him aWay and Says he Sees fir[e]s Burning." Boston boys entertained themselves by crowding around and following some of the distracted strangers, all the while verbally testing and teasing them, a scene which at times created "a Grate noise." James

Dunbar ran "aboute the Streets Calling himselfe a Liberty Man" in July 1770, but the locals knew better. John Barber, who had served in the army, was "holowing and Screeming About the Streets and Swe[a]ring," and, like several mentally disturbed strangers, refused or was unable to tell Love where he lodged or when he came to town.[22]

In the context of Boston's street life, the public face of madness was masculine. Only four of the thirty-two strangers identified by Love with descriptors akin to "crazy" and "underwitted" were women. Most were men who appeared adrift, unanchored by home or kin network. These displaced outsiders included Anthony Serron, a "Stupefide" beggar whom Love called "an Indian to Nasion" (meaning East Indian), and several Britons, most notably a man claiming he had been "an Ofiser under Genrall Gage and [was] Brock [broke] by him." The preponderance of men among "distracted" strangers reflected both the greater mobility men enjoyed in contrast to women and the tendency of Anglo-American culture to represent madness as masculine.[23]

The number of strangers for whom Love noted some sort of physical disability was twice as large as those he perceived to be mentally disturbed. Of sixty-seven in the general category, twelve had lost eyesight, totally or partially; three fit the label "a Deefe man"; one was a shoemaker who happened also to be a dwarf. The adjective *lame* covered a wide range of handicaps. A stranger might be "lame in" the right shoulder; lame "in his back"; lame in a hand, arm, or leg; or suffering from "the Liprose[leprosy] in his Theye or Knee." Three of the sighted were described as using crutches or needing help to walk. Some of these traveling folks would recover full mobility, while others were permanently disabled. Some had survived amputations, severe frostbite, or tragic accidents, such as the black man Cascobay, whom Love described as lame "of both his hands," having lost all of his fingers. James Jackson, found drunk in the street one early August morning, had come to Boston by land from South Carolina; Love wrote, he "has Lost one of his Arms and one of his Eys." As with mental afflictions, physical disability was markedly male. Only two so described were women: one was "Lame of one hand," and the other had lost an eye.[24]

Even though disabled, some men had trades and were seeking work in Boston. Having impaired hearing or a damaged arm did not preclude labor. Benjamin Gabril, "a Dean [Dane] to nasion" and lame in both hands, told Love that he had "Helped to tend taveren" at his previous place of lodging in Boston with Deacon Daniel Jones. One deaf man was "young . . . but verry poor" and "a taylor to traid" who had "been in the pencelvaney servis in the beginning of the Last Ware." Jacob Hendrick, who had come from Newport three months earlier, "is a Lame man and Goes Aboute the town a pedling of Small things such as Butons & Garters." A handful of the lame were "under" a doctor's care when Love encountered them or were seeking an almshouse stay. John McGrath, as a mariner or fisherman who had "Sailed 2 voydg's out of Marblehead," hoped to emerge from the almshouse ready to ship out again.[25]

Three individuals with disabilities whose lives can be traced display characteristics similar to those of many of the able-bodied men who sojourned in Boston and hailed from eastern Massachusetts towns: they were fairly young, belonged to propertied yeoman families, and did not come to town to settle. Timothy Maddin was twenty-four when Love questioned him in May 1766. His father and namesake, a laborer, had died nine years earlier, and the lad had chosen a "gentleman" from his hometown of Uxbridge (west of Boston) as his guardian. According to Love, Maddin was "Almost Blind and is Obliged to be Lead from House to House." Because the warning occurred on Maddin's day of arrival, we do not learn where he found lodging, whether he came to visit kin or consult a physician, or how long he stayed in town. And while we do not know who his escort was, we can conclude that Maddin was not asking for alms from house to house, as Love would have been sure to note such worrisome behavior. By November 1768, and probably long before, Maddin was back in his natal town: in that month, he married Abigail Kibbey. They had two children born in Uxbridge in the next few years, and by the time of the 1790 census, he and his family had done what many in the older, settled parts of southern New England did after the Revolution—he joined his half brother Michael in moving to a frontier settlement farther west in Berkshire County.[26]

Love's records tell us something of what it meant to be ill or plagued by an old war injury. Those whom Love described as "sickly" or "in a poor State of Health" might have "the fever & Eggo [Ague]," be "verry Bad of a Cansere upon" the nose, or be so "ill of the Rumatisam" that one was "not able to help" oneself. Three of the sick were already in the almshouse, and five more would enter soon after being warned. Mariner Lawrence Cooper, a native of Scotland, disembarked from a ship quite ill, was cared for by his landlord for fifteen weeks (at the province charge), and then admitted to the almshouse, still sick. He died there seven weeks later, age twenty-five. Forty-year-old James Miller looked lame and "Not Well in health" to Love;

he died seven days later at the almshouse. Others sweated out their infirmities in their lodgings or paid for a physician's ministrations. Visitors George King ("verry ill of a Grate Cold") and Peter Vallance ("sikly and under the docters hands") probably recovered, reckoned with their Boston landlords, and moved on to other locations.[27]

A wide array of public attitudes—compassion, respect, or disdain— might be expressed in eighteenth-century Boston toward men and women "stricken in years," as the dictionaries of the day put it. Unfortunately, Love's emotional reactions to elderly travelers are opaque to us. He rarely expressed nervousness, disgust, or disdain in noting the seventy parties he called old. Mostly he used the characterization in conjunction with other adjectives of neediness such as poor, begging, disabled, idle, dressed in rags, forced to lodge outdoors.[28] His descriptions shed light on what age range counted as old for colonial New Englanders. Writings of the period contain vague or contradictory statements. Age seventy (the biblical three-score-and-ten) was most often named as the likely end point of a long life. As one Connecticut man put it on reaching seventy, "I may now call myself on Probation." On the few occasions when we can match an individual's approximate age with Love's label "old," the strangers were in their early and midseventies. "Very old" is a moniker that Love seems to have reserved for those in their late seventies and above. James Bailey came last from "the round pond near Pemaquid" and lived in Boston in a house of the widow Gees near the Charlestown ferry: "he is a verry old man aged 84 years." Even considering that New England settlers were among the healthiest and longest-living of early modern European populations, it is remarkable to witness the mobility of older folks like Bailey, and the brothers Phillip and Jonathan Hodgkins, aged eighty-four and sixty-seven, who traveled from Cape Ann to stay in Boston with a kinswoman.[29]

Like many the warner described as old, most of the seventy-five strangers whom Love called drunk, strolling, idle, or "bad" struggled with untreated illnesses and injuries, chronic underemployment, and poverty. Onlookers, however, were less sympathetic to those they saw as voluntarily embracing a life of sloth and moral dissolution. The behavior of these down-and-out folk placed them in danger of criminal prosecution. Massachusetts statutes, echoing those of Britain and her other American colonies, inveighed against idlers and prescribed fines or whippings for convicted miscreants. However, by the early 1700s prosecutorial interest in bringing these sorts of charges to the county courts had waned. Night constables or concerned citizens might haul strollers and common tipplers before a justice of the peace to receive summary discipline, but more often than not they were allowed to go on their way.[30]

Drinking ale or spirits to excess was not unusual behavior in a society in which most of the beverages consumed were fermented or contained alcohol. What drew the attention of authorities was disruptive, public drunkenness manifested by men and women of the laboring classes. In contrast, "gentlemen" of the "better sort" typically courted no official chastisement when they persuaded tavern keepers to keep the "Wine and Arack Punch" coming while making "Merry Drink^g Toasts Singing roareing &c. untill Morning," far past the appointed hour when no liquor was to be served. The two dozen white adults whom Love somewhat scornfully described as drunk or as notorious drinkers appear to have hailed from the laboring class. They had often wandered far from their original homes. John Stanton, a drunken, quarrelsome soldier, had most recently been stationed in Detroit. Nine more were from outside greater New England. Two were carpenters and four had been soldiers. Nearly all were brought to Love's attention on their first or second day in town; only one man had been in Boston as long as three weeks. None were likely to have stayed put in Boston.[31]

In Love's catalog of tippling sinners, one could be a plain "drinking man" or "a *verey* Drinking man." Love sometimes discovered the extreme imbibers incoherent and raging in the town's streets. Among these was William Flin who at "about 9 or 10 a Clock in the morning had a Number of Boys with him [in Milk Street] and he Cursing and Swering at them." James Cammock was also bedeviled by youths: "the Boys [were] Draging him about the Streets." Love spun some lighthearted tales of drunkards—he caught Andrew Cahail "acting verry foolishly"—and some sad ones. Before making it to Boston, the justifiably forlorn John Murphy, whom the warner found "Drunk in the Street," had sailed from Liverpool and been castaway off the Connecticut coast.[32]

Women who displayed public drunkenness risked losing all respectability. Love's attitude about two solo female travelers echoed that of a midcentury Virginian who noted that for a woman to be drunk on the street was "a Condition, which of all others, least becomes the Sex." On a July day in 1770, Katherine Genin [Jennings?] arrived in Boston and ran into the disapproving warner, who recorded that "She is an Old woman & verry

Grate Lier and was in Drink and Wanted Moor." Did Love call her a liar because she was spinning tall tales, because he had encountered her previously telling untruths, because she denied being intoxicated, or because people around her called her by this epithet? Genin, like others whom Love encountered "in Licker," was not prosecuted or physically removed from town as a punishment.[33]

On the streets of Boston, women were prominent among those perceived to be strollers. The descriptor had two valences for Love. Some fit the primary early modern meaning of the verb—to roam from place to place without a settled habitation. Mary Kelton had been in town a few days when Love spoke with her; he described her as "a poor Stroling Woman[;] She says she Belongs No Whare." However, when a woman was strolling within the confines of Boston, Love used the term to suggest loose sexual behavior or prostitution. By the time she was warned in May 1769, Mary Smelledge had been in town three months and was living at the cooper Mr. Salt's. However, Love discovered her "at the house of Mr _____ Lamson upon Boston Neck in a strolling way and seen with the soldiers." Love was probably similarly imputing illicit sexual activities to Polly Barber when he commented that she had arrived in Boston ten months earlier "and has been Stroling Ever Since."[34]

Strolling did not necessarily mean that an adult avoided legitimate work. A tinker or a peddler might be labeled a stroller. Love identified William Wilson and James Cife as strollers. Wilson reported he was "a mason to traid," and Cife told Love that he wanted "Imploy." Claims to respectable occupations might ring hollow, however, because Massachusetts shared in a culture in which strollers were associated with crime and likened to the vagabonds and rogues condemned in statutes. Even though "Stroling man" Thomas Hardin told Love that he was a baker to trade and had worked at various times in the past with "2 or 3 Backers in town," Love was suspicious of this tale because Hardin "Could not tell the Names of any of them." Besides, Hardin was "very" impudent with Love, as were three other strollers (one man and two women).[35]

Love distinguished idle and idling persons from strollers. "Idle" indicated that a man had no trade and was loitering without discernible purpose. Twelve of the sixteen idle, solo male travelers spotted by Love were last from a New England location. Whereas a newcomer from farther away might have been spared Love's scorn for "Idling Aboute the town," for a

New England man to appear in town with "No Business" was accounted a sin. George Stoning, "an Idle man and very Rag[g]ed in his Clothing," was in his mid-thirties when he appeared before Love in May 1766. Probably unknown to the warner was that in his hometown of Salem, Stoning had served in the local militia and volunteered in the Crown Point expedition of 1755. Stoning signed legal documents in an unusual fashion—with a sideways figure-eight. There is no evidence that he ever practiced a trade, married, or took charge of family affairs. Presumably, chronic pain or disability was what left him "Verry much Indisposed, in Body," as he explained in a letter to a judge at age twenty-one. Love missed the backstory not only in Stoning's case but also in that of Indian Sarah Waterman, the only woman to earn the idle label. Waterman was arriving in Boston "to Go to Servis"— thus she had a work goal and perhaps even a particular employer in view. Revealing the damaging stereotypes that Euro-American onlookers often applied to women of color, Love's notation that "She Seems to be an Idle Womon" contrasted with his omission of such a comment for any of the white women who were looking for domestic work.[36]

A final group in the warner's catalog of the immoral poor consisted of those he knew to be thieves, fornicators, or "bad" men and women. John Covey, who had stolen "a Brass Cetle in Charlestown and Sold it [in] Boston," was one of eight people Love visited and warned in the town's jail next to the courthouse on Queen Street. Ann Maxfield was there "upon Suspision of being Concerned in Steeling Money." Some pilferers had already been punished at the pillory and yet kept returning to town. Boston was surely a prime spot for fencing stolen goods. Love knew that James Griffen was "a Noted Thife in this town," and he piled on the pejoratives when describing Mary King: "She has But one Eye," she is "a stroling Woman," and "She has the Name of a Bad Womon and a thief."[37]

The workhouse, a large, narrow brick building next to the almshouse, was the site of twenty-one of Love's warnings. Because almost none of its records survive, we know little of this institution besides that its inmates were vagrants, runaways, and minor miscreants serving short criminal sentences. Under the supervision of keeper Joseph Lasenby and his wife, they were put to tasks such as spinning and picking oakum from old rope in order to recycle it. Women were invariably a majority of the workhouse population of roughly thirty to fifty souls, and, indeed, Love warned slightly more women than men there. Magistrates favored ordering terms in the workhouse, which was also called the house of correction, for disciplining

women they suspected of prostitution. Margaret Smith, a workhouse resident whom Love warned in 1773, was probably the Polly Smith he had
encountered previously who had a reputation for behaving "so ill that thy
Could note Keep her from men."[38]

Christiana Isbister was well known to town officers as a woman of the
lower sort who bore many children out of wedlock. Love warned her in late
1772 when she was lodging in the North End with a woman whose husband
was in jail. Christiana, then in her mid-thirties, had recently arrived from
the Kennebec River area, but she was no stranger to Boston, having been
earlier counted a legal inhabitant. In 1763, Isbister, "spinster" of Boston,
had administered the tiny estate left by her deceased brother William, a
mariner, consisting of his seaman's chest and a few articles of clothing. She
signed the probate documents with a curly "Y." During the 1760s, the town
had paid for her upkeep and lying-in costs through five stays in the almshouse. While in the house, she bore at least four daughters, all of whom
died. Just over a year before being warned, she had confessed in court for
a second time to committing fornication in Boston, for which she received
the punishment of ten stripes "on the naked back."[39]

LOVE introduces us to many adults and families whose lives testify to the
seasonality and uncertainties of employment in preindustrial economies
and to the fact that "laboring people . . . commonly floated in and out of
indigence." Sickness, war wounds, shipwrecks, and house-consuming fires,
combined with the absence of insurance and savings led many working
people to seek poor relief at one or more points in their lives or turn to
itinerancy and strolling. Fortunes could vary from season to season and
year to year. Love might find a New Englander like Patrick Bonner begging
one year and able to afford city lodgings the next. Bonner, like so many
adults circulating over short or long distances in the British colonies, lived
on a very thin fiscal margin.[40]

Some down-and-out strangers passed Love's scrutiny as travelers who
represented themselves honestly and deserved help. Others confirmed his
suspicions that people who appeared to be pursuing legitimate, street-level
work like peddling might be scamming the public or illegally begging. The
ambiguities and multiple personas that were part of many poor folk's survival strategies put Love on his guard. Yet for the most part he described
the ragged persons he interviewed without adding words of moral censure.
Since the warner's role was not to write entertaining poems about street life

or compile a census of all marginal and impoverished residents and visitors, his notes leave us wondering about possible parallels with much more richly documented London. Did Bostonians tolerate charwomen—souls who went to kitchen doors and persuaded the mistress or servants of the house to let them trade an afternoon's work for a night's lodging and some food? Were certain street corners manned by shoeblacks, street sweepers, and scavengers who jealously watched over their piece of urban turf? Despite Boston's colonial reputation for suppressing immorality, a lieutenant of the twenty-third regiment visiting in 1755 claimed—doubtless hyperbolically— that there was "prehaps no town of its size cou'd turn out more whores than this cou'd," thus evoking an underworld largely lost to us.[41]

While many everyday dramas remain hidden, the political theater of the streets drew many chroniclers. Boston's peopling in the ten years before the Revolutionary War comes into sharper focus because Love shone a spotlight on distinct groups of incomers whose distress stemmed from imperial cataclysms.

CHAPTER 9

Warning in the Midst of Imperial Crises

ROBERT LOVE WARNED strangers during extraordinary times. Throughout the British Atlantic, people's lives were changed in the fulcrum of post–Seven Years War reverberations and mounting political protest. Bostonians gained the reputation as the most troublesome of colonial complainants. In summer 1765, townspeople poured into the streets to protest the impending imposition of the Stamp Act. The following May, joyful celebrations accompanied the measure's repeal. Local activists, such as the Sons of Liberty, geared up again when Parliament passed the objectionable Townshend duties and custom officials cracked down on Boston merchants. Town meetings at Faneuil Hall were packed as never before. Merchants who defied the town's orders to cease importing British manufactured goods might be "warned" and threatened with physical removal by vigilantes. To imperial officials, by summer 1768 the Massachusetts capital appeared so frighteningly close to insurrection that they sent four regiments to act as police. On October 1, hundreds of British redcoats disembarked on Long Wharf, and, for the next seventeen months, Boston was an occupied town. Tensions between the military and the citizenry exploded in March 1770 at the event that came to be known as the Boston Massacre—five men were shot dead by the redcoats. As a result, British troops were hastily removed from the city and housed on a harbor island, thereby reducing some of the friction. However, Bostonians continued to take to the streets to express their grievances with imperial policy—up to and beyond Love's death in April 1774.

At first glance, Love's warning activity seems far removed from the political dramas roiling the port town. He used the same formula for entries about strangers over and over. He chose not to punctuate his logs with announcements of the crowd actions, the bonfires, the frightening house assaults, or the dumping of tea. Yet the repercussions of the Seven Years War and the turmoil over parliamentary policies affected how Love did his job and whom he met. As they do our understanding of landlords, middling sojourners, and travelers in need who populated Boston in these years, Love's observations expand our understanding of the imperial crises that afflicted the town before residents could even imagine an independence movement. Love's encounters with those who were on the move because of imperial policy generated what are sometimes the only surviving traces of these individuals' presence in Boston and the shape of their North American journeying. Disabled veterans down on their luck, exiled Acadians determined to return to French communities, women and children left behind by occupying troops, and soldiers jailed for firing into the crowd at the massacre deserve to be included in the stories we tell about pre-revolutionary Boston.

DURING the Seven Years War, sixty thousand redcoats had been shipped from the British Isles and imperial outposts to fight the French and their Indian allies in the campaigns that led France to cede Canada and much of the North American interior. They were joined by thousands of provincial soldiers, a disproportionate number of which were young New England men from middling families drawn to enlist by anti-Catholic fervor and the monetary rewards. At the end of the fighting, most British-born regulars found it nearly impossible to return home, because they rarely qualified for military transport. The army's policy was to encourage veterans to remain in the colonies. Consequently, regimental veterans tramped from place to place seeking part-time employment, often in vain. While their stories and fates have largely been lost, Love's records allow us to glimpse their peram-bulations and their yearnings for homeland, work, and security. In contrast, provincial veterans are barely visible in the warning records. They were less involved than the redcoats in direct combat and experienced far less dislocation.[1]

Of the eighty-three men whom Love identified as veterans, most came to Boston alone. Half were described as injured, impoverished, seeking aid, or in some sort of trouble, such as having head wounds or being in jail. Surely more of the warned strangers had enlisted and served in the recent war; but if the newcomer was not in low circumstances, that biographical detail often went unrecorded. When strangers were asked to account for themselves, previous military service helped to explain disability and neediness.[2]

Soldiers demobilized from "His Majesty's Service" must have been unmistakable, walking the Boston streets in their scarlet coats. They often confirmed their status by presenting various papers. Discharge documents named the regiment in which they had last served and proved they were not deserters. A few of the wanderers possessed additional documents, such as character references from colonial patrons or handmade "briefs" explaining their plight. More than half of the fifty-odd disbanded regimentals whom Love warned were in bad shape. Six were begging, eleven were seriously or permanently injured, two were mentally disturbed, three were chronic drunkards, and at least five ended up in Boston's almshouse, workhouse, or jail. Two complained that "Nobody will Lodge" them. Others had sufficient resources or charisma to have secured accommodations temporarily, but only one, Peter Jackson, reported that he had found steady employment, working for the past seven months with "Mr. Jasper a Cutter in Fore St."[3]

The disbanded regimentals came to Boston from afar. Twenty-two trekked from the major ports of New York and Philadelphia; seven came by ship from Nova Scotia. Others named Crown Point, Detroit, or Fort Stanwix on the Mohawk River as their most recent quarters. Several told Love that, like William Sherwood, who had "been a soldier at Gen. Wolfe's fight at Quebec" and had "a family in Old England," they had "no particular place of abode" on the continent. This last phrase summarized the plight of many demobilized Britons.[4]

Some ex-regimentals had circulated in North America without surcease. Richard Wiggins first encountered the warner in February 1766. Discharged from the Seventeenth Regiment of Foot two years earlier, he had most recently been living in Prince William County, Virginia. This first trip to Boston Wiggins made with his wife, Patience, and son John. Sometime in the following months, the family left town. In summer 1767, Richard returned alone, this time from New Jersey. Because of his war wounds, Richard explained to Love, he was "not able to get his bread." On the very next day, Wiggins was admitted to the almshouse, where he stayed three weeks. The keeper recorded his age as twenty-five. This young man, having temporarily settled his family in northern New Jersey, may have returned to Boston because he knew he could receive medical care on the province account.[5]

Many veterans were much older than Wiggins and had served in several
regiments. Henry Toull had been "a solder in his Magistys Servis 32 years[,]
Last under General Munkton." Thomas Boyfield "is now an old man [who]
. . . pretends to work at the bookbinders business"; he had been "in Brad-
docks fight" in 1755. Forty-year-old Anthony Coffin somehow managed to
make his way to Boston even though at the siege of Quebec he had "Been
fros [froze] in both his feet and [had] part of One Cutt off." William Duffy
was fated to wander from town to town in New England, perhaps picking
up seasonal labor. Love first encountered the veteran of the fifteenth regiment in April 1766, lodging at retailer and mariner Thomas Cunningham's
in the North End. Two years later, Duffy returned, this time from Newport
and in the company of his wife, Sarah. If Duffy fantasized of taking Sarah
back to Britain, he dreamed in vain. He died in New England, impoverished, buried in an unmarked grave. In late summer 1773, Sarah reappeared,
having come on foot from Providence: "she is a begger." Physically, these
former soldiers must have looked to Bostonians like the surviving members
of the Fifteenth Foot did to a major-general who reviewed them on their
1768 return to England: most were old, "very low," and unsteady on their
feet.[6]

Only rarely do we witness veterans managing to secure passage home.
One officer achieved his goal by capturing the attention of Boston's town
fathers: in 1772 they supplied Captain John Ramsey, "an unfortunate Man
who had been a Prisoner at the Havannah with sundry necessaries for his
passage to Liverpool." Some of the veterans passing through Boston had
suffered permanently crippling injuries and imagined—fruitlessly—that
they might earn the army designation "genuine invalid," which came with
a recommendation for a Royal Hospital of Chelsea pension and overseas
passage on a military vessel. But few ever met the criteria.[7]

Not bearing visible marks of disability, William Collier was extraordinarily persistent in attempting to procure passage through military dispen-
sation. Warned three times by Love over a six-year period, Collier had
traveled from various distant spots, armed on each occasion with a different
strategy. At his first appearance in 1765, he had walked or hitched rides
from Casco Bay to Boston. He explained that he had "been a Soldier in the
15 Ragement under Genrall ElmHurest [Amherst] [and] . . . is Gowing to
new york to Genrall Gage to Gett a pasage of him for England." Collier was
destined for disappointment. He continued to trudge the colonial roads.
Back in Boston two years later, he had come "all the way by land" from

South Carolina. The third time Love met up with him was in 1771, when British troops were occupying Boston and military transports were anchored in the harbor. Collier had come the longest distance yet—from East Florida—hoping "to go home in a Man of War."[8]

Most veterans of the provincial regiments, if they sojourned in Boston in the postwar years, found little reason to mention their military service when warned. Given that roughly one-third of white Massachusetts men who were able-bodied and under thirty enlisted for at least one Seven Years War campaign, surely more provincial veterans were present among Love's warned strangers than his count of fourteen implies. Their low visibility can be explained by the circumstances of their service. Soldiers were well remunerated, receiving about twice as much as a redcoat private earned. Furthermore, they were paid in cash—a rare situation for workers in the colonies. Multiple enlistments, traveling to a neighboring colony that offered higher bounties, and getting paid to be a substitute for a higher-class man who had been drafted: all of these were ways to milk the system. A hardy provincial could amass quite a sum, given that single enlistments were short, lasting the duration of a single campaign, from six to eight months, and that fighting lasted in North America from 1754 to 1760. Provincial soldiers found themselves primarily responsible for garrison, fatigue, and support duties. British officers had so little faith in their reliability in the field that the fighting was mostly relegated to the redcoats. Thus, provincial enlistees who survived the disease environment in the army camps could look back on their military service as having given them an economic boost.[9]

Past provincial service was more likely to be elicited by Love when the male stranger was suffering from poverty or disability. Two who had served in Massachusetts regiments were begging. One forty-three-year-old veteran from the New Jersey service needed care at the almshouse (where he died a month later). Three other former provincials were "poorly clothed." Robert Rickes, one of the veterans reduced to begging, told Love that he had served in Captain Samuel Knowles's company in Colonel Thomas Doty's Massachusetts regiment in 1758. Love encountered him eight years later, newly arrived from Philadelphia, an "Old man" and "Lame of an Arme." How Rickes sustained his injury is unclear, but he had experienced privation, as had many provincials, during his service. A Massachusetts minister who observed Doty's men in one of their encampments in 1758 wrote in his journal: "My heart was grieved to find the men so greatly fatigued, and nothing comfortable to take. No sutler [small trader who sold foodstuffs when rations were short], no doctor, no chaplain." Most of the Bay Colony's youths who served and survived had achieved yeoman status by their forties. Rickes, in contrast, resorted to a tramping circuit similar to that of the many demobilized Britons who found themselves without a place of abode in North America.[10]

AT the start of the Seven Years War, the British ordered the twelve thousand French-speaking, Catholic residents of Nova Scotia to leave their homes in the land they called L'Acadie. They were deported immediately or branded as traitors and hunted down. The expulsion, carried out with brutal thoroughness, was justified by declaring the French rebels and their land and livestock forfeit—even though they had pledged neutrality and had lived peaceably next to English neighbors. What British leaders wanted was the territory cleared of subjects they perceived as disloyal, clannish, and unwilling to contribute to the imperial economy. Acadians lost nearly all their possessions and the security that came from forging French communities based on farmland they had made astonishingly productive with ingenious levees. They and their historians termed the expulsion *le grand dérangement*—the great upheaval.[11]

Starting in August 1755, in a logistical feat cloaked in secret planning and falsity, the British commanders, aided by New England officers, soldiers, and sailors, rounded up nearly seven thousand Acadian men, women, and children. They loaded them onto transport ships outfitted below decks like the slavers that bore human cargo from Africa. They then pillaged and burned homesteads to ensure against their return. This first phase of the removal campaign was complete by mid-December. Britain's plan was to distribute the Acadians among its colonies as internees, in order to prevent them from taking up arms and joining the French. While exiles were deposited as far away as Georgia, Massachusetts received the largest number. Roughly eleven hundred—distraught, in poor health, desperately seeking family members from whom they had been separated—became the responsibility of the Bay province for a decade starting in 1756.[12]

Love's often lengthy entries on Acadian families narrate their decade of forced exile in reverse chronological order. On April 30, 1766, he walked the length of Boston Neck and warned four large families staying in the same rented house. All had arrived by foot or wagon five days earlier; another related family of ten joined them two months later.[13] Although

Love mangled the names—Charles Belliveau became Charls Bileybon, Claude Dugas became Cloth Digar—and failed to describe the thirty-three newcomers as "Franch," the strangers were unmistakably Acadians. For them, Boston was a temporary way station. Having spent the previous years in interior Massachusetts towns to which they were assigned, they fervently hoped that the port would serve as the embarkation point for the sea voyage northward, their return from exile.[14]

Since the signing of the Treaty of Paris three years earlier, interned "neutrals" had harbored high hopes that they would be allowed to become free agents again. As one set of petitioning Acadians put it, "We have always understood that in time of Peace . . . the prison doors are open to Prisoners." Why was the provincial government detaining them? After all, it meant ongoing expenses to provide shelter, fuel, and food for "this people," who, as Governor Bernard put it, "was by the exigencies of War rather than any fault of their own . . . removed from a State of ease and affluence and brought into poverty and dependence."[15]

According to the governor and general court, humanitarian and political issues were at stake. If the Acadians were allowed to sail to French Hispaniola, as many of them intended, they would "run into certain destruction" due to "the bad climate" and "the want of subsistence" there. On the other hand, if the way could be cleared for the exiles to go to the other location they requested, Canada, they could then "become a fresh accession of wealth and strength to the British Empire in America." The impasse was resolved when James Murray, Canada's military governor, issued a proclamation welcoming Acadians to Quebec and offering them land, on the condition that male household heads take the oath of allegiance to the British Crown before entering. The Acadian strangers warned in Boston in spring 1766 agreed to the oath. In coming months, they would join the mass exodus of their countrymen from Massachusetts. Mostly by ship but sometimes by foot, they went to live in settlements along the St. Lawrence or on the North Shore of what is now New Brunswick.[16]

Love's notes contain clues as to how Acadians shaped the conditions of exile in important ways. Prior to coordinating their move to Boston, the five families dwelling on the Neck had resided in three adjacent towns in Worcester County—Sturbridge, Charlton, and Dudley. There, although they lived a half day's walk apart from one another and were supposed to procure passports to leave their assigned towns, they had clearly managed regular visits and communication. Furthermore, Love wrote that in Boston they were hiring a house from Gideon Gardiner (who, in turn, rented it from the town). Even though they had endured years of internment and difficulty, not all of the French were poverty stricken and dependent on welfare. Some had managed to secure seasonal and short-term employment, saving part of their wages. Trauma for these displaced persons stemmed as much from family separations and the inability to confess to a priest (though they gathered for lay-led worship) as from economic deprivation.[17]

One survival strategy adopted by some Acadians was the use of Anglicized names when dealing with English colonists. Many of them spoke some English as a result of their successful commercial relationships with Britons and New Englanders prior to expulsion. Thus, Love's rendering of Marie as Mary and LeBlanc as White was not necessarily a reflection of stubborn ethnocentrism. More likely, he wrote down these names phonetically and according to how strangers accounted for themselves.[18]

Love's interviews underscored the key roles played by local grandees in Acadians' experiences. The families of Claude Dugas and "Joseph White" had "lived Nine years under the Care of" Colonel Moses Marcy of Sturbridge, the most prominent man in Sturbridge. Serving for over three decades as moderator of the town meeting, Squire Marcy was a delegate to the General Court and the town's first justice of the peace. Similarly, the families of Joseph Doucet and Charles Belliveau had lived in Charlton "att" Colonel Thomas Cheney's. In New England's social landscape, Cheney and Marcy were powerful gentry, with extensive landholdings, visibility in office holding, and accessibility as creditors and patrons. These men were unusual in having the ability to employ (or broker employment for) Acadians—the men furrowing, planting, haying, plowing, and sawing wood, and the women spinning, weaving, and making clothes. The squires also controlled a variety of housing stock that could accommodate large families.[19]

The families pausing temporarily in Boston Neck in spring 1766 must have considered themselves fortunate when they thought of the hundreds who had perished from English aggression in L'Acadie or from disease, deprivation, melancholy, and old age while in exile. These household heads along with many of their kin were safely in Quebec by 1767. The men, at least, were long-lived. Claude Dugas and François LeBlanc died at St. Jacques de L'Achigan at ages eighty-five and seventy-eight, respectively. Joseph Doucet died at eighty-four in Trois-Rivières; and Joseph LeBlanc survived to the grand age of one hundred, dying in 1818 in St.-Joseph de Carleton.[20]

LOVE's surviving writings give us little sense about whether he attended civic celebrations or participated in impromptu crowd actions. Yet we can infer that this redoubtable public servant witnessed much of the political theater of the day. And of course, as a perambulator intensely attuned to the rhythms of the city, the warner kept himself informed about protests, troop movements, funeral processions, and anything else that might affect foot traffic. In March 1765—when a northeaster brought heavy snow, "the big[g]est Sea in the Harbor that our Oldest men [did] ever see," and extensive damages to the wharves—Love did not warn for two days. When the largest funeral procession "ever known in America" stretched across a third of the town on the last day in February 1770—four hundred schoolboys in pairs preceded the bier and thirty chaises followed it—Love refrained from warning. Love may have been paying his respects to the deceased, eleven-year-old Christopher Seider, shot by an irate merchant who was defending his house from a crowd attempting to terrorize him into halting his importation of British goods.[21]

The great elm that became known as the Liberty Tree was a short stroll along one long block of Orange Street from the Loves' rented quarters on Hollis Street. It is hard to imagine that Love was not present at some of the great rallies held there. The Stamp Act protest of Wednesday August 14, 1765, launched a decade of street theater of homespun ingenuity. That morning, artisans across the town are said to have laid down their tools and joined the growing throng under the tree's boughs, marveling at two effigies that had been strung up the night before and defending them from being cut down.[22] Did Love weave in and out of such crowds, asking after strangers? Elaborately staged entertainments may have held his rapt attention. Each year on November 5, Pope's Day, the Liberty Tree was one site where a twenty-foot wagon stopped to display "very droll" effigies of the hated Catholic leader and other monstrous and diverting characters, such as the devil and "Friends of . . . arbitrary Power." Boys "clad in frocks and trousers well covered with tar and feathers . . . danced about the pope, . . . and frequently climbed up and kissed the devil." During this all-day extravaganza in 1766, Love warned "A Labouring Man," Michael Forman, who had arrived the day before by ship from New York. Perhaps the warner came across him in "Liberty Hall," the wide intersection under the elms where thousands could congregate.[23]

For decades, Bostonians and people throughout the colonies had celebrated great days in their monarch's life: the king's birthday, his spouse's birthday, his ascension and coronation. In addition, once the political scene was transformed by popular protest against parliamentary and ministerial policies, many town residents contributed their energies to annually commemorating the mid-March day on which the Stamp Act was repealed, the town's fondly remembered August 14 protest against the act, and, later, the Boston Massacre. Of the holidays honoring the royal family, George III's natal day, June 4, was the grandest, enjoyed by those of all social ranks. In the morning, at least three outfits of colonial troops paraded on King Street or on the Common. They fired volleys and performed exercises, and in some years, the town militiamen engaged in a "mock fight" to exhibit their preparedness. On the more political days of celebration, colored banners streamed from tree and housetops and masts in the harbor, and nightfall brought out the crowds to admire the wondrous illumination of Faneuil Hall, the largest taverns, and the Liberty Tree—accomplished by the placing of lanterns in each window or on each branch. Love was often out and about the town on these festive occasions, identifying strangers among the hundreds or thousands on the streets.[24]

DURING the winter and summer months bracketing the massacre, Boston's activists kept steady pressure on merchants who either brazenly or surreptitiously imported goods from England. On at least two occasions, protesters appropriated the ritual of warning strangers to pressure obnoxious importers to leave town. These actions were not undertaken by Love; he was too punctilious about his job to indulge in the extralegal use of warning. The episodes tell us that the language of the twinned writs of warning and removal proved useful to public-spirited locals indignant over some strangers' perceived greed and failure to stand with the community against oppressive parliamentary and Crown policies.[25]

In the first episode, the shop owned by three Scottish brothers named McMaster was visited on Friday evening on June 1 by a crowd of "hundreds of Men and Boys." The crowd's leader "commanded" the importers "in a Magisterial tone . . . To keep their House and stores shut and to depart the Province with all their . . . property, at, or before 6 O'Clock on Monday . . . or else to expect the consequence." The crowd did not reappear the following week to enforce their will; rumors were swirling that the McMasters had proposed shutting their shop. But they never took that step, and they told friends privately that they were not willing to leave. After two weeks had elapsed, on Monday afternoon a crowd forced down the shop door,

seized the one brother who was present—twenty-nine-year-old Patrick—
and carted him through town. Made to ride next to a pile of feathers and
barrel of hot tar, McMaster was in the end spared that particular treatment.
By eight in the evening, the ritual of humiliation ended in an extralegal act
of banishment. Taken the two and a half miles through town and across
Boston Neck to the Roxbury line, the men escorting McMaster "made a
lane through which they obliged him to pass, while they spit in his face."
As part of this final coup de grâce, John Ballard, a Bostonian well known
to the McMasters as the manager of the Boston wharf they used, coerced
the thoroughly frightened Scot to take an oath that he and his brothers
would never return to Boston "on pain of death." McMaster fled to Castle
William and from thenceforth used Portsmouth, New Hampshire, as his
mercantile base.[26]

One month later, warning out was explicitly invoked when unofficial
enforcers of nonimportation harassed the McMasters' fellow Scot, James
Selkrig, commanding him to depart. The incident is not well documented;
we know of it because of a pathetic letter of complaint the victim sent to
the selectmen. Throughout his nine-year career in Boston as an importer,
Selkrig tried in various ways to make himself pleasing to the townsfolk. In
August 1769, he and his brother had agreed to stop importing, after initially
refusing to do so. But by July 1770, his actions had attracted the attention
of vigilante enforcers of nonimportation. Selkrig claimed that despite his
conformity "with Every Demand Diserd of me by The Tread[Trade]," he
was attacked "at the Town Dock and Ordred to Leave this place in 48
hours." The merchant asserted that this attempt "to Warne me out of the
place" was without cause and, furthermore, an affront to humanity as his
"only Daughter was then at the point of Death." As far as we know, he was
not physically forced out by a spitting crowd. However, it appears that he
wised up and voluntarily departed to live in Scotland until the spring of
1771, when he was back managing his store at No. 16 on the town dock. Not
surprisingly, he and his family were among the loyalists who evacuated
Boston with the British military in March 1776.[27]

Two artists created dramatic visual depictions of the opening scene of Boston's occupation. An engraving by Paul Revere offers an aerial view of the
town from the harbor. In the foreground are seen the "ships of war landing
their troops" and the soldiers of the fourteenth and twenty-ninth regiments
forming and beginning to march "in insolent parade" down the Long

Wharf into the heart of Boston, "Drums beating, Fifes playing and Colours flying." Christian Remick, an obscure Massachusetts mariner and watercolorist, chose a different approach. He planted himself near the end of Long Wharf and painted the very tip of the wharf surrounded by three-masted British ships and smaller transports, all against a panoramic background of the harbor islands (Figure 10). Remick's "perspective view" captures the moment when hundreds of redcoats were about to disembark and tackle their mission of preventing Bostonians from fomenting insurrection that would spread to other colonies. To most town residents, the presence of soldiers and officers in their scarlet regimental coats spelled a menace—a threat both to their persons and to their system of self-governance.[28]

On a practical level, Boston was ill-equipped to house the approximately twelve hundred men in the regiments. Their number was equivalent to nearly half the town's existing population of adult white men. Town leaders argued that the troops should live at Castle William, the garrison on a harbor island, since it was technically situated within the port town and would thus fulfill the spirit of the Quartering Act. Lieutenant Colonel William Dalrymple, the officer in command, was not persuaded. He ordered the Twenty-Ninth Foot to camp on the Commons, and he asked the province to ready the Manufactory House to accommodate the fourteenth. The tenants in this large, province-owned structure refused to leave. After a two-day standoff between soldiers blockading the building and a vocal but peaceable mob, the effort to quarter troops there was abandoned. In the end, the army leased several large warehouses and stores to use as barracks, while individual officers found their own lodgings nearby.[29]

Both Revere and Remick left out of their detailed illustrations the families that accompanied the British soldiers. While we cannot know the exact number of the "women and children of the regiment" and other dependents accompanying or following the soldiers to Boston, they must have numbered in the hundreds. Some of the regiments had come to North America from Ireland. Because many marriages had occurred there, regiments paid for the transport of far more than the typical allotment of six women per company. Other wives, sweethearts, and children arrived from Halifax. Regimental paymasters expended over £1,200 in housing the dependents, mostly in the South End. Love's warnings capture some forty of these military families. Not only does he provide names and partial life stories for women who otherwise would remain anonymous, he details the living arrangements of some soldiers who played key roles in the Boston Massacre.[30]

FIGURE 10. Pictured here, the Long Wharf with British soldiers preparing to alight. The artist, Cape Cod-born Christian Remick, and his wife were warned by Robert Love on July 15, 1768, after their return to New England from Liverpool, England. Detail, "Perspective View of Boston Harbor."

Image courtesy of the New England Historic Genealogical Society, www.AmericanAncestors.org.

Because the military was supposed to take fiscal responsibility for women and children "of the regiment" while the troops were stationed in Boston, Love did not issue warnings until regiments had been sent elsewhere. His investigations into spouses or families who appeared to be abandoned by male household heads and regimental authorities came in four waves, starting in summer 1769.[31]

The first set of warnings highlights the plight of dependent women left behind and the worries of municipal officials that some were women of loose morals. The warner found three soldiers' wives lodging in a North End; two were married to grenadiers: "th[e]y Belong to Capt. Henery powers Company" in the sixty-fourth, now "Gon to Halifax." All three women would eventually follow their husbands to Nova Scotia before returning together to Boston in 1771, when they were warned a second time by Love. Other women were cut off from their connection to a regiment when soldiers deserted. Hannah Mills—or someone standing nearby when Love warned her in summer 1769—explained that when her husband had been ordered to Halifax, he "Left her Behind Because She Was a Bad Women." Love found Dorothy Williams living with a midshipman. Her husband had deserted her and his regiment in 1769. Soon, Williams sought almshouse admission for herself and a child, who may have been a newborn. The child's fate is unknown; Williams left the house a few weeks later in the company of another soldier's wife. The almshouse provided her shelter again during the next two winters. In the fall of 1772, now identified as a "spinster" "of Boston," she appeared before the Sessions court and was convicted of lascivious conduct. The evidence confirmed that on a late August day she had received "into her Bed, one Joseph Mesial & did permit" him "Lewdly & indecently to be & remain with her Naked in Bed &c." Fined twenty shillings, Williams remained in Boston's jail for a few months until she could pay up. In the end, the county paid her trial and jail costs, as it often did with petty miscreants who were impoverished.[32]

In the next wave, from late April to mid-May 1770, Love warned sixteen parties linked to members of the twenty-ninth regiment. Ten of the women had children with them, for a total of thirty-two persons warned. The late winter and early spring weeks preceding the warnings were the tensest of the occupation. On market days (Thursdays), when no school was held, hundreds of boys joined crowds of adults who gathered outside the shop doors of merchants pegged as violators of the agreement not to import

manufactured goods from England. The collective action included the boo-
ing and hissing of anyone patronizing the stores and the prominent place-
ment of signs painted with a pointing finger and the word "IMPORTER."
By night, shop windows were smeared with dirt and mud. An incident at
John Gray's ropewalks in the South End on March 2 set the stage for the
Boston Massacre. On that Friday morning, Patrick Walker, a private looking to pick up day labor to supplement his army pay, found himself trading
escalating insults with some of the workers at this large manufactory. His
honor at stake, Walker fetched other soldiers from nearby barracks, and
fighting with club and sticks broke out in the ropeyards. Eventually, the
soldiers were pushed back to their quarters; by evening, calm prevailed in
the neighborhood. But all weekend, rumors swirled that many townspeople
were looking forward to "fighting it out with the soldiers on Monday"
evening. Indeed, what occurred that evening on King Street as a result of
confused and frightened sentries firing into a crowd (leaving five dead and
six wounded) was the event that finally persuaded British military leadership that British troops should no longer be housed on peninsular Boston.
Within two and a half months, all would be withdrawn to Castle William.[33]

Walker was one of three soldiers with featured roles in the Boston Massacre or its lead-up who earned a warning. Not only did these strangers
have dependents living in town, but they may have been sought out by
Love or his employers because they had proved especially obnoxious to
townspeople. Love's warning of Walker's wife, Mary, which occurred two
months after the ropewalks incident, tells us that at the time they had no
children with them and that she had found lodging with three other soldiers' wives in a house in a prominent Bostonian's yard a few blocks west
of her husband's would-be workplace.[34]

In the wake of the massacre, Love warned the spouses of two of the
soldiers charged with shooting into the crowd. Both were grenadiers of the
twenty-ninth—a unit comprised of especially tall men. James Hartigan had
married in Boston (in an Anglican church) one year after his arrival; his
bride was living in Boston at the time, but no evidence points to her origins.
Love warned the woman at her lodgings on King Street, close by the scene
of the fatal shootings.[35] Edward Montgomery's wife, Isabella, and their three
children were living in rented house on a stretch of Ann Street near the
Mill Creek. Isabella made herself notorious among townspeople by declaring from her doorway, on the evening the massacre occurred, that she

hoped many of her neighbors would find "their arses . . . laid low by morning." In writing out his warning of this soldier's family, Love revealed his
political allegiances. He explained that the private was "Now Under con-
finment in Our Goal for the murder of our People." Love shared in the
collective outrage over the loss of life in the Boston Massacre. Five months
before the actual trial, the warner in effect offered his personal verdict,
a harsher one than what was handed down. Defended by John Adams,
Montgomery was found guilty of manslaughter but not murder. Within
days, he departed Boston in a man-of-war to rejoin his regiment in New
Jersey. The town clerk's records indicate that the soldier had "left his wife
and 3 children."[36]

By 1771 and 1772, when most of the troops had departed the area, conditions for wives and children left behind tended to be desperate. Nell Puce
and Peggy Carpenter were avoiding starvation by gathering dandelions on
Fort Hill to sell; Love declared the two women to be "in a misarable Con-
dison and allmost Nacked." Polly Vane was living in a foul tenement in the
South End. Eleanor Burrough, a soldier's daughter, was "verry d[est]istute
of Every thing." The selectmen got no satisfaction from the British commander at Castle William when they wrote formally requesting that he
either take in or pay support for several sets of wives and children who
needed succor in the almshouse. The Bostonians' attempt to educate him
on "the Law of this Province" ("whoever is the Occasion of any Person
being brought into this Town & does not acquaint yᵉ Selectmen thereof
becomes liable for the Charge of all such Persons if they shou'd be reduced
to necessitous Circumstances") fell on deaf ears.[37]

ONE of Love's last warnings was delivered on March 25, 1774 to an impoverished Irishman. Although the date's significance would not be apparent to
Bostonians for a few weeks, it was when Parliament passed the first of the
Coercive Acts, several of which singled out Boston and Massachusetts for
special punishment. The draconian Boston Port Act was designed to shut
down all oceangoing commerce by the port's merchants until the East India
Company received compensation for the tea dumped into Boston harbor
the previous December. Other acts closed town meetings and enlarged the
Crown's power to control the province's magistrates. These measures signaled to many New Englanders that the king himself was a tyrant and could
no longer be counted on to protect his people. If Love had lived a few more

days until news of the "cruel edict" (the Port Act) arrived, his people's future would have looked very bleak indeed.[38]

The succession of ragtag strangers dislocated by imperial policies and warned by Love prefigured New Englanders' trajectory toward resistance and revolution. The sight of war's cast-offs—demobilized regimentals in their tattered scarlet coats and world-weary Acadians with their hard-won savings—did not dislodge colonists' loyalties to king and country, but Britain's wartime debts led to a string of taxation schemes that critics argued were threats to civil liberties. Two pivotal moments catalyzed the radicalization of many townspeople—the 1768–70 occupation and the implementation of the Coercive Acts. Love's warnings of soldiers' wives huddling in filthy rooms and scavenging for subsistence coincided with growing disillusionment with the benefits of empire. Yet at the same time that Sons of Liberty condemned parliamentary measures and the ministers who shaped Crown policy, they, like Love, clung to reverence for "His Majesty," believing that the monarch was poorly informed and did not intend them harm. Coincidentally, it was after Love's demise that Massachusetts residents cast their lot with open rebellion. During the summer and fall of 1774, the leaders of Boston and other towns constituted themselves "the sole effective government in the province" in defiance of royal authority. Thus, in the space of a decade, Massachusetts had transformed from one of the most enthusiastic colonial partners of the British Empire to "its most intractable opponent."[39]

✿

Epilogue

AFTER THE REVOLUTION, efforts to warn newcomers slackened in towns across Massachusetts even though high birth rates, increased overseas immigration, and much mobility among the native-born contributed to rising populations. Town officials no longer paid searchers to register strangers; they found other ways to differentiate between town and state poor. Residents might be examined as to where they had settlement when they paid their property taxes or when they asked for admission to the almshouse. A June 1789 statute, however, reinstated warning. In the previous twenty-two years, free persons had been able to gain settlement in a town only by birth, marriage, and explicit vote of the town. The new law created several additional methods, including simple residence for two years without being warned.[1]

Worried about the potential for dramatically increased poor relief costs, towns across the state began issuing warnings again. In Boston, the law was read aloud at a joint meeting of the overseers of the poor and selectmen, who declared it to be "greatly to the disadvantage of the Town" and "impossible" to implement. They voted to petition the General Assembly to amend the law or exempt the commonwealth's largest town. A few months later, when relief had not been granted, the selectmen charged the three men serving in the recently established post of inspector of police to search for newcomers. Their instructions came straight out of Robert Love's playbook: "make a strict inquiry of all Strangers that are or may come into ye Town, and take both the Christian & Sir names of such Persons with the part of the Town they reside in," "what House" they occupy, and where they were last from "or belong to." Missing was the long-standing guideline to warn only those in low circumstances. The inspectors were expected to return the names of "*all*" strangers to the selectmen at their Faneuil Hall room every Wednesday. To comply with the law, the selectmen ordered printed warning warrants in bulk and purchased a folio ledger for listing warned strangers alphabetically. In the ensuing months, slightly over two thousand, one hundred parties received warning in Boston.[2]

A legislative overhaul of the settlement law in 1794 ended the pressure on towns to issue warnings. Boston's protests had been heard. Town officials appear to have gotten wind of the impending legislation. Months before the law passed, the police inspectors who had warned so diligently in the previous two years stopped returning warrants to the town clerk or asking to be reimbursed for warning strangers. Warning in Boston had come to its final end.[3]

From the early eighteenth century until 1793, warning played an important administrative role helping jurisdictions keep tabs on strangers who might drain the town's coffers. It was a familiar, nonthreatening ritual to Massachusetts residents and sojourners. Warning by itself did not disrupt working people's lives by forcing them to move on. Ordinary folk determined on their own where to live and when to relocate. New Englanders knew that warning's significance lay in determining where one had legal settlement and who would be billed for poor relief. Locals taught strangers not to take literally the constable's notice to depart the town in a certain number of days. Our analysis of Boston's warning rolls establishes that people were on the move for many reasons—economic survival, vocational betterment, family reunification—and suggests that being identified as a legal stranger was of little concern.

A story generated by a lawsuit between two towns near Boston captures the spirit with which New Englanders approached warning. In 1766, thirty-year-old Mary Powers, who had never married, needed poor relief when she could not pay her living expenses or medical bills during pregnancy. Overseers of the poor in Woburn, where she lived at the time, paid the costs but sued neighboring Lexington, arguing that Powers was legally their inhabitant because she had not been properly warned there years earlier. What makes the suit distinctive—and probably unique—is that Mary's older sister, Anna, in the course of being deposed, offered a child's view of being warned. Not only that, but she revealed that New Englanders saw humor in the practice.[4]

As young children, Mary and Anna had lived in several towns, first with their mother and then as members of the family formed when she married John Macklewain. When Mary was about nine, the household moved from Woburn to Lexington, where they lived for a year in David Cutler's house along with other lodgers. One February day, constable Benjamin Smith came to call, armed with a warning warrant. Anna recollected that she and Mary "were called up out of the Cellar . . . by name to hear the warrant Read," along with their stepfather, mother, and stepsiblings. The constable "told them they were all warned to depart & leave the Town of Lexington." Anna enhanced the credibility of her memory of the incident by adding that, in the instant after being warned, she "took up A Cat" the family had "brought from Woburn & told the Constable he had not warned out the Cat." John Adams, known for his courtroom wit, was the lawyer for the town of Lexington. With Anna as his star witness, Adams won the suit for his client.[5]

Let's transpose the encounter to a wintry day in Boston in the years of the Stamp Act and Tea Party protests. Knowing the characteristics of Boston's best warner as we do, perhaps we can agree that Robert Love would have acquiesced with a young person's request—and warned the cat.

Traveling Parties and Locations
They Were "Last From"

Last from	Solo males/ females	Parties of two or more	Total warned parties	Percentage of all parties last from this location
Massachusetts	439/463	281	1,183	(49%)
Rest of New England	177/60	71	308	(13%)
Canada	109/54	99	262	(11%)
Rest of Americas	275/45	109	429	(18%)
British Isles	75/11	37	123	(5%)
Europe, Africa	6/0	1	7	(0.3%)
Not given	43/15	39	97	(4%)
Totals (types of parties)	1,124/648	637	2,409	—

Sources for Robert Love's Warning Records, by Date

Love's surviving warnings for the period January 1765 to April 1774 are housed in several repositories, as indicated below. Love created three copies: logbook entries, warrants returned to the county court, and pages delivered to the Boston overseers of the poor. For some dates, only one of these copies survives; for others, two or more exist. Less frequently, none of Love's manuscript warnings have come to light, but the town clerk's Warning Out book summarizes Love's activity. In this key, the Warning Out books are listed only if they contain the single surviving record of a particular warning. Note that these Warning Out books include almost all of Love's otherwise documented warnings, but occasionally the town clerk omitted or garbled the information.[1]

The following abbreviations are used in this appendix.

Adlow	Elijah Adlow Papers, Box 92032, Boston Public Library, Rare Books and Manuscripts. Some of these are warrants; others are copies of logbook pages.
OV	Boston Overseers of the Poor Records, Box 4, Ms. Bos. W2, Box 4, Boston Public Library, Rare Books and Manuscripts.
SF	Suffolk Files, Suffolk File Collection, Judicial Archives, Massachusetts Archives, Boston. For a given month, the file sequence reflects the chronological ordering of warnings.
Warning Out Book	*Boston Overseers of the Poor Records*, microfilm edition, 15 reels. Boston: Massachusetts Historical

Society, 1998, reel 4. These alphabetical indices were created by town clerk William Cooper, who abstracted the information from warrants returned by Love and other warners. One book covers 1745–70, and another 1770–73 and 1791–92.

1765

Jan. 31–Dec.	Robert Love Record Book, 1765–66, Massachusetts Historical Society; various SF 86078–86707; Adlow (Nov. 1–16)

1766

Jan.–Aug.	Robert Love Record Book, 1765–66, Massachusetts Historical Society; various SF 86727–87101; Adlow (Jan. 10–31, July 1–22)
Sept. 3–27	SF 87106
Oct. 1–18	Adlow
Nov. 5–13, 20–29	SF 87276
Nov. 14–16	Warning Out Book
Dec. 3–16	SF 87522
Dec. 17–29	SF 87295

1767

Jan.	OV
Feb.	OV; SF 87552
March	OV; SF 87711
April	OV
May	OV
June	OV; SF 87722, 87900
July	OV; SF 87907
Aug.	OV
Sept.	OV; SF 87913
Oct.	OV
Nov. 2–30	OV; SF 88037, 88040
Dec.	OV

1768

Jan.	SF 88180, 88181

Feb.	Warning Out Book
March 1–24	SF 88340
April 2–13	SF 88355
April 15–29	Warning Out Book
May 1–20	Warning Out Book
May 23–30	SF 88359
June 1–23	SF 88532
June 23–30	Warning Out Book
July 1–18	Warning Out Book
July 18–29	SF 88545
Aug.	SF 88559, 88558
Sept. 5–14	SF 88646
Sept. 15–30	Warning Out Book
Oct.	SF 88654, 88652
Nov.	Warning Out Book
Dec.	SF 88842

1769

Jan.	SF 88847
Feb.	SF 88983
March 3–10	Warning Out Book
March 21–27	SF 88986
March 27–30	Warning Out Book
April 4–20	SF 88997
April 17–25	SF 88998
May 1–23	SF 89009
May 23–27	Adlow
June 1–17	SF 89146
June 14, 19–30	Warning Out Book
July 7–21	SF 89165
July 24–31	SF 89166
Aug. 1–19	SF 89175
Aug. 22–31	SF 89176
Sept. 1–25	Adlow
Sept. 26–28	Warning Out Book
Oct. 2–13	SF 89238
Oct. 17–30	SF 89237
Nov. 1–17	Warning Out Book

Nov. 18–30	Adlow
Dec. 2–10	Warning Out Book
Dec. 12–30	SF 89389, 89387

1770

Jan. 6–20	Warning Out Book
Feb.	Warning Out Book
March	SF 89515, 89513
April	Warning Out Book
May	SF 89545, 89546
June	SF 89757, 89742
July	SF 89794, 89796
Aug.	SF 89793, 89795
Sept.	SF 89879, 89880
Oct. 5–30	SF 89901, 89902
Nov. 2–21	SF 89905
Nov. 24–30	Warning Out Book
Dec. 1–14	Warning Out Book
Dec. 15–31	SF 90077

1771

Jan. 1–15	Warning Out Book
Jan. 16–30	SF 90087
Feb. 2–23	SF 90095
Feb. 25–28	Adlow
March 5–30	Adlow
April 1–13	SF 90296
April 19–30	Adlow
May	SF 90310, 90309
June 1–12	Adlow
June 12–26	SF 90468
June 27–28	Adlow
July 1–9	SF 90481
July 10–13	Warning Out Book
July 15–26	SF 90484, 90483
Aug. 1–12	SF 90480
Aug. 13–19	Warning Out Book
Aug. 22–28	SF 90482

Sept. 2–5	Adlow
Sept. 7–23	SF 90493
Sept. 23–30	SF 90490
Oct. 2–21	Adlow
Oct. 21–26	SF 90522
Oct. 26–28	Warning Out Book
Nov. 1–25	SF 90545, 90542, 90543, 90544
Dec. 11–27	SF 90757

1772

Jan. 1–10	Warning Out Book
Jan. 11	SF 90759
Feb. 1–22	SF 90760, 90758
March 2–23	Adlow
March 24–26	SF 90867
April 11–23	Warning Out Book
May 1–28	Adlow; SF 90916 (May 11–27)
June 4–30	Adlow
July 2–25	Adlow; SF 91133 (July 17–25)
Aug.	SF 91138, 91139; Adlow
Sept. 1–19	Warning Out Book
Sept. 21–26	SF 91302
Oct. 1–13	SF 91305
Oct. 20–27	SF 91306
Nov. 5–30	Adlow
Dec. 7–15	Adlow
Dec. 15–31	Warning Out Book

1773

Jan. 1–30	SF 91623
Feb. 9–25	SF 91630, 91629
March 3–27	SF 91697
March 27–30	Adlow
April 5–23	SF 173564 [torn], supplemented by Warning Out Book
April 24–30	SF 91699b
May	SF 91706, 91705
June 2–14	Warning Out Book
June 17–28	SF 91714

July 2–19	SF 91719
July 20–28	Adlow
Aug.	Adlow
Sept. 18–29	SF 91871
Oct. 4–22	SF 91878
Oct. 22–30	SF 91876
Nov. 2–21	Adlow
Dec. 1–22	SF 92107

1774

Jan.	SF 92114a
Feb. 8–26	SF 92114b
March 2–30	SF 92141

1771 Valn.	*The Massachusetts Tax Valuation List of 1771*, ed. Bettye Hobbs Pruitt. Rockport, Me.: Picton Press, 1998.
1780 Takings	*Assessors' "Taking Books" of the Town of Boston, 1780*. Boston: Bostonian Society, 1912.
Acts and Resolves	*Acts and Resolves, Public and Private, of the Province of the Massachusetts Bay . . . 1692–*. Boston: Wright and Potter, 1869– .
BOPR, MHS	*Boston Overseers of the Poor Records*, microfilm edition, 15 reels, Boston: Massachusetts Historical Society, 1998.
Boston Births	*Boston Births from A.D. 1700 to A.D. 1800*. Boston: Rockwell and Churchill, 1894.
Boston Cems.	*Inscriptions and Records of the Old Cemeteries of Boston*, comp. Robert J. Dunkle and Ann S. Lainhart. Boston: New England Historic Genealogical Society, 2000.
Boston Ch. Recs. database	Records of the Churches of Boston, CD-ROM database. Boston: New England Historic Genealogical Society, 2002.
Boston City Directory 1789	*First Boston City Directory (1789) Including Extensive Annotations by John Haven Dexter (1791–1876)*, ed. Ann Smith Lainhart, with a preface by John A. Schutz. Boston: New England Historic Genealogical Society, 1989.
Boston Deaths	*Deaths in Boston, 1700–1799*, by Robert J. Dunkle and Ann S. Lainhart, 2 vols. (continuously paginated). Boston: New England Historic Genealogical Society, 1999.

Boston Marrs., 1	*Boston Marriages from 1700 to 1809.* Vol. 1: *1700–51*, comp. Edward W. McGlenen. Baltimore: Genealogical Publishing Co., 1997, first published 1898.
Boston Marrs., 2	*Boston Marriages from 1700 to 1809.* Vol. 2: *1752–1809*, comp. Edward W. McGlenen. Baltimore: Genealogical Publishing Co., 1977, first published 1903.
Boston Obits.	*Index of Obituaries in Boston Newspapers, 1704–1800*, comp. Ogden Codman, 3 vols., facsimile of orig. mss. in Boston Athenaeum. Boston: G. K. Hall, 1968.
BPL	Boston Public Library, Rare Books and Manuscripts.
BTR	*A Report of the Record Commissioners of the City of Boston, Containing the Boston Town Records*, vols. 1–27. Boston: Rockwell and Churchill, City Printers, [1876–1909].
Hist. Artillery Company	*The History of the Ancient and Honorable Artillery Company, [Rev. and Enl]. from Its Formation in 1637 and Charter in 1638, to the Present Time; Comprising the Biographies of the Distinguished Civil, Literary, Religious, and Military Men of the Colony, Province, and Commonwealth*, by Zachariah G. Whitman. Boston: J. H. Eastburn, 1842.
Hollis St. Church Recs.	*Hollis Street Church, Boston: Records of Admissions, Baptisms, Marriages, and Deaths, 1732–1887*, comp. Ogden Codman, transcribed by Robert J. Dunkle and Ann Smith Lainhart. Boston: New England Historic Genealogical Society, 1998.
John Adams, *Diary*	*Diary and Autobiography of John Adams*, ed. Lyman H. Butterfield, 4 vols. Cambridge, Mass: Belknap Press, 1961.
MA Archives	Massachusetts Archives, Boston.
Maas, *Divided Hearts*	David E. Maas, ed. *Divided Hearts, Massachusetts Loyalists, 1765–1790: A*

	Biographical Directory. Boston: New England Historic Genealogical Society, 1980.
Mass. SCJ Records	Superior Court of Judicature Records, Judicial Archives, Massachusetts Archives, Boston (MA Archives).
MAVR	The Massachusetts Vital Records Project, John Slaughter, administrator and owner, www.mavitalrecords.org.
MCPF	Middlesex County Probate Files, microfilm, Judicial Archives, Massachusetts Archives, Boston (MA Archives).
MCPR	Middlesex County Probate Records, microfilm, Judicial Archives, Massachusetts Archives, Boston (MA Archives).
MHS	Massachusetts Historical Society, Boston.
NEHGR	*New England Historical and Genealogical Register.*
NEHGS	New England Historic Genealogical Society, Boston.
Nellis and Cecere, *BOPR*	Eric Nellis and Anne Decker Cecere, eds. *The Eighteenth-Century Records of the Boston Overseers of the Poor.* Boston: Colonial Society of Massachusetts, 2007.
Port Arrivals	*Port Arrivals and Immigrants to the City of Boston, 1715–1716, 1762–1769,* comp. William H. Whitmore. Boston: Registry Dept. of Boston, 1900.
Rowe Diary	*Letters and Diary of John Rowe, Boston Merchant, 1758–1762, 1764–1779,* ed. Anne Rowe Cunningham. Boston: W. B. Clarke, 1903.
Schutz, *Legislators*	John A. Schutz, ed. *Legislators of the Massachusetts General Court, 1691–1775: A Biographical Dictionary.* Boston: Northeastern University Press, 1997.
SCPF	Suffolk County Probate Files, microfilm, Judicial Archives, Massachusetts Archives, Boston (MA Archives).

SCPR   Suffolk County Probate Records, microfilm,
                            Judicial Archives, Massachusetts Archives,
                            Boston (MA Archives).
Seybolt, *Town Officials*   Robert Francis Seybolt, *The Town Officials of
                            Colonial Boston, 1634–1775.* Cambridge, Mass.:
                            Harvard University Press, 1939.
SF   Suffolk File Collection, microfilm, Judicial
                            Archives, Massachusetts Archives, Boston
                            (MA Archives).
Sibley's Harvard Graduates *Sibley's Harvard Graduates; Biographical
                            Sketches of those who Attended Harvard College
                            . . . with Bibliographical and Other Notes,* by
                            John Langdon Sibley et al. Boston:
                            Massachusetts Historical Society, 1873–.
Suff. Co. GSP Records   Suffolk County, General Sessions of the Peace
                            Records, Judicial Archives, Massachusetts
                            Archives, Boston (MA Archives).
Thwing database   Annie Haven Thwing, *Inhabitants and Estates
                            of the Town of Boston, 1630–1800, and The
                            Crooked and Narrow Streets of Boston,
                            1630–1822.* CD-ROM database. Boston: New
                            England Historic Genealogical Society and
                            Massachusetts Historical Society, 2001.
Warning Out Book, 1745–70   Warning Out Book, 1745–70, *Boston Overseers
                            of the Poor Records,* microfilm edition, 15 reels,
                            Boston: Massachusetts Historical Society,
                            1998, reel 4.
WMQ   *William and Mary Quarterly,* 3rd ser.
Worc. Co. Warnings   *Worcester County Warnings, 1737–1788,* comp.
                            Francis E. Blake. Camden, Me.: Picton Press,
                            1992, first published Worcester, Mass.: F. P.
                            Rice, 1899.

NOTES

Prologue

1. Love's surviving warnings for 1765 to 1774 are found in several repositories, as indicated in Appendix B. Only a small fraction is missing. This is largely because not only did Love make three copies (in a logbook, in warrants returned to the county court, and on sheets sent to the overseers of the poor), but also the town clerk abstracted the warnings into a ledger. This reconstruction follows Love's logbook entries for July 9, 1766, and is informed by Annie Haven Thwing, *The Crooked and Narrow Streets of the Town of Boston, 1630–1822* (Boston: Marshall Jones, 1920); Samuel G. Drake, *History and Antiquities of Boston . . .* (Boston: Luther Stevens, 1856); Samuel Adams Drake, *Old Landmarks and Historic Personages of Boston* (Boston: James R. Osgood, 1873); SCPF 11581 for Henry King (1757); *Boston News-Letter*, Sept. 22, 1757, 3; and our research on the named warned strangers and landlords. On Scott: Love warnings on Feb. 5, 1765, July 26, 1766; Thwing database 53965; and *Rowe Diary*, 74–75. David Hunt returned to his home-town, where he married in 1777 and raised a family; *Vital Records of Tewksbury, Massachusetts, to the End of the Year 1849* (Salem, Mass.: Essex Institute, 1912), 140, 46–47. After his perambulations on this Wednesday, Love probably attended the selectmen's evening meeting (*BTR* 20:219).

Introduction

1. One researcher called them messengers, because some men appointed prior to 1765 served simultaneously as errand carriers for the selectmen; Seybolt, *Town Officials*, 231, n.525. The quoted phrase is from warnings dated Feb. 19–27, 1767, Boston Overseers of the Poor Records, Ms. Bos. W2, Box 4, BPL. Love used the same phrase in all written copies of his warnings, with occasional variations in spelling, capitalization, and wording.

2. Robert Love Record Book, 1765–66, MHS. The journal is quarto-size, measuring about 7 by 5 inches with a spine three-quarters of an inch thick. It is bound in green vellum (with the green considerably darkened by age), tooled on front and back, with a somewhat uncommon hybrid of hard and soft boards. Thanks to MHS curator Anne E. Bentley for her expert analysis.

3. We have calculated Love's share at 63 percent of the total warnings issued from January 1765 through August 1766; Warning Out book, 1745–70. For Love's first year, our count agrees with Stephen Edward Wiberly Jr., "Four Cities: Public Poor Relief in Urban America, 1700–1775" (Ph.D. diss., Yale University, 1975), 47.

4. Josiah Henry Benton, *Warning Out in New England, 1656–1817* (Boston: W. B. Clarke, 1911; repr., Bowie, Md.: Heritage Books, 1992). Benton's account is largely accurate, but he omitted the Bay province's 1767 act on inhabitancy, removals, and warning and mentioned only on his

final two pages warnings' function of ascertaining where the responsibility for relieving an indigent person rested—with the town or the province. For warning in Rhode Island, see Ruth Wallis Herndon, *Unwelcome Americans: Living on the Margin in Early New England* (Philadelphia: University of Pennsylvania Press, 2001).

5. In practice, warning affected mostly imperial and regional insiders. Almost all of the warned were Britons and nearly three-quarters hailed from New England. For a different argument about the origins of modern deportation law, see Daniel Kanstroom, *Deportation Nation: Outsiders in American History* (Cambridge, Mass.: Harvard University Press, 2007), 38. For a political scientist's perspective on linkages across the centuries, see Susan F. Martin, *A Nation of Immigrants* (New York: Cambridge University Press, 2011). One must take care not to equate the workings of settlement laws with those of vagrancy statutes or confound Rhode Island's quite different application of warning with practice in the rest of New England.

6. On warning as social control, see, for example, Douglas Lamar Jones, "The Strolling Poor: Transiency in Eighteenth-Century Massachusetts," *Journal of Social History* 8 (Spring 1975), 28–54. Note that warning was not practiced from the 1630s to the 1650s, when the Bay Colony's puritan rulers anxiously banished proselytizing Quakers and other outspoken religious dissenters such as Anne Hutchinson and Roger Williams.

7. We used record linkage, piecing together evidence from a variety of primary sources to produce biographies of warned strangers. We focused intensively on those named in Love's first logbook who came to Boston from other Massachusetts towns. We also researched thoroughly people of color and dependents of occupying soldiers. We conducted similar research less systematically for strangers arriving from other locations and in the period after August 1766. For studies profiling the life of a single man or woman not among the elite or learned classes, see Laurel Thatcher Ulrich, *A Midwife's Tale: The Life of Martha Ballard, Based on Her Diary, 1785–1812* (New York: Knopf, 1991); Alfred F. Young, *The Shoemaker and the Tea Party: Memory and the American Revolution* (Boston: Beacon Press, 1999), 3–84; and Keith Wrightson, *Ralph Tailor's Summer: A Scrivener, His City, and the Plague* (New Haven: Yale University Press, 2011). Several studies that track the life stories of hundreds of ordinary folk have inspired us: Billy G. Smith, *The "Lower Sort": Philadelphia's Laboring People, 1750–1800* (Ithaca, N.Y.: Cornell University Press, 1990); Richard Cobb, *Death in Paris: The Records of the Basse-Geôle de la Seine, October 1795–September 1801, Vendémiaire Year IV–Fructidor Year IX* (New York: Oxford University Press, 1978); James S. Amelang, *The Flight of Icarus: Artisan Autobiography in Early Modern Europe* (Stanford, Calif.: Stanford University Press, 1998); and Herndon, *Unwelcome Americans*.

Chapter 1. Mr. Love's Mission

1. Reconstructed plans for the interior spaces of Faneuil Hall are found in the historic structures report *Faneuil Hall, Boston National Historic Park [Historic Structure Report]* (N.p.: National Park Service, ca. 1980).

2. *BTR* 20:129–31.

3. *BTR* 20:130. Cooper copied these orders onto the first page of Love's record book; Robert Love Record Book, 1765–66, MHS.

4. *BTR* 20:139; 23:11, 32, 141. One of the three men, Cornelius Thayer, warned only fourteen persons in the winter of 1765 before giving up the effort (SF 86097). John Sweetser issued 324

warnings to five hundred individuals from the start of 1765 until the end of August 1768, submitting frequent returns. Unlike Love, Sweetser never included children's names, strangers' occupations, marks of distress, or lodgings; see SF 88553 for Sweetser's last return. One of Sweetser's returns is reproduced in Douglas Lamar Jones, "The Transformation of the Law of Poverty in Eighteenth-Century Massachusetts," in *Law in Colonial Massachusetts, 1630–1800*, ed. Daniel Coquillette (Boston: Colonial Society of Massachusetts, 1984), 177–78.

5. *BTR* 20:131, 130. To help remove dung and offensive objects from Savannah's streets, legislators in Georgia in 1768 authorized the appointment of a salaried beadle to patrol the town at least once a week and report back to the parish vestry; Allen Daniel Candler, ed., *The Colonial Records of the State of Georgia*, 25 vols. (Atlanta: Franklin, 1904–16), 18:754.

6. Winthrop was defending an act passed by the General Court in 1637 that required towns to seek approval from a high colony official or magistrate for a "stranger" to stay more than three weeks. He distinguished the granting of "continual" residency from the short-term "hospitality" that was due to strangers who were "in misery" and not a danger to residents. *Winthrop Papers: 1698–1654*, 6 vols. (Boston: Massachusetts Historical Society, 1929–92), 3:422–26. The 1637 statute imposed a penalty on towns or hosts who "intertaine[d]" a stranger more than three weeks without magisterial approval; Nathanial B. Shurtleff, ed., *Records of the Governor and Company of the Massachusetts Bay in New England*, 5 vols. (Boston: William White, 1853–54), 1:196. "Keep off": Kenneth A. Lockridge, *A New England Town, the First Hundred Years: Dedham, Massachusetts, 1636–1736* (New York: W. W. Norton, 1970), 5 (quotation), 6–19.

7. Josiah Henry Benton, *Warning Out in New England, 1656–1817* (Boston: W. B. Clarke, 1911; repr., Bowie, Md.: Heritage Books, 1992), 8–10. For a study stressing the positive legal right to relief over negative aspects of settlement law such as removals, see Lorie Charlesworth, *Welfare's Forgotten Past: A Socio-Legal History of the Poor Law* (New York: Routledge, 2010). In England, the jurisdiction collecting the poor rate and distributing poor relief was the parish; in New England, it was the town.

8. Jonathan Leavitt, *A Summary of the Laws of Massachusetts Relative to the Settlement, Support, Employment and Removal of Paupers* (Greenfield, Mass.: John Denio, 1810), 5, 7–8, 9–16; Leavitt reprints the 1701 Act Directing the Admission of Town Inhabitants (9–12). A 1739 act clarified that being taxed in a town did not give inhabitancy by itself; this was in contrast to English practice (13–16). See also Hendrik Hartog, "The Public Law of a County Court: Judicial Government in Eighteenth Century Massachusetts," *American Journal of Legal History* 20 (Oct. 1976), 293. As Benton points out, towns often admitted new inhabitants "upon conditions," such as that the new resident practice his valuable trade there or set up a mill; Benton, *Warning Out*, 18–19.

9. For the 1659 law, see Shurtleff, ed., *Records of the Governor and Company of the Massachusetts Bay*, vol. 4, pt. 1, 365; and Benton, *Warning Out*, 49. The backdoor route was akin to adverse possession in the realm of property law. We thank Sheila O'Rourke and Bruce H. Mann for their lawyerly perspectives on this issue. For the 1767 act (which also denied inhabitancy to children born in town to newcomers who had not been explicitly approved as legal inhabitants), see *Acts and Resolves*, 5:911–12.

10. Benton, *Warning Out*, 40, 37, 54 (for Plymouth Colony); 1683 use in Boston: Aug. 27, 1683, entry for John Lee, in "A List of Several Persons Returned by the Countie Court . . . [1670/71–1700]," Bonds for Securities Against Strangers, MHS. The printed records for Boston, 1660–1700, reveal no use of the term *warning* in the context of strangers. Once the selectmen

began keeping records of their meetings in a separate book, the term appears regularly, the first being on Dec. 29, 1701: "John Hooper, worsted Com[b]er, is warned to depart the Town unless he Give Security (to indempnifie the Town from Charge) at or before the next monthly meeting of the Select-men" (*BTR* 11:13). The verb *to warn* also had a more common use in England and New England in this period, referring to the act of announcing and summoning hearers or certain parties to a meeting, such as a town meeting.

11. Benton, *Warning Out*, 65–66, 86, 88–90. When Massachusetts, Plymouth, and Connecticut agreed in 1672 to articles of confederation as part of a mutual defense pact, they addressed the problem of the "settleing of vagabonds and wandering persons removeing from one Collonie to another": If any person was found to have had their abode in one place "for more than three monthes and not warned out by the authoritie of the place," and if the person ignored a warning to depart and then was not physically removed, "every such person or persons shalbe accoumpted an Inhabitant," qtd. in ibid., 49–50. Rhode Island adopted warning but implemented the identification, interviewing, and physical removal of strangers in a different fashion from other New England jurisdictions; see Ruth Wallis Herndon, *Unwelcome Americans: Living on the Margin in Early New England* (Philadelphia: University of Pennsylvania Press, 2001), chap. 1.

12. The 1692 law, entitled "An Act for Regulating of Townships . . . ," also explained that near kinsmen were liable for the support of an indigent person and made an exception to the three-month warning rule for "any persons committed to Prison" in the town, or sent there "for Nursing or Education"; John D. Cushing, ed., *Massachusetts Province Laws, 1692–1699* (Wilmington, Del.: Michael Glazier, 1978), 38–43 (quotations p. 42). Benton believed that the legislators relieved town officials of the necessity of actually removing all newcomers because of increased population and mobility at the turn of the century (*Warning Out*, 51). The practice of "returning" the names of strangers "and their qualities" to a court is first mentioned in a June 1650 law (qtd. in ibid., 47). In 1671, Boston selectmen began ordering that the names of strangers who remained in Boston despite not having been admitted as inhabitants of the town or colony be returned to the county court (*BTR* 7:58, 64, 72, 73, 77, 80, 88, 94, 96, 102, 109, 121–22, 123, 125).

13. Richard LeBaron Bowen, *Early Rehoboth: Documented Historical Studies of Families and Events in This Plymouth Colony Township*, 4 vols. (Rehoboth, Mass.: Privately printed, 1945–50), 2:139–66 (a complete set of the town's surviving warning warrants from 1694 to 1768). For men refusing the constable's job, see, for examples, Seybolt, *Town Officials*, 270, 273–74, 276, 303, 310n716. For Salem, see Benton, *Warning Out*, 36, 56.

14. Hartog, "Public Law," 292; Benton, *Warning Out*, 60–61 (on Middlesex County); Bowen, *Early Rehoboth*, 2:153. For less than fourteen days, see *BTR* 11:99; 15:103. Sample Roxbury and Stoughton warrants are SF 85713, 88370, 88354, 88984. Boston used the term *caution* only in the 1670s; *Records of the Suffolk County Court, 1671–1680* (Boston: Colonial Society of Massachusetts, 1933), 424, 594. It is not clear why lawmakers chose fourteen days for the statutory waiting period between first warning and optional removal.

15. Audience: Shurtleff, ed., *Records of the Governor and Company*, 3:205. For the 1701 change: *Acts and Resolves*, 1:452. The captain was to deliver his passenger list to the impost officer (or forfeit £5); the impost officer was to transmit all lists to the town clerk; and the clerk was to "lay all such lists . . . before the selectmen at their next meeting." For examples of captains or ship-owners agreeing or being ordered to return unacceptable passengers to their point of origin (even before they had disembarked in Boston), see *BTR* 19:61, 70–71; 20:266, 294.

16. *Acts and Resolves*, 2:337. An awkwardly worded 1722 law lamented that many vessels arrived in ports where no impost officer was resident, so that no vetting of passengers occurred

at disembarkation point. This statute made the town where the passengers landed responsible for their upkeep (if infirm or indigent), thus giving officials in coastal towns extra incentive to lobby that ship captains be the first line of defense (*Acts and Resolves*, 2:244). This route to residency was quickly closed down, as the 1722 law was repealed in 1724, a fact missed by Kunal M. Parker, "State, Citizenship, and Territory: The Legal Construction of Immigrants in Antebellum Massachusetts," *Law and History Review* 19 (Fall 2001), 589.

17. Obtruding: SF 11927, 12620 (1710s Boston warning lists); *Acts and Resolves*, 1:451 (preamble to the 1701 Act), Bowen, *Early Rehoboth*, 2:145–65; Ann S. Lainhart, "Weston Cautions 1757 to 1803," *NEHGR* 144 (July 1990), 217 ("one Benjamin Stimson a man in very low Circumstances intruded him Self into my House"). June 1723 law: *Acts and Resolves*, 2:283. A February 1736/37 law reduced the time frame for notification to twenty days and the fine to forty shillings (ibid., 2:835). Ross: *BTR* 15:320, and, for other examples, see 55, 63, 103.

18. Note that the directive to identify those in low circumstances came not from the Massachusetts statutes but from some towns' explicit orders. Benton makes a similar point and emphasizes that towns apparently varied in whether they made it a practice to warn all newcomers or just those showing signs of near poverty; Benton, *Warning Out*, 55–62.

19. The records of Boston, Wrentham, Rehoboth, and other Massachusetts towns illustrate that many residents heeded the notification law and that selectmen imposed fines when landlords flouted the requirement. In Boston throughout the century, residents either sent slips to the selectmen or appeared before them in person to give notice of strangers they had taken in. For a contrasting view of notification policies as draconian measures to punish townsmen who wished to hire outsiders as laborers, see Barry Levy, *Town Born: The Political Economy of New England from Its Founding to the Revolution* (Philadelphia: University of Pennsylvania Press, 2009), 40–45.

20. Lainhart, "Weston Cautions," 215, 216. Some of these notifications can be read as residents' bids that their lodgers be admitted to permanent inhabitancy or at least not carried out of town. For narratives that offer detailed migration histories, see *BTR* 17:19–20; 19:62–63, 89.

21. Bowen, *Early Rehoboth*, 2:190.

22. Ibid., 157.

23. "Notable woman": ibid., 148; the man with one cow was shipwright John Killey, Jr., who was accompanied by his wife and one child: ibid., 152.

24. Esther L. Friend, "Notifications and Warnings Out: Strangers Taken into Wrentham, Massachusetts, Between 1732 and 1812 [Part 1]," *NEHGR* 141 (July 1987), 189.

25. Bowen, *Early Rehoboth*, 2:192. This landlord understood the provincial law of settlement—the one-year residency clock for an apprentice did not start until he or she ended the term of apprenticeship.

26. Cato, notification dated May 14, 1759: Lainhart, "Weston Cautions," 215; two-year-old Mary Cory: ibid., 217 (Aug. 28, 1764).

27. *BTR* 20:237 (Nov. 12, 1766).

28. Bowen, *Early Rehoboth*, 2:218 (June 15, 1767).

29. Lainhart, "Weston Cautions," 218–19, 217; as Isaac Jones of Weston put it: "this is to give you notice if you Pleas to warn them out" (218). Nonstigmatizing: Alden M. Rollins, *Vermont: Warnings Out*, 2 vols. (Rockport, Me.: Picton Press, 1995–97), 1:7.

30. A 1735 law acknowledging the special conditions of the port towns of Boston and Salem gave overseers of the poor therein the same power that selectmen had to warn out "all intruders" and back up those warnings with physical removal. In practice, we do not find the Boston

overseers making warnings. See *Acts and Resolves*, 2:758; Gary B. Nash, *The Urban Crucible: Social Change, Political Consciousness, and the Origins of the American Revolution* (Cambridge, Mass.: Harvard University Press, 1979), 126.

31. Town population: G. B. Warden, *Boston, 1689–1770* (Boston: Little, Brown, 1970), 16; Allan Kulikoff, "The Progress of Inequality in Revolutionary Boston," *WMQ* 28 (July 1971), table 5, 393. *BTR* 7:135, 190 (seat of trade), 241 (populous town). The 1701 law included for the first time a criminal penalty—one familiar from the English poor laws—for any stranger removed from town by warrant; if they "presume[d] to return back, and obtrude him- or herselfe" by residing there again, he or she was to "be proceeded against as a vagabond"; *Acts and Revolves*, 1:453. Any such prosecutions would have been at the level of justice of the peace, and records for this do not survive.

32. "A List of Several Persons Returned by the Countie Court . . . [1670/71–1700]," Bonds for Securities Against Strangers, MHS. Fleet: *BTR* 23:106.

33. Lawrence M. Friedman, *A History of American Law*, 2nd ed. (New York: Simon and Schuster, 1985), 90. On the warned who remained, see William Pencak, *War, Politics, and Revolution in Provincial Massachusetts* (Boston: Northeastern University Press, 1981), 202, 211n66; and Friend, "Notifications and Warnings Out," 186. For equations of warning with removal or barring of residence, see Levy, *Town Born*, 39–40, 108–10. Levy finds that in rural towns, unmarried or newly married men who were warned rarely settled in the town, and if they had wed a town resident, the couple moved elsewhere (chap. 3).

34. The only difference between almshouse admissions of town and province poor was that in the latter case, approval of the selectmen was needed in addition to the say-so of two overseers. For more on the origins and the operation of the province account, see Chapter 3 of this volume.

35. The salience of the province account to the warning of strangers is often not recognized by historians. Only on the final two pages of his book did Benton explain that the colony covered the relief of those warned; Benton, *Warning Out*, 120–21. Barry Levy incorrectly asserts that a statewide poor account did not exist until 1793 (*Town Born*, 293). Exceptions are: Carl Bridenbaugh, *Cities in Revolt: Urban Life in America, 1743–1776* (New York: Alfred A. Knopf, 1955), 319–20; Steven Edward Wiberly Jr., "Four Cities: Public Poor Relief in Urban America, 1700–1775" (Ph.D. diss., Yale University, 1975), 54–55 (slightly misreading the 1701 provision); and Parker, "State, Citizenship, and Territory," 590 (characterizing colonial-era expenditure on the province poor as insignificant). For other New England jurisdictions with province and state poor accounts, see Rollins, *Vermont: Warnings Out*, 1:9; and Edward Warren Capen, *The Historical Development of the Poor Law in Connecticut* (New York: Columbia University Press, 1905), 43–44, 81–86.

36. Atkinson: *BTR* 17:92. Others had brought with them £50, "nearly" £200, and £200–300 sterling, or "Effects Sufficient to Indemnify the Town according to Law"; ibid., 15:53. In all, we find twelve such admissions not necessitating bondsmen from Feb. 1737 to May 1751; see *BTR* 15:28, 59, 60, 304, 351; 17:19, 20, 41, 114, 262. The occupations of this group included ironmonger, stationer/bookbinder, wool comber, peruke maker, saddler, wheelwright, and trader.

37. Admitted, with bondsmen: *BTR* 11:26, 221; 13:80, 101, 164, 191; 15:3, 9, 14, 20, 34, 57–58, 78, 207, 255, 288, 299, 301; 17:13–14 (Thomas White), 27, 92, 102. The bond was to indemnify the town for five years; for family groups, the amount averaged about £30 per person. Among those who procured bondsmen (without putting up their own money or assets), occupations included blacksmith, carver, clothier, cooper, cordwainer, cutler, distiller, hatter, locksmith, mariner,

schoolteacher, tailor, tallow chandler, ticket porter, weaver, wheelwright, wig maker, and one cleric (Reverend Samuel Osborne). We have found only two town admissions after 1749 (*BTR* 17:262; 20:111), indicating new caution on the part of the selectmen in the face of the town's economic distress. To avoid warning and to guarantee they could live independently, some newcomers posted security: *BTR* 19:156–57 (Scipio, free negro, with lawyer Benjamin Kent as bondsman).

38. *BTR* 11:78, 13:165, 261, 276, 289, 304; 15:3, 27, 92, 186–187, 224, 237, 240, 320, 322, 350; 17:18, 19. A shop or trade (milliner) was mentioned in only two cases.

39. See *BTR* 10:62; 13: 317–18 (deserters); 15:198–201 (quotation p. 198), 314 (St. Christopher's to Louisburg), 337–43 (illegal trade suspected; quotations pp. 337, 343), 355–57; 17:61 (Maginel), 67, 83 (quarantine); 19:103 (deserter in 1759). More than one man claimed to have come for a few months "to perfect himself in the English Tongue" (*BTR* 15:201, 342), and others had "a Suit in the Law here" (ibid., 356, and see also 200). For the December 1692 "Act for the preventing of Danger by the French residing within this Province," see *Acts and Resolves*, 1:90. For a Frenchman in 1744 who initially kept to his lodgings "for fear of being made a prisoner of war," see Carl Bridenbaugh, ed., *Gentleman's Progress: The Itinerarium of Dr. Alexander Hamilton, 1744* (Chapel Hill: University of North Carolina Press, 1948), 129 (quotation), 140.

40. Robinson: *BTR* 11:226 (April 19, 1715). For face-to-face meetings, see 10:113; 11:215, 238. *BTR* 7:201 (Williams); 11:46, 53, 57 (doubled warnings); 13:85–86 (Marion); 17:36 (practicable). Warnings in 1715–16 were made in person by the selectmen (SF 10569, 10766, 10961). In 1718, the town clerk began to use the phrase "warned by the Order of the Selectmen," indicating that the warning was often made by their designee (SF 12463, 12620). Until the 1730s, the returns are wholly in the handwriting of the town clerk. Dates of various warnings from the 1710s forward confirm they were issued by warners because the selectmen did not meet on that day.

41. Hogreeves were responsible for rounding up stray pigs. On minor town offices, see Edward M. Cook Jr., *The Fathers of the Towns: Leadership and Community Structure in Eighteenth-Century New England* (Baltimore: Johns Hopkins University Press, 1976), 28–33; and Susan Allport, *Sermons in Stone: The Stone Walls of New England and New York* (New York: W. W. Norton, 1990), 54–55. For warners, we have estimated some of these ages, assuming age twenty-five at marriage. One younger person was appointed—Cornelius Thayer, at around age thirty-five.

42. *BTR* 15:50 (keep an account); 17:13 (laws transgressed), 44, 299–300 (province law to be reprinted); 19:43 (copy for the overseers). At first, the town's warning ledger may have been chronological. In 1758, the selectmen ordered that the book be alphabetical; *BTR* 19:83–84. For a 1736 effort to reprint the laws "in the Publick Newspapers," see *BTR* 13:283.

43. Savell: *BTR* 15:363; in chastising him, the selectmen named the page (2) in the current law book where the relevant statute could be found. For Williston, see *BTR* 17:13, 21, 98; Seybolt, *Town Officials*, 228, 231n525, 235; Thwing database 62036. His replacement: *BTR* 17:36. On Larrabee: *BTR* 17:44 (quotation), 56 (salary), 91. For a few months in 1756–57 and again in 1762, two persons were appointed simultaneously as warners; *BTR* 19:48–49, 198. Of course, having a solo warner had the practical effect that no official had to check if a newcomer had already been warned by someone else. Over the colonial period, the only hint that the selectmen ever considered assigning warning by neighborhood came in Larrabee's initial job instructions, which were to warn "Northward of the Draw bridge in Boston"; *BTR* 17:44. However, since Larrabee ended up serving alone for thirteen years, he surely did not confine his warnings to half the town.

44. Adams's appointment: *BTR* 19:55. Testimony by Joseph Adams describing "Sundry times in the summer A.D. 1766," MS f Bos. 7, Boston Town Papers, 7:106, BPL. Adams's neglect (*BTR*

20:130–31) is seen in gaps between roughly 1757 and 1764 in which no strangers with surnames starting in common letters such as *B* (with first vowel *a*) were entered under Adams's name in the Warning Out book, 1745–70.

45. Nash, *Urban Crucible*, 185, 253–54. For increases in the number warned as a percentage of every thousand residents of the town, see Kulikoff, "Progress of Inequality," table 9, 400.

46. Other counties in the province experienced surges in the numbers warned; see Douglas Lamar Jones, "Poverty and Vagabondage: The Process of Survival in Eighteenth-Century Massachusetts," *NEHGR* 133 (Oct. 1979), 245; and Douglas Lamar Jones, "The Strolling Poor: Transiency in Eighteenth-Century Massachusetts," *Journal of Social History* 8 (Spring 1975), 33, table 3.

47. Harsh: J. H. Elliott, *Empires of the Atlantic World: Britain and Spain in America, 1492–1830* (New Haven: Yale University Press, 2006), 262–63; *Acts and Resolves*, 5:911–12. Some towns interpreted the 1767 law as a call to intensify the recording of strangers; see Friend, "Notifications and Warnings Out," 185. After the law took effect, constables were no longer under pressure to find and warn sojourners within a year of their arrival.

Chapter 2. The Warner

1. The Loves probably lived in Ballymoney, given that a Robert Love served as a synod commissioner from that parish in 1692; Charles Knowles Bolton, *Scotch Irish Pioneers in Ulster and America* (Baltimore: Genealogical Publishing 1986; first published 1910), 358. Our estimate of Robert's birth year is based on his obituary notices, which posit he was seventy-seven at death in April 1774. For Richie Love's marriage, see *Boston Marrs.*, 1:83. On Thomas Bridge and his traveling in Europe as a youth and preaching stints at Port Royal, Jamaica, and West Jersey prior to 1705, see Arthur Blake Ellis, *History of the First Church in Boston, 1630–1880* (Boston: Hall and Whiting, 1881), 160–64, and William A. Warden, *The Ancestors, Kin and Descendants of John Warden and Narcissa (Davis) Warden, His Wife . . .* (Worcester, Mass.: Maynard-Gough, 1901), 83.

2. Ethel Stanwood Bolton, *Immigrants to New England 1700–1775* (Baltimore: Genealogical Publishing, 1979), 14–15; Emily Wilder Leavitt, *The Blair Family History of New England* (Boston: D. Clapp and Son, 1900), 135–36, 150; and SCPF 6859 for William Blair. For the warning: *BTR* 13:46; SF 12620.

3. Patrick Griffin, *The People with No Name: Ireland's Ulster Scots, America's Scots Irish, and the Creation of a British Atlantic World, 1689–1764* (Princeton, N.J.: Princeton University Press, 2001); Richard Hofstadter, *America at 1750: A Social Portrait* (New York: Alfred A. Knopf, 1971), 25–27. For details on the 1716–20 Boston arrivals, see R. J. Dickson, *Ulster Emigration to Colonial America, 1718–1775* (London: Routledge and Kegan Paul, 1966), 21–24; and Jane Bramwell, "Irish Immigration to New England, 1714–1722: An Early Example of the Emigrant Trade" (M.A. thesis, University of Miami, 1995), 1–13.

4. There is a single reference to an earlier Robert Love in New England—on a list entitled "The Names of such persons in Brantery [Braintree] who have taken the oath of Allegiance," around October 1678; *Records of the Suffolk County Court, 1671–1680* (Publications of the Colonial Society of Massachusetts, *Collections*, vols. 29–30) (Boston, 1933), 973 (in vol. 30; the two volumes have continuous pagination). It is possible that this was Richie and Robert's father.

5. Robert Love, "his dep[osition] As to people who lived at Rowsick," SF 15770. Love's presence in the area is confirmed by his witnessing a mortgage executed at Georgetown on Feb. 18, 1720/21; *York Deeds*, 18 vols. (Portland, Me.: John T. Hull, 1884–), 10: fol. 180. Timber: Samuel Penhallow, *The History of the Wars of New-England, with the Eastern Indians . . .* (Boston: T. Fleet, 1726), 82.

6. For recruitment of Ulster Scots to the area, see R. H. Akagi, *The Town Proprietors of the New England Colonies: A Study of Their Development, Organization, Activities and Controversies, 1620–1770* (Gloucester, Mass.: P. Smith, 1963, first published 1924), 259–62; and Robert Earle Moody, "The Maine Frontier, 1607 to 1763" (Ph.D. diss., Yale University, 1933). We are grateful to Emerson Baker for advice on the early history of the Kennebec River area.

7. This and the following paragraphs draw on the court documents, including depositions from Abraham Ayers, Thomas Newman, and Luke Noyce (a servant or apprentice of Newman), printed in Charles T. Libby, Robert E. Moody, and Neal W. Allen, eds., *Province and Court Records of Maine*, 6 vols. (Portland: Maine Historical Society, 1928–75), 6:91–92, 103–9.

8. A third incident occurred two days later, when the innkeeper John Butler "passt through the Town with a drawn Sword and a Pistol and declared . . . that he would kill Tho: Newman if he could & that then he should have a fair Tryal for his life"; ibid., 104.

9. Ibid., 106–9. On the fluidity of claiming the label *merchant* in the early part of the century, see Bernard Bailyn and Lotte Bailyn, *Massachusetts Shipping, 1697–1714: A Statistical Study* (Cambridge, Mass.: Belknap Press of Harvard University Press, 1959), 57–58.

10. Myself captive: SF 15770. Barbarous and riotous: *Province and Court Records of Maine*, 6:106. The raid occurred on June 13, 1722; Emma Lewis Coleman, *New England Captives Carried to Canada Between 1677 and 1760 During the French and Indian Wars*, 2 vols. (Portland, Me.: Southworth Press, 1925), 2:133–39. It was a precursor to the French-English conflict known as Governor Dummer's war, fought over who would control settlement of northern New England lands, especially along the Kennebec.

11. Coleman, *New England Captives*, 2:139–44, 418–23; Kenneth M. Morrison, *The Embattled Northeast: The Elusive Ideal of Alliance in Abenaki-Euramerican Relations* (Berkeley: University of California Press, 1984), 185.

12. *Journals of the House of Representatives of Massachusetts*, 52 vols. (Boston: Massachusetts Historical Society, 1919–86), 5:327, 335; 6:35. At one point, two house members from Essex County, John Turner and Symond Epes, Esq., spoke on Love's behalf, stressing "his great Misfortunes and [the] Necessities to which he was reduced by reason of his late Captivity among the Eastern Indians" (6:71–72). For payments to the other captives (including a reward for a man who offered his journal of "Observations &C. of the Indians and French during his Captivity"), see Coleman, *New England Captives*, 2:142–44; and *Journals of the House*, 5:186, 265, 270–71; 6:187, 191, 197–98. In 1724, with Love freed and Trescott still held in Montreal, Love sent Trescott a letter informing him that one of the captive Indian sachems had died in Boston prison; Coleman, *New England Captives*, 2:140–41. With his brother Richie, in December 1723 Robert Love had an unrelated petition approved: *Journal of the House*, 4:77, 104, 143; *Acts and Resolves*, 10:242.

13. He briefly became the joint owner of 240 acres in Barrington but evidently did not hold this tract long; Deed conveying 240 acres in Barrington from Robert Armstrong to Robert Love and James Boyd for £10 of current New England money, Feb. 1, 1726/27, Portsmouth, New Hampshire, New Hampshire deeds, 15:193–95, microfilmed card index, NEHGS.

14. Neither was Love one of several persons admitted as inhabitants with useful trades, upon posting a £100 bond; for examples, see *BTR* 13:165, 170. In SF (MA Archives), there is a gap in the

lists of warned strangers returned between April and May 1727 (for these, see *BTR* 13:167–68) and late spring 1734 (SF 20510, 37760). Town authorities sometimes referred to a newcomer who had been warned and who continued to reside in town as "under warning." For examples, see *BTR* 11:78; 15:36, 205–6; 17:89.

15. SCPF 4918, Richie Love. Richie died insolvent, with the expenses of raising his sons and paying his creditors outweighing the worth of his personal property, which was £59. The first clear documentation of Robert's being "of Boston" is his signing as a bondsman in August 1728, when a new administrator took over the probating of Richie Love's estate, but he had probably moved there by late 1727. For Robert Love, tailor, as guardian, see SCPF 5932. For Copia's remarriage and death, see William Richard Cutter, ed., *Historic Homes and Places and Genealogical and Personal Memoirs Relating to the Families of Middlesex County, Massachusetts*, 4 vols. (New York: Lewis Historical Publishing, 1908), 2:403.

16. All of the Loves' children were baptized at the First Church except Ann. Baptisms, First Church records, Boston Ch. Recs. database. The children's deaths were not recorded but can be inferred from the absence of their names in other records and from the distribution of their father's estate.

17. The Presbyterian congregation met at first in a barn on Long Lane—not far from Robert and Rachel's lodgings in the South End. On Moorehead, see Frederick Lewis Weis, *The Colonial Clergy and the Colonial Churches of New England* (Baltimore: Genealogical Publishing, 1977, first published Lancaster, Mass., 1936), 144.

18. *BTR* 20:129. First Church records, Boston Ch. Recs. database.

19. William Richie Love, SCPF 11771. The personal estate was appraised at £152, and a net of £67 remained after legacies, debts, and fees were paid. Robert Love evidently did not take the lead in the routine settling of this estate; the other executor wrote up the accounts.

20. *Hugh Vans, merchant, v. Robert Love, trader*, 1731, SF 32057 (Auchmuty pleads for Love); Love suing cooper Samuel Burnall for £7 in 1736, SF 44425; mariner Daniel Malcolm sued the Love brothers in 1761 for £17 on a promissory note, SF 81752; *Robert Auchmuty, gentleman, v. Robert Love, yeoman*, 1763, SF 172,687; *Auchmuty v. David Love*, cases in 1757 and 1758, SF 78330, 82182.

21. Account, *Robert Love, yeoman, v. John Barker*, 1756, SF 75866.

22. Love fits the profile that Joyce M. Ellis draws for many inhabitants of England's eighteenth-century towns: they "regarded their occupations as fluid and flexible rather than fixed for the whole of their working lives"; *The Georgian Town, 1680–1840* (London: Palgrave, 2001), 55. Records exist only for Love's purchase of "the half of the third Division" for £25 from Joshua Olds in 1740; Hampshire County Deeds, K366 1740, Hampshire District Registry of Deeds, Northampton, Mass. Even as an absentee owner, Love could be styled a yeoman in legal documents, as was the case in 1756 (as plaintiff, SF 75866) and 1763 (as defendant, SF 172,687). In Love's probate inventories, the land was valued at £102; SCPF 16150.

23. *BTR* 20:222, 264. For renewals, see SF 89125, 89250. Love's nephew Billey had a similar license which Billey's widow, Margaret Ross Love, took up in her own name in 1758, after her husband's death; *Journals of the House*, vol. 34, pt. 2, 439.

24. Petition dated Feb. 17, 1763 MS Bos 11, Boston Town Records, Loose Papers, BPL.

25. According to historian Carole Shammas, 59 percent of Boston residents on the 1798 federal tax rolls were listed as renters; personal communication, March 3, 2013.

26. Inventory dated March 17, 1777, SCPF 16150. Undifferentiated "house linen" was valued at £5.12.0. For illustrations of armchairs, see *The Great River: Art and Society of the Connecticut Valley, 1635–1820* (Hartford, Conn.: Wadsworth Atheneum, 1985), 192–93, 207–9.

27. For a description of tavern furnishings and services, see Sharon V. Salinger, *Taverns and Drinking in Early America* (Baltimore: Johns Hopkins University Press, 2002), chap. 2.

28. The mahogany desk was valued at forty-eight shillings, another "desk" at twenty shillings, and a small desk at twelve shillings. The only other pieces of furniture similar in value to the mahogany desk were a chest of drawers and table appraised together for eighty shillings.

29. Historians often cite a 1729 mob's prevention of the landing of passengers from an immigrant ship from Ireland as evidence of New England settlers' anti-Irish prejudice, but the episode needs to be weighed against the life stories of individual settlers from Ireland. Richard Hofstadter combines the 1729 incident with a misinterpretation of the routine warning in Boston (but not expulsion) of new arrivals from Ireland from 1719 onward; *America in 1750*, 26–27. Carl Bridenbaugh draws a more nuanced portrait in *Cities in the Wilderness: Urban Life in America, 1625–1742* (New York: Capricorn Books, 1964, first published 1938), 250–51.

30. Warn, s.v., *Dictionary of the Older Scottish Tongue* (New York: Oxford University Press, 2003), 12:37. We are grateful to Margo Todd for suggesting this source. On early modern notarial practice, see J. Maitland Thomson, *The Public Records of Scotland* (Glasgow: Maclehose, Jackson and Co., 1922), chap. 4; Donna Merwick, *Death of a Notary: Conquest and Change in Colonial New York* (Ithaca, N.Y.: Cornell University Press, 1999), esp. 187–90; and Laurie Nussdorfer, *Brokers of Public Trust: Notaries in Early Modern Rome* (Baltimore: Johns Hopkins University Press, 2009).

31. Richard L. Bushman, *King and People in Provincial Massachusetts* (Chapel Hill: Omohundro Institute of Early American History and Culture and University of North Carolina Press, 1992); Brendan McConville, *The King's Three Faces: The Rise and Fall of Royal America, 1688 to 1776* (Chapel Hill: Omohundro Institute of Early American History and Culture and University of North Carolina Press, 2006).

32. Sweetser served as constable in 1746. In June 1772, he was included as one of the gentlemen invited to attend the visitation of the free schools; *BTR* 23:133. For his land transactions, see Thwing database 56941. In holding no prior or concurrent town offices, Love was unlike all the men who had served as warners since 1690. Thayer had served as clerk of the market for ten years, measurer of wheat for one year, and sealer of leather from 1758 to 1764 (Seybolt, *Town Officials*, 264–309, passim); on the Thayers, see Thwing database 57414; and Boston Ch. Recs. database. For Peirce (1723–92), see *BTR* 20:265; and Thwing database 49738 and 49742.

33. *Boston Marrs.*, 2:38, 346; obituary: *Boston Post-Boy*, Nov. 8, 1773, 3. Bookkeeper, yeoman: SF 75345, 78330, 82616. For the Watts-Love suit, see SF 84347. Ebenezer Love became the Speaker of the assembly in the Bahamas in 1768, two years before his death there; *Boston Evening-Post*, Aug. 25, 1766, 2; *Boston Post-Boy*, May 14, 1770, 3. In the margins of her second administrator's account, Ann Love noted the debt due from David's estate, implying it was a nonrecoverable asset; SCPF 16150.

34. Boston Ch. Recs. database; Emmons as landlord, living on Milk Street: Robert Love's warning records, Feb. 18, 1765; 1784 petition: SF 95586. Samuel Emmons made no appearance in the 1771 tax valuation, or in Suffolk County deeds and probate records. Three of his daughters never married—an indication of the uneven sex ratio in Boston in the late 1700s; one, Rachel Jr., died in 1816 with a net worth of $3,500; SCPF 25131.

35. Ray: New South, Boston Ch. Recs. database: for her marriage and baptism of one son; for her obituary, see *Independent Chronicle* [Boston], Nov. 18, 1791, 3.

36. *BTR* 25:9, 192; SF 93675, 95587. Her obituary appeared in two Boston papers, the *Independent Chronicle* and the *Columbian Centinel*, and in the *Massachusetts Spy* (Worcester), in their

issues dated Oct. 6 or Oct. 11, 1792. At his death, Robert owed Ann £30 by the deceased's "Own [Account] Books" and £5 by a note; SCPF 16150. In probate documents, Ann's name is sometimes given as Anna.

37. *Boston Marrs.*, 2:25; Thwing database 6833; SCPF 14653; West Church baptisms, Boston Ch. Recs. database; Samuel Bradlee Doggett, comp., *History of the Bradlee Family, with Particular Reference to the Descendants of Nathan Bradley, of Dorchester, Mass.* (Boston: Rockwell and Churchill, 1878), 10–24; *Boston Cems.*, 541 (Granary Burial Ground). Robert Love also served as bondsman when Agnes became guardian of her son Samuel; SCPF 14652.

38. SCPF 16150. That the Monson land sold in 1779 for £223 (lawful money) prevented insolvency; as with many modest estates of the time, Love's £117 in debts plus the costs of settling the estate exceeded the value of his movables. Construction artisans (whose median personal wealth was £60 in pounds sterling, N = 19): Gary B. Nash, *The Urban Crucible: Social Change, Political Consciousness, and the Origins of the American Revolution* (Cambridge, Mass.: Harvard University Press, 1979), 314, and see figures 7–8 on 415–16. For the 1771 valuation's missing 225 polls in Ward 12, where Love lived, see James A. Henretta, "Economic Development and Social Structure in Colonial Boston," *WMQ* 22 (Jan. 1965), 82. Conversion to pounds sterling is based on Alice Hanson Jones's formula for Massachusetts province currency in 1774; *Wealth of a Nation to Be: The American Colonies on the Eve of the Revolution* (New York: Columbia University Press, 1980), 9.

39. Alfred F. Young, "George Robert Twelves Hewes (1742–1840): A Boston Shoemaker and the Memory of the American Revolution," in *The Shoemaker and the Tea Party: Memory and the American Revolution* (Boston: Beacon Press, 1999), 18, 28–29. For correlation of wealth and life-cycle stage, see Jackson T. Main, *The Social Structure of Revolutionary America* (Princeton, N.J.: Princeton University Press, 1965) and Jones, *Wealth of a Nation to Be*, 381–88.

40. Young, "George Robert Twelves Hewes," 31–32, 36–57, 67–68, 75–77. Voting requirements: G. B. Warden, *Boston, 1689–1772* (Boston: Little, Brown, 1970), 42; Robert J. Dinkin, *Voting in Provincial America: A Study of Elections in the Thirteen Colonies, 1689–1776* (Westport, Conn.: Greenwood Press, 1977), 39–42. One needed £40 in rateable estate to vote in colony-wide elections. Only certain types of property were rated at the province level; see Robin L. Einhorn, *American Taxation, American Slavery* (Chicago: University of Chicago Press, 2006), 65–75.

41. Number of voters: Alan Day and Catherine Day, "Another Look at the Boston Caucus," *Journal of American Studies* 5 (April 1971), 27–28. Our calculation assumes that adult males made up 22 percent of the town's population of 15,500. On "the Body of the People," see Nash, *Urban Crucible*, 356–62; Warden, *Boston*, 218–20, 243; and Richard D. Brown, *Revolutionary Politics in Massachusetts: The Boston Committee of Correspondence and the Towns, 1772–1774* (New York: W. W. Norton, 1976, first published 1970), 161–62.

42. Urban gradations: P. J. Corfield, *The Impact of English Towns, 1700–1800* (New York: Oxford University Press, 1982), 132–38. Rowe, a onetime selectman, recorded the names of those in attendance at civic and private dinners and other elite social gatherings he was present at, never mentioning Robert Love; for examples, see *Rowe Diary*, 116, 125–26, 129, 133, 139, 148, 149, 169, 174–75, 178–79, 185. Ruffles: Young, "George Robert Twelves Hewes," 56. In contrast to shoemaker George Hewes, Love was not among the five hundred men at the August 14, 1769, Sons of Liberty dinner in Dorchester ("An Alphabetical List of the Sons of Liberty, Aug. 14, 1769 . . . ," Miscellaneous Bound Collections, MHS).

43. Gillian B. Anderson, "The Funeral of Samuel Cooper," *New England Quarterly* 50 (Dec. 1977), 650; T. H. Breen, *The Marketplace of Revolution: How Consumer Politics Shaped American*

Independence (New York: Oxford University Press, 2004), 213–17; Alice Morse Earle, *Customs and Fashions in Old New England* (Rutland, Vt.: Charles E. Tuttle, 1973, first published New York, 1893), 379–80.

44. Unlike the estates of the likely pallbearers, Love's was not sufficient for the purchase of rings and gloves for the mourners. Love's most substantial debts were to Jackson (£49), Bradford (£31), and Ann Love. When Ann took out letters of administration, Bradford and Sever served as bondsmen. The estate paid £2.18.0 for two coffins (one was for widow Rachel, who died soon after her husband) and £2.17.6 for "the gravediggers, etc."; SCPF 16150.

45. Eaton; *Essex Gazette* [Salem], July 26, 1774, 3. On obituaries of illustrious locals, see Charles E. Clark, *The Public Prints: The Newspaper in Anglo-American Culture, 1665–1740* (New York: Oxford University Press, 1994), 223–28, 231.

46. Isaiah Thomas, *The History of Printing in America* . . . , 2nd ed. (Worcester, Mass.: American Antiquarian Society, 1874), 1:145–47.

47. *Boston News-Letter*, April 28, 1774, 3. The first line of this obituary (or a variant) appeared in four additional papers, in issues published between May 2 and 5 (*Boston Evening-Post, Boston Post-Boy, Massachusetts Spy,* and *Essex Gazette*). In the last, Love's obituary appeared with those of only two other Bostonians of the several whose deaths had been announced in the previous week. This indicates that the Salem printer knew or knew of Robert Love and believed that some of his readers would wish to learn of his death. Of about eighty death notices for town residents published in the *News-Letter* in the previous year, only four included a character description.

48. "Refinement," *Universal Magazine* [London] 77 (December 1785), 288–89, qtd. in Richard Godbeer, *The Overflowing of Friendship: Love Between Men and the Creation of the American Republic* (Baltimore: Johns Hopkins University Press, 2009), 70; "acts of humanity": William Livingston to Noah Wells, Dec. 16, 1751, Johnson Family Papers, Yale University Library, qtd. in ibid., 63. For elegies, see Earle, *Customs and Fashions*, 365–67.

Chapter 3. Origins

1. Valentin Groebner, *Who Are You? Identification, Deception, and Surveillance in Early Modern Europe* (New York: Zone Books, 2007), 204. The same traveler described a similar system in Geneva in 1595 involving metal badges rather than tickets (ibid., 203). Similarly, the dukes of Ferrara demanded to be informed each day of the travelers lodging overnight in the jurisdiction (25). At the national level, seventeenth-century French royal decrees prohibited anyone from leaving the country without permission, and Spain implemented elaborate vetting and certification of emigrants to New Spain in order to prevent Moors, Jews, and others perceived as dangerous sorts from becoming settlers (201, 191–93).

2. Ibid., 200. For the curfew, see *Acts and Resolves*, 1:535; *BTR* 17:24, 26. While interned in Massachusetts, Acadians were required by law to have written permission from the selectmen when they went beyond town boundaries, although enforcement was probably spotty; Richard G. Lowe, "Massachusetts and the Acadians," *WMQ* 25 (April 1968), 219.

3. Groebner, *Who Are You?* 229, 232, 201, 50–51 (Nuremberg), 178–79 (Bern). The registers ordered by the synod of Salzburg perhaps came closest to a full accounting of a city's population; they were to include parish members by age and status, births, and deaths, but also immigrants and those who moved away (200–201). For methods of marking the poor in cities such as Grenoble, Rouen, Lyons, and Valladolid, see Bronislaw Geremek, *Poverty: A History*, trans. Agnieszka Kolakowska (Cambridge, Mass.: Blackwell, 1994), 148–63.

4. John Torpey notes that divergent histories of state-building in Europe, including variation in registration approaches, are reflected in language. English lacks "equivalents for the German *'erfassen'* [to grasp, as in register] and the French verb *'surveiller'* "; "Revolutions and Freedom of Movement: An Analysis of Passport Controls in the French, Russian, and Chinese Revolutions," *Theory and Society* 26 (Dec. 1997), 842.

5. Josiah Henry Benton, *Warning Out in New England, 1656–1817* (Boston: W. B. Clarke, 1911; repr., Bowie, Md.: Heritage Books, 1992), 4–5, quoting Francis Palgrave, *The Rise and Progress of the English Commonwealth* (London: J. Murray, 1832), pt. 1, 83, on the laws of the Salic Franks. James Stephen Taylor similarly believes that the earliest settlement restrictions can be seen "in the laws of Anglo-Saxon kings" and seventh-century practices of hospitality to travelers; James Stephen Taylor, "The Impact of Pauper Settlement, 1691–1834," *Past and Present* 73 (Nov. 1976), 47–48. Born in Vermont, Benton (1843–1916) was the son of a congregational minister and a descendant of early New England settlers, about whom he wrote genealogies. Called Colonel because of his service in the Union army, he practiced law in Vermont and New Hampshire before settling in Boston in 1873. He lectured on railroads and corporations at the Boston University Law School and published several books on historical subjects. See H. L. Motter, ed., *The International Who's Who in the World, 1912* (New York: International Who's Who Publishing, 1911), 117; *New England Medical Gazette*, 52 (March 1917), 171; and Walter Muir Whitehill, *Boston Public Library: A Centennial History* (Cambridge, Mass.: Harvard University Press, 1956), 166.

6. Ex officio c. D. Thomas Morgan, chaplain of Eastchurch (Canterbury 1492), KAO, Act book P.R.C. 3.1, f.26: "Postea judex decrevit et monuit predictum dominum Thomam quod amoveat se ab ista jurisdictione citra festum Michaelis [Afterward, the judge decreed and warned the aforesaid Master Thomas that he remove himself from that very jurisdiction before the feast of (Saint) Michael]." Richard Helmholz, personal communication, Feb. 5, 2007, enclosing his transcription of five cases. In the four other cases, a verb such as "recedat" was used instead of monuit. Thanks to Professor Helmholz, and to Professor Allen Ward for translation.

7. Christopher Dyer, "Poverty and Its Relief in Late Medieval England," *Past and Present* 216 (Aug. 2011), 41–78; Margo Todd, *Christian Humanism and the Puritan Social Order* (New York: Cambridge University Press, 1987), chap. 5.

8. Geremek, *Poverty*, 186–205, 136–41; Todd, *Christian Humanism*, 137–46. See Geremek, *Poverty*, chaps. 3–5, for a tour-de-force synthesis of reform attempts across Europe related to poverty and for the cross-fertilization of ideas from city to city.

9. Martin Dinges, "Self-Help and Reciprocity in Parish Assistance: Bordeaux in the Sixteenth and Seventeenth Centuries," in Peregrine Horden and Richard Smith, eds., *The Locus of Care: Families, Communities, Institutions, and the Provision of Welfare since Antiquity* (London: Routledge, 1998), 111–25 (quotation p. 117). In this period, England welcomed small streams of Protestant refugees from the Continent, who then put the Reformed relief system into effect for congregants of their "Stranger churches" and influenced English puritan thinking; Paul Slack, *From Reformation to Improvement: Public Welfare in Early Modern England* (Oxford: Clarendon Press, 1999), 39, 43, 85. In Boston, Increase Mather managed to obtain a scribal copy of one of the "Disciplines" French Calvinists had used as a guide to ecclesiastical and civic government; Mather Family Papers, American Antiquarian Society, Worcester, Mass. Thanks to Robert Kingdon for telling us about the manuscript's existence.

10. Steve Hindle has written extensively on effective welfare regimes. For an early use of the concept, see Hindle, "The Birthpangs of Welfare: Poor Relief and Parish Governance in Seventeenth-Century Warwickshire," *Dugdale Society Occasional Papers*, no. 40 (2000), 4. On

Norwich, see E. M. Leonard, *The Early History of English Poor Relief* (Cambridge: Cambridge University Press, 1900), 103–7 (quotation p. 103), and appendices 2 and 3. Leonard notes that the Norwich system worked for about ten years in the utopian way that its creators had hoped for; their pride in providing better for the town's poor and in achieving fiscal efficiency comes through clearly in the mayor's books and other records (106–7).

11. Robert Jenison, *The Cities Safetie* . . . (London, 1630), 11, 29, qtd. in Slack, *From Reformation to Improvement*, 29; see also 30–31. On the fact of Geneva as a model, see William Hunt, *The Puritan Moment: The Coming of Revolution in an English County* (Cambridge, Mass.: Harvard University Press, 1983), 83–84, 252. On Geneva's policies toward the poor, see Robert M. Kingdon, "Social Welfare in Calvin's Geneva," *American Historical Review* 76 (Feb. 1971), 50–69; William C. Innes, *Social Concern in Calvin's Geneva*, ed. Susan Cembalisty-Innes (Allison Park, Pa.: Pickwick Publications, 1983); and Jeannine E. Olson, *Calvin and Social Welfare: Deacons and the "Bourse Française"* (Selinsgrove, Pa.: Susquehanna University Press, 1989). On puritan social reform, see Marjorie K. McIntosh, "Local Responses to the Poor in Late Medieval and Tudor England," *Continuity and Change* 3 (Aug. 1988), 212, 237n12; and Steve Hindle, "Exclusion Crises: Poverty, Migration and Parochial Responsibility in English Rural Communities, c. 1560–1660," *Rural History* 7 (Oct. 1996), 131–38. For an interpretation that does not stress puritans, see Anthony Fletcher, *Reform in the Provinces: The Government of Stuart England* (New Haven: Yale University Press, 1986), 351–73. For Anglican involvement, see Marjorie K. McIntosh, "Networks of Care in Elizabethan Towns: The Example of Hadleigh, Suffolk," in Horden and Smith, eds., *Locus of Care*, 75–76.

12. Leicester: Philip Styles, "The Evolution of the Law of Settlement," in Styles, *Studies in Seventeenth Century West Midlands History* (Kineton, Eng.: Roundwood Press, 1978), 178. Searchers: Leonard, *Early History of English Poor Relief*, 108; Nathaniel Bacon, *The Annalls of Ipswiche. The Lawes Customes and Government of the Same. Collected out of the Records Bookes and Writings of that Towne*, ed. William H. Richardson (Ipswich, Eng., 1884), 249, 319; see also 337, 351 (ordering weekly searches, February 1587). For searches by ward ordered by the common council of London in 1574, see Leonard, *Early History of English Poor Relief*, 307. Surrey: Helen Raine, "Christopher Fawsett Against the Inmates: An Aspect of Poor Law Administration in the Early Seventeenth Century," *Surrey Archaeological Collections* 66 (1969), 79–85 (quotation p. 80).

13. "Chargeable" was the shorthand phrase meaning a person was in need of public relief. On bonds, see McIntosh, "Local Responses to the Poor," 232–33; Styles, "Evolution of the Law of Settlement," 178–84; and Leonard, *Early History of English Poor Relief*, 109. Styles points out that many of these methods were attempts to get around the fact that prior to 1662, town officials could not legally order removals except under the vagrancy laws. Placing the burden on the landlord rather than the inmate preserved "the common law right to freedom of movement of all who could not be classed as rogues and vagabonds" (177–78). When parish officials became aggressive about ordering removals (often illegally), a tussle between local officials and supervising justices of the peace ensued, especially from 1630 to 1660 (181, 185). See also Fletcher, *Reform in the Provinces*, 202–4.

14. Norma Landau, "Who Was Subjected to the Laws of Settlement? Procedure Under the Settlement Laws in Eighteenth-Century England," *Agricultural History Review* 43, pt. 2 (1995), 139–59, and Landau, "The Application of the Laws of Settlement in Eighteenth-Century England," Working Paper Series, no. 67, Agricultural History Center, University of California, Davis, June 1992. Note that the vast majority of migrating workers rented for under £10. After

1685, newcomers not qualified for settlement were required to give notice of their presence within days of arrival, and only if they did so did the "residency" clock start; few migrants gave notice.

15. Richard Burn, *The Justice of the Peace and Parish Officer . . .* 11th ed., vol. 3 (London: W. Strahan and M. Woodfall, 1769), 285–515.

16. Miller: Nov. 2, 1767.

17. Roger Wells, "Migration, the Law, and Parochial Policy in Eighteenth- and Early-Nineteenth-Century Southern England," *Southern History* 15 (1993), 103–4, quoting "Questions to be asked on Examining Persons to their Settlement" formulated by eighteenth-century officials in the port town of Southampton. Because Massachusetts did not grant settlement on the basis of renting for a certain annual sum, or paying rates, the last four questions were irrelevant. Oaths: Styles, "Evolution of the Law of Settlement," 200. On examinations, see Norma Landau, "The Laws of Settlement and the Surveillance of Immigration in Eighteenth-Century Kent," *Continuity and Change* 3 (Dec. 1988), 400–409, 412–15.

18. Relaxation: Styles, "Evolution of the Law of Settlement," 204; Taylor, "Impact of Pauper Settlement," 55. At some English examinations, justices gave the resident two to three months to return to the home parish to get a certificate; examinations could also lead the receiving parish to dun the home parish for what historians have called nonresident relief payments. On the latter, see Wells, "Migration, the Law, and Parochial Policy," 105–7. Commons: Norma Landau, "The Regulation of Immigration, Economic Structures and Definitions of the Poor in Eighteenth-Century England," *The Historical Journal* 33 (Sep. 1990), 558–59, 562; the preamble to the 1697 Certificate Act, qtd. in Styles, "Evolution of the Law of Settlement," 190–91. K. D. M. Snell disagrees with Landau on many points; see Snell, "Pauper Settlement and the Right to Poor Relief in England and Wales," *Continuity and Change* 6 (Dec. 1991), 397–402.

19. [Richard Kilburne,] *Choice Presidents Upon all Acts of Parliament, Relating to the Office and Duty of a Justice of Peace . . .* 5th ed. (London: Printed for Mary Tonson, 1694), 385–86. Warning in this sense is not found in Burn, *Justice of the Peace and Parish Officer.* We have also searched in the removal orders in *Warwick County Records*, vol. 2, *Quarter Sessions Order Book, Michaelmas 1637 to Epiphany 1650*, ed. S. C. Ratcliff and H. C. Johnson (Warwick: L. E. Stephens, 1936–37); *Records of the Borough of Leicester . . .* , ed. Mary Bateson, rev. by W. H. Stevenson and J. E. Stocks, vol. 3 (Cambridge: C. J. Clay, 1905); and consulted legal compendia such as the 1635, 1677, and 1742 London editions of Michael Dalton, *The Country Justice . . .* ; Edmund Bott, *Decisions of the Court of King's Bench upon the Laws Relating to the Poor. Originally published by Edmund Bott, Esq. . . . Now Revised, Corrected, and Considerably Enlarged . . . The Third Edition . . .* by Francis Const, 2 vols. (London: Printed for Whieldon and Butterworth, 1793); and James Burrow, *A Series of the Decisions of the Court of King's Bench upon Settlement-Cases; from the Death of Lord Raymond in March 1732 . . .*, 2 vols. (London: J. Worrall and B. Tovey, 1768).

20. Bacon, *Annals of Ipswiche*, 391; Styles, "Evolution of the Law of Settlement," 199; Norma Landau, personal communication, Sept. 29, 2006.

21. George Lee Haskins, *Law and Authority in Early Massachusetts: A Study in Tradition and Design* (New York: Macmillan, 1960), 114–15. For a fresh look at the reception issue, see William E. Nelson, *The Common Law in Colonial America*, vol. 1, *The Chesapeake and New England, 1607–1660* (New York: Oxford University Press, 2008), esp. 3–5, and 70–71.

22. Hewes: *BTR* 13:57 (the year was 1719). For early certificates, see *BTR* 7:148, 149, 182, 188–89, 199, 11:77, 225, 228. For a 1750s example, see Nellis and Cecere, *BOPR*, 835. For a typical town-to-town negotiation that produced a certificate, see *BTR* 13:294–95, 312, 313, 317. For the

wording of English certificates, see Styles, "Evolution of the Law of Settlement," 195–96. At least three of the eleven certificates issued by Boston from 1708 to 1751 involved a person currently in need of relief; others promised that Boston would cover any future relief expenses or would receive the person if he or she became chargeable.

23. Prov. Laws, 1700–1701, chap. 23, sect. 2, and Prov. Laws, 1701–2, chap. 9, sect. 2, in *Acts and Resolves*, 1:452, 469; also 5:911; and Robert Wilson Kelso, *The History of Public Poor Relief in Massachusetts, 1620–1920* (Boston: Houghton Mifflin, 1922), 121–22.

24. Trifle: Executive Records of the Governor's Council, vol. 16 (1765–74), Reel 9, 219–20 (microfilm), MA Archives; Massachusetts Archives Collection 125 (Treasury Records, 1759–70): 270, 293, 352, 382, MA Archives; ibid., Treasury 1, Series 2262x, Box 1, Sewn folio size booklet for May 1770–: entry for March 25, 1771; *Acts and Resolves*, 19:537, 833; *Worc. Co. Warnings*, 80. Williams: *Acts and Resolves*, 18:430. Province account reimbursements can be tracked in the resolves passed by the General Court, the records of the governor and council, and the province treasury records. In a pioneering discussion of colonial poor relief, Marcus Wilson Jernegan wrongly linked Massachusetts warnings to "deportation." The poor strangers who were warned and whose passage was paid to Britain were rarely being forcibly removed; they desired to return and were unable to foot the bill. *Laboring and Dependent Classes in Colonial America, 1607–1783: Studies of the Economic, Educational, and Social Significance of Slaves, Servants, Apprentices and Poor Folk* (Chicago: University of Chicago Press, 1931), 194–95, 208.

25. The 1769–70 totals have been calculated based on Massachusetts Archives Collection 125 (Treasury): 363–91. In addition, the Boston selectmen were paid £5 lawful money for one man's pension (374). Province poor expenditures in other years: ibid., 340–59 (1768–69), and treasury records for 1770–72, Treasury 1, series 2262x, Box 1. Counties, as the intermediate level of government between towns and province, regularly paid for the diet of indigent prisoners in county jails; see, for example, payments ordered from the county treasury, Suff. Co. GSP Records, record book for 1764–68 (unpaginated), Nov. 8, 1765, Jan. 7, 1766, Oct. 7, 1766, and Jan. 27, 1767 sessions.

26. Costs for Acadians: *Acts and Resolves*, 3:887, 917–18; Lowe, "Massachusetts and the Acadians," 220–21. The funding basis shifted in 1760 so that towns would treat any needy among the Acadians assigned to them as town rather than province poor; legislators evidently believed that the towns would keep a firm cap on expenditures. *Acts and Resolves*, 4:103–4. For aid to Indians, see Jean M. O'Brien, *Dispossession by Degrees: Indian Land and Identity in Natick, Massachusetts, 1650–1790* (New York: Cambridge University Press, 1997), 193–98. After independence, the province poor account became the state account. In the years 1767–69, all of the persons described as negro or mulatto and admitted to the Boston almshouse were town poor; in 1788, all nine were state poor; our counts are based on the admissions records reprinted in Nellis and Cecere, *BOPR*.

27. John Cannon, April 10, 1771; see also George Downing, Feb. 20, 1772.

28. Stephen Edward Wiberly Jr., "Four Cities: Public Poor Relief in Urban America, 1700–1775," (Ph.D. diss., Yale University, 1975), 48–56. For the burden of covering almshouse admissions of the nonsettled, see Gary B. Nash, *The Urban Crucible: Social Change, Political Consciousness, and the Origins of the American Revolution* (Cambridge, Mass.: Harvard University Press, 1979), 255, 327, and Robert E. Cray Jr., *Paupers and Poor Relief in New York City and Its Rural Environs, 1700–1830* (Philadelphia: Temple University Press, 1988), 73.

29. Rhode Island typically used warning to end a nonsettled resident's stay rather than as a marker of nonsettlement upon the person's arrival; see Ruth Wallis Herndon, *Unwelcome Americans: Living on the Margin in Early New England* (Philadelphia: University of Pennsylvania Press, 2001), 4–15.

30. We cannot answer the question definitively for Philadelphia because the file papers do not survive. The extant quarter sessions docket books for Philadelphia County contain many removal orders by justices of the peace that were appealed, but these lack the level of detail that might include references to warning (Dockets, 1753–60, 1773–80, Philadelphia City Archives). William E. Nelson shared with us his notes on the docket books for Northampton, Lancaster, and York Counties in Pennsylvania: these contain litigation over removal orders, but no language of warning; personal communication, Oct. 27, 2010.

31. Testimony of overseer Joseph Nicklin and the Quarter Session Court order dated Feb. 28, 1728, in the folder on Margaret Power; see also the cases of William Evans, Ann Worrilaw, Ann Noys, Elizabeth Knight, and Mary Massia, Chester County Court of Quarter Sessions, Clerk of Courts, Overseer of the Poor Petitions, 1722–98, Chester County Archives (hereafter, CCA). We are grateful to legal historian Holly Brewer for alerting us that she had seen warning mentioned in Chester County records. See Brewer, *By Birth or Consent: Children, Law, and the Anglo-American Revolution in Authority* (Chapel Hill: Omohundro Institute of Early American History and Culture and University of North Carolina Press, 2005), 257n45. Thanks also to CCA archivist Cliff Parker for help in piecing together the Power case.

32. Warning is also missing from surviving township books that contain financial accounts relating to poor relief; East Bradford Township Book, Ms. 76209; West Bradford Township Accounts, Ms. 76214; East Caln Township, Accounts of the Poor, 1735–1757, Ms. 13524; and Goshen Township Account book, 1718–1869, Chester County Historical Society.

33. Cray, *Paupers and Poor Relief*, 55. For New Jersey, see Jean R. Soderlund, "The Delaware Indians and Poverty in Colonial New Jersey," in Billy G. Smith, ed., *Down and Out in Early America* (University Park: Pennsylvania State University Press, 2004), 289–311; John A. Grigg, "'Ye relief of ye poor of sd towne': Poverty and Localism in Eighteenth-Century New Jersey," *New Jersey History* 125, no. 2 (2010), 23–35; and the Nottingham Township Minute Book, published in *Proceedings of the New Jersey Historical Society* 58 (1940), 22–44. On southern colonies, see Zachary Ryan Calo, "From Poor Relief to the Poorhouse: The Response to Poverty in Prince George's County, 1710–1770," *Maryland Historical Magazine* 93 (Winter 1998), 393–427; John K. Nelson, *A Blessed Company: Parishes, Parsons, and Parishioners in Anglican Virginia, 1690–1776* (Chapel Hill: University of North Carolina Press, 2001), 70–83; Alan D. Watson, "Public Poor Relief in Colonial North Carolina," *North Carolina Historical Review* 54 (Oct. 1977), 347–66.

34. For county-level relief, see the February 1724 case of Elizabeth Roost, Chester County Court of Quarter Sessions, Clerk of Courts, Dockets, vol. for 1723–33, and the February 1748 ruling in the case of Jane Andrews, Overseer of the Poor Petitions, 1722–1798, both at CCA; Grigg, "'Ye relief of ye poor of sd towne': Poverty and Localism in New Jersey," 33 ("an old Indian" who was evidently not accounted a legal inhabitant). More research is needed on the extent to which provincial treasuries paid for relief for the nonsettled other than Acadian exiles. In 1767, Savannah vestrymen petitioned the assembly for help in ministering to the transient poor, but the outcome is unknown; Allen D. Candler, ed., *The Colonial Records of the State of Georgia*, 25 vols. (Atlanta: Franklin, 1904–16), 14:439.

35. Michael Dane Byrd, "White Poor and Poor Relief in Charles Town, 1725–1775: A Prosopography" (Ph.D. diss., University of South Carolina, 2005), chap. 8; and Tim Lockley, "Rural Poor Relief in Colonial South Carolina," *Historical Journal* 48 (Dec. 2005), 955–76. Not surprisingly, poor relief taxes in Charles Town rose astronomically between 1732 and 1775; Timothy James Lockley, *Welfare and Charity in the Antebellum South* (Gainesville: University Press of Florida, 2007), 6.

36. For north-south comparisons, see Lockley, *Welfare and Charity in the Antebellum South*, 5–12 (quotations pp. 6, 7); and Wiberly, "Four Cities," 157–59. Differences in regional practices are often overstated: as in Charles Town, recipients in Massachusetts sometimes received public support for decades. Christian charity: Lockley, *Welfare and Charity in the Antebellum South*, 6; Virginia Bernhard, "Poverty and the Social Order in Seventeenth-Century Virginia," *Virginia Magazine of History and Biography* 85 (April 1977), 153–54. On changing views among Boston clergymen, see J. Richard Olivas, " 'God Helps Those Who Help Themselves': Religious Explanations of Poverty in Colonial Massachusetts, 1630–1776," in Smith, ed., *Down and Out in Early America*, 262–88.

37. For the point that poor relief analyses must not ignore wider contexts of immiseration, see Philip D. Morgan, "Slaves and Poverty," in Smith, ed., *Down and Out in Early America*, 93–96. For a comparison of Massachusetts's "sophisticated" and quite democratically based province tax system with those of Virginia and other colonies, see Robin L. Einhorn, *American Taxation, American Slavery* (Chicago: University of Chicago Press, 2006), pt. 1.

38. There was no dedicated provincial poor rate in Massachusetts, but taxpayers' tax burden was higher due to province poor account expenditures. Research is needed on the terms and patterns of African New Englanders' and Indians' engagement with poor relief in the northern colonies.

39. Slack, *From Reformation to Improvement*, 46–52 (quotation p. 49). For more on the debate over the degree of puritan leadership, see Margaret Spufford, "Puritanism and Social Control?" in Anthony Fletcher and John Stevenson, eds., *Order and Disorder in Early Modern England* (New York: Cambridge University Press, 1985), 41–57, and Paul A. Fideler, "Introduction [to Symposium on the Study of the Early Modern Poor and Poverty Relief]: Impressions of a Century of Historiography," *Albion* 32 (Autumn 2000), 381–407.

40. Slack, *From Reformation to Improvement*, 52.

Chapter 4. Walking and Warning

1. Gillerest: Aug. 5, 1766; Doty: Sept. 19, 1765.

2. Only a small percentage of entries in the surviving 1765–66 logbook have cross-outs, careted additions, or corrections, suggesting that Love used a preliminary notebook and then transferred the information into the bound logbook, writing the final entries (and the copies that went to the county court and to the overseers of the poor) at his mahogany desk in his rented quarters.

3. For examples, see Richard LeBaron Bowen, *Early Rehoboth: Documented Historical Studies of Families and Events in This Plymouth Colony Township*, 4 vols. (Rehoboth, Mass.: Privately printed, 1945–50), 2:145–65. For examples of warning returns from Medway and Needham, see SF 85684 and 85685. In writing their returns, country town constables did not include the same extent of information as Love did; at most they noted peoples' names, where they were from, and when they arrived in town (e.g., three months ago); more typically, they simply wrote: I have warned [name], [date warned]. Evidently, to be valid, warnings had to be delivered verbally and in person. None of the surviving returns of warrants for Suffolk County towns, 1764–74, are subscribed by the constable "left at the abode of" (as was permissible for court summonses).

4. *BTR* 20:130.

5. In Love's surviving warnings, the arrival date is given for 66 percent of the parties (N = 1608). Prior to March 1767, a year's residency without being warned conferred settlement. There are no recorded cases in which Love's failure to warn a stranger within one year resulted in the stranger becoming chargeable to the town. For a consequential failure to warn within a year by one of Love's predecessors, see the case of Priscilla Hayden, *BTR* 23:58–59; Nellis and Cecere, *BOPR*, 204, 217, 630. Only in two instances, both after 1767, did it appear that a newcomer warned by Love had been in town more than a year (Moore: April 30, 1773; Winter: Feb. 18, 1772).

6. Joyce M. Ellis, *The Georgian Town, 1680–1840* (London: Palgrave, 2001), 110. Knew every person: "Diary of James Allen, Esq., of Philadelphia, Counsellor-at-Law, 1770–1778," *Pennsylvania Magazine of History and Biography* 9 (1885), 185. On the "memory economy," see Laurel Thatcher Ulrich, *A Midwife's Tale: The Life of Martha Ballard, Based on Her Diary, 1785–1812* (New York: Alfred A. Knopf, 1990), 86.

7. Thick-set, swarthy: Notice about John Cammel, *Boston Gazette*, June 8, 1767, 4. Slender-bodied: Notice about suspected thief John Gowdy, ibid., Dec. 7, 1767, 2. Straight-limbed: *New-Hampshire Gazette*, June 1, 1764, 3. Middling aged man and woman (also, he had a "smooth Face" and was wearing a cinnamon colored superfine broad cloth coat; the woman was "pretty tall, pock freckled"): *Boston Post-Boy*, May 25, 1767, 3. Speech impediments: *New-Hampshire Gazette*, April 19, 1764, 4; *Boston Gazette*, March 5, 1764, 3. Speaks like a Scotchman: ibid., Jan. 16, 1764, 3. Gray yarn stockings: ibid. and, for another example, see Notice about James Mertho, *Essex Gazette* [Salem], Dec. 8, 1772, 75. Clothing worn by reported runaways can be surveyed in Antonio T. Bly, *Escaping Bondage: A Documentary History of Runaway Slaves in Eighteenth-Century New England, 1700–1789* (Lanham, Md.: Lexington Books, 2012).

8. Thompson: Feb. 28, 1766, and Aug. 21, 1767 (both times from Scotland, but on different ships); Harris: Sept. 20, 1765, Dec. 16, 1766, Aug. 6, 1767, May 15, 1770. Of the fifteen warned three to four times times, eight were solo men, three were women with a child, and one was a solo woman. At times, the town clerk did not include the second or third warning in the Warning Out book, 1745–70—either by oversight or because he believed it was not needed.

9. None of the passengers warned on "this day" had arrived by sea. Love often waited at least three days before warning them, suggesting that he waited for ship captains to report the passengers they had disembarked. For examples of gaps between arrivals by sea and warning, see Peter Rose (shoemaker), July 9, 1766; butcher John Demont and wife: July 10, 1766, and *Port Arrivals*, 55; Andrew Acker, Aug. 18, 1767; and Katherine Bronnock, May 27, 1772.

10. Green: April 8, 1766; Smith: Aug. 2, 1765; Chatot: Jan. 10, 1766. We are grateful to Kariann Yokota for pointing out Love's possible brokerage role.

11. Rodgers: Nov. 28, 1765; Conway: March 7, 1766; Townsend, Feb. 1765 Return for the north division of the watch, MS f Bos. 7, Boston Town Papers, 7:9, BPL.

12. Griffin: March 27, 1770; Lemey: March 16, 1772; Wolfindine: March 2, 1770. Samuel Farrington, accompanied by his three sons, told Love he intended "to Go into the country with them"; Love explained, "Least he should Not I Warned them" (June 16, 1767).

13. *BTR* 17:44. The quotation is from warner William Larrabee's 1743 instructions; he was also to note "their Occupation & Circumstances & the Persons that Entertain them." Love was just about the only warner of the twelve who served Boston to take heed.

14. Solo men lodging with Enoch Brown: May 13, 1772, and July 12, 1773; Hardwick: Sept. 5, 1771. Similar clusters (same-day warnings listing the identical landlord for strangers who did not come into town together) occurred on: Sept. 25, 1766, Feb. 27, 1767, Dec. 8, 1768, April 14, 1769, July 11, 1769, Aug. 18, 1769, July 26, 1770, Dec. 11, 1772, and Feb. 25, 1773.

15. William Johnston, Sept. 30, 1771; strollers: William and Margaret Robinson, March 16, 1773. Morning drunkards: William Flin, June 26, 1770, and July 6, 1770; physically disabled James Jackson, Aug. 6, 1767.

16. Surviving records show that Love walked and warned 1,362 days from January 1765 to April 1774. The frequencies for number of groups warned per day break down as follows: one per day, 54 percent ($N = 731$); two per day, 27 percent; three per day, 12 percent; four per day, 5 percent; five to six per day, 2 percent; seven to twelve per day, 0.04 percent.

17. For examples of two or more warnings on such days, see May 6, 1766, Aug, 14, 1767; for information on Love's activity on days when crowds carried out political protests, see Chapter 9 in this volume. On the days when the selectmen met, Love at times issued several warnings, sometimes none.

18. Over the first two years of warning, Love warned an average of 134 days per year. At the peak of warnings, in 1767 and 1768, when three warners were paid by the head, Love warned an average of 178 days annually. Once he took over as sole warner, he delivered warnings on fewer days—on average, 122. During his tenure, he occasionally warned no one for seven to nineteen consecutive days; these gaps may have been due to bouts of illness or physical injury or trips out of Boston or may reflect missing warrants (see Appendix B). There were thirty-seven such gaps (twenty-four of them in months November to February), with an annual average of 2.6 prior to 1773, when there were nine.

19. For the phrase "under warning," see Petition of the Brookline selectmen, Suff. Co. GSP Records, record book for 1764–68 (unpaginated), Nov. 11, 1768, session. We identified removal orders and warrants by combing the selectmen minutes, sessions court papers, and the Warning Out books for 1745–70 and 1770–73, 1791–92 (MHS). On the cost (on average, several pounds) and disincentives to remove, see E. M. Hampson, *The Treatment of Poverty in Cambridgeshire, 1597–1834* (Cambridge: Cambridge University Press, 1934), 137; and James Stephen Taylor, "The Impact of Pauper Settlement, 1691–1834," *Past and Present* 73 (Nov. 1976), 62.

20. SF 88845: Gammons removal warrant, Jan. 21, 1769. Four months later, Gammons appeared in the sessions court to answer fornication charges; she named Francis Welch of Boston as the father of her child; Suff. Co. GSP Records, record book for 1769–73, 10. For selectmen ordering removals, see *BTR* 20:286; 23:2. Constables typically handed off the removed person to their counterparts in the adjacent town on the route.

21. Watchmen's powers: *BTR* 13:129–30. On typical parties removed, see Norma Landau, "The Laws of Settlement and the Surveillance of Immigration in Eighteenth-Century Kent," *Continuity and Change* 3 (Dec. 1988), 412; and Steve Hindle, *On the Parish? The Micro-Politics of Poor Relief in Rural England, c. 1550–1750* (Oxford: Clarendon Press, 2004), 337, 359. Burglary defendants: Lawrence McGuire: Warning Out book, 1745–70 (carried to Cambridge Nov. 28, 1767); Patrick Marrough or Marach: SF88351. Their Aug. 1767 indictment is found at SF 101,114.

22. Pernam: June 5, 1766; Warning Out book, 1745–70, June 5, 1766, entry; *BTR* 23:165 (Feb. 24, 1773). Green: July 18, 1768. "Carry" in this context meant escort; for example, when suspected miscreants were apprehended by constables, they were said to be carried before a magistrate. Of the thirty removal orders, fifteen were for solo women; three were for solo men, two of whom were the subjects of pauper support litigation between towns.

23. McIntosh: Nov. 14, 1770 (emphasis added); Tombs: April 4, 1768; Chase: Oct. 15, 1767. For another case alleging Roxbury's failure to warn, see Thomas Sturme: Feb. 19, 1767. It appears that in the case of Frenchman Anthony Sharrow (warned Aug. 19, 1768), Love was able to confirm

the absence of a warning by checking a written record: Sharrow lived at Charlestown "he Says this 3 years and Never was Warnned Oout [as] I found in Our Common _____ [book?] and Was Afraid to take his Word therefor." On the 1767 law that eliminated settlement by a year's residency, see Chapter 1 of this volume.

24. Gray: Jan. 22, 1768; Fosdick: Jan. 4, 1769. Many of these defiant travelers could not afford to lodge anywhere, but some may have successfully protected a landlord from paying a fine for not notifying the selectmen of taking in a lodger.

25. Michael Vane: April 17, 1766.

26. Johnston: March 7, 1766. Hollering: John Holland, Oct. 14, 1768; openly begging: Jonathan Whittemore: April 4, 1768. Almost all cases in which Love deployed the first-person involved men. Twenty-seven such entries survive: seventeen in Love's 1765–66 logbook and eleven in the surviving 1767–74 warnings. Probably, there was a smattering of others, in warnings for which the whole text of what Love wrote does not survive.

27. Boma: July 17, 1767 (emphasis added). "Do not Like Verry Well": John Ryan, May 2, 1770; Ryan came in from New York and told Love that he had lived with the wealthy merchant Charles Ward Apthorp (of Braintree) for four years. Conaway: Oct. 2, 1769.

28. "Let him go:" John Holland: Aug. 7, 1770; this may well have been the same Holland whom Love warned on Oct. 14, 1768, described as crazy and hollering in the streets. Other examples of strangers giving "slender" or no accounts: John Cowan: April 15, 1766; Elizabeth Shaw, March 2, 1767; Moses Sanders, Sept. 4, 1770; Thomas McGlochlin, Dec. 9, 1772; and John Harward, March 3, 1773.

29. Lawrence: July 17, 1770; Filch: July 21, 1768; Ewing: June 9, 1766. For more on the sixteen solo men, twelve solo women, six couples, and one woman with her child identified as strollers, see Chapter 8 of this volume.

30. Smith: Aug. 15, 1770; Colden: Nov. 20, 1772; Mott: Aug. 22, 1769; Hebier: Aug. 23, 1771 (emphasis added).

31. Thompson/White: April 15, 1767, Oct. 12, 1767. Shays/Dasson: Oct. 26, 1771, March 12, 1773; Nellis and Cecere, *BOPR*, 222. In the 1773 warning, Love recorded that he warned Shays previously, on Sept. 29, 1772, a date for which his warnings do not survive. See William Chappell, *Old English Popular Music*, ed. H. Ellis Wooldridge (New York: Novello, Ewer, 1893), 2:186–87. Dawson was also a figure featured in Boston's Nov. 5 (Pope's Day) theatrical displays; see Chapter 9 of this volume. Our thanks go to Al Young for identifying the meaning of the alias. Another user of an alias was Mary Kinsay/Jean Wilson: Sept. 23, 1769, Oct. 3, 1771.

32. Unnamed woman: Aug. 19, 1768. Man child: May 28, 1772 (never baptized: see page 1 of the warrant). This was one of three cases in which Love warned a nursing infant. The other cases involved two-month-old Ruth Chamberlain (whose parents and siblings had already been warned) and eight-month-old William Langley; see their warnings, June 23, 1772, and March 9, 1768.

33. Haley: July 18, 1772; Mumford: May, 16, 1772; Gosey: Sept. 5, 1768. For another Frenchman who "Cannot Speake English," see Joseph Gochee, Sept. 5, 1767.

34. Lee: June 16, 1769; Smithers: May 18, 1770; Mason (Love wrote Eseby Masson): Oct. 15, 1771.

35. For example, George Peele, who carried "fish, timber," and more in his sloop, the *Mary*, back and forth from Salem to Boston for twenty years prior to 1776, was never warned; Daniel Vickers with Vince Walsh, *Young Men and the Sea: Yankee Seafarers in the Age of Sail* (New

Haven: Yale University Press, 2005), 113. For a description of market women and their trips to Boston, see William S. Tilden, ed., *History of the Town of Medfield, Massachusetts, 1650–1886* . . . (Boston: G. H. Ellis, 1887), 197. Twelve local adults, in addition to the diarist and his wife, made shopping trips of a few days to Boston from New Hampshire, 1755–70; none of them was warned; *The Diary of Matthew Patten of Bedford, N.H. from 1754 to 1788* (Camden, Maine: Picton Press, 1993), 15, 24, 44, 49, 50, 56, 58, 61, 66, 77, 93, 131, 139, 154, 185, 187, 219.

36. Love noted two ship's cooks and one ship's carpenter but no ordinary seamen. In contrast, in a spurt of warnings issued in 1791, seventy-seven of 197 strangers warned in the port town of Salem (and for whom occupations were noted) were labeled mariners; Douglas Lamar Jones, "The Strolling Poor: Transiency in Eighteenth-Century Massachusetts," *Journal of Social History* 8 (Spring 1975), table 6, p. 38. We thank John Murrin for drawing our attention to mariners' omission from Boston warnings. On sailors, see Vickers with Walsh, *Young Men and the Sea*; Marcus Rediker, *Between the Devil and the Deep Blue Sea: Merchant Seamen, Pirates, and the Anglo-American Maritime World, 1700–1750* (New York: Cambridge University Press, 1987), 10–12 (quotation p. 11), 117–18, 141–42; Peter Earle, *Sailors: English Merchant Seamen, 1650–1775* (London: Methuen, 1998), 34–35; and Simon P. Newman, *Embodied History: The Lives of the Poor in Early Philadelphia* (Philadelphia: University of Pennsylvania Press, 2003), 12–13, 104–24.

37. Arrivals with Brown the wagoner: Sept. 7, 1765, Nov. 7, 1765, July 17, 1766, Sept. 3, 1766, June 25, 1767, and June 6, 1771 (two parties). For the White Horse, see Annie Haven Thwing, *The Crooked and Narrow Streets of the Town of Boston, 1630–1822* (Boston: Marshall Jones, 1920), 170.

38. Mary More: *BTR* 23:58. For landlord notifications followed up by Love's warnings, see *BTR* 20:130, 149, 180, 188, 215; 23:47. For almshouse admissions that occurred prior to the warning, see *BTR* 20:140, 182, 183, 186, 261; 22:34, 65.

39. William Hudson or Hutson: *BTR* 20:175, and Love warning on Sept. 12, 1765. In other cases where almshouse admissions occurred after Love's warning, the stranger had not expressed to Love a wish to be admitted (according to his warning, at least), and the gaps between warning and admission might be short (one to three weeks) or long (several months or a few years). Almshouse inmates also had to be recommended by one or two overseers of the poor, and in many cases it was probably the overseers' action, not Love's earlier warning, that was the immediate precipitant of the admission.

40. Family of four (Mitchell): *BTR* 20:294, and Love warning: May 30, 1768. In several other cases, Love's warning occurred on the same day as the landlord notification or selectmen's order for almshouse admission, but the documents contain no clues as to whether the warning came first or second. For two other cases of ship captains or owners being summoned after Love informed that they had allowed passengers to disembark who were sick or "in poor Circumstances," see *BTR* 20:167 (Lawrence Cooper, sick, warned June 6), 240 (Wright family, warned Dec. 11).

41. For a profile of the overseers and their duties, see Nellis and Cecere, *BOPR*, 41–56. For one overseer's walking ritual, see the entry for June 12, 1770, in vol. 34 ("Town Book"):1, Samuel Abbot Collection, Baker Library Historical Collections, Harvard Business School, Cambridge, Mass.

42. *BTR* 13:113; 19:167–68. The journals were the constables' monthly returns, which at a minimum noted how many nights each watchman worked in order for him to be paid; they are found in MS f Bos. 7, Boston Town Papers, 6 and 7, BPL. For more on the night watch, see J. L. Bell, "'I Never Used to Go Out with a Weapon': Law Enforcement on the Streets of Prerevolutionary Boston," in Peter Benes, ed., *Life on the Streets and Commons, 1660 to the Present* (Boston: Boston University, 2007), 41–55.

43. Murray: May 23, 1768. This was probably an evening warning; one wonders if constable Wallace brought the man to Love's residence. Murray was warned again by Love on Oct. 18, 1770; he was then serving time in Boston jail for an unknown minor crime, having arrived two weeks earlier from New York.

44. These comments are informed by Jane Caplan and John Torpey's astute historical comments on the development of modern identity documentation, and its emancipatory and repressive aspects; *Documenting Individual Identity: The Development of State Practices in the Modern World*, ed. Jane Caplan and John Torpey (Princeton: Princeton University Press, 2001), 1–12.

45. On May 24, 1771, Love encountered four women, wives of British soldiers, all now living "at the Castle," noting "I have 3 of them on my Books." Although the logbooks do not survive, warrants confirm that he had warned the three women previously, on Aug. 2–3, 1769.

46. For several months between March 1765 and March 1766, town clerk William Cooper filled out Love's warrants. The reason for this is unclear; Love continued to write his logbook during these months, so there is no evidence that his writing hand was injured. Cooper used more standardized spellings of surnames and places than Love but otherwise copied, almost verbatim, Love's logbook entries. See the returned warrants, SF 86106, 86336, 86431, 86466, 86467, 86648, 86707, 86727, 86848.

47. Only Love's copied sheets for the year 1767 survive; Boston Overseers of the Poor Records, Ms. Bos. W2, Box 4, BPL. Our thanks go to Ruth Herndon for alerting us of this and sharing digital images of the pages.

48. These ledgers are not known to survive; for their existence, see *BTR* 19:83–84. Two alphabetical warning ledgers copied for the overseers survive, one covering 1745–70, and the other 1770–73 and 1791–92; BOPR, MHS mss. The headings in the alphabetical ledgers that were copied for the overseers are: "Persons Warnd," "Time when," "By whom," "Towns they came from," "Time they have been here." A typical entry (abstracted from Love's logbook) is: "Berry, Esau May 2d 1771 R. Love Bedford 3. weeks."

49. For example, see SF 87106.

Chapter 5. The Warned and Why They Came

1. Oldest and youngest: James Bailey: Oct. 19, 1773; "man child": May 28, 1772.

2. For another study that stresses sojourning, see Alan Karras, *Sojourners in the Sun: Scottish Migrants in Jamaica and the Chesapeake, 1740–1800* (Ithaca, N.Y.: Cornell University Press, 1992). For betterment and subsistence migrants, see P. Griffiths et al., "Population and Disease, Estrangement and Belonging, 1540–1700," in *The Cambridge Urban History of Britain*, vol. 2, *1540–1840*, ed. Peter Clark (Cambridge: Cambridge University Press, 2000), 199.

3. Gary B. Nash, "Urban Wealth and Poverty in Prerevolutionary America," in *Race, Class, and Politics: Essays in American Colonial and Revolutionary Society*, by Nash (Urbana: University of Illinois Press, 1986), 186 (quotations); Gary B. Nash, *The Urban Crucible: Social Change, Political Consciousness, and the Origins of the American Revolution* (Cambridge, Mass.: Harvard University Press, 1979), 185–86, 253; Douglas Lamar Jones, "The Strolling Poor: Transiency in Eighteenth-Century Massachusetts," *Journal of Social History* 8 (March 1975), 28–54.

4. Love attached descriptors of neediness to 462 of 2,409 parties (19 percent) and to 12 percent of individuals warned ($N = 484$). They are the subject of Chapter 8 of this volume. P. J.

Corfield makes the point that those seen as "the poor" at any given point were not all in need of relief; many "supported themselves by casual labour or semi-licit dealings"; *The Impact of English Towns, 1700–1800* (New York: Oxford University Press, 1982), 134.

5. Not surprisingly, a very high percentage of those coming from Suffolk County towns had lodgings when Love warned them. See Appendix A for a breakdown of type and size of traveling parties and the location they were said to be "last from."

6. Charles E. Clark, *The Eastern Frontier: The Settlement of Northern New England, 1610–1763* (Hanover, N.H.: University of New England Press, 1983; first published 1970); Julian Gwyn, "Comparative Economic Advantage: Nova Scotia and New England, 1720s–1860s," in *New England and the Maritime Provinces: Connections and Comparisons*, ed. Stephen J. Hornsby and John G. Reid (Montreal: McGill-Queen's University Press, 2005), 94–108, esp. 94–97.

7. Bernard Bailyn with Barbara De Wolfe, *Voyagers to the West: A Passage in the Peopling of America on the Eve of the Revolution* (New York: Alfred A. Knopf, 1986), 205–18.

8. Besides the 123 parties "last from" the British Isles, fifty-five of the warned (not including occupying soldiers' dependents) told Love they were originally from or "belonged" to England, Ireland, or Scotland, and a few more reported having started their journey there. This is an undercount of Britons, given that Love may not have noted origins in some instances and that the Love warnings gleaned from the warning out ledger omit his comments about nationality and geographic origins. Love's warnings for which only the Warning Out book, 1745–70 survives consist of 348 warned parties: 102 solo females, 168 solo males, and seventy-eight kin parties, adding up to 537 individuals in all. See Appendix B.

9. Kelley: Jan. 12, 1773; the solo "Dutch" travelers were last from Albany, New York (city), and Philadelphia. Love did not mention the German birth or heritage of several families and solos arriving from Broad Bay (present-day Waldoboro) in Maine, an area settled by German immigrants in the 1750s. Examples are Philip Ulmer (June 17, 1768); Adam Shoemaker with wife, Sofia, and five children including Jacobina (Aug. 22, 1769); and Michael Remingham [Rominger] with family (Oct. 26, 1770). The last were part of a cluster of four families sojourning in Boston in summer and fall 1770, who were probably among those moving to North Carolina with their Moravian pastor, Georg Soelle. See Jasper J. Stahl, "Diary of a Moravian Missionary at Broad Bay, Maine, in 1760," *New England Quarterly* 12 (Dec. 1939), 759.

10. Jamison: June 6, 1769; Desilver: Dec. 17, 1771; Serron: March 26, 1773; Peterson, Sept. 22, 1772. The number of strangers identified by Love as non-Britons was small—forty-four parties in all. These included a Dane; three Prussians, two Portuguese men, a German couple, eleven Acadian parties, and twenty-two French.

11. This discussion of twenty-two parties labeled French omits the ten Acadian families whom Love classified as neutral French or did not bother to tag as French.

12. Love omitted "last from" in ninety-seven entries, often because someone refused to tell him (or was unable to do so because drunk or raving) or reported having no place of abode. During Boston's occupation, he assumed that soldiers living in town and their dependents were the responsibility of the British army and "belonged" to a man-of-war. He also omitted "last from" on some occasions when he was flustered. In a few cases, we are unable to interpret or identify the location he wrote down.

13. Constables in other towns, when returning warrants, sometimes used slightly different formulas than the vague "last from." Dorchester constables wrote that a stranger "had removed from" Boston (say) to Dorchester a certain number of days or months previously (SF 96483,

88860–61, 89401). Roxbury constables wrote that her/his "last abode" or "last place" was (for example) Philadelphia (SF 89772–73, 89903, 91633). Medfield returns in 1773 noted that strangers were "late residents of . . ." (SF 91703, 91707, 91868).

14. Gershom Adams, May 23, 1769; Nichols: Nov. 16, 1770. We count 108 entries noting the stranger "properly," "originally," or "formerly" belonged to a specified town or a nation.

15. Solo strangers made up 70 to 78 percent of those warned in each of Love's years except 1769 and 1772, when they dipped to 62 and 65 percent respectively. Douglas Lamar Jones found somewhat similar percentages of "single" men and women being warned in Essex County towns, 1760–64: 32 percent were men alone, and 37 percent were women alone or with children ("Strolling Poor," 35).

16. Unlike Gary B. Nash, we choose not to label these incomers "single adults" because, first, many were under twenty-one, the age of majority, and, second, some were married. Note also that Nash included single-parent families in his counts of "single" men and women; see Nash, "Urban Wealth and Poverty," in *Race, Class, and Politics*, 186, and Nash, *Urban Crucible*, 253, 498n106. Because Love did not typically give a stranger's age, we cannot provide profiles by age.

17. Last from Halifax were thirty solo females and twenty-six solo males. Boston's annual intake of warned solo females was highest in 1767 ($N = 92$). In 1772 and 1773, when warnings dropped off somewhat, fifty-four and forty-two solo women were warned, respectively. Annually in 1765–73, between four and eighteen women traveling with one child were warned by Love.

18. The warnings registered more solo women than solo men coming from Suffolk and Middlesex counties and the District of Maine ($N = 202$ females, 161 males for Suffolk, seventy-eight and fifty-six for Middlesex, and fifty-two and thirty-three for Maine locations). Incoming from other province counties, males outnumbered solo females, with the significant streams being from Essex County (sixty-four males and fifty-two females), Plymouth (fifty-one and forty-two), and Worcester (twenty-three and twenty-two).

19. Peter Clark and David Souden, eds., *Migration and Society in Early Modern England* (London: Hutchinson, 1987), 34–35; Corfield, *Impact of English Towns*, 99; Joyce M. Ellis, *The Georgian Town, 1680–1840* (London: Palgrave, 2001), 30–31, 59; Ellen Hartigan-O'Connor, *The Ties That Buy: Women and Commerce in Revolutionary America* (Philadelphia: University of Pennsylvania Press, 2009), chap. 1.

20. The number of eleven females "last from" the British Isles does not include the wives of soldiers occupying Boston starting in fall 1768 who presumably arrived on army transport ships from other parts of the war theater, sometimes in the company of husbands, sometimes not.

21. Overall, 10 percent of warned female parties were marked as needy. Love described as needy 36 percent of solo males arriving from outside New England and Canada in contrast to 25 percent coming last from a Massachusetts location.

22. Amblert (last from Ireland by way of Newfoundland): Feb. 18, 1772. Two of Dehone's lodgers were identified as barbers, and all had been lodging there two weeks to six months when warned. Among all white male parties (solo or nonsolo), Love mentioned occupation in 193 cases, for a total of sixty-eight occupations. Forty-three of the solo males with stated occupations were also indicated as needy in some way (poor, ragged, etc.). Love never included trades when he wrote entries for men he described as of African or Native American ethnicity.

23. Richard Middleton, *Colonial America: A History, 1565–1776*, 3rd ed. (Oxford: Blackwell, 2002), 226. For the number of offspring accompanying spouse pairs, the median was three and

the mode was one (117 couples came with one child, eighty-three with two, seventy-seven with three to four, thirty-six with five to six, and seven with seven to eight).

24. Rhodes party, warned Dec. 3, 1765. The terminology of stepfamilies was not yet in use. Love typically explained that one or more children were the mother's "by another [or first] husband." Love also noted if a couple had a child born to them in Boston between their arrival and their warning.

25. Elizabeth Filis: Nov. 2, 1770; her husband had been warned by Love on June 22, coming (like Elizabeth and their children) "last from" nearby Lincoln. Sarah Berry: Sept. 7, 1770. The 11 percent of mothers with children marked as needy contrasts with Love's labeling only 3 percent of male-headed households consisting of three or more persons as needy.

26. According to censuses that surely gave undercounts, people of African heritage made up about 2 percent of the Massachusetts population and about 5 percent of Boston's in 1765. Indians were either not counted or were lumped with "negroes" in these counts. At midcentury, a few thousand indigenous Americans—Wampanoag, Nipmuc, and others—resided in and claimed lands in southeastern New England as their homelands. In Rhode Island, where nonsettled residents were warned out of towns and forced to leave at the end of extended sojourns, 10 percent of warned strangers in the years soon after 1750 were identified as persons of color; the proportion rose to 40 percent after gradual emancipation statutes passed in the 1780s. See Ruth Wallis Herndon, *Unwelcome Americans: Living on the Margin in Early New England* (Philadelphia: University of Pennsylvania Press, 2001), 18–19.

27. In no entry did Love record tribal affiliation. He called one solo woman "mustee," by which he probably meant someone of Indian and African ancestry: Thankful Ned ("She was born in Newport"), Aug. 4, 1772. Six of the seven newcomers whom he marked as enslaved went—at this stage in their lives—by the surname of their current or a previous owner.

28. In all, Love's surviving warnings name 127 people of color. These paragraphs omit nine because they were dependents traveling as part of white-headed households or, in one case, a former slave accompanying a white man where their relationship was not explained by Love.

29. Only five parties designated nonwhite came last from New York or Pennsylvania, and three from England—all black or mulatto men traveling solo. No woman of color warned by Love arrived "last from" a location outside of New England or Canada. On seasonal movements, see Ruth Wallis Herndon and Ella Wilcox Sekatau, "The Right to a Name: The Narragansett People and Rhode Island Officials in the Revolutionary Era," *Ethnohistory* 44 (Summer 1997), 442–43, 449–50. Forty percent of the people of color warned by Love ended up lodging with a black Bostonian.

30. Mohawk: June 19, 1771. Love added: "his father was a Mohock Indin his mother Was a Malato Womon." For indentures, see Margaret Ellen Newell, "The Changing Nature of Indian Slavery in New England, 1670–1720," in *Reinterpreting New England Indians and the Colonial Experience*, ed. Colin G. Calloway and Neal Salisbury (Boston: Colonial Society of Massachusetts, 2003), 106–36.

31. Belongs to Barnes: Eunice Gunion [Gunney], July 3, 1767; Mingo Otis: Oct. 12, 1772. On the aged turned adrift, see Lorenzo Johnston Greene, *The Negro in Colonial New England, 1620–1776* (New York: Columbia University Press, 1942; repr., Bowie, Md.: Heritage Books, 1998), 295. Boston newspapers contained notices offering to give away enslaved black infants or children. For seven of the nineteen parties whose status was not stated, we do not have Love's entries, only the town clerk's abstracted information.

32. Daniel R. Mandell, *Behind the Frontier: Indians in Eighteenth-Century Eastern Massachusetts* (Lincoln: University of Nebraska Press, 1996), 128–32; Jean M. O'Brien, *Dispossession by Degrees: Indian Land and Identity in Natick, Massachusetts, 1650–1790* (New York: Cambridge University Press, 1997), 198–209; William D. Piersen, *Black Yankees: The Development of an Afro-American Subculture in Eighteenth-Century New England* (Amherst: University of Massachusetts Press, 1998), 20; Greene, *Negro in Colonial New England*, 93–94. Historians assume that the unbalanced sex ratio among blacks stemmed from the priority that slave traders and purchasers placed on males. Love warned thirty-three solo black males and twenty-eight females.

33. Hesilrige: April 10, 1766. Biographical data comes from C. Frederick Adams, Jr., "Notices of the Walter Family," *NEHGR* 8 (July 1854), 209–14; *Sibley's Harvard Graduates*, 8:630–34 and 16:3–4; *Complete Baronetage. Edited by G.E.C [George E. Cokayne]*, 5 vols. (Exeter, Eng.: W. Pollard, 1900–1906), 1:203; *Boston Deaths*, 453 (the Trinity Church record of her death reads "Lady"). Sarah's siblings were socially distinguished members of the Boston orbit, and her children made advantageous marriages starting in 1776. Her father, however, declined into intemperance and dysfunction before his death in 1776.

34. John Carnes: Aug. 11, 1766; *Sibley's Harvard Graduates*, 11:137–42; Robert Brand Hanson, ed., *Vital Records of Dedham, Mass, 1635–1845*, rev. ed. (Camden, Maine: Picton Press, 1997), 500; Suff. Co. GSP Records, record book for 1769–73, 19.

35. For the exodus of artisans, see Robert Blair St. George, *Conversing by Signs: Poetics of Implication in Colonial New England Culture* (Chapel Hill: Omohundro Institute of Early American History and Culture and University of North Carolina Press, 1998), 208, 238–42.

36. Carl Bridenbaugh, *Cities in Revolt: Urban Life in America, 1743–1776* (New York: Alfred A. Knopf, 1955), 76 (quotation), 224–28; Nash, *Urban Crucible*, 235–36, 246–47, 314–18; Fred Anderson, *Crucible of War: The Seven Years' War and the Fate of Empire in British North America, 1754–1766* (New York: Alfred A. Knopf, 2000), 588–91; William Pencak and Ralph J. Crandall, "Metropolitan Boston Before the American Revolution: An Urban Interpretation of the Imperial Crisis," *Proceedings of the Bostonian Society, 1977–83* (1985), 57–79.

37. Nash, *Urban Crucible*, 240–47, 251–54, 402–4, 415–17; Edmund S. Morgan and Helen M. Morgan, *The Stamp Act Crisis: Prologue to Revolution* (Chapel Hill: Omohundro Institute of Early American History and Culture and University of North Carolina Press, 1953), 21–30; Robin L. Einhorn, *American Taxation, American Slavery* (Chicago: University of Chicago Press, 2006), 53–78. According to Nash's calculations, the annual tax per taxable in Boston declined from a high of £4.4 in 1755–59, to £3.2 in 1765–69 and £2.5 in 1770–74. In New York and Philadelphia, it never rose above £2.3 (403).

38. Nash, *Urban Crucible*, 242–45; Alfred F. Young, "'Persons of Consequence': The Women of Boston and the Making of the American Revolution, 1765–1776," in *Liberty Tree: Ordinary People and the American Revolution* (New York: New York University Press, 2006), 103–7; *BTR* 14:180 (for an observation in 1750 that widowed retailers "get a poor subsistenc"); and Eric Nellis, "The Working Poor of Pre-Revolutionary Boston," *Historical Journal of Massachusetts* 17 (Summer 1989), 156–57. The Bay province's smaller maritime towns, such as Marblehead and Gloucester, had adult sex ratios similar to Boston's ratio of 0.814 (Nash, 495n61). "Widow capital": Al Young, personal communication to the authors, July 2008.

39. Newport's population had reached ninety-two hundred by 1774, while Halifax's was well under four thousand.

40. Clark and Souden, eds., *Migration and Society*, 24 (quotations); Corfield, *Impact of English Towns*, 99.

41. On the New England labor market, see Daniel Vickers, *Farmers and Fishermen: Two Centuries of Work in Essex County, Massachusetts, 1630–1850* (Chapel Hill: Omohundro Institute of Early American History and Culture and University of North Carolina Press, 1994), 206, 235–37, 247–58. As in England, the number of formal apprenticeships was declining while the number of live-in servants was rising (Corfield, *Impact of English Towns*, 128). We need an in-depth study of domestic servants in New England, especially of women. We are unable to measure if the warned newcomers who stayed in town depressed wages.

42. Darby: April 26, 1/66. Born in Salem, Samuel and his wife (Sarah Estes) had named one of their daughters Philadelphia. Between 1765 and 1774, this landlord, three of his grown sons, and his widow hosted a total of twenty parties of warned strangers, all of whom except for Darby and two men from New York were "last" from New England towns. The majority were women traveling to Boston alone. One was kin (Samuel Sr.'s daughter visiting with her two children), and one man was a whitesmith.

43. Isaac Hammon: Sept. 4, 1771; Mary Hammon: May 9, 1771. With two of her children, she first lived with Judge Samuel Welles (who died in May), but by September she was renting a house from Jones Fitch. Two months apart, Love warned laborer Patrick Marach and blacksmith Lawrence McGuire (McGuire was accompanied by his wife), both incoming from New York City. The men lodged separately, but on a July night they broke into merchant John Rowe's warehouse and stole £100 in textiles. After their Superior Court trials, the selectmen ordered them carried out of town. Warnings, March 16, 1767; May 28, 1767; *Boston Post-Boy*, Aug. 3, 1767, 4, Aug. 17, 1767, 3; *Rowe Diary*, 140, 146; SF 101,114 (Indictment), 88351 (removal order); Warning Out book, 1745–70.

44. Ellis, *Georgian Town*, 54–57. Clark and Souden suggest four types of mobility based on "individual motivation": local (moving short distances "within a local area" and "within a labour, agricultural, or marriage market"), career (by which you end up in a place somewhat randomly due to your profession or match-up with the expert who will train you), circular (moving away and then returning to the "starting point"), and chain (following family or acquaintances along a patterned path); *Migration and Society*, 15–17.

45. Nash, *Urban Crucible*, 314–15, 320; Samuel Eliot Morison, "The Commerce of Boston on the Eve of the Revolution," *Proceedings of the American Antiquarian Society*, n.s., 32 (April 1922), 24–51.

Interlude. A Sojourner's Arrival

1. For data on the town center (Wards 6, 8, and 9), see Allan Kulikoff, "The Progress of Inequality in Revolutionary Boston," *WMQ* 28 (July 1971), 394–97. For a similar prose tour, see Walter Muir Whitehill, *Boston: A Topographical History*, enl. 2nd ed. (Cambridge, Mass.: Harvard University Press, 1968), 26–46. Love warned thirty-six parties whom he reported lodged in King Street, eleven of whom were staying with barbers.

2. John Drayton, *Letters Written during a Tour through the Northern and Eastern States of America* (Charleston, S.C.: Harrison and Bowen, 1794), 91.

3. For the North End, see Annie Haven Thwing, *The Crooked and Narrow Streets of the Town of Boston, 1630–1822* (Boston: Marshall Jones, 1920), 26–77; Kulikoff, "Progress of Inequality," 394–98 ("poorest section," p. 398); David Hackett Fischer, *Paul Revere's Ride* (New York: Oxford University Press, 1994), 10 ("to and fro"); map of Boston, c. 1775, Lester J. Cappon, ed., *Atlas of*

Early American History: The Revolutionary Era, 1760–1790 (Princeton: Princeton University Press, 1976), 9. We follow Thwing, *Crooked and Narrow Streets*, in defining the bounds of the various districts such as the North End.

4. *Boston Gazette*, July 30, 1770, 4 ("afternoon"), and July 8, 1771, 4. See also Carl Bridenbaugh, *Cities in Revolt: Urban Life in America, 1743–1776* (New York: Alfred A. Knopf, 1955), 326.

5. Whitehill, *Boston*, 5–8, 15 (quoting visitor John Josselyn in 1663), 35; Samuel Adams Drake, *Old Landmarks and Historic Personages of Boston* (Boston: James R. Osgood, 1873), 349. In updating John Bonner's 1722 map, William Price in his editions of 1754 and 1769 for the most part failed to include new details of the built environment and often omitted newly laid-out streets, especially in the West End.

6. Cow-path: Drake, *Old Landmarks*, 333. On Fort Hill and environs, see ibid., 284–88.

7. Kulikoff, "Progress of Inequality," 394–98 Thwing (*Crooked and Narrow Streets*, 152–85) comments on the many gardens giving the South End a "village" appearance; see also Whitehill, *Boston*, 33–34.

8. On the Neck, see Thwing, *Crooked and Narrow Streets*, 228–43. Row of trees, gallows: *BTR* 17:135, 261–262. The Neck, like Boston Common, was where troops could bivouac or parade (Thwing, *Crooked and Narrow Streets*, 242).

Chapter 6. Lodgings

1. Anderson: July 5, 1765 (her husband joined them in October); shoemaker: Thomas Smith, Aug. 16, 1773; St. John (last from Montreal): Sept. 26, 1770.

2. Quotation: *Geographical Gazetteer of the Towns in the Commonwealth of Massachusetts* (Boston: Greenleaf and Freeman, 1784–85), 6, qtd. in Henry Wilder Foote et al., *Annals of King's Chapel from the Puritan Age of New England to the Present Day*, 3 vols. (Boston: Little, Brown, 1882–1940), 2:340; Allan Kulikoff, "The Progress of Inequality in Revolutionary Boston," *WMQ* 28 (July 1971), 393; Walter Muir Whitehill, *Boston: A Topographical History*, 2nd ed. (Cambridge, Mass.: Harvard University Press, 1968), 27. For a calculation of seventeen hundred residential buildings and over 250 commercial ones on the peninsula, see G. B. Warden, "The Distribution of Property in Boston, 1692–1775," *Perspectives in American History* 10 (1976), 89. Kulikoff calculated that the number of persons per house in 1765 and 1771 was 9.26 and 9.12 respectively; "Inequality in Boston," 393. One can zoom in on the 1769 Price map at the Bostonian Society's website, http://www.bostonhistory.org/sub/mappingrevolutionaryboston/.

3. For 1,482 of the 2,409 warned parties, Love noted the name of the person with whom they were staying or renting. In another seventy-four entries, the name of the landlord is illegible ($N = 11$) or only the lodging location was given. Overall, 1,567 warned parties had lodgings with private individuals (not all of whom were named) or in taverns. A further eighty-four were in the almshouse, jail, or workhouse when warned (or on their way there), and six boarded on a vessel. Note that at least another fifty were warned as they were arriving and thus did not give lodging information.

4. Hancock's renters in Union Street were Augustus Moore (with wife, Abigail, son, Ethan), warned July 15, 1769, and Ruth Peterson (whom Love noted was born in nearby Pembroke), warned Dec. 24, 1770.

5. Widow Scott: July 20, 1773. Love reported a kin connection in fifty-nine cases; a surname was shared in sixteen additional cases.

6. Love's records provide the only documentation of specific addresses for many Bostonians, given that the vast majority is not in the deeds and the first city directory was not published until 1789.

7. Compare Love's warning data to the May 1765 census taken by town officials. The census listed 6,553 whites over age sixteen, 510 negro males and 301 females, twenty-one Indian males and sixteen females, making no distinction between dependents such as youths and servants and independent families; "An Account of the Houses, Families, White People, Negros Mulattoes and Indians in the Town of Boston," May 16, 1765, MS f Bos. 7, Boston Town Papers, 7:24, BPL.

8. Male landlords were more likely than female ones to house "strangers" repeatedly—43 percent did so in contrast to 22 percent of women.

9. Locations can be ascertained for 1,541 warned parties: four were on harbor islands; 902 were housed in the South End (59 percent); 246 in the town center (16 percent); 248 in the North End (16 percent); seventy-five in New Boston (5 percent); and sixty-six on the Neck (4 percent). On shifting patterns of residence, see Kulikoff, "Progress of Inequality," 394.

10. Warden, "Distribution of Property," 85–86, 109 (quotation). Of the 365 householders who submitted claims for losses in the 1760 fire in the town center, 75 percent did not own; William Pencak, "The Social Structure of Revolutionary Boston: Evidence from the Great Fire of 1760," *Journal of Interdisciplinary History* 10, no. 2 (Autumn 1979), 267–78.

11. Commodious: *Boston News-Letter*, Jan. 18, 1770, 3. Rooms on a floor: ibid., July 4, 1771, 3, 4; *Boston Gazette*, Nov. 29, 1773, 3. Apartments: ibid., March 26, 1770, 3. Ready furnished: *Boston News-Letter*, July 4, 1771, 3, 4; May 3, 1773, 4. Sober, etc.: *Boston Gazette*, May 8, 1769, 3; June 15, 1767, 2 suppl.; March 19, 1770, 3; *Boston News-Letter*, May 7, 1772, 3; May 13, 1773, 3. Mary Speakman charged eight shillings per week for girls boarding to attend her school; ibid., June 1, 1769, 3. Most advertisements did not indicate who was offering the lodging; instead they directed interested parties to enquire of the paper's printer. They also did not state the amount of rent charged. In the 1720s, a house worth £100 rented for about £16; Warden, "Distribution of Property," 86n. In 1769, John Boyle reported renting a house on Marlborough Street for £20 lawful New England money; *NEHGR* 84 (July 1930), 259.

12. The factory house had been built as a work-for-welfare project that lasted 1753–59; see Gary B. Nash, "The Failure of Female Factory Labor in Colonial Boston," in *Race, Class, and Politics: Essays on American Colonial and Revolutionary Society*, by Nash (Urbana: University of Illinois Press, 1986), 119–40; *Sibley's Harvard Graduates*, 7:187. Love's warnings of seven solo males, four solo females, a couple, and four families living there were dated between April 15, 1767 and Aug. 26, 1772. He listed over half of them as living with or in another person's apartment or room. For how the building and its tenants featured in a struggle over the occupying British troops in 1768, see Chapter 9 of this volume.

13. Dunbar: Mercy Wright warning, Aug. 2, 1770. Love was inconsistent about using *Mr.* for Quakers; he did so in four out of seven entries for landlord Samuel Pope and not for Elijah Collins (Dec. 12, 1772). In the case of two dozen or so of the repeating landlords, Love withheld a title the first time he listed them, after which they became "Mr." This included Frenchman Joseph Harvey (Feb. 18, 1765, and Sept. 9, 1767, warnings) and Irishman Michael Carroll (Nov. 16, 1765, July 13, 1767, April 9, 1768).

14. Crafts: Aug. 11, 1766 (taking in James Mallown, a painter); Hoskins: April 14, 1769.

15. Love recorded ninety-two parties as staying with a widow, fifty-nine with a mistress, and three with a madam. In the eighteenth century, *Mrs.* stood for the honorific Mistress and did not

necessarily mean the woman in question had a husband living. A family of three, for example, was living in a house of "Mrs." Mary Butler, whose spouse, a prosperous merchant and saddler, had died eight years earlier. The three black landladies were Hitty Winship, Hannah Peters, and Cato Jackson's wife, Susa (née Susanna Primus, a freewoman at their 1765 marriage; *Boston Marrs.*, 2:55); their lodgers were warned June 18, 1767; June 18, 1768; and Aug. 4, 1772.

16. On the Mackays, see Dan Berwin Brockman, "Mackay-Hunt Family History," 1983, typescript at NEHGS; *BTR* 20:188. Jones evidently never married; she died at age eighty in her hometown; *BTR* 21:141, 246.

17. Marshall: April 11, 1769, warning; John Adams, *Diary*, 1:339; *Milton Records: Births, Marriages and Deaths, 1662–1843* (Boston: Alfred Mudge and Son, 1900), 45. If she was the Sarah Marshall of Milton who died in Boston in 1807, she was nineteen when living with the Adamses in Boston. The Adamses, perhaps because of their wealth, were not warned. Welles's lodger was Esther Hegar, who had arrived five months earlier, last from Needham (Feb. 28, 1771). Prior to this, families as large as six rented houses owned by Welles in the South End.

18. Condon as landlord: March 29, 1765; May 27, 1765; July 16, 1765, Jan. 28, 1767, Sept. 23, 1767; July 24, 1770; Boston Ch. Recs. database (Christ Church). Historians studying early modern cities have found that the lower one was in the ranks of wealth, the more likely one was to move within a town and to leave altogether after a decade.

19. Davis, last from Leicester, Mass.: March 2, 1772. On short-term work contracts in England, see P. J. Corfield, *The Impact of English Towns, 1700–1800* (New York: Oxford University Press, 1982), 128–29.

20. April 25, 1769, warning; *Boston Post-Boy*, April 24, 1769, 3 (quotation). Cranch lived on Mackerel Lane near Oliver's Dock in a house she rented from housewright Jeremiah Russell; see Love warnings of Elizabeth Haley and daughter on April 25, 1769 and Elizabeth Dorran and her daughter on Sept. 2, 1767; Pencak, "Social Structure of Revolutionary Boston," 276, and *Boston Gazette*, March 24, 1760, 1.

21. Carl Bridenbaugh, ed., *Gentleman's Progress: The Itinerarium of Dr. Alexander Hamilton, 1744* (Chapel Hill: University of North Carolina Press, 1948), 106, 114–15, 147 (quotation). Hamilton took breakfast at his lodgings but dined and supped elsewhere in town. Fictive kin: Joyce M. Ellis, *The Georgian Town, 1680–1840* (London: Palgrave, 2001), 113; P. Clark, "Migrants in the City: The Process of Social Adaptation in English Towns, 1500–1800," in *Migration and Society in Early Modern England*, ed. Peter Clark and David Souden (London: Hutchinson, 1987), 280–86.

22. For an extended portrait of social and wealth groupings, based mostly on 1790 information, see Kulikoff, "Inequality in Boston," 379–89. Pencak argues convincingly that the distribution of personal property is better represented by what people held (and lost) in the 1760 fire than by the 1771 tax valuation or probate inventories. We use his table 4 as a rough guide, equating the lower sort with those owning less than £40, the middling £40–499, and the better sort more than £499; "Social Structure of Revolutionary Boston," 272.

23. *Rowe Diary* (index). William Stoddard's father, Simeon, set him up as a merchant with a gift of £1,000, after he left Harvard without graduating because of his unacceptably violent behavior; *Sibley's Harvard Graduates*, 5:648–51.

24. Warned May 14, 1767, Tilden had arrived the previous fall. He would have been fourteen years old when he arrived in Boston if he were the Elisha Tilden who was born in Coventry, Conn., in 1751 and died in Montague, Mass., in 1834, serving twice in the Continental army from Connecticut and receiving a pension in 1818 in which he claimed he had no other property.

25. Pierpoint's bills to the town for improvements to roads, bridges, the town dock, and almshouse in the 1760s and 1770s were in an elegant hand—his or his clerk's; MS f Bos. 7, Boston Town Papers, 6:257; 7:201, 253, 268, BPL. Pierpoint, a coroner for the county from 1761, presided over the inquest on Crispus Attacks's body. He died with an estate valued at £3,232, including two chaises, "goloshoes," and a scarlet cloak; SCPF 18800. The young carter was Aaron Hartshorn (warned Oct. 31, 1768).

26. On Rowe, see the introduction by Anne Rowe Cunningham, *Rowe Diary*, 2–60; Thwing database 53035; William H. Whitmore, *The Massachusetts Civil List for the Colonial and Provincial Periods, 1638–1774* . . . (Albany: J. Munsell, 1870), 129–30; *Salem Mercury*, Feb. 24, 1787, 3. Hobby: April 24, 1767, warning and the related warning of Mary Shattuck, who came from Reading to live with widow Hobby, March 24, 1768; *Sibley's Harvard Graduates*, 4:300–303, 7:530–37. Widow Hobby died in Reading (now Wakefield) in 1785.

27. Williams: M. F. Sweetser, *King's Handbook of Boston Harbor* (Cambridge, Mass.: Moses King, 1883), 111; *Boston News-Letter*, Feb. 2, 1764, 3; ibid., Aug. 13, 1767, 3. Porter family: April 11, 1768. Love also twice warned solo men who were living with Williams on the island (Sept. 5, 1766, May 3, 1773). Noddle's Island became East Boston and Chelsea.

28. Quincy: *Sibley's Harvard Graduates*, 13:478–88; Hinkley: March 21, 1765, warning; SCPF 13512 (Ebenezer Hinkley, 1764); *Boston Marrs.*, 2:51; Thwing database 21816; *Boston Obits.*, 1:129. The busiest landlord among the handful of physicians in Love's records was North End mansion owner William Clark, who rented houses to eight families and two solo sojourners.

29. Bowen: *Sibley's Harvard Graduates*, 15:196–200; March 30, 1773, and May 20, 1773, warnings. After the revolution, Bowen found his true calling as an Episcopal preacher in South Carolina. Mather: *Sibley's Harvard Graduates*, 7:216–38; as landlord: July 25, 1772, warning.

30. Appleton: *Sibley's Harvard Graduates*, 12:355–59; Vose: July 23, 1772. At least twenty-three of the elite or middling landlords named in Love's records were slave owners, including widow Sarah Bean, merchants Gilbert Deblois and Oliver Wendell, and lawyer Samuel Swift.

31. Calef: SCPF 16097; Nov. 19, 1765, and Jan. 5, 1767, warnings. For an astute assessment of those of "the middle station" in eighteenth-century England, see Peter Earle, *The Making of the English Middle Class: Business, Society and Family Life in London, 1660–1730* (London: Methuen, 1989), chap. 1.

32. Indian boy, "James Mohawk": June 19, 1771. On Eddy, see Thwing database 17998. On Parker: *Boston Gazette*, March 12, 1770, 2; *Boston Marrs.*, 2:60; *Massachusetts Soldiers and Sailors of the Revolutionary War: A Compilation from the Archives*, 17 vols. (Boston: Wright and Potter, 1896–1908), 11:846 ("stature, 5 ft. 8 in.; complexion, ruddy"); *Vital Records of Roxbury, Massachusetts to the End of the Year 1849* (Salem, Mass.: Essex Institute, 1925), 1:266; Thwing database 48432. Parker recovered from his wound, married in Boston the following year, and listed himself as a wheelwright upon purchasing a house on Milk Street in 1778. On Preston, see Thwing database 50579. On Scott: SCPF 14849; Thwing database 53965; Boston Ch. Recs. database (Hollis Street baptisms).

33. On Boston shoemakers, see Alfred F. Young, *The Shoemaker and the Tea Party: Memory and the American Revolution* (Boston: Beacon Press, 1999), 18–19, 27; and Gary B. Nash, *The Urban Crucible: Social Change, Political Consciousness, and the Origins of the American Revolution* (Cambridge, Mass.: Harvard University Press, 1979), 398 (table 5 for the wealth of Boston shoemakers at death, 1756–75). On Murray: *Boston Marrs.*, 2:12; Boston Ch. Recs. database (King's Chapel christening, June 16, 1753); Mass. SCJ Records, vol. for 1771: 235–36; *Boston Evening-Post*,

Aug. 12, 1771, 3; *Massachusetts Gazette*, Aug. 12, 1771, 3. Love found Mary Baldridge lodging with the Murrays on May 12, 1766.

34. For Shepard, see *Boston News-Letter*, Oct. 18, 1764, 3; June 11, 1767, 2; Aug. 13, 1767, 3 (snuffbox stolen), June 23, 1768, 2; *1780 Takings*, 33; Thwing database 54412. On Coley: SCPF 14565; Thwing database 16215; two warned parties, Nov. 16, 1765.

35. The three lodging with McFadden were Charles Richie (Aug. 25, 1772), John Connery (Aug. 1, 1772), and John Fogerty (March 27, 1773). Love wrote that Connery "has Been in town Several times But not to be an Inhabitant." On McFadden, see *BTR* 23:85, 87; Thwing database 44026; and Boston Ch. Recs. database (New South). On Dawes, see Thwing database 23593 and David Hackett Fischer, *Paul Revere's Ride* (New York: Oxford University Press, 1995), 97, 287. Other South End leather dressers and landlords in the leather trades taking in solo males were Ebenezer Dorr, Joseph Dorr, Thomas Crawford, Robert Davis, and Thomas Eades.

36. On Cunningham: Thwing database 17624; *Hist. Artillery Company*, 309; March 28, 1770, and May 4, 1770, warnings. On Byles: Thwing database 10617; Arthur Wentworth Hamilton Eaton, "The Byles Family," *NEHGR* 69 (April 1915), 101n.; some of the nine warnings associated with Byles were on April 5, 1766, Aug. 7, 1766, Sept. 12, 1768, and July 17, 1772 ("in fields").

37. Mitchell died in May 1776 owning a modest estate consisting of a house on the lane leading to Wentworth's wharf and £44 in clothing and household goods. On Mitchell: SCPF 15941; Thwing database 45878; *1771 Valn.*, 0101–2309; *Port Arrivals*, 32, 83; and warnings, June 14 and 16, 1766, Dec. 13, 1766, Aug. 19, 1767, and April 7, 1769. On seafarers retiring, see Daniel Vickers with Vince Walsh, *Young Men and the Sea: Yankee Seafarers in the Age of Sail* (New Haven: Yale University Press, 2005), 156–60.

38. On Lucas: *Vital Records of Plympton, Massachusetts, to the Year 1850* (Boston: New England Historic Genealogical Society, 1923), 134, 344; *BTR* 20:168; *Port Arrivals*, 41, 56, 77; *Boston News-Letter*, Feb. 25, 1768, 3 suppl; *1771 Valn.*, 0101–4023. The Lucases took in as lodgers the family of Barnabas Fagan, who had come with Lucas on the sloop *Gloria* from Canso, Nova Scotia, Aug. 6, 1766.

39. Cordis as landlord: Aug. 8, 1770, and Aug. 21, 1766, warnings. Cordis began his career as a sugar-baker and merchant in the West End, but was declared bankrupt in 1758. As the coffeehouse proprietor, he did well, leaving personal estate apprised at £480 at his death in 1772, including two enslaved males, Caesar and Prince (SPCF 15192; *1771 Valn.*, 0101–4121). The selectmen remunerated Cordis for providing madeira, punch, biscuits, and dinners for their meetings; MS f Bos. 7, Boston Town Papers, 7:39, BPL. Other innholder–landlords (each with several warned parties to their name) with matching data include John Coleman, John Fisk, Ephraim May, and Rosanna Moore. Roughly half of the scores of warned strangers housed by tavern keepers were noted as "living with" the proprietor and half as "lodging at."

40. Young man to hire: *Boston News-Letter*, May 6, 1773, 3; property for sale (the Sign of the Black and White Horse): ibid., April 23, 1772, 2 suppl. Despite the fact that in dispensing licenses, Boston officials differentiated between innholders and liquor retailers (*BTR* 20:170, 183–84, 221, 253, 264), contemporaries tended to use the terms inn, tavern, public house, and licensed house interchangeably, leading to modern-day confusion. Love used the term "tavernkeeper," not "innholder." Love warned relatively few persons staying at public houses in the town center compared to other districts.

41. For similarly large houses catering to the genteel and offering a range of services, see Sharon V. Salinger, *Taverns and Drinking in Early America* (Baltimore: John Hopkins University Press, 2002), 54–58.

42. Property description: *Boston Evening-Post*, March 8, 1756, 2; Thwing database 4976, 20599. Freemason feasts: *Boston Post-Boy*, June 13, 1763, 3; June 17, 1765, 2; *Rowe Diary*, June 25, 1771, June 24, 1773. Sleigh rides, horseman's performance: *Rowe Diary*, Dec. 19, 1767, Nov. 1, 1771. Brackett announced his taking the house, now called the King's Arms, in the *Boston Gazette*, March 19, 1770, 3; in late May Nancy Holdin, last from Bristol in the District of Maine, arrived to live with him (July 11, 1770, warning). Gardner and his family left in 1769 to occupy his cousin Dr. Sylvester Gardiner's property on the Kennebec River; *Boston Evening-Post*, Aug. 30, 1773, 2. Starting in June 1769, Edward Bardin of New York tried for a few months to make a go of running the tavern, posting an elaborate ad boasting about his elegant garden, "choice New-York Mead and Cakes" for sale, "Turtles, [and] Barbicues" for dinner, a coach to shuttle guests from the town center, and even "hot Chicken Pies for ready Suppers"; *Boston Gazette*, Aug. 7, 1769, 3. Love's records tell us that Bardin brought in one solo woman and four men to staff his short-lived establishment (warnings dated July 11, July 24, Aug. 18, and Dec. 19, 1769).

43. Warnings (for Gardner) dated April 10 and 30, 1766, July 11 and Aug. 21, 1767, and March 3, 1768. A tenement was defined as a building with one roof under which there were separate domiciles or shops; see Robert Blair St. George, *Conversing by Signs: Poetics of Implication in Colonial New England Culture* (Chapel Hill: University of North Carolina Press, 1998), 236–38, and advertisements presenting tenements as suitable for small families: *Boston Evening-Post*, Aug. 12, 1771, 3; *Boston News-Letter*, May 13, 1773, 3.

44. On the Perrys: Charles Nelson Sinnett, *Our Perry Family in Maine; Its Ancestors and Descendants* (Lewiston, Maine: Journal Printshop, 1911); *NEHGR* 58 (Oct. 1904), 374. The family was warned in Boston by Abijah Adams, SF 86056; for landlord notifications by Perry, see *BTR* 20:149, 238. Their lodgers were warned between Feb. 1, 1765 (Lydia Twitchell) and March 23, 1769 (Benjamin and Hannah Morrow). On Enoch Brown, who later styled himself merchant and bought up properties in all parts of Boston, including the famous Thomas Hutchinson estate: *BTR* 20:221, 23:11, 19, 64; *Boston Gazette*, July 2, 1770, 3; Thwing database 8297; [Timothy Newell], "A Journal During the Time Yt Boston Was Shut Up in 1775–76," *Massachusetts Historical Society Collections*, 4th ser., 1 (1852), 264, entry for July 10, 1775. His live-ins plus two tenants who hired a house from him were warned between Nov. 15, 1766, and April 23, 1773.

45. Landladies are difficult to profile because in the case of thirty-four individuals, Love did not give a first name, writing only "Widow Deacon," "Mrs. Clough," or "their daughter." We have been able to identify some of these. On Ann Love, see Chapter 2 of this volume. Rosanna, widow of William Moore: July 1761 petition, MS Bos 11, Boston Town Records, Loose Papers, BPL; July 1762 petition, MS f Bos. 7, Boston Town Papers, 7:156, BPL; approved as innholder, Nov. 5, 1765, *BTR* 20:183–84; landlady to warned strangers: Sept. 28, 1765, March 31, 1766, and April 28, 1773.

46. Dousett "keeps at" Mrs. Robicheaux's: Oct. 5, 1768, last from Newbury. Advertisements offering lodging rooms: shopkeeper Jolley Allen, *Boston Gazette*, May 17, 1773, 3; auctioneers Moses Deshon, *Boston News-Letter*, July 4, 1771, 3, and John Gerrish, *Essex Gazette*, Feb. 13, 1770, 4; needlework schoolmistresses Mary Speakman, *Boston News-Letter*, June 1, 1769, 3, and Sarah Bramham, *Boston Post-Boy*, May 12, 1760, 2.

47. Butt (in Fitches Alley): Feb. 22, 1766, Aug. 22, 1766, warnings; *1771 Valn.*, 0101–4016; Thwing database 10551; Ethel Farrington Smith, "Seventeenth Century Hull, Massachusetts, and Her People," *NEGHR* 143 (Oct. 1989), 336. Culbertson (in Marlborough Street opposite to Bromfields Lane): July 26, 1769, May 3, 1770, June 24, 1772, warnings; *BTR* 20:304. For a later era, see

Wendy Gamber, *The Boardinghouse in Nineteenth-Century America* (Baltimore: Johns Hopkins University Press, 2007).

48. Dinsdale: her niece Deborah Wood, warned May 4, 1771, last from Stoughton. Taylor: Sept. 18, 1766, Oct. 28, 1768, warnings; for the land Taylor owned on Marlborough Street, Thwing database 57184. These are the only two landladies for whom Love gave an occupation. Among the warned strangers, we have not been able to document girls who were boarding in Boston to receive training at needlework schools.

49. Holmes: warned July 16, 1765; Thomas W. Baldwin, comp., *Vital Records of Cambridge, Massachusetts, to the Year 1850*, 2 vols. (Boston: Wright and Potter, 1914), 2:203; Boston Ch. Rec. database; SCPF 15830. Lodging with the Holmeses: Patience Ayres (July 16, 1765, warning; *Boston Cems.*, 528; she was also warned in Brookline in 1769, SF 89153); peruke maker William Bosson (Aug. 17, 1765; William R. Cutter, ed., *Genealogical and Personal Memoirs Relating to the Families of Boston and Eastern Massachusetts* [New York: Lewis, 1908], 3:1169–76), and others warned on May 1, Aug. 14, and Dec. 29, 1767, and July 21, 1769. Rodgers: Thwing database 52867; *Boston News-Letter*, April 10, 1766, 2; *Worc. Co. Warnings*, 67; Worcester County Probate File 51123 (1805) (microfilm), Judicial Archives, MA Archives. For an illuminating parsing of the lower ranks of the laboring classes, see Billy G. Smith, *The 'Lower Sort': Philadelphia's Laboring People, 1750–1880* (Ithaca, N.Y.: Cornell University Press, 1994), 4–6; see also, Corfield, *Impact of English Towns*, 134.

50. Androwson: Nellis and Cecere, *BOPR*, 177–78; Oct. 14, 1768, warning of the French girl, Françoise Ways. It is striking that only one of the 480-odd strangers whom Love described as needy in some way appeared among the nine hundred landlords named in Love's warnings. The exception was John Williams, a castaway off Rhode Island who walked into Boston on Aug. 7, 1770, the day he was warned by Love ("he properly belongs to Old England"). When warning Williams again on Jan. 4, 1774 (last from New York), Love gave more details: "Lame in one of his hands, originally from" White Fryer in London. In between these episodes, on May 9, 1771, Moses Cummings, arriving from Douglastown, Mass., told the warner he expected to live with Mr. John Williams, a lame man, in Union Street.

51. "Ill govern'd" appeared frequently in the charges against disorderly house proprietors; see, for example, the prosecution of James and Mary Roach, Suff. Co. GSP Records, record book for 1764–68, Oct. 30, 1764 session. None of these six defendants had a liquor retailing or tavern license. Three were acquitted: peruke maker Nicholas Butler, laborer Robert Doran, and rope maker Gilbert Anderson. Laborer John Skinner was fined twenty shillings and brewer Patrick Carroll was found "Guilty [of the charges] Except of Harbouring Negroes" and fined £3. At his residence near Fort Hill, "just by the shipyard," Carroll housed one man, Patrick Norris (warned May 18, 1772), during the time his house was said to be disorderly. In 1773–74, he took in two solo women. See Suff. Co. GSP Records, record book for 1769–73 (unpaginated), Aug. 7, 1770, Jan. 29, 1771, April 14, 1771, and July 14, 1772 (Carroll) sessions.

52. Hubbard: Suff. Co. GSP Records, record book for 1764–68, Jan. 28, 1766 session; BTR 20:122; O'Bryant warning, Oct. 2, 1765 (he had arrived from London in July); Thwing database 39292 on her husband, Francis (whose inventory amounted to £115); *Boston News-Letter*, Feb. 9, 1769, 2; Nellis and Cecere, *BOPR*, 295. O'Bryant, sometimes styled Bryant: Suff. Co. GSP Records, record book for 1764–68, April 16, 1766 session; SF 100810. At the same location as in 1765, Widow Hubbard took in a lame man, Robert Low (July 28, 1768, warning). Hubbard's rowdy, unlicensed tavern may have been exposed when O'Bryant was captured in Salem (shortly after Oct. 19, 1765)

with the bay gelding he had stolen from a stay maker who lived in the West End. Bryant and Hubbard were charged in the same month.

53. None of the Love landlords prosecuted for running disorderly houses were located in New Boston or near Mount Whoredom, one area of the city mentioned in the rare references to sex for sale. The docks were another: merchant John Rowe noted on July 24, 1771, that last night "the mob Routed the Whores at the house of Joseph Henderson at Olivers Dock"; *Rowe Diary*, 218. On prostitution in Boston, see Salinger, *Taverns and Drinking*, 113–14; and D. Brenton Simons, *Witches, Rakes, and Rogues: True Stories of Scum, Scandal, Murder, and Mayhem in Boston, 1630–1775* (Beverly, Mass.: Commonwealth Editions, 2005), 99–101.

54. For unlicensed houses, see Salinger, *Taverns and Drinking*, 281n54. One defendant and landlord, master mariner, and trader, Murtaugh McCarroll, was convicted three times and fined the statutory £6 on the third occasion. He died two years later, leaving a wife and two minor children, possessed of £37.6.0 in personal estate and a house worth roughly £48; Thwing database 43855; *1771 Valn.*, 0101–5536; Suff. Co. GSP Records, record book for 1769–73, May 1, Aug. 7, and Oct. 2, 1770, sessions. McCarroll rented his house near New South meetinghouse to a family of four arriving from Glasgow (Feb. 11, 1771, warning).

55. Lorenzo Johnston Greene, *The Negro in Colonial New England, 1620–1776* (New York: Columbia University Press, 1942; reprint Bowie, Md.: Heritage Books, 1998), esp. chap. 11; Catherine Adams and Elizabeth H. Pleck, *Love of Freedom: Black Women in Colonial and Revolutionary New England* (New York: Oxford University Press, 2010).

56. *1771 Valn.*, 0101–3616 and 0101–3617. Fayerweather: Thwing database 9946; July 22, 1767, July 18, 1770, and June 10, 1771, warnings. For a similar account of Fayerweather, Locker, and Boston Smith (mentioned below) occupying this site, see Kathryn Grover and Janine V. da Silva, "Historic Resource Study: Boston African American National Historic Site," Dec. 31, 2002, 27–30, http://www.nps.gov/history/history/online_books/bost/hrs.pdf. Jacob Price's 1769 map (see this book's endsheets) omitted changes to the west end, including Belknap Street.

57. Locker: Thwing database 10033; *1780 Takings*, 28. Work at the courthouse complex: SF 89168, 89273. Highway work: *BTR* 19:195–96, 240; 20:218, 236; MS f Bos. 7, Boston Town Papers, 7:98, 101, BPL. Tobias may have been the son or nephew of Scipio Lock/Locker, to whom he mortgaged his land in late 1764. Locker lodged Lucy Pernam (June 5, 1766, warning); for more on her, see Chapter 8 in this volume.

58. On Bill: *BTR* 19:195; Nellis and Cecere, *BOPR*, 152, 157, 177, 637; lodgers: Feb. 19, Feb. 24, June 6, July 22, 1766, warnings. Bill had had an earlier stay in the almshouse, from May to November 1764.

59. Gunney: Boston Ch. Recs. database (Old South); Thwing database 9947; lodgers: Dec. 2, 1765, Nov. 26, Dec. 13, 1766, June 12, 1767, and July 3, 1767, warnings. Halsey: May 22, 1770, Nov. 20, 1772, warnings; SCPR, 76:549; SCPF 17345; for an instrument maker's business, see William Williams's advertisement, *Massachusetts Spy*, Feb. 13, 1772, 3. In listing lodgers for Gunney, Love was not consistent in calling him "a negor man." This was true with some other black landlords, especially subsequent to the first such entry Love made. Gunney remained in Boston after the wartime occupation and was named as executor by two free black men (Thwing database for mariner John Day: 23630, and 16140, for laborer Nero Cogswell). Halsey may have been formerly enslaved to the Halsey family that included several mathematical instrument makers. Other black landlords included Pompey (no surname given), who lived in a South End house of the glazier James Cunningham and was named as landlord four times in May–June 1770.

60. Abraham and Elizabeth (Lee) Millrow: *Boston Marrs.*, 2:421; Dec. 13, Jun. 19, 1766, and Jan. 5, 1767, warnings. Esau, Peggy, and Dinah Millrow were warned Jan. 20, 1767; on Cato Jeffries, see *Boston Marrs.*, 2:46. Overall, the seventeen black landlords took in thirty-seven warned parties, ten of whom (four solos and six families) were unmarked racially by Love and thus were probably perceived as whites.

61. Whitehill, *Boston*, 5–8 (quotation p. 5), 60–63, 577–84, chap. 7; Drake, *Old Landmarks*, 284–88; Marilynne K. Roach, "A Map of Revolutionary Boston," available in the National Park Service store, Boston; Jane Holtz Kay, *Lost Boston* (Boston: Houghton Mifflin, 1980). For superimpositions of the original peninsula on modern maps, see Whitehill, *Boston*, 4, and Alex Krieger and David Cobb, eds., with Amy Turner, *Mapping Boston* (Cambridge, Mass.: MIT Press, 1999), 16, and the accompanying website (see "Composite Map of Boston").

Chapter 7. Sojourners of the Respectable Sort

1. Hall's birth and parents: July 8, 1766; Priscilla R. Ritter and Thelma Fleishman, comps. and eds., *Newton, Massachusetts, 1679–1779: A Biographical Directory* (Boston: New England Historic Genealogical Society, 1982), 45; *Vital Records of Newton, Massachusetts, to the Year 1850* (Boston: New England Historic Genealogical Society, 1905), 83; MCPF 10147, Josiah Hall.

2. For similar arguments that for English parish officers "successful judgements about potential indigence must have been extraordinarily difficult to make" and that the attributes of laborers shaded, often imperceptibly, into those who were (wrongly or rightly) denigrated as vagrants, see Steve Hindle, *On the Parish? The Micro-Politics of Poor Relief in Rural England, c. 1550–1750* (Oxford: Clarendon Press, 2004), 359, and Rab Houston, "Vagrants and Society in Early Modern England," *Cambridge Anthropology* 4 (1980), 25.

3. Some profiles in this chapter are the result of tracing we did selectively, not systematically, on persons Love warned from September 1766 to March 1774. Others resulted from our concentrated research sample, in which we systematically attempted to trace all parties incoming from a Massachusetts location (not including the District of Maine, where few vital records were kept) who appeared in Love's surviving logbook covering his warnings from January 1765 through August 1766. Of sixty-six solo males in the sample, we traced forty-four to some extent, including thirty both before and after warning. We can attach age-at-warning to thirty-nine: ten were fourteen to nineteen, and fourteen were in their twenties; the median age was twenty-four. Some of the twenty-four untraceables had common names, such that several men of that name appear in the vital records of the town where the traveler was last from or in the Massachusetts records as a whole.

4. William Doty: Sept. 19, 1765; *Vital Records of Plymouth, Massachusetts, to the Year 1850*, comp. Lee D. van Antwerp (Camden, Me.: Picton Press, 1993), 117, 265; Plymouth County Probate Records, 45:125, 129 (microfilm), Judicial Archives, MA Archives. Others fitting this profile include: nineteen-year-old Roger Bates of Hingham, who returned to his natal town to marry and soon after moved his family briefly to Boston before settling in Vermont (March 11, 1765, and Nov. 17, 1770, warnings; George Lyman Davenport and Elizabeth Osgood Davenport, *The Genealogies of the Families of Cohasset, Massachusetts* [Somerworth, N.H.: New England History Press, 1984, first published 1909], 52–53); and Ebenezer Townsend, son of a Charlestown saddler, arrived at fifteen to lodge with saddler Sutton Byles, married in his hometown in 1772 (Aug. 7,

1766, warning; Thomas Bellows Wyman, *The Genealogies and Estates of Charlestown, in the County of Middlesex* . . . , *1629–1818* [Boston: D. Clapp and Son, 1879], 948–49).

5. Goodenow: June 6, 1765, warning; *Vital Records of Sudbury, Massachusetts, to the Year 1850* Boston: New England Historic Genealogical Society, 1903), 54, 202; MCPF 9315, Aaron Goodenow (1788); MCPF 9336, Elisha Goodenow (1798). Goodenow's Boston landlord was cordwainer Ebenezer Topliff. Kittery-born Lemuel Gowen (warned March 14, 1765) illustrates a slight variation: he arrived in Boston at about age twenty-five, having last resided (possibly as an apprentice) in Sudbury; by 1771, he was farming modest holdings in his hometown, where he married in 1777 (*1771 Valn.*, 1705–0522; Joseph Crook Anderson II and Lois Ware Thurston, eds., *Vital Records of Kittery, Maine to the Year 1892* (Camden, Me.: Picton Press, 1991), 79, 97, 155; John E. Frost, comp., *Maine Probate Abstracts*, vol. 1, *1687–1775* (Camden, Me.: Picton Press, 1991), 315, 667.

6. Sabin: Feb. 28, 1765; *Vital Records of Attleborough, Massachusetts, to the Year 1849* (Salem: Essex Institute, 1934), 546; *The Descendants of William Sabin of Rehoboth, Massachusetts*, comp. Gordon Alan Morris, Thomas J. Prittie, and Dixie Prittie ([Camden, Me.]: Penobscot Press, 1994), 40; Esther Friend, "Wrentham Notifications and Warnings Out," *NEHGR* 141 (July 1987), 201; *1771 Valn.*, 0919–0604.

7. Haven: July 1, 1766; Josiah Adams, *The Genealogy of the Descendants of Richard Haven of Lynn* . . . (Boston: W. White and H. P. Lewis, 1843), 16, 26–27; MAVR, for births of the couple's children in Framingham, Lancaster, Pepperell, Dedham; *Worc. Co. Warnings*, 10; *Massachusetts Soldiers and Sailors of the Revolutionary War: A Compilation from the Archives*, 17 vols. (Boston: Wright and Potter, 1896–1908), 7:538; *1771 Valn.*, 0424–0601; SCPF 17714, Daniel Haven (Asa's father), 1782.

8. *Boston News-Letter*, Dec. 17, 1767, 3; *Boston Gazette*, June 15, 1772, 3; *Boston Post-Boy*, Dec. 6, 1773, 4. George: Feb. 10, 1773 (last from Braintree, came on Nov. 3, 1772); BTR 20:248. On Thomas Trott Sr., see Thwing database 58489. Love seems to have reserved the label "child" for incomers under ten years old.

9. Goodale: March 31, 1766; *Vital Records of Marlborough, Massachusetts, to the Year 1849* (Worcester: F. P. Rice, 1980), 81, 361; Will of Nathan, MCPF 9312; *Massachusetts Soldiers and Sailors*, 6:560; *Vital Records of Conway, Massachusetts, to the Year 1850* (Boston: New England Historic Genealogical Society, 1943), 53, 236. In the final disbursement from the estate in 1780, Solomon was to receive, besides "what I have alr[e]ady given him," one-fifth of his father's lands in New Marlborough and New Hampshire, plus one cow and one-third of the husbandry tools and clothes.

10. Pratt: June 26, 1766; Ann S. Lainhart, "Weston Cautions 1757 to 1803," *NEHGR* 144 (July 1990), 216; *Vital Records of Needham, Massachusetts: Births to 1845, Marriages to 1850, Deaths to 1850* (n.p., 1959), 82; SCPF 8529, Zebediah Pratt (Simeon's father), 1746; Ancestry.com, *1790 United States Federal Census* [database on-line] (Provo, Utah: Ancestry.com Operations, 2010), Roxbury, Mass., Series M637, Roll 4, 516; Norfolk County Probate File 15144 (1805) (microfilm), Judicial Archives, MA Archives. Given the vagaries of probate record survivals and the difficulties of tying warned strangers to their parents' estates, it is impossible to determine what proportion of Massachusetts-born solo youths warned in Boston were not inheritors of land.

11. Ames: Feb. 10, 1767 (last from Waltham); Samuel Mather, *Christ Sent to Heal the Broken Hearted.: A Sermon* . . . . *To Which is Added, His Life Written by Himself* (Boston: William M'Alpine, 1773), 31 ("credible"), 36.

12. Clark: July 15, 1765; Sylvester Judd, *History of Hadley Including the Early History of Hatfield, South Hadley, Amherst, and Granby Massachusetts with Family Genealogies by Lucius M.*

Boltwood (Springfield, Mass.: H. R. Huntting, 1905), 339, 20–21 (the latter, in the genealogies' pagination); *1771 Valn.*, 0510–0317.

13. Tyler: July 7, 1765; Robert B. Hanson, ed., *The Vital Records of Dedham, Massachusetts, 1635–1844*, 3 vols. (Bowie, Md.: Heritage Books, 1989), 1:295; *Sibley's Harvard Graduates*, 10:329–34; Abner Morse, *Genealogical Register of the Descendants of Several Ancient Puritans* (Boston: H. W. Dutton and Son, 1861), 3:110–11. In 1778, Joseph served as administrator of his deceased father's estate, appraised at £220 in goods (SCPR, 77:151).

14. Hide: March 28, 1765; *1771 Valn.*, 0101–3124 for David Hide, 0611–0168 for his father, Enoch; *Vital Records of Newton*, 107; deeds summarized in Thwing database 39756; *History of Monson, Massachusetts* (Monson: Monson Historical Society, 1960), 82.

15. Cox: Oct. 7, 1767; William Richard Cutter, ed., *Historic Homes and Places and Genealogical and Personal Memoirs Relating to the Families of Middlesex County, Massachusetts*, 4 vols. (New York: Lewis, 1908), 1:367; *The Bi-Centennial Book of Malden . . .* (Malden: G. C. Rand, 1850), 245, via Google Books; *Boston Marrs.*, 2:47, 421, 426; Suff. Co. GSP Records, record book for 1764–68 (unpaginated), May 4, 1768, session. Dickinson: Nellis and Cecere, *BOPR*, 189, 192. The Malden histories omit Cox's Boston activities; Cutter asserts that Cox died in Malden "at an advanced age."

16. Observers stated that just under seven thousand Bostonians remained in town one month after the blockade began, and that figure was down to 2,719 by early 1776. The city population did not exceed its colonial peak of sixteen thousand or so until 1785. See Jim Vrabel, *When in Boston: A Time Line and Almanac* (Boston: Northeastern University Press, 2004), 72–73, and Jacqueline Barbara Carr, *After the Siege: A Social History of Boston, 1775–1800* (Boston: Northeastern University Press, 2005).

17. Stutson: April 5, 1765; John Stetson Barry, *A Genealogical and Biographical Sketch of the Name and Family of Stetson; from the Year 1634, to the Year 1847* (Boston: W. A. Hall, 1847), 93, 95–96 (quotation p. 95); Brigitte Burkett, *Genealogical Data Extracted from the Boston Selectmen's Minutes, 1730s–1776* (Bowie, Md.: Heritage Books, 1993), 401. Ascertaining definitively if warned strangers stayed in Boston is hampered by the paucity of death records kept by early New Englanders, who were more assiduous about registering births and marriages.

18. Hogan: Aug. 9, 1768 (Love spelled the surname Hugins); *Massachusetts Spy*, Aug. 8, 1771, 3; *Boston Evening-Post*, Aug. 12, 1771, 3.

19. Woodhouse: Dec. 3, 1766; *BTR* 20:238; *Milton Vital Records, 1662–1843*, 78, www.new englandancestors.org. Our concentrated research sample consists of the sixty-five white solo females incoming from New England and Nova Scotia locations and recorded in Love's 1765–66 logbook, surnames A–H. We traced thirty-three to some extent. Ages are known or estimated for thirty-two, yielding an average age of twenty-one, a median age of twenty, and a range of fifteen to sixty-three. In the same period, Love warned six Indian or African-descended solo females (they are discussed below) and 2 whites last from Pennsylvania (no further evidence of them emerges in New England records).

20. White: *BTR* 20:180, and Oct. 23, 1765, warning; Barker: Dec. 15, 1772. Short: Feb. 1, 1772; Ledeer: June 1, 1769. Love mentioned that a solo female was "in service" or hoped to get a place in sixteen cases. Three of the sixteen were labeled "Indian" and one "negro."

21. Scamp or Scramp: May 3, 1770; for her marriage to Thomas Carnes, see *Boston Marrs.*, 2:363. For his father, John Carnes, see Chapter 5 in this volume.

22. Flint: Aug. 7, 1766; *Boston Marrs.*, 2:400; *Hollis St. Church Recs*, 195; *Boston Cems.*, 115.

23. Cobb: April 5, 1765; *Genealogical Notes of Barnstable Families, Being a Reprint of the Amos Otis Papers* . . . , 2 vols. (Barnstable: F. B. and F. P. Goss, 1888–90), 1:176; *Sibley's Harvard Graduates*, 16:43–46. Hall: *Boston Marrs.*, 2:363 (to Nathaniel Rogers); *Vital Records of Newton*, 168. Most of the young women warned by Love and marrying in Boston were considered, for purpose of the marriage records, "of Boston" at their weddings, even though they had legal settlement elsewhere.

24. Sullivan: April 19, 1768 (last from Pownalboro); Suff. Co. GSP Records, record book for 1769–73, 16. After being warned, it appears that Sullivan left Boston and returned, to be warned by Love again on July 19, "last from" Georges, Maine. Four days later, she was admitted to the almshouse, "sick," on the province account. She gave birth there on Jan. 25, 1769. She may be the "Kata. Sullivan" discharged and "sent to Ireland," in 1770; Nellis and Cecere, BOPR, 191, 211, 233, 629. Besides Christian Isbister, who is discussed in Chapter 8 of this volume, the names of two other solo warned women match the names of women "of Boston" charged with fornication: Ann Salter (warned May 16, 1765, convicted in October 1767; she may be the Anna Salter who married John Phillips, Nov. 2, 1767; *Boston Marrs.*, 2:348) and Elizabeth Harris (warned July 16, 1765; convicted in August 1770; named as her child's father housewright Daniel McLester of Boston, "now absconded").

25. Gay: Jan. 28, 1771; SF 102016 (inquest), 90897, 90905–907 (escape from justice: 90897); *Boston News-Letter*, April 16, 1772, 2 ("disowned"). On Daniel Whitney: May 15, 1769, warning; BTR 23:11, 19; MAVR: Brookline birth and marriage, Warwick death. She may have been one of the two Mary Gays who married in Boston in the next four years (*Boston Marrs.*, 2:43, 88). On infanticide, see Peter C. Hoffer and N. E. H. Hull, *Murdering Mothers: Infanticide in England and New England, 1558–1803* (New York: New York University Press, 1981), esp. 74–91, and Cornelia Hughes Dayton, *Women Before the Bar: Gender, Law, and Society in Connecticut, 1639–1789* (Chapel Hill: Omohundro Institute of Early American History and Culture and University of North Carolina Press, 1995), 207–13.

26. For example, George Clark, warned June 15, 1765; his three daughters arrived separately and were warned Oct. 28, 1765 (Hannah and Margaret) and March 13, 1766 (Betsy). Love's notes reveal that Clark père moved over the eight month period, lodging initially at Roger McNight's, then renting a house first from Stephen Rodgers and then from Judge Samuel Welles—all South End locations.

27. Unchet: Oct. 23, 1772. Sisters Ann and Jane Clark (warned March 28, 1766) had been born in Boston or lived there as children; their father, tallow chandler Thomas Clark, died in 1748 (Thwing database 15685). In 1768, they were rejoining their mother and stepfather, housewright Ezekiel Averill, after all four had lived in Halifax. Another example is Sarah Delhonde, warned May 15, 1766, last from Salem; she had been baptized as an infant in 1744 in Boston's New South Church (Boston Ch. Recs. database).

28. Kingston: April 22, 1769; *1771 Valn.*, Paul Kingston: 0462–0511. Hardwick: Sept. 5, 1771. Love explicitly described thirty-three solo incomers as wives and twenty-four as widows; our research shows that he did not always note when a traveler was married or widowed. Love commented that one incomer had been "Lately Disvorced" and gave her maiden name (McDonnell): Charlotte Ford, last from Wilmington, Dec. 27, 1771.

29. Allen sisters: Aug. 9, 1765 warning; Ward: Dec. 13, 1765. Arrest: *Boston Evening-Post*, Jan. 6, 1766, 3; *Connecticut Courant*, Jan. 20, 1766, 2; *Newport Mercury*, Jan. 13, 1766, 3. Grievous: SF 100815. Love or the children themselves overstated their ages as eleven and nine; they were nine

and seven. He noted that their guardian, a Natick man, had "£85.0.0 Lawful money of the Childrens in his hands." Their mother was originally from Boston. See *Town of Weston: Births, Deaths, and Marriages 1707—1850* . . . , ed. Mary Frances Peirce (Boston: McIndoe Bros., 1901), 89, 92, 98.

30. In cases involving child victims, penetration was hard to prove. See Marybeth Hamilton Arnold, " 'The Life of a Citizen in the Hands of a Woman': Sexual Assault in New York City, 1790–1820," in *Passion and Power: Sexuality in History*, ed. Kathy Peiss and Christina Simmons (Philadelphia: Temple University Press, 1989), 42–45; Barbara S. Lindemann, " 'To Ravish and Carnally Know': Rape in Eighteenth-Century Massachusetts," *Signs* 10 (1984–85), 75–76; and Dayton, *Women Before the Bar*, 233, 249–56. For male coercion as a culturally accepted part of courtship, see Sharon Block, *Rape and Sexual Power in Early America* (Chapel Hill: Omohundro Institute of Early American History and Culture and University of North Carolina Press, 2006).

31. SF 100815, 100811; *Boston Post-Boy*, May 26, 1766, 3; Suff. Co. GSP Records, record book for 1764–68, July 8, 1766, session. Among the five witnesses were the McCurdys and a male physician they must have called to examine and tend to Betty. It appears that a court-appointed attorney, Samuel Winthrop, defended Ward. Hopestill Foster, named three times a landlord in Love's warnings, was foreman of the grand jury. A similar sentence handed down in 1770 was carried out at the pillory in King Street; *Boston News-Letter*, Jan. 18, 1770, 3.

32. There are marriages for several Elizabeth and Tamar Allens in various Massachusetts towns, including Boston, in the 1770s; see, for example, *Boston Marrs.*, 2:339. The McCurdys moved to Orrington, Maine, by 1771; Donald Bradford Macurda, *Early McCurdys in Maine (Their Antecedents and Descendants)* (Privately published, 1979), typescript at NEHGS, 57–60.

33. Warning, July 18, 1770 (the children were listed as John, Caesar, and Fillis Peirpoint); Boston Ch. Recs. database (Second Church of Roxbury). It is possible that the "negro" woman, Sepro, who attended Walter's married daughter, Lady Sarah Hesilrige, when she came to Boston in 1766, was Cuffee and Grace's daughter Zipporah (Hesilrige warning, April 10, 1766). It is quite likely that a black woman Love warned and did not mark as either enslaved or free was their daughter: Phyllis Walters, last from Roxbury, warned Jan. 5, 1767, arrived in August 1766, lived first "with Mr. Samuel Bragdon the brewer near the Whipping post in King St." and then with free black Abraham Millrow.

34. Feittis: Sept. 2, 1771. Scipio married free black Judy Oliver out of Christ Church, Boston, in winter 1769; *Boston Marrs.*, 2:336. He had been a slave of the wealthy Brinley family, who owned a Framingham farm and a mansion in Roxbury; see Finding Aid, Brinley Family Papers (Ms. 161), Special Collections and University Archives, W. E. B. DuBois Library, University of Massachusetts Amherst.

35. "Both Indians": Thomas and Abigail Simons, last from Dartmouth, Oct. 22, 1767. Wamsquan (Love wrote the surname "Wainscutt"), last from Southborough, with children Eunice and Solomon: Sept. 26, 1767, warning; *Vital Records of Natick, Massachusetts, to the Year 1850*, comp., Thomas W. Baldwin (Bowie, Md.: Heritage Books, 1991), 192. "No Pretension": qtd. in Jean M. O'Brien, *Dispossession by Degree: Indian Land and Identity in Natick Massachusetts, 1650–1790* (New York: Cambridge University Press, 1997), 193. Parker: Feb. 9, 1774. Meers: May 6, 1771; Nellis and Cecere, *BOPR*, 210, 228; Love noted that Elizabeth belonged "properly to" Stoneham and that her daughter was born in Lancaster. Note that, as with across-status marriages among blacks, Love gave different surnames for the Meers-Collins couple. On Indian-white marriages, see Daniel R. Mandell, "The Saga of Sarah Muckamugg: Indian and African American Intermarriage in

Colonial New England," in *Sex, Love, Race: Crossing Boundaries in North American History*, ed. Martha Hodes (New York: New York University Press, 1999), 74 ("custom frowned"), 80, and O'Brien, *Dispossession by Degrees*, 202n.

36. Chase, Oct. 15, 1767; Fletcher, Oct. 2, 1769; Short, Feb. 1, 1772. Gummer/Gomer: Jan. 10, 1766, warning; Boston Ch. Recs. database (Hollis Street Church) for her March 21, 1742, baptism and Aug. 15, 1745, marriage; *Vital Records of Natick*, 191. On Vitter (or Vitto), see Lorenzo Johnston Greene, *The Negro in Colonial New England, 1620–1776* (Bowie, Md.: Heritage Books, 1998, first published New York: Columbia University Press, 1942), 309, 313–14. For William Gummer's manumission, see *Sherborn Past and Present, 1674–1924* (Sherborn: Sherborn Historical Society, 1924), 70.

37. "Form for a Negroe Marriage" of Andover minister Samuel Phillips, in George E. Howard, *A History of Matrimonial Institutions*, 3 vols. (Chicago: University of Chicago Press and Callaghan, 1904), 2:225–26, quoting George H. Moore, "Slave Marriages in Massachusetts," *Dawson's Historical Magazine*, 2nd ser., 5 (1869), 137. For Dinn, who married freeman Newton Prince (a Love landlord), see July 30, 1767 (Dinn, renting a house called the Three Horse Shoes), and Oct. 15, 1767 (Prince as landlord to Elizabeth Chase) warnings; *Boston Marrs.*, 2:56. For Short's December 1773 marriage intention, see *Boston Marrs.*, 2:434. Sarah Prince was warned July 11, 1769, one month after her marriage to Will, a slave of Captain Thomas Newell; Love listed her as living in Newell's residence on Wentworth wharf; *Boston Marrs.*, 2:329.

38. When warned on Nov. 3, 1767, Surrance was living in a house of distiller Andrew Johonnot's in Long Lane, and possibly working for him. The Warning Out book, 1745–70, but not Love's entry, notes that Surrance had a child with her when she was warned. *Boston Marrs.*, 2:422 ("neg. svt. of the Governor's"); Nellis and Cecere, *BOPR*, 193, 638, 643n30.

39. Pernam: June 5, 1766, warning (lodging with Tobias Locker); Warning Out book, 1745–70, June 5, 1766; Divorce libel of Lucy Pernam, with Scipio's answers, and depositions, SF 129751 (profane, distracted, vile); "A Descriptive List of the State's Poor, 1795," loose paper in the Overseers of the Poor Account Book (1805–43), City Clerk's Office, Newburyport, Mass. ("raving"); *Essex Journal and New Hampshire Packet* (Newburyport), Dec. 19, 1787, 3 ("negro wench"). Pernam was physically removed from Boston in February 1773 (*BTR* 23:165) and was jailed there in August 1775 ("A Journal Kept by John Leach, During his Confinement by the British, in Boston Gaol, in 1775," *NEHGR* 19 [July 1865], 259). On other divorces by black New Englanders, see Catherine Adams and Elizabeth H. Pleck, *Love of Freedom: Black Women in Colonial and Revolutionary New England* (New York: Oxford University Press, 2010), 113–14.

40. Waban, Feb. 23, 1768; O'Brien, *Dispossession by Degrees*, 198–99, 141–42; MCPF 23397 (Isaac Wabourn, 1746), 23398 (Mary Waban, 1746), and 23688 (John Wamsquon, her grandfather, 1746); *Vital Records of Natick*, 95; *Vital Records of Barre, Massachusetts, to the End of the Year 1849* (Worcester: F. P. Rice, 1903), 211. It is not clear if Mary Waban ever sold the two Natick parcels she inherited in 1749.

41. Wamsquan, Nov. 25, 1765; O'Brien, *Dispossession by Degrees*, 200; *Vital Records of Natick*, 11, 192. Selling land, being disappointed: administrator's account, MCPF 23690 (Rhoda Wamsquam, 1769). Her estate administrator was Joseph Perry of Sherborn, substantial farmer, former selectman, town clerk, and legislator, who became a justice of the peace in 1766; Schutz, *Legislators*, 309.

42. Speen (whom Love called Beulah Rodgers): June 18, 1767; *Vital Records of Natick*, 45, 87, 145, 191, 179, 184, 245; *Boston Marrs.*, 2:336; O'Brien, *Dispossession by Degrees*, 202; and, on Pateshall, *Sibley's Harvard Graduates*, 9:558–60. For the life of Sarah Burnee (1744–1821), daughter of

Nipmuc woman Sarah Muckamugg and her husband, Fortune Burnee, see Mandell, "Saga of
Sarah Muckamugg," 81. Burnee was warned by Love July 22, 1766, last from Grafton, arrived July
18, lodged at negro man Joseph Bill's, New Boston.

43. Diego: July 14, 1768, and Aug. 12, 1771 (tall); Travel: Sept. 12, 1768, and June 28, 1771;
Cromwell: Oct. 1, 1767 (for his landlord Robert Pierpoint, see Chapter 6 in this volume).

44. Ephraim: Aug. 21, 1767, warning; *Vital Records of Natick*, 37; George Quintal Jr., *Patriots
of Color: "A Peculiar Beauty and Merit": African Americans and Native Americans at Battle Road
and Bunker Hill* (Boston: Boston National Historical Park, 2004), 40, 96. A few years earlier,
Ephraim was posted as a runaway by "his Master," Seth Dwight of Medfield, and described as
wearing "his own black Hair," "a blue Woolen Coat, a green Baize Waistcoat, Leather Breeches,
grey Yarn Stockings, and a Pair of old Shoes"; *Boston Evening-Post*, Oct. 22, 1764, 3. He died in
January 1777, just before he was due to start service in the Continental army. In 1753, he had
inherited a cash share of his father, Peter's, estate valued at £394, but no land; O'Brien, *Dispossession by Degrees*, 155.

45. Francis/Peters: Dec. 13, 1766, warning; Deposition of Snow Francis, dated Dec. 21, 1780,
SF 129933; B. B. Thatcher, *Memoir of Phillis Wheatley, A Native African and a Slave* (Boston:
George W. Light, 1834), 26–30. See also Vincent Caretta, *Phillis Wheatley: Biography of a Genius
in Bondage* (Athens: University of Georgia Press, 2011), chap. 7.

46. Brown: Oct. 12, 1770, "with Dr. Church and Mr. Price," meaning the physician Benjamin
Church and, presumably, Ezekiel Price, both of whom were later loyalists; *Boston Marrs.*, 2:68.
As landlord: Chloe Prescott, warned Jan. 1. 1773, last from Groton. Brown served in the Revolutionary War; upon his death in January 1820 he left household items worth $25 plus $38 from the
Pension Office; SCPR, 118:209, 239. His funeral was from King's Chapel. An obituary notice called
him "a man of colour, aged 67; an honest and industrious man"; *Independent Chronicle*, Feb. 2,
1820, 3; Boston Ch. Recs. database (King's Chapel).

47. Allen, last from Providence: Feb. 5, 1765. Ebenezer and Meribah had two sons baptized
at Old South (Boston Ch. Recs. database); their apprentice Silas Allen married in Boston and
appeared in the 1771 tax valuation (*Boston Marrs.*, 2:43; *1771 Valn.*, 0101–1631). McNabb (Love
wrote "McNobb"), last from Halifax: Jan. 31, 1769; James New, the head of household for a family
of eight arriving on the same day, worked with McNabb (Jan. 27, 1769, warning).

48. Chase: Jan. 1, 1772, warning; *Boston Marrs.*, 2:338; Charles Edward Banks, *The History of
Martha's Vineyard, Dukes County, Massachusetts*, 3 vols. (Boston: George H. Dean, 1911, 1925),
2:18, 58, 3:71–80. Stoneman: Oct. 19, 1770; *BTR* 23:69; *Boston Gazette*, Dec. 24, 1770, 4, and June 15,
1772, 3; *Newport Mercury*, July 6, 1772, 1; and see Ellen Hartigan-O'Connor, *The Ties That Buy:
Women and Commerce in Revolutionary America* (Philadelphia: University of Pennsylvania Press,
2009), 1–2, 74–75. Love noted twenty-nine instances in which arriving householders brought with
them apprentices, servants, or enslaved persons.

49. Nutting: May 20, 1766 (the servant was David Malcomb); William T. Ruddock, "Four
Jonathan Nuttings of Cushing, Maine," *Maine Genealogist* 31 (Aug. 2009), 104–8. Anderson: April
14, 1766; Henry R. Stiles, *The History and Genealogies of Ancient Windsor . . .*, 2 vols. (Hartford,
Conn.: Case, Lockwood, and Brainard, 1891–92), 2:37; probate file of Ashbel Anderson of E.
Windsor, 1777 (microfilm), Connecticut State Library, Hartford.

50. Ament: July 24, 1765; *Collections of the New-York Genealogical and Biographical Society*
(New York: Printed for the Society, 1890), 2:363, 484; *Ecclesiastical Records, State of New York*
(Albany: J. B. Lyon, 1905), 6:3970. According to the 1790 federal census, Eldert Ament was then a
resident of Schenectady. Williams: April 25, 1767, and March 24, 1768.

51. Simmons: Dec. 29, 1768; *Port Arrivals*, 85; *Boston Gazette*, March 19, 1770, 3; Boston Ch. Recs. database. Beatty: Feb. 15, 1765, and July 9, 1766; *Boston Post-Boy*, Aug. 18, 1766, 3; *1771 Valn.*, 0101–3120; Maas, *Divided Hearts*, 11; Anne Borden Harding, "The Port Roseway Debacle: Some American Loyalists in Nova Scotia," *NEHGR* 117 (Jan. 1963), 11.

52. Richards: May 29, 1766; *Vital Records of Weymouth, Massachusetts, to the Year 1850* (Boston: New England Historic Genealogical Society, 1910), 2:163; George Walter Chamberlain, *Genealogies of the Early Families of Weymouth, Massachusetts*, 2 vols. in 1 (Baltimore: Genealogical Publishing, 1984, first published 1923), 593; Seybolt, *Town Officials*, 324; Thwing database 52153; Boston Ch. Recs. database; *New England Chronicle* (Cambridge), Jan. 25, 1776, 3. The couple named one son born in Boston for the landlord they had when they first arrived: Edmund Quincy.

53. Bradley: Feb. 7, 1765; *Vital Records of Haverhill, Massachusetts, to the Year 1849* (Topsfield, Mass.: Topsfield Historical Society, 1910), 1:44, 2:41; Thwing database 6825; *Boston City Directory 1789*, 22; SCPR, 93:294–95. Note that the "prentis boy" John Pecker, who accompanied the Bradleys, was still their tenant or lodger in 1771; *1771 Valn.*, 0101–1820 and 0101–1821. Moore: July 15, 1769; Ethel Stanwood Bolton, "Some Descendants of John Moore of Sudbury, Mass.," *NEHGR* 57 (Oct. 1903), 367–68; *Boston Gazette*, Feb. 1, 1768, 2; Maas, *Divided Hearts*, 107; Thwing database 46034; SCPF 17962.

54. Forder: July 25, 1765; *Port Arrivals*, 41; *Boston Marrs.*, 2:25; Boston Ch. Recs. database (First Church, marriage; King's Chapel, infant baptisms); *1771 Valn.*, 0101-3628. Winter: Feb. 26, 1765; *Boston Births*, 118; *Boston Marrs.*, 1:229, 329; Thomas W. Baldwin, comp., *Vital Records of Cambridge, Massachusetts, to the Year 1850*, 2 vols. (Boston: Wright and Potter, 1914), 1:776 (for the baptism of daughter Mary in September 1763); *Sibley's Harvard Graduates*, 16:291–93 (the sketch is incorrect that Francis's parents had no other children); *Hollis St. Church Recs.*, 22; Thwing database 62342; *Boston Evening-Post*, March 29, 1762, 4.

55. Barrell: Dec. 10, 1767; *1771 Valn.*, 1010–4603; Adams, *Diary*, entry for June 6, 1771, 2:26. The Yale graduates were Daniel Humphreys (warned with wife, Mary, July 26, 1770, lodging with Barrell), and Titus Smith (Jan. 23, 1768). Another Yale graduate and Sandemanian convert arrived solo: Theophilus Chamberlain (warned Jan. 25, 1768; had marriage banns published in Boston the next April, *Boston Marrs.*, 2:427). Quotations: Samuel Pike, *A Plain and Full Account of the Christian Practices Observed by the Church in St. Martin's-le-Grand, London, and Other Churches (Commonly Called Sandemanian) in Fellowship With Them: In a Letter to a Friend* (Boston: Z. Fowle, 1766), 13 (italics in orig. are omitted), 18, 12, qtd. in Williston Walker, "The Sandemanians of New England," *Annual Report of the American Historical Association for 1901* (Washington, D.C.: Government Printing Office, 1902), 148; and, for more on the Yale graduates drawn to Sandeman, see 155.

56. "Middling stature": Ezra Stiles, qtd. in Walker, "Sandemanians of New England," 151n; David and Ann Mitchelson, April 2, 1767, Dec. 10, 1767; Maas, *Divided Hearts*, 107 (Mitchelson). Love showed no disapproval or contempt for Sandemanians. In fact, he accorded Sandeman and Mitchelson, the former elder of the London church, with the honorific "Mr.," which he rarely applied to strangers. For more on the sect, see John Howard Smith, *The Perfect Rule of the Christian Religion: A History of Sandemanianism in the Eighteenth Century* (Albany: State University of New York Press, 2008); Henry H. Edes, "The Places of Worship of the Sandemanians in Boston," *Publications of the Colonial Society of Massachusetts*, 6 (1901), 109–23; and Jean F. Hankins, "A Different Kind of Loyalist: The Sandemanians of New England During the Revolutionary

War," *New England Quarterly* 60, no. 2 (June 1987), 223–49. In Danbury, Sandeman, an associate traveling with him, and his landlord were prosecuted for not observing the notification and warning rules; however, the justice of the peace who sentenced them to pay a fine let the execution lapse; Walker, "Sandemanians of New England," 154n.

57. "Draws Faces in crayon," George Mason, *Boston News-Letter*, Jan. 7, 1768, 3; "takes faces:" *Boston News-Letter*, Nov. 26, 1773, 3; "Tender affection": Obituary for Robert Love, ibid., April 28, 1774, 3.

Chapter 8. Travelers in Distress

1. Benjamin and Hannah Morrow: March 23, 1769; Abigail Harris: June 14, 1768; Terence and Mary Bryan: Oct. 17, 1769; Robert Campbell, Sept. 1, 1769. This portrait of neediness is approximate because, on the one hand, some people warned by Love must have been needy but did not attract his labels of "ragged," "poor," etc.; and on the other, as we note below, some whom he identified as disabled or elderly were able to make their livings. The 462 parties break down into: 346 solo men, sixty-seven solo women, twenty-two married couples, thirteen family groups consisting of parents and at least one child, eleven mothers with child or children, two male twosomes, and one sister pair who were children. Twenty percent of these 462 parties had lodging in Boston, a far smaller proportion than for the overall population of incomers warned by Love. Two-thirds were "last from" a location outside of Massachusetts.

2. Although the enslaved men and women whom Love encountered were not described in these categories of neediness, they experienced more immiseration, physical and spiritual, than any other group in the colonial Atlantic. Philip D. Morgan, "Slaves and Poverty," in Billy G. Smith, ed., *Down and Out in Early America* (University Park: Pennsylvania State University Press, 2004), 93–131. For African New Englanders, free and enslaved, see Chapter 7 in this volume.

3. Miller: Aug. 11, 1773; young man: James Cobbett, July 17, 1770 (last from Saco [in Maine]); Robinson: March 16, 1773; "in spite of": John Linaker, Sept. 7, 1768. The principal statute that mentioned begging was one that encouraged towns to establish workhouses; "An Act for the Suppressing and Punishing of Rogues, Vagabonds, Common Beggars, and other Leud, Idle & Disorderly persons," was passed in 1700 and revived often thereafter; *Acts and Resolves* 1:378–81. Two other begging parties promised Love they would leave town the next morning or within a few days. Manifesting boldness were William Filch (July 21, 1768) and John and Elizabeth Fetheringell ("they are Begers and the woman is verry Bould"; July 10, 1769). For beggars and their strategies in London, see Tim Hitchcock, *Down and Out in Eighteenth-Century London* (New York: Hambledon and London, 2004).

4. Money: John Williams: March 27, 1773. Help: Jonathan Robbins: March 3, 1768. Bread: Alexander Berrett: Feb. 3, 1767, and Thomas Simons: June 19, 1767. Complete beggar: Richard Wiggin: June 1, 1767 (wounded while serving in the seventeenth regiment under Colonel John Campbell). Wood: Oct. 26, 1772; Barker: June 13, 1769; Davis: Sept. 27, 1765; Harris: Aug. 6, 1767. Love called one stranger "a travelling beggar" and four parties "strolling beggars" or a variant. Curiously, Love's warnings contain no strangers described as children who were begging. Of sixty-eight parties begging, fourteen were characterized as disabled.

5. Young or stout/healthy men begging, idle, or in rags: Robert Montgomery, June 8, 1769; William Hines, Aug. 26, 1768; Jonathan Menner, Aug. 18, 1768; Thomas Brinley, Nov. 13, 1767,

and five others. Eleven (16 percent) of beggars were described by Love as old, but surely many more were beyond their fifties.

6. Bonner: July 9, 1766, and Oct. 27, 1767. On the second occasion, Love reported that Bonner was lodging with Ephraim Perry at the South End; for Perry's many down-and-out lodgers, see Chapter 6 in this volume. Simpson: Dec. 12, 1765, Aug. 19, 1767, and Jan. 22, 1768. Love warned sixty-one solos who were begging, four of whom were women.

7. Whittemore: April 4, 1766; Bradford Adams Whittemore, comp., "The Whittemore Family in America," *NEHGR* 107 (Jan. 1953), 34–35; 106 (Jan. 1952), 97–98.

8. Bowen: Aug. 19, 1766. Bowen had been in town a few days and had perhaps secured lodgings but did or could not tell Love with whom. In surviving Westford tax lists for 1731, Bowen was at the bottom of the ranks, with no real or personal estate. There is no record that Bowen married or had children. For his school teaching and his last years, see Edwin R. Hodgman, *History of the Town of Westford . . .* (Lowell, Mass.: Westford Town History Association, 1883), 307–8; William B. Prescott, *Westford, Mass.: Eight Tax Lists, 18 October 1730 to November 1731* (Round Brook, N.J.: William B. Prescott, 1998).

9. Want of clothes: John Whitney, June 13, 1768. Most were warned on the day they came to Boston or within three days (82 percent of the fifty-seven ragged parties for whom arrival dates are recorded). In terms of the seasonality of warnings, the "ragged" were not skewed toward the harsh months; only 8 percent (N = 6) arrived in winter. For discussion of the language of nakedness, see Wendy Lucas Castro, "Stripped: Clothing and Identity in Colonial Captivity Narratives," *Early American Studies* 6 (Spring 2008), 104–36.

10. Johnston: March 7, 1766. Linda Baumgartner, *What Clothes Reveal: The Language of Clothing in Colonial and Federal America* (Williamsburg, Va.: Colonial Williamsburg Foundation and Yale University Press, 2002), esp. chaps. 2–5. On mending, see Marla Miller, *The Needle's Eye: Women and Work in the Age of Revolution* (Amherst: University of Massachusetts Press, 2006). On ordinary working persons' apparel, see Jonathan Prude, "To Look upon the 'Lower Sort': Runaway Ads and the Appearance of Unfree Laborers in America, 1750–1800," *Journal of American History* 78 (June 1991), esp. 143–49.

11. Willard: Nov. 6, 1767; Chillman: Oct. 26, 1769 (Love gave her maiden name, White, suggesting she may have been an abandoned wife). Toye, Nov. 2, 1767. Nearly four weeks later, Toye (here, Tay) was admitted to the Boston almshouse on the province account and described as "a poor Lame man," age thirty-five; he "went away" from the house without formal discharge one month later (Nellis and Cecere, *BOPR*, 185, 263n35). For the parties warned when they were almshouse inmates, the warner did not bother to note the condition of their clothing (even though many must have been poorly clothed), since their need for poor relief was already instantiated.

12. Highnots: June 17, 1773. For example, Betsy Whipple (June 5, 1766), warned on her second day in town, "an Indin woman Last from" Coventry, Connnecticut, "She Says She Lodges in the Streets anywhere."

13. Giles: Aug. 22, 1766; Shipsces (a former soldier): May 1, 1769. Ferrell: July 25, 1768; Love warned a man of the same name on Aug. 19 and Dec. 3, 1773, describing him as emigrating ten years earlier from Ireland and (in December) as "Crasey" and then in the almshouse. Other spots in the city where those without money slept were porches, watch houses, and "a shade or warehouse" on the Long Wharf: William Cowell, June 10, 1767 (porches); Lee Wolfindine, March 2, 1770; John Lewis, Nov. 20, 1765 (shed or warehouse).

14. Taylor: Sept. 8, 1767; Mary McCarthy, Aug. 8, 1770; Nellis and Cecere, *BOPR*, 210, 212, 630; *BTR* 23:64, 67 (quotation). For similar strangers hoping for charity to pay for overseas passages, see John Warren, Oct. 18, 1766, and Thomas Williams, Sept. 7, 1768. Boston town records from the 1730s to the 1770s show about twenty instances of such requests made or payments authorized. For example, William Robinson, about to be released from Boston's jail in January 1765, promised "to work for his passage" but convinced the selectmen that they should "provide for the Passage of his Wife and Child on the best terms they can" (*BTR* 20:126).

15. For descriptions of the almshouse, see Nellis and Cecere, *BOPR*, 57–69; Thwing, *Crooked Streets*, 222; and Stephen W. Becker, "The Rhetoric of Architecture: Civic Republican Space in Early Boston" (Ph.D. diss., Northwestern University, 2000), 343–46. Lester J. Cappon's reconstruction of the map of Boston portrays it as a long building paralleling Beacon Street; Lester J. Cappon, ed., *Atlas of Early American History: The Revolutionary Era 1760–1790* (Princeton: Princeton University Press, 1976), 9.

16. McNeil: Oct. 18, 1770; William Hudson, Sept. 12, 1765; John McGrath ("to Be Cured"), Oct. 21, 1771; Nellis and Cecere, *BOPR*, 166, 221. The town paid an annual salary to one physician who was expected to make daily visits; Nellis and Cecere, *BOPR*, 65–66. For several inmates who, under the care of Dr. John Gorham, recovered from serious manic spells after a few weeks of treatment, including opium doses, see Jacques M. Quen, "Early Nineteenth-Century Observations on the Insane in the Boston Almshouse," *Journal of the History of Medicine and Allied Sciences* 23, no. 1 (Jan. 1968), 80–85. For almshouse admissions that occurred on the same day as Love's warning, see the examples offered in Chapter 4 of this volume.

17. Leader: March 21, 1765; *BTR* 20:140; Nellis and Cecere, *BOPR*, 161, 166.

18. Dolbeare, Feb. 20, 1772. From June 1767 on, Love dealt with Proctor's successor, Paul Farmer and his wife, Thankful.

19. Guttridge: June 3, 1767; Nellis and Cecere, *BOPR*, 181–82. Fitzgerald: Dec. 7, 1772; Nellis and Cecere, *BOPR*, 235, 268. Davis: Nov. 20, 1771; Nellis and Cecere, *BOPR*, 222, 240. For ages of a larger pool of inmates, see ibid., 75. Length of stay could be determined for sixty-three solo residents or family heads in our unsystematic sample of province charges warned by Love. The findings break down as follows: one month or under, $N=12$ (including two deaths); 1.25–3.5 months, $N=15$ (one death); 4–5.5 months, $N=12$ (two deaths); six to eight months, $N=11$ (one death); nine to thirty-seven months, $N=13$.

20. Norcross: June 7, 1766; *BTR* 20:240; MCPF 16028, 1761 guardianship. Most white New Englanders who struggled with mental disorders were cared for at home and rarely manifested violence or disrupted their communities with dramatic scenes.

21. Odd: Samuel Towns, Sept. 4, 1766. Ferdinando: Aug. 15, 1765; Sturgis: Aug. 8, 1765. Sturgis's family arranged for him to be taken care of in Dorchester, where he died in 1779; John B. Carney, "In Search of Fayerweather: The Fayerweather Family of Boston," *NEHGR* 144 (Oct. 1990), 347–48. Dwyer: Jan. 9, 1769, warning; *BTR* 23:28; this is probably the same John Dwyer who was admitted to the Boston almshouse at age thirty-two in January 1768 (Nellis and Cecere, *BOPR*, 187, 196). Love would have been familiar with Abraham-men, beggars known for tramping the English roads claiming, often falsely, to have been inmates of London's hospital for the insane. See Roy Porter, *Mind-Forg'd Manacles: A History of Madness in England from the Restoration to the Regency* (Cambridge, Mass.: Harvard University Press, 1987), 37.

22. Carroll: Aug. 25, 1770. Boys mocking: Lee Wolfindine, March 2, 1770 (great noise); Esseby Masson [Azubah Mason], Oct. 15, 1771. Dunbar: July 4, 1770; he had arrived three days earlier

from New York and had no lodging. Barber: May 15, 1769. Mason was a Medfield woman in her late thirties, who lived out her life in her hometown until her death at age eighty-four (*Vital Records of Medfield, Massachusetts, to the Year 1850* (Boston: New England Historic Genealogical Society, 1903), 68–69, 222. Love mentioned disruptive, raving behavior by those described as mentally ill on six occasions.

23. Serron: March 26, 1773; "broke": Isaac Jemison, Sept. 8, 1768. Two others reported having served in the British army. For the iconography of madness, see Porter, *Mind-Forg'd Manacles*, 33–38. All thirty-two arrived in Boston alone.

24. Deaf: Moses Dickson, Oct. 15, 1767; James Nothey, Dec. 11, 1767; William Cook, Aug. 13, 1768. Dwarf: Robert Milton, Oct. 16, 1770. Blind, for example: William Organ, Aug. 28, 1769; James Holden, Sept. 25, 1766. Leprosy: fisherman John Connal, March 22, 1769. Examples of lameness: Philip Ulmer: June 17, 1768; Ichabod Whitney: Nov. 21, 1770. Crutches or needing help to walk: James Sanders: Jan. 23, 1768; Nathan Pettingell: June 3, 1766; Samuel Scott, July 15, 1767. Cascobay, "who Says he is free," last from Taunton: Sept. 11, 1767. Jackson: Aug. 6, 1767. Lame of one hand: one of the two women traveling with James Wall, warned March 18, 1767. Lost an eye: Mary King: July 11, 1770.

25. Gabril: Feb. 22, 1772; deaf: Dickson: Oct. 15, 1767; Hendrick: May 22, 1770. McGrath: Oct. 21, 1771; Nellis and Cercere, *BOPR*, 221, 267n514. For a tavernkeeper with an amputated arm, see Sharon V. Salinger, *Taverns and Drinking in Early America* (Baltimore: Johns Hopkins University Press, 2002), 190. Thirteen of those identified as disabled were begging; another four asked for charity or to get into the almshouse. Twelve in all (16 percent of the lame or disabled) had almshouse stays. Five of the disabled reported that no one would lodge them or that they lodged outdoors. Fifteen were discharged soldiers.

26. Maddin: May 7, 1766; *Vital Records of Uxbridge, Massachusetts to the Year 1850* (Boston: Wright and Potter, 1916), 105–6; Worcester County Probate Records, 461:144, 199:382 (microfilm), Judicial Archives, MA Archives; 1790 federal census for Partridgefield, Mass.

27. Sickly, for example: Collom McClellan, Oct. 12, 1772; poor state: Michael Carry (a butcher to trade, traveling with his wife, Katherine), Oct. 30, 1773; fever and ague: Thomas Willard, Nov. 6, 1767; cancer: Richard Hickney, Sept. 5, 1768; rheumatism: Samuel Whippey, Dec. 12, 1767. Cooper: June 6, 1765; *BTR* 20:167 (Cooper, identified as sick but unnamed, arriving on Schooner Unity with Capt. Thatcher Rich), 174; Daniel McKeen's bill, MS f Bos. 7, Boston Town Papers, 7:84, BPL; Nellis and Cecere, *BOPR*, 165, 635. Miller: Nov. 2, 1767; Nellis and Cecere, *BOPR*, 185. King ("Belongs to providanc" in Rhode Island), Nov. 9, 1765. Vallance (last from Marshfield): Nov. 2, 1767. King and Vallance had been in town fourteen and eighteen days, respectively, and both had lodgings. Overall, Love identified twenty-eight people as sick or wounded, twenty-six of whom were solo males.

28. Forty of the "old" fit one or more of the listed rubrics. Another eleven were described as sick, drunk, resistant, or wanting a passage. Of all those labeled elderly, fifty-nine were solo men, four were couples, six were solo females, and one party consisted of two men traveling together—one seventy-five-year old man leading his blind "master." Only six of these strangers landed in the almshouse, where a couple of them died.

29. Probation: Elisha Niles, Diary, Feb. 28, 1834, Connecticut Historical Society, qtd. in Paula Scott, *Growing Old in the Early Republic: Spiritual, Social, and Economic Issues, 1790–1830* (New York: Garland, 1997), 9. Bailey: Aug. 19, 1773; Nellis and Cecere, *BOPR*, 255. Hodgkins [Hodskins]: Jan. 14, 1774. On the Hodgkins brothers, see Roger D. Joslyn, "The Descendants of John Stockbridge," *NEHGR* 134 (Jan. 1980), 146. For a discussion of how concepts of manhood intersected

with old age, see Lisa Wilson, *Ye Heart of a Man: The Domestic Life of Men in Colonial New England* (New Haven: Yale University Press, 1999), chap. 7.

30. For the declining rate of drinking- and tavern-related crimes prosecuted in Massachusetts and elsewhere, see Salinger, *Taverns and Drinking*, 141–43, and chap. 4. From late 1764 to early 1773, the three most common misdemeanors tried at the court of general sessions for Boston and surrounding towns were fornication, theft, and assault; Suff. Co. GSP Records, record books for 1764–73.

31. Punch and merry toasts: "Extracts from Capt. Francis Goelet's Journal, Relative to Boston, Salem and Marblehead, &c., 1746–1750," *NEHGR* 24 (Jan. 1870), 59–63 (quotations p. 61), as quoted and described in Salinger, *Taverns and Drinking*, 142–43, 221–22. Stanton: May 27, 1769. Ten were warned on the same day they arrived; seven had come in the day or night before. For the four for whom Love recorded no arrival date, the strong likelihood is that they arrived "this day" as none had lodgings. Of the twenty-four parties, only three had lodgings.

32. Drinking man: Love used this phrase five times, including for John Hood and James Dunlap (both warned July 21, 1770) and Barnaby Maran (June 7, 1770). "Very drinking" (emphasis added) and cursing at boys: William Flin, July 6, 1770; Cammock, July 24, 1770. Cahail: Nov. 1, 1771. John Murphy, April 30, 1773.

33. Least becomes the sex: "Journal of William Black," *Pennsylvania Magazine of History and Biography* 1 (1877), 416, qtd. in Salinger, *Taverns and Drinking*, 224. Genin: July 4, 1770. The other woman warned drunk was Elizabeth Stewart ("a Common Stroler is orignaly from Irland"), Aug. 7, 1772. The phrase "in Licker": Flin, June 26, 1770; John Hood, July 21, 1770. Such women might have been sentenced to a short term in the workhouse; no admission ledgers survive.

34. Kelton: Dec. 8, 1766; Smelledge: May 23, 1769; Barber: Feb. 18, 1769 (now in the workhouse; according to the Warning Out book, 1745–70, she soon was physically removed from town). Two other strollers had "the name of a Bad Womon" (Mary King, July 11, 1770, and Anna Caterina Boma, July 17, 1767). The *Oxford English Dictionary* does not include sexual laxity or prostitution among the meanings of *stroll, stroller, strolling*. Of thirty-eight strolling parties, thirteen were solo women, eighteen were solo men, one consisted of a woman traveling with a child, and six were couples. Contrast this with two women among the drunks, one among the idle, two among the lame, and 10 percent of the "old" traveling singly.

35. Strolling tinkers: John McCan, traveling with his wife, Oct. 21, 1771, and Jonathan Lawrence, July 17, 1770; peddler: John Clark, July 26, 1769. Wilson: July 3, 1773; Cife: Aug. 1, 1771; Hardin: July 14, 1770. For attitudes and policies toward vagrants in the early modern period, see Robert Jutte, *Poverty and Deviance in Early Modern Europe* (New York: Cambridge University Press, 1994), 146–50, and A. L. Beier, *Masterless Men: The Vagrancy Problem in England, 1560–1640* (New York: Methuen, 1985).

36. Idling about town: Moses Sanders, Sept. 4, 1770. No business: Charles Lee, June 16, 1769, and David Ranstead, July 2, 1767. Stoning/Storing: May 29, 1766; *Vital Records of Salem, Massachusetts, to the End of the Year 1849*, 6 vols. (Salem, Mass.: Essex Institute, 1916–25), 4:356 (his parents' marriage); *Massachusetts Officers and Soldiers of the French and Indian Wars, 1755–1756*, ed. K. David Goss and David Zarowin (Boston: New England Historic Genealogical Society, 1985), 184; Essex County Probate File 26764 (his father, 1752), Judicial Archives, MA Archives. Waterman: Jan. 2, 1769. Love used the word vagabond only once (William Marcy, June 27, 1766). Only two strollers were described as old.

37. Covey: Oct. 15, 1770; Maxfield: May 16, 1771; Griffin: Sept. 7, 1768 (was "in prison Sometime ago[;] he is Latly Come to town I warned him"); King (lodging with a woman in the North End): July 11, 1770. Similarly, Michael Forman, June 22, 1768 (Prussian, third warning by Love, last from Hartford, "has Been a thife, He Lives Now in the Work House").

38. Smith: March 30, 1773, and Aug. 15, 1770. Love warned twelve women and nine men at the workhouse, and three women and five men at the jail. On the workhouse, see Nellis and Cecere, *BOPR*, 70–74.

39. Isbister: Nov. 24, 1772; Nellis and Cecere, *BOPR*, 75, 132, 155, 161, 167, 171, 215, 219, 628–30, 636–38, 641; SCPF 13251; Suff. Co. GSP Records, record book for 1764–68, Oct. 21, 1768 session, and record book for 1769–73, April 1771 session. In 1771, it appears that she came into court a few days after giving birth. She named mariner William Buckley as the child's father.

40. Billy G. Smith, ed., *Down and Out in Early America* (University Park: Pennsylvania State University Press, 2004), introduction (quotation p. xvii). Bonner (almost blind): July 9, 1766, and Oct. 27, 1767.

41. *Discord and Civil Wars Being a Portion of the Journal Kept by Lieutenant Williams of His Majesty's Twenty-Third Regiment While Stationed in British North America During the Time of the Revolution* (Buffalo: Salisbury Club, 1954), 5. For a lengthy poem about urban life, see *Walking the Streets of Eighteenth-Century London: John Gay's Trivia (1716)*, ed. Clare Brant and Susan E. Whyman (Oxford: Oxford University Press, 2007). On "pauper professions" such as shoe blacking and charring, see Hitchcock, *Down and Out*, 49–74.

Chapter 9. Warning in the Midst of Imperial Crises

1. Stephen Brumwell, *Redcoats: The British Soldier and the War in the Americas, 1755–1763* (New York: Cambridge University Press, 2002), 297–98.

2. Daniel Fowler, Aug. 28, 1772; Murray Frasier, Jan. 12, 1768; Thomas Gyles, Sept. 26, 1772; Peter Murray, Oct. 18, 1770. Love recorded the British regiment served in (by number, name, or commander) for fifty-four veterans; for another seven, he used the phrases "regular" or "army." He indicated provincial or "country" service for seventeen, and made vague statements about five ("has Been a soldier"). Eighteen arrived with wives or wives and children.

3. Love recorded discharge dates for ten men, all from 1763 to 1765. Others mentioned serving in a given year but gave no discharge date. Briefs and passes: William Filch, July 21, 1768; John McDonel, discharged by Amherst and last from Johnston Hall in New York, had "a pass to travel to Boston": April 8, 1768. Robert Donelson (blind, with multiple injuries, and traveling with his wife) "prodused a pasport signed H Moor Governor of New York to admite him to travel to Virginie": July 23, 1767. Nobody will lodge: John Hamilton, Jan. 13, 1768; Murray Frasier, Jan. 12, 1768. Jackson, July 17, 1772. Twenty-one army veterans had found Boston lodgings, whether for a few days or several weeks; twenty-one others were warned by Love on the day they arrived, so no lodgings were noted.

4. Sherwood: July 18, 1769. Only one-fifth had resided or sojourned last in New England.

5. Wiggins: Feb. 13, 1766, June 1, 1767; Nellis and Cerere, *BOPR*, 181–82. In 1767, Wiggins was last from "Bowtown," which we take to be the village of Boonetown on the Rockaway River.

6. Henry Toull: Sept. 6, 1765; Boyfield: June 9, 1769; Coffin: Aug. 29, 1767; four months later, he entered the Boston almshouse for a two-week stay (Nellis and Cecere, *BOPR*, 186). William

Duffy: April 30, 1766; Sarah Duffy: June 16, 1768 (with William), Aug. 18, 1773. Very low: Brumwell, *Redcoats*, 295, and see also 46–47.

7. Ramsey: *BTR* 23:134; June 25, 1772, warning. Before shipping out, Ramsey had an almshouse stay (Nellis and Cecere, *BOPR*, 229). Royal Hospital of Chelsea website, http://www .chelsea-pensioners.co.uk; Brumwell, *Redcoats*, 297.

8. William Collier: Oct. 7, 1765, Sept. 9, 1767, July 26, 1771.

9. Fred Anderson, *A People's Army: Massachusetts Soldiers and Society in the Seven Years' War* (New York: W. W. Norton, 1984), 58–60, 38–39, 78–83, 90–107, 231. Consulting muster and billeting rolls, we matched a few ex-provincials who identified themselves as such to Love and confirmed that they served as they reported: Darby (or Daniel) Bryant: warned Sept. 23, 1767; Massachusetts Archives Collection, 99:156, MA Archives.. John Smith: ibid., 93:135, 139a; warned Aug. 2, 1765.

10. Begging: John Bryan, Jan. 4, 1768; New Jersey service: John Whelan, Nov. 7, 1765, and Nellis and Cecere, *BOPR*, 167, 635. Poorly clothed: James Howard, June 15, 1767; Joseph Williams, Jan. 15, 1768; William Rodgers, Nov. 28, 1765. Robert Rickes: April 19, 1766; the Reverend Daniel Shute, qtd. in Anderson, *A People's Army*, 88. Half (seven of fourteen) of those identified as serving in provincial service were marked as needy.

11. Echoing others, John Mack Faragher calls it "the first episode of state-sponsored ethnic cleansing in North American history"; *A Great and Noble Scheme: The Tragic Story of the Expulsion of the French Acadians from Their American Homeland* (New York: W. W. Norton, 2005), 473. See also Christopher Hodson, *The Acadian Diaspora: An Eighteenth-Century History* (New York: Oxford University Press, 2012), 15–46.

12. Faragher, *Great and Noble Scheme*, 335–75. Thousands fled into the woods, with some men mounting a guerilla resistance that lasted until the surrender of Quebec in 1760; others managed to escape to the native Míkmaq in the interior or to French protection (366).

13. The four warnings: April 30, 1766; the fifth was Francis White's family, July 12, 1766. On June 9, 1768, Love warned three more Acadian families (ten people in all) who had coordinated their trips, arriving on the sloop *Eagle* from New London, Connecticut, the day before. Love noted no landlord for them but reported "th[e]y talk of Gowing to Canada verry soon[;] they are franch Nutrels." Love rendered the names of the household heads as Charles Gould, Charles Janvere, and Joseph Marrow.

14. The other household heads were Joseph Doucet (with wife, Ann) and brothers Joseph and François White (LeBlanc) ("old Man . . . Lame in his Wrist," Love wrote, of François). Doucet was sixty-six; he had been born in Port Royal, married there in 1731, and had ten children before being expelled in 1755. All twelve Doucets were on a 1763 list of Acadians who had been distributed to the Bay province, but only three of the children (aged twelve, fifteen, and twenty-three) were with their parents in April 1766 in Boston. By June 2, a fourth child had joined them there. Janet B. Jehn, *Acadian Exiles in the Colonies* (Covington, Ky.: Jehn, 1977), 177, 186.

15. Jan. 1, 1765, petition, qtd. in Pierre Belliveau, *French Neutrals in Massachusetts: The Story of Acadians Rounded Up by Soldiers from Massachusetts and Their Captivity in the Bay Province, 1755–1766* (Boston: K. S. Giffen, 1972), 231; Bernard, on Feb. 13, 1766, qtd. in Belliveau, *French Neutrals*, 237.

16. Governor Bernard qtd. in Belliveau, *French Neutrals*, 232. On Murray's policy, see Faragher, *Great and Noble Scheme*, 436–37. At least two boatloads left in summer 1766, and more followed the next spring, after the legislature authorized the province treasury to pay the passage

for those who could not afford it; Richard C. Lowe, "Massachusetts and the Acadians," *WMQ* 25 (April 1968), 228. One exiled group went from St. Domingue (Haiti) to Louisiana, but the more significant immigration to the Gulf bayous did not occur until the 1780s and later (Faragher, *Great and Noble Scheme*, 428–36). Some Acadian exiles returned to Nova Scotia—mostly to the southwest and not to their original villages, which were now settled by immigrants from New England, Scotland, and Ireland; Faragher, *Great and Noble Scheme*, 438–71.

17. On visiting, see Belliveau, *French Neutrals*, 98–99, 202; on work, ibid., 212–17, 223, 228, 230, 236 37. On religion, see Thomas Hutchinson, *The History of the Colony and Province of Massachusetts-Bay*, ed. Lawrence Shaw Mayo, 3 vols. (Cambridge, Mass.: Harvard University Press, 1936), 3:30–31. Exiles' agency is most visible in their frequent petitioning of the General Court to protest egregious instances of mistreatment. As a result, the legislature rebuked towns for not providing adequate food, firewood, and shelter and for separating families. See Placide Gaudet, "Acadian Genealogy and Notes," Public Archives of Canada, *Report 1905* (Ottawa, 1906), 100–102, 125, 128, 129. We thank John Mack Faragher for sharing his notes on the Acadian petitions. In effect, the Acadians were engaging in a dialogue about human rights and what constituted humanitarian treatment of "strangers." Their talking points included testimonials to their own compassion and saving services to shipwrecked British seamen in Nova Scotia, appeals to the ethical concepts of due process and equitable treatment, and insistence that they wished to find work in order to support themselves.

18. On pre-1755 commerce, see Hodson, *Acadian Diaspora*, 29–30. On exiles' strategic use of Anglicized names, we thank audience comments we received on presenting "Boston Waystation: A Snapshot of Acadian Journeys, 1755–66," at the French Colonial Historical Society annual meeting, Wolfville, Nova Scotia, in June 2005. Claude Dugas's name was rendered variously in town records, including Gloit Legoy and Gload Dewger (Massachusetts Archives Collection, 23:401, 550, MA Archives).

19. Schutz, *Legislators*, 282; George Davis, *A Historical Sketch of Sturbridge and Southbridge* (West Brookfield, Mass.: O. S. Cooke, 1856), 10–11, 135. We do not know the type of overlords that Marcy and Cheney were. Some similarly situated gentlemen were abusive to Acadians; see Faragher, *Great and Noble Scheme*, 379–80. Marcy's reimbursed expenditures on Acadians in 1757 and 1759 included the provision of shoes, yards of linen, axes, and foodstuffs such as beef and pigeons, plus "Land to plant corn, Beans & Potatoes," "Team & cart to carry wood," and "House rent"; Massachusetts Archives Collection, 23:550, 550a, 24:194–95, MA Archives. For family lore suggesting Cheney was given a cache of coins by a dying French naval officer at Louisburg, see Charles Henry Pope, *The Cheney Genealogy* (Boston: C. H. Pope, 1897), 63–65. Historians have noted the roles played by educated elites like the Reverend Ebenezer Parkman and councillor Thomas Hutchinson as patrons, translators, and scribes for Acadians (particularly high-status ones), but have not explored in any depth the roles of rural grandees as brokers for Acadian exiles.

20. Bona Arsenault, *History of the Acadians* (Carleton, Que.: CHAU-TV, 1988), 170; Stephen A. White et al., *Dictionnaire Généalogique des Familles Acadiennes*, 2 vols. (Moncton, N.B.: Centre d'études acadiennes, Université de Moncton, 1999), 1:575, 548, 2:1019. The mother of these two LeBlanc brothers, widow Marguerite, made it from Boston in 1766 or 1767 to Miquelon, where she headed a household that included two of her grown sons (3:217); Jehn, *Acadian Exiles*, 182, 184. Occasionally, Acadians chose to remain in New England: a boy named "Gload" was born in Charlton in 1774 to a Charles and Sarah Dugar, and he married there in 1797; *Vital Records of*

Charlton, Massachusetts, to the End of the Year 1849 (Worcester, Mass.: F. P. Rice, 1905), 39–40, 152.

21. Biggest sea: *Deacon Tudor's Diary; or, "Memorandoms from 1709, &c., by John Tudor, to 1775 and 1778, 1780 and to '93." A Record of More or Less Important Events in Boston, from 1732 to 1793, by an Eyewitness,* edited by William Tudor (Boston: Press of Wallace Spooner, 1896), 17; "largest" (perhaps): Thomas Hutchinson, qtd. in Jim Vrabel, *When in Boston: A Time Line and Almanac* (Boston: Northeastern University Press, 2004), 68. For the Seider shooting, see Hiller B. Zobel, *The Boston Massacre* (New York: W. W. Norton, 1970), 173–78.

22. On the Aug. 14, 1765, protest, see Dirk Hoerder, *Crowd Action in Revolutionary Massachusetts, 1765–1780* (New York: Academic Press, 1977), 97–101. Prior to fall 1766, the tree was referred to as Deacon Eliot's tree, for the landowner; Alfred F. Young, *Liberty Tree: Ordinary People and the American Revolution* (New York: New York University Press, 2006), 327.

23. "Droll" and "power": *Boston News-Letter,* published as a supplement to the *Massachusetts Gazette,* Nov. 6, 1766, 1; see also *Rowe Diary,* Nov. 5, 1766, 114. Boys: an unnamed elderly resident's reminiscence in the *Boston Advertiser,* Nov. 9, 1821, qtd. in Esther Forbes, *Paul Revere and the World He Lived In* (Boston: Houghton Mifflin, 1942), 95. According to the 1821 account, on some Pope's Days one of the figures featured on the cart was a dancing woman "they called Nancy Dawson"; for a warned stranger who adopted Dawson's alias, see Chapter 4 in this volume. In England, this holiday was Guy Fawkes Day. Forman: Nov. 5, 1766. Forman had at least two almshouse stays, one starting a week after this warning and one for three months in 1771: Nellis and Cecere, *BOPR,* 177, 218. Liberty Hall: Forbes, *Paul Revere,* 102.

24. *Boston News-Letter,* March 19, 1767, 3; March 24, 1768, 2 suppl.; June 9, 1768, 4; June 10, 1773, 2 suppl. Love warned on June 4 in 1765, 1766, and 1770–72. In 1767, he warned three parties on March 18 and Aug. 14, and, in addition, one on March 18, 1768. On the first anniversary of the Boston Massacre, he warned three (March 5, 1771).

25. Suffering after two years of nonimportation, many merchants believed they were justified in importing after January 1 because it marked the expiration date of the agreement most had signed. Gary B. Nash, *The Urban Crucible: Social Change, Political Consciousness, and the Origins of the American Revolution* (Cambridge, Mass.: Harvard University Press, 1979), 356–57.

26. Colin Nicolson, "A Plan 'to banish all the Scotchmen': Victimization and Political Mobilization in Pre-Revolutionary Boston," *Massachusetts Historical Review* 9 (2007), 55–102, esp. 76 (quoting McMaster's petition to Thomas Hutchinson, June 5, 1770, Colonial Office 5/759, fol. 271, The National Archives, Kew, Eng.), and 81 (pain of death); Zobel, *Boston Massacre,* 233 (spit in his face); and *Boston News-Letter,* June 21, 1770, 3.

27. *New Hampshire Gazette,* Aug. 18, 1769, 2; James Selkrig to the selectmen, June 21, 1770, MS f Bos.7, Boston Town Papers, 7:254, BPL. Selkrig thanked the committee of inspection for their "Sincer Endavours to find out who assaulted me which as yet is not been done." By happenstance, both victims of extralegal action appear in Love's records as onetime landlords: for Patrick McMaster, see the warning of Hannah Turner, Jan. 16, 1769; for James Selkrig, see Mary Eades, warned Oct. 21, 1768.

28. Paul Revere Jr., *"A View of Part of the Town of Boston in New-England and Brittish [sic] Ships of War Landing their Troops! 1768,"* Boston Athenaeum; see http://www.bostonathenaeum.org/node/311. For more on the engraving, see Forbes, *Paul Revere,* 139, and Benjamin L. Carp, *Rebels Rising: Cities and the American Revolution* (New York: Oxford University Press, 2007), 39. On Remick's life and the several surviving versions of the October 1768 scene, see D. Brenton

Simons, *Boston Beheld: Antique Town and Country Views* (Lebanon, N.H.: University Press of New England, 2008), 122; Winifred Lovering Holman, *Remick Genealogy* (Concord, N.H.: Rumford Press, 1933), 91–94; and Henry Winchester Cunningham, *Christian Remick, an Early Boston Artist: A Paper Read by HWC at the Meeting of the Club of Odd Volumes of Boston, Massachusetts, February 24, 1904* (Boston: Club of Odd Volumes, 1904).

29. Zobel, *Boston Massacre*, 96–104.

30. When regiments were at full strength, there were five companies to a regiment and one hundred soldiers to a company. The information on payments for housing women and children and on debates within the British military over how to handle and transport women and children attached to soldiers comes from Serena Zabin, "Desertion and Military Families in Occupied Boston, 1768–1772," chap. 5 of her book-in-progress, "Occupying Boston: An Intimate History of the Boston Massacre" (August 2012, chap. in possession of the authors, courtesy of Zabin). "Of the regiment": ibid., 19, quoting General Alexander L. S. Mackay to General Thomas Gage, June 19, 1769, American Series, Gage Papers, Clements Library, Ann Arbor, Michigan.

31. In many of these entries, Love named the male household head even though the soldier was officially "at the castle" or no longer in the province. It was often the case that Love never personally met the soldier.

32. Grenadier's wives: Mary Hall, warned Aug. 2, 1769, and Katherine Carpenter, Aug. 3, 1769. Third woman at the same location: Mary Mason, Aug. 3, 1769. These women's second warning was on May 24, 1771. On their second sojourn, these transatlantic travelers and military wives were taken in by British troops occupying Castle William. Mills: July 26, 1769. Dorothy Williams: Aug. 5, 1769, warning; Nellis and Cecere, *BOPR*, 206, 208, 214, 220, 226; Suff. Co. GSP Records, record book for 1769–73 (unpaginated), Oct. 6, 1772 and Jan. 5, 1773 sessions.

33. Crowd harassment of importers: Zobel, *Boston Massacre*, 172–78. Nonimportation was a strategy meant to exert pressure on London merchants and Parliament to repeal the Townshend duties. For most of these sixteen soldiers, Love wrote "now at Castle William." Walker incident, "fighting it out": ibid., 181–83 (quotation p. 183). In Sept. 1770, Castle William was transferred from the control of the town to the British military; ibid., 238–40.

34. Walker: May 4, 1770, warning (and see two others warned on that day); the landlord was glazier James Cunningham, a major in Boston's regiment, who lived on Newbury Street between Essex and Pond (Thwing database 17624). Walker's wife, Mary, was probably the woman of that name who gave birth in the Boston almshouse in mid-November to a boy described as "Molatto"; she was discharged seven weeks later in the company of military wife Dorothy Williams; Nellis and Cecere, *BOPR*, 210, 214, 630.

35. Hartigan (Love wrote "Hartick"): May 4, 1770. For what we know of the couple, see John L. Bell's Oct. 29, 2006, blog post, http://boston1775.blogspot.com/2006/10/elizabeth-hartigan-newlywed.html.

36. Edward Montgomery, wife, Isabella, and children, Mary, Esther, and William: May 18, 1770; Warning Out book, 1745–70, notation with the May 18, 1770, entry. "Arses": Testimony of Caleb Swan, in *A Short Narrative of the Horrid Massacre in Boston, . . . to Which is Added, an Appendix, Containing the Several Depositions . . .* (Boston: Edes and Gill, and reprinted for W. Bingley, London, 1770), Appendix: 11. For the trials, see Zobel, *Boston Massacre*, 270–94. Zobel wrongly assumed that the selectmen ordered the wives of Montgomery and Hartigan warned and that the warning was the equivalent of an ejection for vagrancy (228, 268). For further confirmation that Montgomery's given name was not Hugh, see John L. Bell, "Boston 1775" blog post

for March 1, 2007, http://boston1775.blogspot.com/2007/03/edward-montgomery-private-family-man.html.

37. Puce and Carpenter (their husbands, both of the sixty-fourth, were "gone for Old England"): May 7, 1772. Vane: Nov. 9, 1772. Burrough: June 13, 1771. *BTR* 23:141–42, 147 (quotation).

38. Benjamin L. Carp, *Defiance of the Patriots: The Boston Tea Party and the Making of America* (New Haven, Conn.: Yale University Press, 2010), 195, quoting Samuel Adams, and see 189–203 for the Coercive Acts as they applied to Boston.

39. Richard D. Brown, *Revolutionary Politics in Massachusetts: The Boston Committee of Correspondence and the Towns, 1772–1774* (New York: W. W. Norton, 1976; first published 1970), 236; Anderson, *A People's Army*, 223. For radicalization, see also Richard Archer, *As If an Enemy's Country: The British Occupation of Boston and the Origins of the Revolution* (New York: Oxford University Press, 2010), 226–29, and Brendan McConville, *The King's Three Faces: The Rise and Fall of Royal America, 1688–1776* (Chapel Hill: Omohundro Institute of Early American History and Culture and University of North Carolina Press, 2006), 281–311.

Epilogue

1. Records of Personal Property, 1790–1834, City of Gloucester [Mass.] Archives; Description of State Poor from January 1794 to January 1795, in Volume of Miscellaneous Records, 1746–1832, Records of the Overseers of the Poor of Salem, Phillips Library, Peabody Essex Museum, Salem. On the 1767–89 period and the 1789 law and its amendments, see Jonathan Leavitt, *A Summary of the Laws of Massachusetts, Relative to the Settlement, Support, Employment and Removal of Paupers* (Greenfield, Mass.: John Denio, 1810), 17, 23–27, and Robert Wilson Kelso, *The History of Public Poor Relief in Massachusetts, 1620–1920* (Boston: Houghton Mifflin, 1922), 57–59. Sect. 6 of the 1789 law gave the warning writ to be used; constables were directed to give notice, "in the name of the Commonwealth," to persons lately arrived "for the purpose of abiding . . . , not having obtained the town's consent therefore," to depart within fifteen days.

2. *BTR* 27:96, 104, 106 (emphasis added), 135; Nellis and Cecere, *BOPR*, 54–55, 97n120. The selectmen specified three districts so that each inspector was responsible for identifying strangers only in one-third of the town. In the alphabetical listings copied for the overseers of the poor, warnings were issued en masse on three Wednesdays—Nov. 23, 1791, and Feb. 22 and 29, 1792; Warning Out book, 1770–73, 1791–92, BOPR, MHS. The two surviving warning out books fail to record scores of warnings by Love's successor, Isaac Peirce, from 1776 to 1779; see his returned warrants, Elijah Adlow papers, Box 90302, BPL. Local historians note the indiscriminant nature of the 1790–92 warnings, with wealthy and prominent residents warned along with laborers; see Josiah Henry Benton, *Warning Out in New England, 1656–1817* (Boston: W. B. Clarke, 1911; repr., Bowie, Md.: Heritage Books, 1992), 56, 62, 102–4. The 1789 law made no mention of the need for constables to file warning returns with the county sessions court.

3. On the 1794 statute, see Leavitt, *Summary of the Laws*, 28–34. The law specified eleven paths to inhabitancy, none of which involved residency without being warned. The Settlement Act was paired with "An Act providing for the relief . . . and removal of the poor," which continued the colonial-era dual poor relief system, with the state reimbursing towns for relief dispensed to those with no in-state settlement; see ibid., 34–53. For the cessation of warning by inspectors, see Benjamin Homan, bill, MS Bos 11, Boston Town Records, Loose Papers, folder for

March 1794, BPL. Warning lasted until 1818 in Vermont; see Alden M. Rollins, *Vermont Warnings Out*, 2 vols. (Rockport, Me.: Picton Press, 1995–97), 1:4–9, 2:ix–xi.

4. *Inhabitants of Woburn v. Inhabitants of Lexington*, Middlesex County General Sessions of the Peace Records, file papers, 1768, Judicial Archives, MA Archives. Thanks to Robert A. Gross for leading us to this case. See also Hendrik Hartog, "The Public Law of a County Court; Judicial Government in Eighteenth Century Massachusetts," *American Journal of Legal History*, 20 (Oct. 1976), 297.

5. Deposition of Anna Powers, sworn on March 23, 1768, *Woburn v. Lexington*, file papers; Middlesex County General Sessions of the Peace Records, record book for 1761–71, Judicial Archives, MA Archives.

Appendix B. Sources for Robert Love's Warning Records, by Date

1. After we had written this book, Serena R. Zabin reported finding four more pages of Love warnings, covering January and February 1770, in the MS Bos 11, Boston Town Records, Loose Papers, BPL. These contain six parties and sixteen total individuals not noted elsewhere and not included in the analysis of Love warnings offered in this volume.

INDEX

Page numbers in italics refer to figures or tables

Dawson, Sarah, 91

Dawson, Sarah, 91
deaf persons, among warned individuals,
    141–42
Dedham, Massachusetts, seventeenth-
    century residency restrictions in, 8
Dehone, Theodore, 81, 206n22
Delaware, as source for migrants to Boston,
    77, 106
Delhonde, Sarah, 221n27
demographics. *See* warned strangers, demo-
    graphics of
Demont, John, and wife, 200n9
deportation, 17, 124, 154, 182n5, 197n24. *See
    also* removals, forced
Desilver, Josey (José), 79
Detroit, as source for migrants to Boston,
    144, 151
Dickinson, Sarah, 120
Diego, Anthony, 128
Dinn, Phyllis, 126
Dinsdale, Elizabeth, 110
disabled persons among warned individuals:
    begging by, 229n25; employment, 141–42;
    mental disabilities, 140–41, 151; physical
    disabilities, 141–42, 229n25
disorderly houses, prosecutions of landlords
    for, 111, 216n51, 217n53
distressed travelers, 134–48; beggars, 135–37,
    229n25; breakdown by sex and family
    status, 226n1; criminals and bad persons,
    88, 146–47, 209n43; drunkards, 144–45, 151;
    elderly, 143, 229n28; homeless individuals,
    137–38, 227n13; idlers, 143–46; Love's
    descriptions of, as unembellished, 147–48;
    men solo travelers as majority of, 134;
    mental disabilities, 140–41, 151; number of
    in Love's records, 134; physical disabilities,
    141–42, 229n25; people of color rarely
    described as, 83; and range of risks faced
    by common folk, 134–35; shabbily or inad-
    equately dressed individuals, 136–37; sick
    and injured, 142–43, 146, 150–52, 229n25;
    strollers, 67, 143–47; types of distress, 134.
    See also almshouses in Boston
divorce, 127, 221n28
Dolbeare, David, 139
Donelson, Robert, 231n3
Doran, Robert, 216n51
Dorchester, Massachusetts, 119, 192n42,
    228n21; hills of, 93; as source for migrants

to Boston, 80, 99; warning system in, 9,
    205n13
Doty, Abigail Sylvester, 117
Doty, Thomas, 153
Doty, William, 57, 117
Doucet, Ann, 232n14
Doucet, Joseph, 156, 232n14
Dousett, Peter, 110
Draper, Richard, 39
drunkards: among warned individuals, 62,
    67, 72, 141, 143–45, 151, 206n12, 229n28;
    definition of as class-based, 144; reported
    on by the night watch, 55; tormenting of
    by town children, 144; town tolerance of,
    144, 230n30
Duffy, Sarah, 152
Duffy, William, 152
Dugas, Claude, 155, 156
Dunbar, James, 140–41
Dunbar, Samuel, 99
Dupee, Isaac, 18
Dwyer, John, 140

economy of Boston: and absorption of
    newcomers, 86–88; and home ownership
    rates, 98; opportunities of large seaport,
    87, 89; slowdown of mid-eighteenth
    century, 86–87; Sugar Act of 1764 and,
    86–87. *See also* labor market in Boston
Eddy, Benjamin, 105
Edgar, Henry, 26
elderly persons, 13, 52, 117, 156, 157; among
    warned individuals, 60–62, 66, 75, 84, 88,
    123, 134, 136, 143, 153, 198n34, 229n28,
    230n34, 230n36, 232n14; attitudes toward,
    143; as beggars, 135, 136, 225–26n5; defi-
    nition of in eighteenth-century New
    England, 143; need for paid in-home assis-
    tance, 99–100
Eliot, John, 127
elites ("better sorts"): absence of some
    families from warning records, 101; charac-
    teristics of, 101; clothing of, 38; definition
    of, 101; family migrations with servants,
    129–30; as landlords, 101–4; sociability of,
    38, 144
Ellis, Joyce M., 190n22
Emerson, John, 122
Emerson, Sabra Cobb, 122
Emmons, Rachel Love (daughter), 34–35, 37

Love, Robert, as warner (*continued*)
  forced removals, role in, 64; hiring of, 6–7;
  investigations conducted by, 68–71;
  literacy of, and record-keeping, 54–55;
  logbooks of, 1, 2, 3, 58, 73; memory for
  people, high quality of, 5, 59–60; monitoring of illegal dumping as, 7–8; and
  notarial tradition, familiarity with, 32–33;
  number of warnings per month, 19;
  obsessive pursuit of duty by, 2, 5; pay, 7,
  30; persistence of, 66, 68–69; pride of, 57;
  reporting responsibilities of, 7, 18, 19,
  73–74; and selectmen as source of information, 71; selectmens' happiness with, 30;
  as source of information on lodging, 62;
  typical daily route of, ix–xi; work schedule
  and working hours, 62–63, 201n18; writing
  implements, as mark of official status, 57.
  See also warning reports by Love; warnings
  by Love
Love, William Richie ("Billey") [nephew],
  27, 29, 190n23
lower sorts: and excessive alcohol
  consumption, 144; definition of, 101, 218n2;
  frequent moves as characteristic of, 117;
  laborers' average annual income, 98; as
  landlords, 101, 110–14; and Love's social
  status, 32; precarious economic situation
  of, 134–35, 147; women, reliant on sharing
  lodging, 80. See also distressed travelers
loyalists, 39, 102, 103, 131, 132, 159, 224n46
Lucas, Abiel, 107–8
Lucas, John, 95
Luce, Cuffee, 125
Luce, Grace, 125
Luce, Zipporah, 222n33

Macgowen, Lodowick, 24–25
Mackay, Mungo, 99
Macklewain, John, 167
Maddin, Timothy, 142
Maginel, John Baptist, 16–17
Maine: Love's early residence in, 23–25;
  mercantile ties to Boston, 76; as source for
  migrants to Boston, 14, 76, 77, 121, 143, 147,
  152, 205n9, 206n18, 215n42, 221n24, 226n3
Mallown, James, 211n14
Manufactory House, 99, 160, 211n12
Marach, Patrick, 201n21, 209n43
March, Alice, 82

March, Mary, 82
Marcy, Moses, 156, 233n19
Marion, John, 17, 18
marriage(s): divorce, only black woman in
  colonial Massachusetts to receive, 127;
  between free and enslaved persons, 126,
  128; interracial, among couples warned by
  Love, 125; of Love, 27; of nonwhites, white
  perception of, 126; pregnancy outside of,
  122, 147
marriage partner, search for, as reason for
  travel to Boston, 120, 126
Marrow, Joseph, 232n13
Marshall, Sarah, 99
Maryland: poor relief in, 52; as source for
  migrants to Boston, 77
Mason, Azubah, 70, 228–29n22
Massachusetts: as originator of warning
  system in New England, 4, 9; soldiers
  supplied to colonial wars, 87; as source for
  migrants to Boston, 57, 65, 75–76, 78,
  79–81, 83, 117, 118, 135, 142, 155, 169, 206n18
Massachusetts Gazette, 39
Massachusetts poor relief: British model and,
  48–49; and certificate system, 48–49;
  generosity vs. other colonies' systems, 53;
  innovative features of, 54; provisions for
  relief of strangers, 15; puritan influence
  and, 54; range of needs covered by, 49–50;
  volume of itinerant persons and, 49. *See
  also* Boston poor relief; province poor
  account
Massachusetts Spy (newspaper), 98
Mather, Cotton, 104
Mather, Increase, 194n9
Mather, Samuel, 104, 219n11
Maxfield, Ann, 146
May, Ephraim, 214n39
Mayhew, Jonathan, 35
McCarroll, Murtaugh, 217n54
McCarthy, Mary, 138
McCurdy, Robert, 123, 124
McDaniel, Mrs., 11
McFadden, John, 69, 106–7
McGrath, John, 142
McGuire, Lawrence, 209n43
McIntosh, Moses, 65
McKeen, Daniel, 62
McKnights, Rodger, 61, 221n26
McLester, Daniel, 221n24

18–19; early practice of personally interviewing strangers, 17; hiring of Love as warner, 6–7; information about strangers provided to Love by, 71; and liquor licensing, x, 29–30, 85, 110; and mob enforcement of British imports ban, 159; night constables' reports to, 72; oversight of poor relief, 15–16, 49, 50, 71, 139, 164; oversight of warning and inhabitancy issues, 8, 9, 16–18, 19, 23, 59, 64, 71, 209n43; post-Revolution reinstatement of warning system and, 166; and public order, oversight of, 72; and public service requirements, oversight of, 113; requirements to report strangers to, 11, 12, 12–14, 71, 118, 121; social class of, 38
Selkrig, James, 159, 234n27
sensibility, culture of, 40
Sepro (enslaved black), 222n33
Serron, Anthony, 79, 141
settlement. See inhabitancy, legal
Settlement Act of 1662, 46
Seven Years War: British abandonment of discharged soldiers, 150; British veterans of, as warned strangers, 150–54; and demobilized soldiers, influx of, 20, 80, 86; depression following, 86; echoes of in Love's records, 150. See also Acadians
Sever, Ebenezer, 38
Sewall, Samuel, 104
sexual assault, 123–24, 222n31
Shammas, Carole, 190n25
Sharrow, Anthony, 201–2n23
Shattuck, Mary, 213n26
Shays, Nancy, 68
Shepard, John, 106
Sherwood, William, 151
ship captains: as informants, 71; as landlords, 107–8; responsibility for indigent passengers, 11, 71; responsibility for seaman, 70; responsibility to report strangers, 11, 184–85n16, 184n15, 200n9
Shipsces, Moses, 137
shipwrecks. See castaways
shoemakers: economic and social standing of, 105–6; as landlords, 106
Short, Chloe, 121, 125–26
Simmons, Elizabeth, 130–31
Simpson, William, 136
Skinner, John, 216n51

slavery: of Indians, 83; opponents of among Boston elite, 104; poverty and, 119n37, 226n2
slaves: among warned individuals, 83–84, 114, 125, 129, 130, 224n48; children, advertised by owners, 207n31; curfews for, 42; held by Boston residents, 36, 106, 121, 213n30, 214n39; marriages with free persons, 114, 126, 128; marriages with Indians, 126, 128; runaway advertisements for, 200n7; self-freeing of, in New England, 83, 84; settlement criteria for, 8, 50; transition to freedom from, and migration to Boston, 125; unsettled status of in mid-eighteenth century, 84; wedding vows for, 126
Smith, Benjamin, 168
Smith, Boston, 113, 217n56
Smith, John, 61
Smith, Margaret, 147
Smith, Polly, 68, 147
Smith, Titus, 225n55
Smithers, Joseph, 69–70
social class: of city dwellers, and likelihood of moving, 212n18; clothing as indication of, 136; and drunkenness, stigma of, 144; of landlords, Love's use of titles and, 99, 211–12n15, 211n13; and warnings to strangers, 5, 7, 11–12, 15, 185n18. See also elites; landlords; lower sorts; middling sorts
Soelle, Georg, 205n9
sojourners in New England towns: betterment vs. subsistence, 76; described, 12–14; as epitomizing warned individuals, 75–76, 116; French, 16–17; and province account, 46; registered through warning system, 42; tour of Boston by imagined, 90–94. See also distressed travelers; warned strangers
soldiers, British, in occupation of Boston, 145, 159–64: families accompanying, 86, 107, 160–64, 204n45, 205n12, 206n20, 227n13, 235n34; harassment of, 163; quartering of, 160
soldiers, former: as beggars, 67, 135, 151, 153; disability pensions, as unavailable to, 152; drunkenness in, 144, 151; in England, 46; illness and injury in, 146, 150–52, 227n13, 229n25; mental illness in, 141, 151; place of origin for, 151; poverty in, 150, 151; seeking passage home, 86; veterans of Seven Years

Trifle, Mary, 50
Trott, Thomas, 118
Turner, Dorothy, 96
Twing, John, 69
Tyler, Joseph, 119

Ulster Scots: Boston residents, 28, 29; immi-
	grants to New England, 23; Love as, 22,
	32–33, 82; in scuffle with law, 24–25; New
	England residents, 119
Unchet, Mary, 123
utopian communities, as goal of New
	England settlements: and oversight model
	of government, 21, 54, 72–73; and right to
	deny inhabitancy status, 8

vagrancy: Boston officials' concerns about,
	67–68; Love's threats to charge strangers
	with, 61; penalty for, 61, 65. See also idlers;
	strollers
Vallance, Peter, 143
Vane, Michael, 66
Vane, Polly, 164
Vermont, as source for migrants to Boston,
	77, 112
veterans. See soldiers, former
Violet (Indian woman), 130
Virginia, poor relief in, 52; as source for
	migrants to Boston, 151; tax system of,
	199n37
Vitter, Prince, 126
Vives, Juan Luis, 43–44
Vose, Susanna, 104

Waban, Mary, 128
wagon service from Providence to Boston, xi,
	71
Walas, Mr., 72
Waldo, Mrs. (widow), 99
Walker, Mary, 163, 235n34
Walker, Patrick, 163
Walter, Nathaniel, 125
Walters, Phyllis, 222n33
Wamsquan, Rhoda Babesuck, 128
Wamsquan, Sarah, 125
Wamsquan, Sarah Jones, 125
Wamsquan, Solomon, 125
Ward, John, 123–24, 222n31
warned strangers: age range of, 75; increasing
	number of in eighteenth century, 20, 41,

51–54; infants as, 202n32; no surviving
	accounts of warning experience by, 56;
	percentage with lodging, 96; physical attri-
	butes of, Love's failure to record, 59–60;
	refusals to cooperate, 57, 66–69, 119,
	205n12; responses to warning, 63–64,
	167–68; strangers repeatedly warned,
	60–61; testimony by, 167–68; untruthful,
	68; warning history, Love's recording of,
	65–66. See also distressed travelers; French
	strangers; Boston, reasons for departure
	from; Boston, reasons for travel to
warned strangers, demographics of, 75–86;
	betterment sojourners, 76, 87–88; children,
	number per family, 82, 206–7n23; family
	groups, 81–82, 88–89; gender and family
	status, 79; Massachusetts residents, 75–76,
	78, 80, 81, 206n18; migrant settlers, 75,
	88–89, 123, 129, 131; people of color, 82–84,
	88, 207nn27–29; places of origin, 75–79, 77,
	78, 169; refugees, demobilized soldiers, and
	military families, 85–86; social elites,
	84–85; solo travelers, 79–81, 83,
	206nn15–18; subsistence sojourners, 76, 81,
	89; travelers, 75, 88; wide range of, 5, 75, 84,
	116, 166; widows, 82
warner, Love as: disreputable individuals,
	special treatment of, 61–62, 66–68; duties,
	formal statement of, 7; early competitors
	for job, 2, 6, 7, 182–83n4; effectiveness of,
	59, 71, 200n5; establishments routinely
	visited by, x–xi, 62, 71; and forced
	removals, role in, 64; hiring of, 6–7; inves-
	tigations conducted by, 68–71; literacy of,
	and record-keeping, 54–55; logbooks of, 1,
	2, 3, 58, 73; memory for people, high
	quality of, 59–60; monitoring of illegal
	dumping as, 7–8; and notarial tradition,
	familiarity with, 32–33; number of
	warnings per month, 19; pay, 7, 30; persis-
	tence of, 2, 5, 66, 68–69; pride of, 57;
	reporting responsibilities of, 7, 18, 19,
	73–74; and selectmen as source of infor-
	mation, 71; selectmen's happiness with, 30;
	as source of information on lodging, 62;
	typical daily route of, ix–xi; work schedule
	and working hours, 62–63, 201n18; writing
	implements, as mark of official status, 57.
	See also warning reports by Love; warnings
	by Love

ACKNOWLEDGMENTS

In the course of this project, we have benefited enormously from the generosity and support of many institutions. Before the revolution in digitiza-
tion, we camped out for long stretches of time at the New England Historic
Genealogical Society, leaning heavily on their knowledgeable staff, including Jerome Anderson, David Dearborn, Julie Otto, and Marie Daly, and
profiting from the stalwart support of D. Brenton Simons, president and
CEO. At the Massachusetts Historical Society, Peter Drummey, Brenda
Lawson, Jennifer Smith, Jennifer Tolpa, Conrad Wright, Anna Cook, and
others were of inestimable help. At the Massachusetts State Archives, Elizabeth Bouvier put up patiently with our many requests. Laurie Rofini, direc-
tor of Chester County (Pa.) Archives and Records Services, helped us
extend our search for warning outside of New England.

Wonderful graduate students assisted us. Keith Pacholl, while studying
at the University of California, Riverside, supported us at the project's
inception, shaping the initial database and calmly taking our phone calls
while we were on the East Coast and he was in the West. Andrea Maester-
juan, also of the University of California, Riverside, helped with data management, as well. In Boston, archival hounds Sharon Braslaw Sundue, at
Harvard University, and David Byers, Brian Carroll, Rob Haberman, and
Patrick Blythe, all of the University of Connecticut, followed the warning
trail. Michael Limberg in Connecticut, and Alisa Wankier in Irvine, were
ace fact-checkers. We owe the staff in the Dean's office in the Division of
Undergraduate Education at the University of California, Irvine, an enormous debt for bailing us out of technical problems, giving us crash courses
on Excel, and performing wizardry in formatting: Roxanne Taylor, Jennifer
Aaron, Cassandra Jue Low, Matt Dobashi, and Sabella Hess. Tony Soeller,
in the Office of Information Technology at the University of California,
Irvine, contributed the figures on movement into Boston.

We were also extremely fortunate to have a full draft or sizable portions
of the manuscript critiqued by Richard D. Brown, Elaine Fordham Crane,

Ruth Wallis Herndon, Daniel Kanstroom, Norma Landau, Lori Miller, Gary B. Nash, Carla Pestana, Seth Rockman, Carole Shammas, Billy G. Smith, and Daniel Vickers. Fred Anderson, Emerson Baker, Patricia Cleary, Brendan McConville, Marcus Rediker, Jean Soderlund, Alan Taylor, Lorena Walsh, and Serena R. Zabin patiently answered research queries. The late Al Young, who read the manuscript as a referee and repeatedly offered to read subsequent revisions, was unflagging in his encouragement. We very much wish he had lived to see the book completed.

We received invaluable feedback when pieces of the project were presented at conferences and seminars, including the USC-Huntington Early Modern Studies Institute seminar; the McNeil Center for Early American Studies; the Massachusetts Historical Society; the Conference on Law, Religion, and Social Discipline in the Early Modern Atlantic World (hosted by the Newberry Library, Chicago); Boston College Law School's legal history seminar; the British Group in Early American History; the Bay Area Seminar; the French Colonial Historical Society; and the Organization of American Historians. An earlier version of Chapter 3 appears in Daniel J. Hulsebosch and R. B. Bernstein, eds., *Making History Legal: Essays in Honor of William E. Nelson* (New York: New York University Press, 2013). We thank the publisher for permission to reprint the revised work.

One summer, the Huntington Library provided us with concurrent two-month fellowships, as well as an office with an Internet connection, and, of course, access to the gardens, the art collections, and even a blooming corpse flower for inspiration. We also received financial assistance from the University of Connecticut, the University of California, Riverside, and the University of California, Irvine. Dayton worked on parts of the book while a fellow at the American Antiquarian Society and the University of Connecticut's Humanities Institute.

At the University of Pennsylvania Press, Robert Lockhart and Daniel Richter have been extremely helpful, especially in guiding the final revisions. Kathleen Kageff did a superb job of copyediting, as did Noreen O'Connor-Abel in shepherding us through the final phases.

Over the years, our family, friends, and neighbors have sustained our collaboration and pretended not to be fatigued with talk of Robert Love and the strangers he warned. Our profound thanks go to Aaron Salinger, Maria Ambriz, James Boster, Thérèse Wilson and the extended Wilson clan, Susan Foster, Susan Rose, Susan Jarratt, Donna Schuele, Carolyn Beck, Carolyn Boyd, and other boosters.